The European Union and Direct Taxation

Within the European Union, direct taxation is an area which often provokes controversy due to tensions between the tax sovereignty of the individual Member States and the desire for an integrated internal market. This book offers a critical review of the legislative and case law developments in this area at the EU level, and reviews the European Commission's proposed solutions in light of their concerns regarding the proper functioning of the EU's internal market.

Luca Cerioni sets out a series of benchmarks determined from the objectives expressed by the European Commission, including: the elimination of double taxation and double non-taxation; the simplification of cross-border tax compliance; the reduction of abusive forum-shopping practices and general aggressive tax planning strategies; legal certainty for all businesses and individuals carrying on activities and receiving income in more than one EU Member State. Cerioni uses these benchmarks to ask which Directives and/or rulings have left legal uncertainty, and which have ended up creating or increasing the scope for aggressive tax planning. The book puts forward a comprehensive solution for a new optimal regime relating to tax residence, which would contribute to the EU project to the mutual benefit of Member States and taxpayers.

As a thorough and critical discussion of EU tax rules in force, and of the European Court's case law in direct taxation, this book will be of great use to academic researchers and students of EU law, tax practitioners and policy-makers at the EU and national level.

Luca Cerioni, Lecturer in Tax Law, School of Law, University of Edinburgh. He was previously the winner of the Rita Levi Montalcini research grants programme for the legal studies area in the Department of Management, Faculty of Economics at the Università Politecnica delle Marche, Italy.

The European Union and Direct Taxation

A solution for a difficult relationship

Luca Cerioni

LONDON AND NEW YORK

First published 2015
by Routledge
2 Park Square, Milton Park, Abingdon, Oxon, OX14 4RN

and by Routledge
711 Third Avenue, New York, NY 10017

Routledge is an imprint of the Taylor & Francis Group, an informa business

© 2015 Luca Cerioni

The right of Luca Cerioni to be identified as author of this work has been asserted by him in accordance with sections 77 and 78 of the Copyright, Designs and Patents Act 1988.

All rights reserved. No part of this book may be reprinted or reproduced or utilised in any form or by any electronic, mechanical, or other means, now known or hereafter invented, including photocopying and recording, or in any information storage or retrieval system, without permission in writing from the publishers.

Trademark notice: Product or corporate names may be trademarks or registered trademarks, and are used only for identification and explanation without intent to infringe.

British Library Cataloguing in Publication Data
A catalogue record for this book is available from the British Library

Library of Congress Cataloging-in-Publication Data
A catalog record has been requested for this book

ISBN: 978-0-415-73079-2 (hbk)
ISBN: 978-1-315-81867-2 (ebk)

Typeset in Baskerville by
Florence Production Ltd, Stoodleigh, Devon, UK

 Printed and bound by CPI Group (UK) Ltd, Croydon, CR0 4YY

Contents

Foreword   xi
Dr. Prof. Franco Roccatagliata

Preface and Acknowledgments   xiii
Luca Cerioni

Updates   xvii

Introduction   1

PART I
A review of legislative and case-law developments in the direct taxation area at EU level against the "benchmarks": which shortcomings?

1   The 'benchmarks' for a critical review of legislative and case law developments at EU level in the area of direct taxation: a proposed framework   3

   1.1   Direct taxation and the EU: a difficult relation 3
   1.2   The objectives set out by the European Commission: benchmarks for an analysis (and for the search of a solution) 13

2   The development of EU law in the area of direct taxation and the related case law versus Member States' competence   19

   2.1   The sources of EU tax law 19
       2.1.1   The Treaty's legal bases for EU action in the tax area and the development of sources of EU tax law in respect of indirect taxation and direct taxation: overview 19
       2.1.2   The sources of EU law in the area of direct taxation and the interaction with international tax law: background on the attempts of harmonisation throughout the history of the internal market 19

2.2 The Parent–Subsidiary Directive and the Merger Directive: a common, ultimate objective 25
2.3 The Parent–Subsidiary Directive 26
    2.3.1 The directive's key provisions 26
    2.3.2 The directive's text against the benchmarks 28
    2.3.3 The case law on the Parent–Subsidiary Directive 31
    2.3.4 The implementation of the Parent–Subsidiary Directive in Member States; overview 41
    2.3.5 The Parent–Subsidiary Directive, the related case law and its implementation against the benchmarks 43
2.4 The Merger Directive 49
    2.4.1 The directive's key provisions 49
    2.4.2 The text of the Merger Directive against the benchmarks 52
    2.4.3 The case law on the Merger Directive 55
    2.4.4 The implementation of the Merger Directive 66
    2.4.5 The directive, its implementation and the case law against the benchmarks 69
2.5 The Arbitration Convention on Transfer Pricing 73
2.6 The Interest and Royalties Directive 76
    2.6.1 The text of the directive against the benchmarks 76
    2.6.2 The case law on the Interest and Royalties Directive 78
    2.6.3 The implementation of the Interest and Royalties Directive 79
    2.6.4 The Interest and Royalties Directive and its implementation against the benchmarks 81
2.7 The Savings Directive 83
2.8 The Recovery Assistance Directive 86
    2.8.1 The directive's key provisions 86
    2.8.2 The directive against the benchmarks 90
2.9 The Administrative Cooperation Directive 91
    2.9.1 The directive's key provisions 91
    2.9.2 The directive against the benchmarks 95
2.10 Concluding remarks 96

3 The ECJ's case law on the application of fundamental TFEU's freedoms of movement to direct taxation versus Member States' competence   98

3.1 The freedom of establishment and the ECJ landmark rulings on the key issues 98
    3.1.1 The treatment of branches versus subsidiaries in the host Member State 98
    3.1.2 The cross-border compensation of costs and losses for individual and corporate taxpayers 101

        3.1.3 The application of exit taxes 111
        3.1.4 The application of national anti-abuse rules 117
3.2 *The free movement of workers or self-employed and the resident versus non-resident distinction* 122
3.3 *The free movement of capital and the elimination of double taxation on dividends* 133
3.4 *An assessment of the case law against the benchmarks: which shortcomings?* 145
        3.4.1 The complete elimination of double taxation and of unintended double non-taxation 145
        3.4.2 Administrative simplification and greater legal certainty 147
        3.4.3 The fight against cross-border tax evasion and fraud, against abusive practices and against aggressive tax planning 149
3.5 *Final remarks in light of the benchmarks* 151

PART II
Meeting the "benchmarks": a proposal for a new solution aimed at benefiting both the interest of taxpayers with cross-border economic links and Member States' revenues

4 Direct taxation and the proper functioning of the internal market   155

4.1 *The CCCTB project versus the benchmarks* 155
        4.1.1 The salient features 155
        4.1.2 The crucial issues and the CCCTB proposal against the benchmarks 162
4.2 *The other proposed initiatives: overview* 170
4.3 *The 'optimal conditions' for minimising tax-induced distortions in the functioning of the internal market* 173
4.4 *The optimal conditions for minimising tax-induced distortions in the internal market versus tax governance issues for taxpayers, for Member States and for the EU* 179
4.5 *The residence-based jurisdiction in direct taxation versus the protection of tax sovereignty of Member States* 186
4.6 *The quest for alternatives to the national tax-residence: which solutions?* 189

viii   Contents

5   The response to the challenge of achieving on a long term basis the objectives set by the Commission: hypothesis for a new 'comprehensive solution' in the direct taxation area   198

    5.1   The quest for a new solution: hypothesis for an optional 'European Regime for Tax Compliance Simplification' (ERTCS) based on a new 'EU tax residence' 198
        5.1.1   The hypothesis for a comprehensive solution for taxpayers with interests in more Member States 198
        5.1.2   The proposed solution versus the *acquis communautaire* 200
    5.2   Structuring the 'EU tax residence' scheme: suggestions 201
        5.2.1   The EU tax residence solution versus the simplification of tax compliance 202
        5.2.2   The 'EU tax residence' solution versus the removal of all remaining tax obstacles to cross-border business activity within the internal market and the achievement of greater legal certainty 204
        5.2.3   The 'EU tax residence' solution versus the safeguard of the remaining tax sovereignty of Member States 210
        5.2.4   The 'EU tax residence' solution vs. the minimisation of the scope for abusive practices and for aggressive tax planning strategies by multinational businesses 212
    5.3   The individual aspects of the suggested solution versus the individual objectives set out by the Commission 214
    5.4   The feasibility of the 'EU tax residence' solution by enhanced cooperation 215

6   Assessing the effectiveness of the proposed solution   219

    6.1   The actions suggested by the Commission vs. the proposed 'EU tax residence' solution: the EU perspective 219
    6.2   The proposed solution and the safeguard of Member States' revenue interests 225
    6.3   An overall 'impact assessment' of the proposed solution: first indications for future research 232

7   Conclusions   237

    Index   241

"the only way in which a human being can make some approach to knowing the whole of a subject, is by hearing what can be said about it by persons of every variety of opinion, and studying all modes in which it can be looked at by every character of mind. No wise man ever acquired his wisdom in any mode but this; nor is it in the nature of human intellect to become wise in any other manner."

John Stuart Mill, On Liberty

Foreword

Although, as Community law stands at present, direct taxation does not as such fall within the purview of the Community, the powers retained by the Member States must nevertheless be exercised consistently with Community law. In this paragraph of the famous 1995 *Schumacker* case (judgment given twenty years ago), are still contained all essential elements of the EU direct taxation.

The powers retained by the Member States must be exercised consistently with Community law (at the present time: EU Law). Domestic provisions concerning taxation reflect the fundamental preferences of national legislators in economic policies. However, are these national choices 'neutral' with regard to the European dimension? Traditionally, domestic tax rules apply within a strictly national framework. By definition, they do not take account of cross-border considerations. Unless they do so, these domestic rules may impede the exercise of the fundamental freedoms of the treaty or may give rise to inconsistent tax treatment when applied in a cross-border context. In practice, this legal uncertainty and the (partial) absence of coordination between the tax policies of the Member States has increased the EU Court of Justice's work in the field of direct taxation in the last twenty years. Today, the importance of the decisions of the Court on taxation is so great that, curiously, the EU supranational legal system, originally modelled on codified Roman-Germanic systems is currently much more similar to a Common Law system.

Direct taxation does not fall within the purview of the Community. It was true in 1995, it is still true today. The taxation constitutes the essence of sovereignty exercised by national parliaments. Without a fundamental reform of the European institutions and, in particular, the allocation of powers (totally comparable to those normally allocated to national parliaments) to the European Parliament it is difficult to conceive radical changes. The unanimity vote on tax matters is the sovereignty's seal on the EU decision making process; as its corollary, each of the 28 Member States can use its *veto* power blocking any tax proposal. Until now, on direct taxation, Member States have unanimously voted tax proposals which only positively affected their revenue – as the Savings Directive or the recent Directive on the automatic exchange of information – or directives which, *de facto*, did not really harmonised tax legislation at EU level but have just coordinated national rules through EU legislation, leaving national regimes as such untouched, like

Parents/Subsidiaries and Mergers Directives which leave domestic rules on groups of companies and business reorganisations intact.

As Community law stands at present. Nothing – legally speaking – impedes to change EU fundamental law or to adopt, unanimously, real harmonising measures on direct tax matters. The EU Court of Justice, in 2006 *Kerckaert* case, reasoning on the compatibility on the juridical double taxation with the principles of the Single Market – probably one of the most evident incoherence of the EU Law – says that EU law, *in its current state*, does not lay down any general criteria for the elimination of (juridical) double taxation within the EU when it results from the exercise in parallel by two Member States of their fiscal sovereignty. It could be interpreted as an invitation for the legislative EU institutions: to each its own job, you change the legal rule and we, consequently, will change our interpretation. The Commission, in the past, has proposed the harmonisation of systems of company taxation (1975) or deductibility of losses incurred by permanent establishments and subsidiaries (1991) but never obtained the unanimous consensus in the EU Council. Lastly, the common consolidated base project (CCCTB) has been launched in 2001 but it is still under discussion in the Council working groups. About EU primary law, the Commission sent contributions to intergovernmental conferences preparing Nice and Lisbon treaties proposing to introduce qualified majority voting instruments in the areas of taxation but the suggestions have never been accepted by Member States.

It is difficult to predict how the EU policy in the area of direct taxation will evolve in the long term. Certainly tax policy is not the most robust in terms of EU competence and, apparently, priorities of the Member States are more related with the fight of the tax evasion and avoidance than to ensure the total elimination of the tax obstacles in the Single Market. Taking into account the negative experiences of the past, the EU should avoid making – as bad tailors – a one-size suit for 28 countries, at least until all Members are placed under a common diet. *In its current state* to go step by step sounds more reasonable. The first step might be an EU coordination of the interpretation and application of common principles of the international tax law, like the concept of 'tax residence'. It could be the starting point to finally reach a common and uniform concept of 'EU tax resident', as Luca Cerioni in this book eventually proposes, which will make the life easier for all taxpayers earning incomes at two or more Member States and which, probably, can also better serve the revenue interests of all Member States. This double challenge, addressed by this book, is certainly a significant one for tax policy developments, especially in the current historical phase of the EU project.

Brussels, 13 January 2015
Dr. Prof. Franco Roccatagliata, Principal Administrator
Governance, International Issues and Double Taxation,
European Commission, Directorate-General for
Taxation and Customs Union, Brussels

Visiting Professor in Tax Law
European Legal Studies Department, College of Europe, Bruges

Preface and acknowledgments

Over the last few years, the objectives which have been set out by the European Commission as regards the desired developments in the area of direct taxation within the EU (in parallel with the increasing concern at the wider international level to fight cross-border tax evasion and avoidance), have made it clear, in my view, that EU tax policy faces a difficult challenge: to reconcile the protection of Member States' tax revenues with the elimination of all tax obstacles to cross-border taxpayers' investments and activities, and with the simplification of the overall framework concerning direct taxation within the EU.

Personally I believe that, to meet this key challenge, it would be necessary to achieve all objectives that have been set out by the European Commission, and to pursue – in addition to the well known CCCTB (common consolidated corporate tax base) project – *another "supranational"* and *optional solution*, to be conceived to the benefits of all taxpayers having cross-border economic links: a solution that would successfully "compete" with national tax regimes and which would simplify cross-border tax compliance for such taxpayers whilst reaching, in the mutual interest for the protection of revenue interests, an "administrative integration" between Member States' tax authorities. As the proposed new supranational solution would be optional, the current EU directives in the area of direct taxation, and the national regimes resulting from their implementation, would continue to apply to all taxpayers not opting for the new solution. However, in my view, this solution could be initially tailored to a sub-group of these taxpayers as a pilot project (as it will be argued) with a view to a subsequent extension, in the longer term, to all taxpayers having economic interests and links in at least two Member States.

Accordingly, the ultimate goal of this book consists of suggesting such a solution (although without a claim to be exhaustive) and of offering inputs capable of opening new research avenues for further analysis and proposals. The idea elaborated in this monograph is – for the direct taxation area – a specific development of an approach already proposed in a previous one, published in 2007: "EU Corporate Law and EU Company Tax Law". In that work, the ultimate issue was whether in two interconnected areas, such as corporate taxation and company laws, it would be possible to find a supranational solution to the inter-jurisdictional competition between Member States, and a positive response was proposed, subject to the condition of designing both an EU company taxation regime and an EU company law vehicle more attractive than the national ones. The events that have marked the time passed since then (such as: the efforts by the Commission to pursue the CCCTB project; the economic-financial crisis and the quest for an "economic governance" at least within the Euro-area; the increasing consensus about promoting automatic exchange of information between national tax authorities) have been persuading me that this approach can still be proposed, but that it would need to focus, first, on the direct taxation area, with a specific goals of formulating a hypothesis for a direct taxation framework that would need to be more beneficial, than the current one, both for all taxpayers having cross-border incomes and for Member States revenues.

The construction of this argument benefited from exchange of ideas with EU officials on the one hand and with academics on the other hand, and I wish to express my sincere thanks to all of them.

On the one hand, I'm therefore very grateful to Franco Roccatagliata, Principal Administrator of the European Commission for Governance, International Issues and Double Taxation, who, as early as 1996, first mentioned an idea which inspired the solution eventually proposed in this monograph, and with whom I've had several exchanges of views. I'm also thankful to Ioanna Mitroyanni, working for the Commission's CCCTB Team, with whom before beginning this work I had useful discussions about the idea developed in this book.

On the other hand, I'm very grateful to all tax law Professors (both full Professors and other academics) with whom, in chronological order, over the last six years, at the occasion of Conferences and/or through further individual contacts, I had the occasion to discuss, on a one-to-one bases, about some key arguments that are submitted in this work: Prof. Pedro M.Herrera (UNED, Universidad National Espanola de Education a Distancia, Madrid), Prof. Daniel Gutman (Université de Paris I-Sorbonne), Prof. Michael Lang (Vienna University of Economics and Business Administration), Prof. Christiana HJ Panayi (Queen Mary, University of London), Prof. Pasquale Pistone (Vienna University of Economics and Business Administration, IBFD and University of Salerno, Italy) and Prof. Hans van der Hurk (University of Maastricht). Those discussions were useful for me to consider potential observations and arguments that could be raised about the idea that was bound to be developed in this work, and to elaborate responses that helped to build the overall proposal.

My gratitude extends to all tax law Professors and other tax law experts which, on 11 June 2013, at the IBFD in Amsterdam, at the occasion of a special event for young academics, listened my presentation of the research project which eventually resulted in this book – Prof. Maria Teresa Soler Roch, Prof. Dennis Weber, Dr. Maria Cruz Barreiro Carril, Dr. Joao Félix Pinto Nogueira – and raised comments which stimulated my reflection on the issues which are involved.

I'm also thankful to the three anonymous academic tax referees on whom the Publisher, before accepting the work, relied for an assessment of its merit, for their useful comments and observations.

Admittedly, the ultimate solution proposed in this book can be regarded – to a certain extent – as going off the already beaten tracks in the area of EU (and of international) tax law. However, for this reason too, it can hopefully contribute useful inputs to the debates at an academic and decision-making level, at a historical time when the future directions of EU policies in the area of direct taxation should, more than ever before, be conceived with a view to meeting simultaneously the interests of both Member States and taxpayers.

Luca Cerioni
10 April 2015

Updates

During the period subsequent to the submission of this book– in particular, the subsequent period of its formatting and preparation by the Publisher – the ECJ issued new rulings, and several other cases concerning direct taxation are still pending (April 2015).

Amongst the new rulings, a significant one for the arguments submitted in Chapter 3, 3.1.2. of the text, concerning cross-border loss compensation, is the ruling delivered on 3 February 2015 for Case C-172/13, *Commission v. UK*, deriving from an allegedly improper response of national legislator to the *Marks & Spencer* ruling, discussed in Chapter 3, 3.1.2..

In this ruling, the ECJ dismissed the Commission's claim that the provisions of the UK Corporation Tax Act (CTA)2010, setting out specific conditions for the deduction by resident parent companies of losses incurred by non-resident companies, run against *Marks & Spencer*. Under those provisions, a non-resident company must have exhausted all possibility of having the losses taken into account in the accounting period in which the losses were incurred or in previous accounting periods, and there must be no possibility of the losses being taken into account in future accounting periods. The CTA 2010 requires that the determination as to whether losses may be taken into account in future accounting periods must be made 'as at the time immediately after the end' of the accounting period in which the losses were sustained. The Commission argued that these rules would make it virtually impossible for a resident parent company to obtain cross-border group relief, since in practice it allows the resident parent company to take such losses into account in only two situations: (i) where the legislation of the Member State of residence of the subsidiary concerned makes no provision for losses to be carried forward and (ii) where the subsidiary is put into liquidation before the end of the accounting period in which the loss was sustained. Nonetheless, the Court found that the first situation referred to by the Commission was irrelevant because, where the legislation of the Member State of the subsidiary precludes all possibility of losses being carried forward, the Member State in which the parent company is resident may refuse cross-border group relief without thereby infringing freedom of establishment (para. 33) . As regards the second situation, the Court found that the Commission had not established the truth of its assertion that the CTA 2010 requires the non-resident subsidiary to be liquidated before the end of the accounting period in which the losses were sustained in order for its resident parent company to be able to obtain cross-border group relief (para. 34). In rejecting the Commission's claim concerning the first situation, the ECJ relied on its 2013 K ruling concerning individuals, which is analyzed in Chapter 3, 3.1.2., and according to which a taxpayer cannot claim to have exhausted the possibility of deducting losses suffered in a source State if the deduction of losses was not granted under the law of that State. In so doing, the ECJ reached a solution which may be regarded as inconsistent with its 2005 *Marks & Spencer* ruling from the viewpoint of taxpayers' interest to have losses always taken into account somewhere within the EU.

Introduction

The importance of the subject in the current phase of EU law development

Over the last few years, the economic and financial crisis which since 2007–2008 has been hitting the Western economies, and the subsequent 'sovereign debts crisis' within the Euro-area which has been leading to austerity policies deepening the recession in some EU countries, have opened for the European project the most difficult period in its 60 year history. In this period, tensions have arisen between Member States due to certain macroeconomic policies, which were regarded as beneficial in certain countries but harmful in other countries, and due to migrations of persons and capital from some Member States in difficult economic conditions to other Member States in a better economic situation and offering – among other issues – a more favourable direct taxation regime. In this problematic scenario, the debates at a decision-making level and at an academic level have on various occasions stressed the need for an 'economic governance' at least of the Euro area, and for a 'tax coordination' concerning the area of direct taxation too, which, more than any other area, has been regarded by Member States as being at the heart of their national sovereignty.

In fact, there has been an increasing awareness – in the debates as well as in the Communications presented and in the initiatives undertaken by the European Commission – that the future developments in the area of direct taxation are bound to have a very important role in the future of the single EU market, *either* by helping to overcome the currently perceived tax-induced malfunctioning in the working of the internal market *or* by risking to multiply the tax-related distortions which occur at the present time. In the former case, future developments would help achieving the economic integration objectives set out by the Treaty; in the latter, they would risk increasing the tensions as between Member States and threatening the future of the European project.

After attempts at harmonisation in the area of direct taxation, which have resulted only in few tax Directives, and after a 'negative integration' deriving from ECJ rulings, which have struck down from time to time national tax provisions incompatible with fundamental freedoms, two kinds of distortions are currently perceived. On the one hand, the persisting obstacles to cross-border activity deriving from the overlapping between uncoordinated national systems. On the other hand, the aggressive tax planning strategies by businesses whose scope is created by the inter-jurisdictional competition between Member States in the direct taxation area. Communications issued by the European Commission over the last three years have highlighted the concern to overcome these distortions – by stressing the need to remove cross-border tax obstacles for EU citizens, to eliminate double taxation, to fight cross-border tax evasion and aggressive tax planning strategies damaging Member States' revenues – and have suggested a series of targeted actions to achieve such objectives. In this context, however, key questions seem to arise as to: *which* legislative developments and which ECJ rulings have resulted in (or maintained the scope for) the current distortions, and thus have been inconsistent with this objective; *whether* the targeted actions that the Commission wishes to pursue would be sufficient or whether an additional solution would be appropriate and, in this last case, *which solution* would be the optimal one, and for *which reason*.

The present work is aimed at providing a response to these questions. The first one – which essentially implies analysing how far the current tax environment is from the achievement of the objectives set by the Commission – is dealt with in the first part, which includes Chapters 1, 2 and 3. This part, after indicating the objectives set out by the European Commission, will take these objectives as 'benchmarks' against which the developments in the direct taxation area will be critically reviewed, to identify the shortcomings which occurred, as well as which legislative measures or which rulings contributed to generating them. The second part, which includes Chapters 4, 5 and 6, will attempt at offering a response to the other questions. After highlighting which conditions would be necessary for overcoming the current shortcomings, Chapters 4 and 5 will formulate the hypothesis for a new 'supranational' solution which – in addition to the well known Common Consolidated Corporate Tax Base (CCCTB) for multinational businesses – could be considered at EU level to the benefit of all taxpayers carrying on activities and/or having links in at least two Member States. Finally, Chapter 6 will attempt at assessing the effectiveness of this solution in contributing to the achievement of all objectives which are assumed as 'benchmarks', and in ensuring the proper functioning of the internal market which the Treaty's drafters aimed to ensure.

PART I
A review of legislative and case-law developments in the direct taxation area at EU level against the "benchmarks": which shortcomings?

PART I

1 The 'benchmarks' for a critical review of legislative and case law developments at EU level in the area of direct taxation

A proposed framework

1.1 Direct taxation and the EU: a difficult relation

At the time of the drafting (1957) of the European Economic Community (EEC) Treaty – which was bound to become later the European Community (EC) Treaty in 1992 and the Treaty on the Functioning of the European Union (TFEU) in 2009 – the founders perceived that different tax provisions of Member States would adversely affect the functioning of the future single market based on the free movement of goods, persons, services and capital, the so-called 'fundamental freedoms'. Consequently, they inserted, in the Treaty, specific provisions dealing with indirect taxation and a general provision concerning 'the abolition of double taxation', without distinction between direct and indirect taxation. The provisions concerning indirect taxation, included in the Treaty's Chapter on 'Competition, Taxation and State Aids', were regarded as directly connected to an undistorted free movement of goods, and were aimed at preventing Member States from using indirect taxation for protecting domestic products vis-à-vis products imported from other Member States.

The general provision concerning 'the abolition of double taxation', originally found in Article 220 of the EEC Treaty (later Article 293 of the EC Treaty) and subsequently repealed from the TFEU, only committed Member States to enter into negotiations, 'as far as necessary', for removing what the Treaty's drafters regarded as a tax obstacle – double taxation – to cross-border economic activity within the single market. Unlike the provisions concerning indirect taxation, this general provision could not, and did not, instigate a harmonisation process in the area of direct taxation, which latter, however, has not remained extraneous to the European integration process.

Ever since the early years of the EEC, the first reports and analysis highlighted that different corporate tax regimes from one Member State to another would adversely affect the functioning of the common market as regards investment decisions and competition. The 1962 Report of the Financial and Fiscal Committee, known as the 'Neumark Report', explained the findings of a group of experts who had been charged with the task to examine two issues: first, whether, and if so to what extent, the differences between the tax systems of

Member States could create an impediment, even if only a partial one, to the creation of a common market having the purpose of ensuring conditions analogous to those of an internal market; and, secondly, whether, and to what extent, these differences could have been eliminated had they considerably affected the establishment and functioning of the common market. Although the Committee should have mainly dealt with indirect taxation, the Commission's mandate also committed the report to investigate the economic effects of disparities amongst the national direct taxation systems.[1]

The report at that time only considered the six states who were members of the EEC – France, Germany, Italy and the Benelux countries – and therefore analysed an overall legal environment which was much more homogeneous than the current one, since all these states had a civil law system. Nonetheless, the report found wide differences between the tax systems of these states and highlighted that these differences resulted from different social and historical conditions, as well as from the different characters of their inhabitants.[2] It considered the structural differences as between national direct taxation systems as justified by the different goals pursued by individual states in terms of social and economic policies and argued that, given the multiple factors lying behind these differences, any attempt at unifying completely the structures of national tax systems was undesirable and bound to fail.[3]

It also stressed that, to deter the delocalisation of profits in Member States applying the most favourable tax regimes, the transnational income, deriving from cross-border activities, should be shared as between Member States, by taking as a model the sharing formula of a German local business tax.[4]

In the first years of the single market, the risk of a tax-driven investment decision was thus already perceived as a distortion. The report submitted that a certain degree of approximation of national tax systems would be desirable for eliminating double taxation, and that an increasing cooperation as between national tax authorities would also be needed. In the Committee's view, these should have been the first steps of a process of convergence, whose desired conclusion would be the introduction (for companies engaged in business activity in more than one Member State) of common rules on the taxable base and the carrying on of assessment procedures in only one country[5] but, for the time being, the report only recommended a limited harmonisation of corporate income taxes of Member States and the adoption of reduced tax rates for distributed profits.

Finally, the report interpreted the 'abolition of double taxation' in Article 220 EEC Treaty as covering both international juridical and economic double taxation. International juridical double taxation refers to the taxation of the same taxpayer on the same income by two states, whereas international economic double taxation

---

1 Report of the Financial and Fiscal Committee, Annex A, 95 (Bruxelles, 1962).
2 Ibid 3.
3 Ibid 31.
4 Ibid.
5 Ibid.

refers to the taxation of the same income in the hands of two different taxpayers by two different countries. With hindsight, the 1962 Neumark Report had already anticipated, in substance, the core issues that, in the following 60 years, were bound to mark the history of the EU intervention on the area of direct taxation, and that will be dealt with in Chapters 2, 3 and 4.

In the years following the Neumark Report, the Commission tried to start various programmes which were intended to develop the convergence lines indicated by the report as regards direct taxation too. In 1966, a report on European capital markets strengthened, with regard to the taxation of income from capital, what had already been concluded in the Neumark Report. The new report, which was written at a time when, owing to the incipient ending of the transitional period, the removal of restriction to the free movement of capital already suggested that different national laws on the taxation of capital income would risk causing revenue losses to Member States, analysed the distorting effects that different national taxation regimes would generate on the free movement of capital.

At the outset, this report defined a tax system as a 'neutral' one if affecting neither the location of direct investments nor the location of indirect investments and if, in the long run, the tax benefits granted would not affect the choice between different types of investments. Additionally, it stressed that the creation of a truly European capital market would require the elimination, in particular, of three tax obstacles: juridical and economic international double taxation, tax benefits granted to taxpayers for investments in their country of residence and differences in the tax treatment between resident and non-resident taxpayers.

In 1967, a Commission document, the 'Programme for tax harmonisation',[6] set out the economic and social objectives to be pursued. In so doing, it stressed that undistorted market competition require that production costs and returns on investments should not be significantly affected by the different national taxation regimes, and that, in order to ensure the optimal utilisation of both productive factors and of financial resources, the choices concerning investment location and capital movement should be mainly driven by economic and social reasons, and not by tax reasons. Once again, the idea whereby tax systems should be as 'neutral' as possible – which had already been formulated in the report on European capital markets – was therefore stressed. Consistently, the document at stake – whilst acknowledging that tax systems should be structured in such a way as to allow companies to develop and to restructure – ultimately found that tax policies of Member States needed to be coordinated.

The conclusion of the 'transitional phase' of the single market (31 December 1969) marked a period of steady progress of harmonisation in the indirect taxation area; the introduction of the first VAT Directives was driven by a common perception amongst Member States that a uniform system of value added tax, rather than different turnover taxes applied in different jurisdictions, would facilitate the free movement of goods from one country to another under conditions of

---

6 'Program on Tax Harmonization', Commission Communication of 8 February 1967, Bulletin Supplement n. 8.

undistorted market competition. Further to the decision by the December 1969 European Council to proceed from the 'common market' to the 'economic and monetary union' phase, a new Committee was entrusted to examine the various aspects concerning the new phase of the European integration process, amongst which was the removal of tax obstacles preventing full market integration.

The report produced in 1970 by this Committee, known as the 'Werner Report', stressed the importance of quickly harmonising the area of indirect taxes – VAT and excise duties – but, with regard to direct taxation, only highlighted the desirability of a future coordination of those taxes which would be bound to have an impact on the free movement of capital and of corporate taxes. The 'Werner Report' formulated the case for introducing a 'classical system' of dividend taxation, without going further in recommending coordination of direct taxation systems.

Nonetheless, the Commission perceived that the objectives set out in the 1967 programme of tax harmonisation were still topical. In 1975, it submitted a proposal for a directive aimed at harmonising corporate tax rates within a range from 45 per cent to 55 per cent and at introducing an imputation system for dividend distributions – with the granting of a tax credit for the recipient – irrespective of the investor's state of residence.[7] However, this proposal was never analysed in depth, as Member States wanted to retain complete control over their choices in the direct taxation area, which they perceived as the area most related to their national sovereignty. The requirement of a unanimity agreement in the Council for introducing harmonising measures in the direct taxation area proved to be an obstacle for the adoption of any measure, to an even greater extent after the enlargement of the (at the time) EEC.

The Commission's proposal only dealt with corporate tax rates, without even mentioning the harmonisation of corporate tax bases: in this respect, the proposal was therefore not in line with the desirable outcomes of the convergence process which had been contemplated by the Neumark Report (in terms of final introduction of uniform rules on the tax base). The inconsistency of an attempt at harmonising corporate tax rates without approximating the rules concerning the tax base was highlighted in 1979 by the European Parliament,[8] and it attracted criticism both by states that were against the harmonisation and by those who were in favour of harmonisation. The former considered the proposal to be in contrast with their tax sovereignty and with the need to retain autonomy in setting the tax rates; the latter regarded this initiative as insufficient. The proposal, after various announcements of a complementary project to harmonise the tax base, a project which was never presented, was formally withdrawn in 1990.

---

7 Commission Proposal for a Directive concerning the harmonisation of corporate tax system and of withholding tax regimes on dividends distribution, 23 April 1975, in OJ EC C 253 of 5 November 1975.
8 European Parliament observations on the Commission Proposal, 8 May 1979, in OJ EC C 140 of 5 June 1979.

Although Member States' desire to retain their autonomy in the direct taxation area and the requirement for a unanimous agreement in the Council caused the stalemate of the Commission's proposal, Member States perceived that it would be in their interest to rely on a supranational legal measure that could prove more effective, for the exchange of information and in general for administrative cooperation purposes, than the provisions contained in double tax conventions (DTCs). As a result, after the introduction in 1976 of a directive on the assistance on tax recovery as between Member States covering the area of indirect taxation too,[9] in 1977 it was possible to introduce a directive on administrative cooperation in the area of direct taxation,[10] which offered Member States specific channels for exchange of information and for tax verifications. Only the second convergence line which had been recommended by the Neumark Report – i.e. a move toward administrative cooperation as between Member States – thus found the start of its implementation.

However, in light of the failure in the attempts at harmonisation up to that time, in 1990 the Commission changed its approach concerning company taxation:[11] it regarded 'horizontal harmonisation' of company taxation regimes of Member States to be no longer the appropriate way forward and it decided to replace the attempts at overall harmonisation with a 'piecemeal approach' lying in the elimination, on a case-by-case basis, of specific tax obstacles to the fair competition between companies within the single market.

In its communication setting out this new approach,[12] the Commission indicated in particular five specific obstacles relating to direct taxation that would hinder cross-border business activity: the disadvantaged tax treatment of capital gains resulting from cross-border business restructuring operations (mergers, divisions and others) in comparison with the tax treatment of corresponding operations as between companies resident in the same Member State; the application of withholding taxes in case of distribution of dividends from a subsidiary resident in a Member State to a parent company resident in another Member State; the application of withholding tax on interests and royalties payments as between affiliated companies resident in different Member States, which was normally not levied for interest and royalties payments taking place as between affiliated companies resident in the same Member State; the economic double taxation resulting from transfer pricing adjustments by national tax authorities in the event of transactions as between associated companies resident in different Member States; and the absence of national provisions allowing the cross-border offsetting of losses within group of companies with parent companies and subsidiaries resident in different Member States.

---

9 Directive 76/308/EEC of 15 March 1976, in OJ EC L 73 of 19 March 1976.
10 Directive 77/799/EEC of 19 December 1977, in OJ EC L 336 of 27 December 1977.
11 Communication of the Commission to the Council and to the European Parliament about the policy in the area of business taxation, COM (90) 601.
12 Ibid.

8   *The European Union and Direct Taxation*

Member States regarded the Commission's new approach as more respectful of their national sovereignty in the direct taxation area and, as a result, in July 1990 it was possible to reach agreement in the Council for the introduction of legal instruments – two directives and a multilateral convention under Article 293 – which were deemed to tackle three amongst the five obstacles to cross-border business activity that had been indicated by the Commission.

The taxation of capital gains resulting from cross-border restructuring operations within the single market was addressed by Directive 434/1990/EEC (the Merger Directive), aimed at ensuring the tax neutrality of restructuring operations as between companies of different Member States.[13] The application of withholding tax to dividend distributions from a subsidiary to its parent company located in another Member State, which would risk giving rise to a (juridical) double taxation of the parent company, was addressed by Directive 435/1990/EEC (the Parent–Subsidiary Directive), aimed at eliminating both the juridical double taxation on the parent company and the economic double taxation of subsidiary and parent company on the same profits.[14] The adjustment of transfer pricing by national tax authorities in connection with transaction as between associated enterprises, was governed by Arbitration Convention 436/1990/EEC, which ensured mechanisms to avoid economic double taxation in the event of mismatching adjustments by the tax authorities concerned.[15]

Therefore, the new piecemeal approach made it possible to introduce the first legal instruments intended to overcome double taxation, but the deep-rooted differences as between national direct taxation systems, the desire of Member States to keep their autonomy to the greatest possible extent and the unanimity requirement in the Council limited the effectiveness of the introduced directives, as will be described in Chapter 2.[16] Nevertheless, even this approach was not bound to last. At the start of the 1990s the Commission had also charged a new Committee to assess the perspective of integration of national taxation systems. In 1992 this Committee produced a report – the 'Ruding Report'[17] – which, once again, just like the Neumark Report had done 30 years earlier, concluded that the differences as between national (direct) tax systems created considerable distortions in the functioning of the single market, such as the delocalisation of businesses and investments.

---

13   Directive 434/1990/EEC of 23 July 1990 on the common system of taxation applicable to mergers, divisions, transfers of assets and exchanges of shares concerning companies of different Member States, in OJ EC L 225 of 20 August 1990, at 1–5.
14   Directive 435/1990/EEC of 23 July 1990 on the common system of taxation applicable in the case of parent company and subsidiaries of different Member States, in OJ EC L 225 of 20 August 1990, at 6–9.
15   Arbitration Convention 436/1990/EEC.
16   See ch 2, at 2.2.
17   European Commission, Report of the Committee of Independent Experts on business taxation (Ruding Report), SEC(92) 1118.

The Ruding Report focused particularly on corporate taxation systems and was prepared at a time when the systems of the (then) 12 Member States showed wide differences from each other with regard to the taxation of dividends, the corporate tax rates, the determination of the taxable base in terms of the relation between taxable profits and financial accounts, the availability of tax reliefs and of free zones. For example, with regard to the taxation of dividends distributions, Germany, France, Italy, Ireland and the UK offered shareholders a tax credit for the corporate income tax paid by the distributing company; Belgium, Denmark and Portugal applied reduced rates on distributed dividends; Luxembourg and the Netherlands adopted 'classical' taxation systems and thus left double taxation. The corporate tax rates used to vary from 10 per cent in the case of Ireland to 50 per cent in Germany; moreover, in Denmark, Ireland, the Netherlands and the UK, the determination of the taxable amount was almost entirely unconnected to accountancy profit, whereas in Belgium, France, Germany, Greece, Italy, Luxembourg and Spain it was strictly dependent on accountancy profit.

There were, finally, further differences as regards the application of withholding taxes to outbound payments of interest, royalties and dividends. In the backdrop of these wide differences, the Ruding Report highlighted the distortions in the working of the single market and expressed the view that a spontaneous coordination induced by an inter-jurisdictional competition between Member States would not be sufficient to overcome them and that legislative measures would be necessary. The report indicated three priorities that the legislative measures should have followed to eliminate or reduce the distortions: the elimination of national provisions of Member States causing discrimination and distortions; the establishment of a minimum corporate tax rate and of common rules on the determination of the taxable base, to limit the tax competition; and the full transparency about all tax reliefs granted by Member States to attract investments.

In the meantime, since the mid-1980s, companies and individuals had started exercising the freedom of establishment granted by the Treaty and challenging, before the European Court of Justice (ECJ), national direct tax provisions for compatibility with this freedom, and the ECJ had started finding national provisions placing non-resident companies at a disadvantage with resident companies to be incompatible with the Treaty,[18] thereby marking the start of the so-called 'negative integration' process via ECJ case law, removing national direct tax provisions conflicting with fundamental free movement rights. The phase from the second half of the 1980s to the start of the 1990s was characterised by the introduction of a directive on the free movement of capital,[19] which removed all restrictions to the freedom of capital transactions, thereby fully implementing one of the fundamental freedoms which, in 1992, was enshrined in the new Maastricht Treaty.

18 Case C–270/83, *Commission v France (avoir fiscal)* [1986] ECR 273.
19 Directive 88/361/EEC of 24 June 1988.

Since then, the Treaty has prohibited all restrictions on capital movements and payments, both between Member States and between Member States and third countries, thereby making the free movement of capital the broadest amongst all fundamental freedoms due to its unique third-country dimension. However, at the time of introduction of the directive on free movement of capital, some Member States were afraid about the risk of capital outflows and others regarded the free movement of capital as an occasion to attract foreign capital owing to their more favourable tax rules.

The final outcome of the necessary negotiation process resulted in Articles 56 to 59 of the EC Treaty – currently, Articles 63 to 66 of the TFEU – which, whilst prohibiting as a general rule restrictions on the free capital movements, also allow Member States to continue applying the provisions of national laws distinguishing between residents and non-residents, as well as other substantive and procedural measures to safeguard national laws, public policy or public security,[20] *provided* that these provisions or measures do not constitute arbitrary discrimination and disguised restrictions.[21] Articles 63 to 66 resulted from a compromise allowing some states relying on inflow of foreign capital to maintain favourable tax provisions for non-residents, and some other states to control capital movement for direct tax purposes.

Nonetheless, the 1992 Maastricht Treaty introduced the 'subsidiarity criteria' for any European Community (EC) legislative action, a criteria which was regarded as necessary for preserving the social, economic, cultural, political and legal features of each Member State to an extent that would be compatible with the proper functioning of the single market. The introduction of the 'subsidiarity criteria' implied that any legislative measure, in any area which was not within the exclusive competence of the EC such as the taxation area, could be introduced only subject to the condition that a better outcome could not be achieved by actions of individual Member States.

The introduction of the subsidiarity principle did not help initiatives in the direct taxation area, as some Member States took this occasion to oppose the introduction of new legislative measures which they perceived as damaging to their own revenue interests. The Commission – at a time when the 'negative integration process' via the ECJ's case law was progressing and gradually eroding national tax sovereignty, but the 'subsidiarity principle' set a political and legal constraint to EC action – reviewed again its approach in the direct taxation area. In the awareness about the difficulties of reaching agreement about new measures in the direct taxation area, derived by the unanimity requirement in the Council, the Commission could only try to encourage Member States to seek greater coordination of their direct tax policies, and it launched a debate about how to overcome those disparities between national taxation systems that were preventing the completion and the proper working of the internal market.

---

20 Article 58(1)(b) of the EC Treaty, currently Article 65(1)(b) of the TFEU.
21 Article 58(3) of the EC Treaty, currently Article 65(3) of the TFEU.

The debate eventually resulted in a document – setting out the priorities of EC tax policy[22] – which emphasised that the stabilisation of Member States' tax revenues, the proper functioning of the internal market and the increase of employment ought to be the focus of European fiscal policy, and highlighted, for the first time, the need to define the concept of 'harmful tax competition'. This attention to the phenomenon of tax competition was induced by increasing evidence that, in a context of free movement of persons and capital, through this competition Member States would cause revenue losses to each other, and that tax competition would also gradually shift the tax burden from the most mobile factors – such as savings and investment income – to the less mobile ones, such as labour income.

In the aftermath of this debate, in 1997 the Commission presented a new 'tax package',[23] which started a 'global strategy': whilst respecting the 'subsidiarity principle', the policy in the direct taxation area had to be integrated with policies pursued in other areas for completing the internal market and had to be consistent with this objective. This 'tax package', in its final version, contemplated the adoption of a 'Code of good conduct on business taxation', of legislative measures capable of eliminating distortions deriving from different taxation regimes of capital income and of further measures abolishing withholding taxes on cross-border interests and royalties payments. This 'Code of good conduct' was a political commitment not to introduce 'special tax regimes' – such as regimes granting more favourable treatment to non-residents in certain geographical areas – causing revenue losses to fellow Member States, and to repeal such tax regimes when already in force. Although not a legally binding measure, this 'Code' eventually proved to be highly successful and resulted in the repeal of 'special' tax regimes within a few years' time.

The 'tax package' and the 'Code of Good Conduct', on the other hand, marked the start of the still accepted conception distinguishing between 'harmful tax competition' and 'fair tax competition', a distinction which would depend on the type of tax provision through which Member States would try to attract capital, investment and taxpayers into their jurisdictions: whereas 'special tax regimes' had to be banned, the competition using elements of the 'normal' tax regimes, such as tax base and rates, would be a 'fair' tax competition and would need to be accepted. That would hold true, apparently, irrespective of the effects that the 'fair' tax competition would generate on Member States' revenues and on the working of the internal market, although some of the actions proposed by the Commission in its later Communications, as will be seen, appear to be difficult to reconcile with this unconditional acceptance of the 'fair tax competition'.[24]

---

22 Discussion document 'Tax policy of the European Union', SEC(96) 487 of 20 March 1996.
23 COM(1997) 564 final.
24 See 1.2 below.

The other measures contemplated in the 1997 'tax package' were eventually re-proposed, in 2001, in a Communication setting out a 'two track strategy'[25] for overcoming tax obstacles to cross-border business activity in the internal market, which was accompanied by a detailed report on 'Company taxation in the internal market'.[26] This report stressed, as obstacles hindering the proper functioning of the internal market, the risks of economic and juridical double taxation, the risk of transfer pricing disputes, the inadequacy of bilateral DTCs as between Member States and the lack of cross-border offsetting of losses within groups of companies. It prompted the Commission to propose amendments to the Merger Directive and to the Parent–Subsidiary Directive to widen their scope of application; the amendments were approved by the Council and introduced in 2003. In the same year, the Council adopted legislative measures which had been contemplated by the Commission since the 1997 'tax package': a directive abolishing withholding tax on interests and royalties payments within EC groups of companies,[27] and a directive concerning the tax treatment of savings income accrued in a Member State by individual taxpayers resident in another Member State.[28]

However, whereas the progress at legislative level was quite limited, the ever-increasing number and range of national provisions challenged before the ECJ by companies and individuals on grounds of compatibility with the fundamental freedoms, particularly with the freedom of establishment and with the free movement of capital, caused the expansion of the 'negative integration process' by ECJ rulings.

This process has been gradually eroding national tax sovereignty in very important aspects of national direct taxation systems, such as, for example: the different treatments for residents and for non-resident individuals with regard to the granting of deductions for personal and family circumstances and with regard to tax rates; the extension to permanent establishments of non-resident EU companies of tax benefits granted to resident companies by double tax conventions (DTCs) with third countries; the application of exit taxes in cases of transfers of the tax residence of individuals and companies from one Member State to another; the cross-border offsetting of losses within groups of companies with parent companies and subsidiaries in different Member States; the granting of deductions by the employment state to a non-resident taxpayer for negative immovable property income in its state of residence, in light of the taxpayer's overall ability to pay; and the application to inbound dividends received from another Member State of the same taxation as domestic dividends, in spite of withholding taxes already applied in the state of origin.

In turn, although the Commission has been inviting Member States to coordinate with each other in amending their national laws in response to ECJ

---

25 COM(582) 2001 final of 23 October 2001.
26 SEC(2001) 681 final of 23 October 2001.
27 Directive 2003/49/EC.
28 Directive 2003/48/EC.

rulings, individual states appear to have responded to the ECJ case law in a largely uncoordinated manner from each other, so that these rulings, just like the implementation of the European tax directives, have left wide differences as between national direct taxation systems. These differences end up maintaining or even increasing the occasions for tax planning strategies, thereby causing revenue losses to Member States.

Finally, in 2009 the Lisbon Treaty entered into force: with regard to taxation, this Treaty – which strengthened the European institutional structure and replaced the EC with the European Union (EU) – stirred a lively debate in the academic literature due to its repealing Article 293 of the former EC Treaty, i.e. due to its deleting the provision committing Member States to enter into negotiation to abolish double taxation 'as far as necessary'. In fact, this left commentators wondering whether the repeal of that provision had any implication in terms of the abolition of double taxation still being an objective of the EU,[29] although the remaining risks of double taxation certainly represent a major obstacle to cross-border activity, as recognised by the Commission itself in a 2011 Communication.

Ultimately, the relation between the EU and the direct taxation area has therefore been a difficult one from the beginning of the European project up to the current time. Member States' desire to retain as much of their sovereignty in this area and the unanimity requirement prevented any real harmonisation[30] for 30 years, as individual states often considered harmonisation as damaging their revenue interests, but a real threat to their revenues came eventually from that tax competition which found its scope exactly in the absence of harmonisation. Paradoxically, after their reluctance to give up a greater 'portion' of tax sovereignty in this sensitive area, Member States have been suffering a gradual and uncontrolled erosion of this sovereignty – by the 'negative integration process' lying in the ECJ case law and by the multiplication of occasions for aggressive tax planning strategies – to a greater extent than would have occurred had they accepted a greater degree of legislative harmonisation or had they spontaneously coordinated their tax legislations.

1.2 The objectives set out by the European Commission: benchmarks for an analysis (and for the search of a solution)

Over the last decade, the European Commission has issued several Communications in which, whilst highlighting the direct tax-related shortcomings in the internal market, it has indicated specific objectives to be achieved for overcoming those obstacles.

---

29 See ch 2 about the different positions.
30 See Foreword by Dr. Prof. Franco Roccatagliata.

Specifically, in a 2006 framework Communication concerning the coordination of Member States' direct tax systems in the internal market,[31] the Commission set out three objectives to be achieved: the elimination of discriminations and of double taxation, the elimination of unintended double non-taxation and of abusive practices and the reduction of compliance costs associated with being subject to more than one tax system. It stressed that, although Member States may eliminate discriminations of cross-border situations in comparison with domestic ones by unilateral actions, these may not be sufficient without a coordination between national legislators and that mismatches between national rules could still give rise to situations of double taxation, of unintended double non-taxation and of abusive practices, all of which may be detrimental to the internal market.[32]

After this general Communication, the Commission issued specific communications providing Member States with guidelines about the interpretation of ECJ rulings relating to specific provisions of national tax systems – such as cross-border losses offsetting,[33] exit taxes[34] or anti-abuse measures[35] – and about how to coordinate their tax systems with regard to those provisions. However, it also issued other general communications stressing the persisting obstacles and distortions relating to direct taxation in the internal market: a 2009 Communication about promoting good governance in tax matters,[36] a 2010 Communication about removing cross-border tax obstacles for EU citizens,[37] a 2011 Communication about double taxation in the internal market and possible actions to remove it,[38] two Communications in 2012 concerning ways to reinforce the fight against tax fraud and tax evasion, including in relation to third countries[39] and setting out an 'Action Plan to strengthen the fight against tax fraud and tax evasion'[40] and a Communication in 2013 about creating an expert group ('Platform for Tax Good Governance, Aggressive Tax Planning and Double Taxation') to help elaborate solutions for tackling aggressive tax planning, ensuring good tax governance and definitively overcoming double taxation.[41]

In the midst of the economic and financial crisis and of the consequent pressure on most Member States to protect their tax base from erosion, the Commission also issued in December 2012 a recommendation against aggressive tax planning,

---

31 COM(2006) 823 final, Co-ordinating Member States' Direct Tax Systems in the Internal Market.
32 Ibid., at 5–6.
33 COM(2006) 824 final, The Tax Treatment of Losses in Cross-Border Situations.
34 COM(2006) 825 final, Exit Taxation and the Need for Coordination of Member States' Tax Policies.
35 COM(2007) 725 final, Direct Taxation: Communication on the Application of Anti-Abuse Measures within the EU and in Relation to Third Countries.
36 COM(2009) 201 final, Promoting Good Governance in Tax Matters.
37 COM(2010) 769 final, Removing Cross-Border Obstacles for EU Citizens.
38 COM(2011) 712 final, Double Taxation in the Internal Market.
39 COM(2012) 351 final, On concrete ways to reinforce the fight against tax fraud and tax evasion in relation to third countries.
40 COM(2012) 722 final, An Action Plan to strengthen the fight against tax fraud and evasion.
41 Commission Decision of 23 April 2003 on setting up a Commission expert group to be known as Platform for Tax Good Governance, Aggressive Tax Planning and Double Taxation, 2013/C 120/7.

which it identified in those strategies aimed at 'taking advantage of the technicalities of a tax system or of mismatches between two or more tax systems for the purpose of reducing tax liability'[42]. Importantly, because all these soft-law pieces have been issued by the Commission after the few harmonisation directives to date introduced in the direct taxation area, and in light of the ECJ rulings concerning the application of fundamental freedoms to direct taxation, they can be regarded as indicating objectives (in terms of proper functioning of the internal market) which *neither* the limited harmonisation *nor* the 'negative integration' process brought about by ECJ rulings have managed to achieve up to the present.

Some of the literature has argued that, in order to promote further European tax integration, a *combination* of soft-law instruments, of 'negative integration', of positive integration via hard-law and of tax competition when leading to a market – driven convergence, can be an effective way forward[43]. However, if 'tax integration' refers to Member States bringing their national direct taxation systems better in line with one another,[44] it could be realised that the combination of positive integration, negative integration, soft-law instruments and tax competition, up to the present, has largely failed to achieve tax integration. Again, this inability of the combination of different legal instruments and of tax competition to achieve tax integration is widely proved by the objectives which are *yet* to be achieved in terms of elimination of double taxation, of elimination of double non-taxation, of contrast to aggressive tax planning, to tax fraud and evasion, and of reduction of administrative compliance onus for taxpayers carrying out cross-border activities and receiving cross-border income.

Achieving the stated objectives would undoubtedly ensure the *optimal* direct tax-related conditions for the working of the internal market: as was already implicitly highlighted by the Neumark Report and by the Ruding Report, these conditions would exist when a sufficient degree of *tax neutrality* from one Member State to another were achieved. In fact, both reports had highlighted the risk of tax driven investment decisions that would be caused by wide differences between national direct taxation systems, and that would prevent the efficient allocation of resources within the internal market. The same concern – i.e., the concern to ensure that choices concerning the allocation of capital sums and the location of investments be mainly based on economic and social reasons, and not on tax reasons – had also been expressed in the 1967 'Programme for tax harmonization'.[45]

In taking this position, that programme had anticipated the subsequent findings of the ECJ's case law on abusive practices in the exercise of fundamental freedoms. In fact, this case law[46] has been consistently stating that the 'wholly artificial

---

42 Commission Recommendation of 6 December 2012 on aggressive tax planning C(2012) 8806 final.
43 E. C. C. M. Kemmeren, 'Sources of EU Law for European Tax Integration: Well-Known and Alternative Legal Instruments' in D. Weber (ed), *Traditional and Alternative Routes to European Tax Integration*, IBFD, 2010, at 48.
44 Ibid., 3.
45 See 1.2 above.
46 See ch 3.

arrangements', i.e. the operations carried out for circumventing the otherwise applicable national tax provisions and for benefiting from more favourable tax regimes of other Member States without any genuine economic integration in the host country, justify restrictions to the freedom of establishment and are therefore to be considered as distortions that need to be prevented: tax savings objectives can thus be *amongst* the reasons for exercising the free movement rights, but cannot be the *sole* or *main* reason.

In other words, from the direct tax perspective, the optimal conditions for the working of the internal market would not impose on Member States a requirement to make their national tax systems identical to each other's, but would require a degree of tax neutrality such as to ensure a twofold outcome. On the one hand, the remaining direct tax differences from one Member State to another would *never* motivate, by themselves, the exercise of free movement rights granted by the Treaty. On the other hand, both double taxation and all the other remaining direct tax obstacles should be definitively overcome for all natural and legal persons, from any Member State, wishing to invest and to carry out cross-border activities within the internal market.

The realisation that the objectives at stake have not been achieved by the current routes to European tax integration and by their combination, suggests that an *alternative solution* for achieving these direct taxation-related objectives would need to be considered. These objectives – as set out by the European Commission's Communications – need to be achieved for the proper functioning of the internal market and for helping to ensure the long-term future of the European project: in this respect, it has been highlighted that 'taxation may ... work as a lever to integrate or disintegrate state and group structures'[47] and historical precedents of forerunners of the current EU have been indicated to demonstrate that taxation could work, in parallel with political, economic and social developments, as a factor of integration or as a centrifugal force for disintegration.[48]

Accordingly, if the achievement of these objectives is necessary for the long-term future of the EU project and an alternative solution for attaining them would be appropriate, the elaboration of hypothesis for an alternative solution can be based, first, on an analysis of the shortcomings which have occurred to date.

Consequently, in such an analysis, these objectives could also be assumed as 'benchmarks' for assessing in what respects the legislative and case law developments which have been taking place up to the present time at EU level in the area of direct taxation have failed to remove completely the tax obstacles to cross-border business activity, to reduce the costs for compliance with different national tax systems and to eliminate the scope for abusive forum-shopping practices, for cross-border tax evasion, for aggressive tax planning etc.

In particular, each of the objectives set out by the European Commission in its Communications – i.e., the complete elimination of double taxation and of

---

47 L. Hinnekens, 'Story and Fundamentals of Direct Taxation at Work in the EU' in *EC Tax Review* 2012, 2.
48 Ibid.

double non-taxation, the reduction of administrative costs for direct tax compliance within the EU together with the achievement of greater legal certainty, the fight against cross-border tax evasion and fraud, against abusive practices and against tax planning – can provide a *yardstick* against which the direct tax directives to date issued and the ECJ jurisprudence in the direct taxation area can be analysed from the perspective of identifying its shortcomings in reaching the objective itself. Therefore, these objectives, taken together, can offer a set of cumulative benchmarks for an analysis of the 'effectiveness' of legislative and case law developments in direct taxation.

Although this analysis would imply taking benchmarks which have not been assumed by the ECJ, no inconsistency arises between this analysis and the legal analysis carried out by the ECJ in its rulings. In fact, the ECJ – when finding about the compatibility or incompatibility of national direct taxation provisions with the provisions of the Treaty or of secondary legislation – carries out an assessment of *individual* national provisions against *individual* provisions of the Treaty or of secondary legislation, by considering the effects of the national provision at stake against the objective of the individual Treaty (or secondary legislation) provision(s) at stake from time to time. Instead, the analysis taking the objectives to be achieved as a benchmark would ultimately assess the consistency of legislative and case law developments, as a whole, with direct tax-related objectives concerning the *proper* functioning of the internal market.

In turn, the proper functioning of the internal market, by definition, must be regarded as inherent in the founding Treaties themselves, and in the ultimate economic and social goals which are stated both in the Treaty on the European Union (TEU) and in the TFEU: wellbeing of people throughout the EU, balanced economic growth and price stability, highly competitive social market economy, aimed at high employment and social progress, solidarity between Member States,[49] economic and social cohesion,[50] promotion of high levels of employment[51] and other economic and social goals.[52]

In other words, the ultimate economic and social goals set out in the TEU and in the TFEU would be jeopardised without a functioning of the internal market that was consistent with these goals, i.e. without a proper functioning of the internal market, which latter requires – from the direct taxation standpoint – the achievement of the objectives indicated by Commission's Communications. Consequently, an analysis taking these objectives as cumulative benchmarks for a review of all legislative and case law developments in the direct taxation area – with a view to identifying their shortcomings (towards the achievement of optimal direct tax conditions for the working of the internal market) – does not contrast with the legal analysis carried out by the ECJ to assess the compatibility of individual national direct tax provisions with individual EU tax law provisions, but rather

---

49 Art. 3, TEU.
50 Art. 4 TFEU.
51 Ibid.
52 Art. 4 and Art. 9 TFEU.

complements it. This holds true because the proper interpretation and application of individual Treaty provisions or secondary legislation provisions (which the ECJ has the task of ensuring) also needs to be regarded as necessary for achieving the ultimate economic and social goals set out in the TEU and in the TFEU.

The 'contribution' of direct taxation to the attainment of these ultimate goals must be ensured *both* at the level of compatibility of individual national tax law provisions with individual Treaty provisions and with individual secondary EU law provisions *and* at the level of consistency of legislative and case law developments as a whole with the objectives indicated by the Commission and which are necessary for the proper functioning of the internal markets. Ensuring the former level falls within the responsibility (of national legislators and) of the ECJ; ensuring the latter level ultimately falls on the direct tax policy choices made by the EU legislator. Arguably, these choices should consider alternative solutions to the extent that the patterns already followed have resulted in being partly inconsistent with the proper functioning of the internal market.

On these premises, Chapters 2 and 3 will therefore review all the legislative and case law developments and will assess them by taking these objectives as benchmarks.

Bibliography

L. Hinnekens, 'Story and Fundamentals of Direct Taxation at Work in the EU' in 21 *EC Tax Review* 2, Alphen aan den Rijn, Wolters Kluwer, 2012, 57–66.

E. C. C. M. Kemmeren, 'Sources of EU Law for European Tax Integration: Well-Known and Alternative Legal Instruments' in D. Weber (ed), *Traditional and Alternative Routes to European Tax Integration* (IBFD, Amsterdam, 2010).

A. Schrauwen, 'Sources of EU Law for Integration in Taxation' in D. Weber (ed), *Traditional and Alternative Routes to European Tax Integration* (IBFD, Amsterdam, 2010).

2 The development of EU law in the area of direct taxation and the related case law versus Member States' competence

A critical review in light of the defined 'benchmarks'

2.1 The sources of EU tax law

2.1.1 The Treaty's legal bases for EU action in the tax area and the development of sources of EU tax law in respect of indirect taxation and direct taxation: overview

Seven principal sources of EU law can be identified: the TEU and the TFEU are primary sources which set out the objectives of the EU, establish the working mechanisms of its institutions and identify the areas of EU competence; the 'secondary legislation' – i.e. regulations, directives and decisions – issued under specific provisions of the Treaty; the 'soft law', namely recommendations or communications issued by the European Commission, which are not legally binding but may help the interpretation and/or application of the Treaty, of secondary legislation and/or application of EU law; the related Treaties made between the Member States, which either amend or enlarge (such as, e.g. the Accession Treaties for new Member States) the original Treaty; the international Treaties negotiated by the EU, as a legal person of international law; the rulings issued by the ECJ in performing its function of ensuring the uniform interpretation and application of EU law; lastly, the general principles of law and fundamental rights which are common to constitutional laws of Member States and which are expressly indicated by Article 2 and by Article 6(1) and 6(3) of the TEU.[1]

Under Article 5 of the TEU, the EU only has the competences conferred on it by the TEU and the TFEU. The areas of EU competence are divided into three categories: 'exclusive competencies' under Article 3 of the TFEU;[2] shared

---

1 J. Fairhurst, *Law of the European Union*, 8th edn (Longmans, London, 2010), ch 2, pp. 56–85.
2 Customs union; competition rules; monetary policy for Member States adopting the Euro as a currency; common fishery policy; common commercial policy; conclusion of an international agreement when provided for in a legislative act of the EU or necessary to enable the EU to exercise its internal competence.

competencies *with pre-emption* in the areas listed in Article 4,[3] where both the EU and Member States are competent and where the exercise of competence by the EU deprives Member States of their competence; shared competence *without pre-emption*, in the areas listed in Article 6 TFEU,[4] where the EU can support, coordinate or supplement the actions of the Member States, without suppressing their competence.

Within the areas of customs union and competition rules (exclusive competence areas), the TFEU imposes 'negative obligations' on Member States in terms of tariffs, excise duties and indirect taxation; within the internal market area (shared competence area with pre-emption); it also offers legal bases to be used for issuing secondary legislation. In particular, tax provisions are contained in Articles 28 and 30 TFEU, which prevent 'charges having equivalent effect' to tariffs amongst which charges of fiscal nature, and in Title VII on 'Common rules on competition, taxation and approximation of laws', whose Chapter 2 ('Tax provisions') sets out rules on indirect taxation. Articles 110 to 112 prevent Member States from imposing any tax creating advantages for domestic products vis-à-vis products from other Member States, and Article 113 commits the Council to adopt provisions for the harmonisation of consumption taxes in the EU.

Whereas indirect taxation was perceived as affecting the trade in goods and services between Member States and was addressed by the Treaty, no provision expressly concerning direct taxation was included. After the repeal of Article 293 of the EC Treaty, which required Member States to negotiate so far as necessary to abolish double taxation, and which covered both direct and indirect taxation,[5] direct taxation – even if not expressly mentioned – falls within the scope of the internal market competence listed in Article 4(2)(a) TFEU. In fact, both indirect and direct taxation affects the internal market in terms of intra-EU cross-border trade, investment, service provision and employment.[6] For the same reason, direct taxation also falls within the scope of the general approximation-of-law provisions under Article 114 to 118, although the requirement of unanimity in the Council for introducing tax harmonisation directives under Article 115 has historically proven to be a major obstacle in this area.[7]

Article 116 offers another legal base for legislative action when differences between national laws distort the conditions of competition in the internal market and, unlike Article 114(2), it does not exclude tax measures. Accordingly, Article 116 provides a further base for EU legislation in the direct taxation area too,[8]

---

3 Internal market; social policy, for the aspects defined in the Treaty; economic, social and territorial cohesion; agriculture and fisheries; environment; consumer protection; transport; trans-European networks; energy; area of freedom, security and justice; common safety concerns in public health matters for the aspects defined in the TFEU itself.
4 Protection and improvement of human health; industry; culture; tourism; education, vocational training; civil protection; administrative cooperation.
5 See ch 1 at 1.1.
6 B. M. Terra, P. J. Wattel, *European Tax Law*, 6th edn (Wolters Kluwer, 2012), at 9.
7 See ch 1, at 1.1.
8 C. H. J. I. Panayi, *European Union Corporate Tax Law* (CUP, 2013), at 4.

although it has not been used to date. Article 352, empowering the Council (acting unanimously on a proposal from the Commission and after obtaining the consent of the European Parliament) to adopt appropriate measures if action by the EU proves necessary but the Treaties have not provided the necessary power, also contains a general legal basis capable of being used for achieving objectives related to the internal market and, impliedly, in both indirect and direct taxation. The Treaty drafters provided, therefore, the legal basis for EU action in the direct taxation area too, when necessary for the proper functioning of the internal market.

In the area of indirect taxation, extensive harmonisation creating a common VAT system and shaping the turnover tax of Member States has been achieved since the end of the 1960s, mainly through directives based on Articles 113 and 114.[9] The common VAT system is currently laid down by the 'recast Directive' 2006/112[10] and its implementing regulations. In this area, Member States retain a marginal competence which is limited to aspects not yet affected by EU harmonising secondary legislation. In turn, Directive 69/335 and Directive 2008/7/EC, relating to indirect taxes on the raising of capital, were intended to design the structure of these taxes completely in terms of *both* tax bases and tax rates. Arguably, the latitude of harmonisation in the *indirect* taxation area could qualify this field, on its own, as a shared EU competence with pre-emption (just as in the internal market area) in respect of 'positive obligations', i.e. of obligations for Member States to adapt their internal systems to EU law.

By contrast, the area of direct taxation – according to the ECJ – falls within the competence of Member States, which, nonetheless, must exercise that competence consistently with EU law.[11] Exercising the competence consistently with EU law implies – for national legislators – adapting national direct tax provisions to any EU directives and refraining from introducing or maintaining any provision in contrast with the fundamental non-discrimination principle enshrined in Articles 18, 45 and 49 of the TFEU. Articles 115 and 352 have been used for introducing direct tax legislation too, in the form of directives, initially in the area of administrative cooperation – Directives 608/76 and 79/779 respectively on recovery assistance and information exchange, subsequently replaced by Directives 2010/24/EU and 2011/16/EU – and subsequently with regard to corporate and individual taxation – i.e. the Merger Directive, the Parent–Subsidiary Directive, the Interest and Royalties Directive and the Savings Directive – as already mentioned.[12]

---

9 Directive 67/228/EEC, 11 April 1967, OJ 71, First VAT Directive; Directive 69/463/EEC, 9 December 1969, OJ 1969 L 320, Third VAT Directive; Directive 71/401/EEC, 20 December 1971, OJ 1971, Fourth VAT Directive; Directive 72/250/EEC, 4 July 1972, OJ 1972, Fifth VAT Directive; Directive 77/388/EEC, 17 May 1977, OJ 1977; Sixth Directive.
10 Directive 2006/112/EC on the common system of value added tax, in OJ L 347/1, 11.12.2006.
11 For example, Case C–35/98, *Verjooijken* [2000] ECR I–4071, para. 32; Joined Cases C–397/98 & C–410/98, *Metallgesellschaft and Others* [2001] ECR I–1727, para. 37.
12 See ch 1 at 1.1.

22 *The European Union and Direct Taxation*

Although harmonisation in the direct taxation area has been a limited one, Articles 115, 116 and 352 can be used for introducing new harmonisation directives *whenever* three conditions are met: (a) in the assessment of the EU legislator, the differences between national tax laws prevent the proper functioning of the internal market; (b) action by Member States would be insufficient to achieve the desired objectives (under the subsidiarity principle); and (c) new EU legislation would be necessary to tackle the problem at stake (under the proportionality principle). These legal bases therefore leave room for a potentially wider and wider EU action. In turn, the procedure for 'enhanced cooperation' (allowing the introduction of EU legislation addressed only to a group of Member States), set out in Article 20 TEU and in Articles 326–34 of the TFEU, can be used in the direct taxation area as well.

Moreover, the potential for EU legislation in this area is bound to expand owing to the increasing number of issues addressed by the European Commission through soft-law pieces. In fact, the increasing movement of taxpayers from one Member State to another results in a greater and greater overlapping of national direct taxation systems, which can give rise to new issues that individual actions by Member State would not be able to tackle. The soft-law pieces concerning the fight against cross-border tax evasion and fraud,[13] and the need to contrast aggressive cross-border tax planning strategies[14] indicate issues on which, in the future, new EU legislation might become necessary should the soft-law pieces fail to achieve their purpose.

Nonetheless, as long as new EU legislation in the direct taxation area is not introduced and the distribution of taxing powers between Member States, in this area too, is still largely based on DTCs, i.e. on international law sources, the intra-EU direct taxation environment is shaped by the interaction between EU law sources and international tax law sources.

2.1.2 The sources of EU law in the area of direct taxation and the interaction with international tax law: background on the attempts of harmonisation throughout the history of the internal market

Well before the foundation of the EEC, the international tax law order had already been shaping itself through bilateral conventions against double taxation (DTCs). After the first DTCs at the end of the 19th century, the perception that double taxation would hinder cross-border trade and investments led the League of Nations in the inter-war period, and subsequently the OECD and the UN, to draw up a set of recommendations addressed to states about how to allocate taxing powers between themselves, through DTCs, for different categories of cross-border income. These sets of recommendations, i.e. the OECD Model and UN

---

13 Ibid at 1.2.
14 Ibid.

Model, are not legally binding, but have become universal points of reference for countries entering into DTCs. There is currently a worldwide network of more than 3000 bilateral DTCs, which are largely similar in structure as well as in the terminology and constitute an international tax regime, which has definable underlying principles that are common to tax treaties[15] and that have been creating a customary international law.[16] Because EU Member States have been entering, as between themselves, DTCs based on the OECD Model, the international tax regime and the obligations that it has been creating as between Member States in terms of allocation of taxing powers and of treatment of non-residents, has come under the scrutiny of the ECJ in cases when natural or legal persons of Member States alleged that their tax treatment, *even if deriving* from DTCs, created a discrimination or a restriction hindering the exercise of fundamental freedoms.

As will be seen in Chapter 3, the ECJ, whilst stating that the Treaty's provisions on fundamental freedoms are *unconditional* and Member States cannot make compliance with those provisions subject to the contents of DTCs,[17] has been accepting that Member States can use the OECD Model when *allocating* taxing powers between themselves, but has stressed that the *exercise* of the taxing powers so allocated must be consistent with EU law. In certain instances, the ECJ regarded the exercise of taxing powers allocated by DTCs as incompatible with EU law on grounds of *discriminations* or of *restrictions* on the exercise of fundamental freedoms arising within an individual Member State to the detriment of non-resident taxpayers, who were in situations comparable with those of resident taxpayers. In these cases, the ECJ went as far as imposing Member State obligations going *beyond* the contents of DTCs, despite the balance of taxing powers established by DTCs.[18]

As a source of international tax law, DTCs are therefore compatible with EU tax law too, *subject to the condition* that the exercise of the taxing powers they allocate to any individual Member State does not result in discriminations or restrictions within a single country. DTCs and the Treaty are 'natural friends of each other'[19] as they pursue objectives which integrate with each other, because the elimination of double taxation, which is the goal of DTCs, also helps the achievement of the internal market. This was acknowledged by the drafters of the Treaty in Article 220 of the EEC Treaty (subsequently Article 293 of the EC Treaty) when they committed Member States to enter, 'as far as necessary', into (bilateral or multilateral) agreements for the abolition of double taxation: the bilateral DTCs entered into between the Member States (according to the OECD Model) pursue this objective, although they were not stipulated under Article 220(293).

---

15 R. S. Avi-Yonah, International Tax as International Law: An Analysis of the International Tax Regime (Cambridge Tax Law Series, CUP, 2007) 3,
16 Ibid., at 5,
17 Case 270/83, *Commission v France (avoir fiscal)* [1986] ECR 273, para. 26.
18 See Chapter 3, 3.2.
19 E. Kemmeren, Principle of Origin in Tax Conventions: A Rethinking of Models (Pijenburg, Dongen, 2001), 121.

As this provision did not have direct effect and thus could not confer any rights on individuals which they might enforce before their national courts,[20] part of the literature argued that, since its repeal by the Treaty of Lisbon, the objective of abolition of double taxation can be pursued by the EU more widely.[21] It also highlighted that Article 293 was complementary in its character ('so far as necessary'), and it could be used only where other legal bases such as the current Article 115 TFEU would not suffice to prevent international double taxation.[22] This argument assumes that, as international double taxation directly affects the functioning of the internal market, EU action to eliminate international double taxation should be based on Article 115 and take the form of a directive.[23]

Other literature submitted that, as the ECJ literally regarded the abolition of double taxation as being an objective of the Treaty due to Article 293, it would no longer be an objective of the TFEU after the repeal of such provision.[24] Nonetheless, the ECJ – in certain situations where it regarded itself as unable to remove juridical double taxation[25] owing to the absence of a general harmonising EU secondary legislation – *stressed the responsibility of Member States* to remove (juridical) double taxation through bilateral DTCs. Arguably, the ECJ would not have emphasised this responsibility of Member States, even after the repeal of Article 293 EC Treaty, if it had not regarded double taxation as incompatible with the very objective of the internal market enshrined in Article 26 of the TFEU.

This conception about international double taxation being incompatible with the internal market is also implied in the 2011 Commission Communication against double taxation.[26] Therefore, after the repeal of Article 293, the abolition of double taxation within the internal market could be regarded as an EU task to be pursued by way of harmonisation under Article 115 TFEU: secondary EU legislation measures become even more necessary than they were under Article 293 *if* the existing DTCs and/or unilateral measures by Member States do not manage to achieve the abolition of double taxation.

Ultimately, with regard to the interaction between the sources of EU tax law and DTCs as a source of international tax law, DTCs are currently 'replacing' a missing EU law measure of general character intended to abolish double taxation, and are playing the same role that would otherwise be played by this would-be EU directive (or regulation). As a result, DTCs as between Member States can also be regarded in a subordinate position to the Treaty – specifically, to internal

---

20 Case C-336/96, *Gilly* [1998] ECR I-2793; Hans Van der Hurk, 'The European Court of Justice knows its limits (a discussion inspired by the *Gilly* and *ICI* cases)', *ECTR* (1999), at 213.
21 E. Kemmeren, 'After Repeal of Article 293 EC Treaty under the Lisbon Treaty', *EC Tax Review* 2008, p. 145 ff.
22 Terra and Wattel, *European Tax Law* (n 6), at 20.
23 Ibid.
24 T. O'Shea, 'European Tax Controversies: A British-Dutch Debate: Back to Basics and Is the ECJ Consistent?' (2013) *World Tax Journal* 100, at 105.
25 See Chapter 3, at 3.3.
26 COM(2011) 712 final, at 3 and 6.

market and free movement provisions – and the ECJ has actually been assessing, from time to time, whether the exercise of taxing powers allocated by DTCs is consistent or inconsistent with the TFEU's provisions. This understanding of DTCs is strengthened by considering that, in the direct taxation area, each individual directive aims at eliminating economic and juridical double taxation for the specific kinds of operations meeting the requirements for falling within its scope. In so doing, such directives leave DTCs a *general* role for eliminating double taxation with regard to all cross-border incomes and operations *falling outside* the scope of each of the directives, although the Commission, since 2001, has been considering DTCs as inadequate to meet the needs of the internal market in terms of elimination of international juridical and economic double taxation.[27]

Against this backdrop, the legislative and related case law developments which have been taking place to date in the direct taxation area can be reviewed in light of each of the objectives still to be achieved – set out by the Commission communications[28] and which can be taken as 'benchmarks' – for fully identifying the shortcomings and considering the most effective way forward.

2.2 The Parent–Subsidiary Directive and the Merger Directive: a common, ultimate objective

The preambles of both Directive 133/2009/EC, the 'Merger Directive'[29] and Directive 2011/96/EU, the 'Parent-Subsidiary Directive',[30] stress the need for 'tax rules which are neutral from the viewpoint of competition',[31] which necessitate a 'common system of taxation'. They recognise, in fact, that the restructuring operations (for the Merger Directive) and 'the grouping together of companies' (for the Parent–Subsidiary Directive) involving companies of different Member States may be necessary to create within the EU 'conditions analogous to those of an internal market and in order thus to ensure the effective functioning of such an internal market',[32] so that these operations should not be hampered by restrictions, disadvantages and distortions caused by the different tax provisions of Member States.[33]

---

27 Commission Staff Working Paper, Company Taxation in the Internal Market, SEC(2001) 582 final, at 284–89.
28 See ch 1 at 1.2.
29 Directive 2009/133/EC, on the 'Common system of taxation applicable to mergers, divisions, partial divisions, transfers of assets and exchanges of shares concerning companies of different Member States and to the transfer of the registered office of an SE or SCE between Member States', OJ EU L 310 (25 November 2009); originally, Directive 434/1990/EEC, OJEC L 225 (20 August 1990).
30 Directive 2011/96/EU on the 'Common system of taxation applicable in the case of parent companies and subsidiaries of different Member States', OJ EU L 435 (29 December 2011); originally Directive 435/1990/EEC, OJEC L 225 (20 August 1990).
31 Directive 2009/133/EC, Preamble, Recital (2); Directive 2011/96/EU, Preamble, Recital (4).
32 Ibid.
33 Ibid.

This goal would certainly be achieved in a situation where competing companies falling within the scope of Article 54(2) of the Treaty[34] found the location in a Member State or in another one as *immaterial* from the tax viewpoint for carrying out – at either intra-EU or domestic level – the operations falling within the scope of the two directives. In this case, tax rules would be completely neutral in the broadest sense, which would be fully coherent with the TFEU's objectives in terms of proper functioning of the internal market and undistorted market competition and would also imply the achievement of all 'benchmarks'.[35] Nonetheless, in this respect the provisions of both directives, the related case law and the directives' implementation show a number of shortcomings, which will be highlighted below for each directive.

2.3 The Parent–Subsidiary Directive

2.3.1 The directive's key provisions

The Parent–Subsidiary Directive aims at eliminating the risk of both economic and juridical double taxation of profits distributions between subsidiaries, including lower-tier subsidiaries, or permanent establishments (PEs), and parent companies resident in different Member States. It applies to companies that, cumulatively: (a) take the national legal forms of private or public limited liability companies, cooperatives and others which are listed in an Annex to the directive[36] or the legal forms of European companies (SE) or of European cooperative societies (SCE);[37] (b) are considered to be tax resident in a Member State under its domestic law and, under a DTC, are not considered as tax resident outside the EU; (c) are subject to corporate income taxes in each Member State without the possibility of an option or of being exempted.[38] It defines 'parent company' as a company of a Member State meeting these eligibility conditions and having a minimum holding of 10 per cent in the capital of a company of another Member State fulfilling the same conditions, or in the capital of a company of the same Member State held through a PE located in another Member State.[39]

Member States may replace, through DTCs, the criterion of a holding in the capital with that of a holding of voting rights, and may require a two-year minimum holding period.[40] Moreover, because any charges related to the holding, and any losses resulting from the distributions of profits of the subsidiary, are costs

---

34 Which includes all profit-making entities.
35 See ch 1 at 1.2.
36 Art. 2, Annex I, Part A.
37 The SE was introduced by Regulation 2157/2001 of 8 October 2001 on the Statute for a European Company (SE), complemented by Directive 2001/86 on the involvement of employees; the SCE was introduced by Regulation 1435/2003 on the Statute for a European Cooperative Society, complemented by Directive 2003/72 on the involvement of employees.
38 Art. 2.
39 Art. 3.
40 Ibid.

relating to exempt income, the directive allows Member States to provide that these costs may not be deducted from the taxable profits of the parent company.[41]

The directive refers to an undefined concept of 'profit distributions', which is generally regarded as being more extensive than the term 'dividends' and as including disguised or hidden dividend distributions.[42] Article 1 includes in the directive's scope three types of possible profit distributions: direct distributions from subsidiaries to parent companies resident in another Member State; distributions from a subsidiary resident in one Member State to a PE located in another Member State of a parent company resident in the same Member State as the subsidiary; distributions from subsidiaries resident in a Member State to PEs located in another Member State of parent companies resident in a third Member State.[43]

To eliminate *economic double taxation* that would occur if distributed profits were taxed *first* in the hands of the distributing company and *again* in the hands of the receiving parent company, Article 4(1) provides two alternative methods, the *exemption method* and the *indirect tax credit method*, to be applied by the Member State of the parent company to inbound 'profits distributions' received by this company *or* by the Member State of location of the PE receiving these distributions. The indirect tax credit method deducts the tax paid by the subsidiary and by any lower tier subsidiary up to the amount of the corresponding domestic tax. The exemption method – after amendments approved as a result of the latest Commission proposal[44] – must be denied to parent companies (or PEs) for inbound distributions of profits that are deductible by the paying subsidiary in its state of residence. This new provision avoids instances of (economic) double non-taxation that would otherwise arise on remuneration paid on hybrid financial loan arrangements regarded as deductible expenses by the subsidiary state and as exempted dividends by the parent company state.

To eliminate the *juridical double taxation* that would be suffered by the parent company (or its PE) receiving the distributed profits if these were subjected both to withholding tax by the subsidiary state of residence and to corporate tax by the residence Member State of the parent company, Article 5(1) requires complete exemption from withholding tax.[45] Moreover, if a parent company state of residence considers a subsidiary located in another Member as fiscally transparent, this state is allowed to tax the resident parent company on the subsidiary's profits as and when they arise, but – to avoid juridical double taxation – it must not tax the distributed profits of the subsidiary in the hands of the parent company.[46]

---

41 Art. 4(3).
42 C. H. J. I. Panayi, *European Union Corporate Tax Law* (n 8), at 34.
43 Directive 2011/96/EU (n 30), Art. 1(c) and (d).
44 Commission Proposal for a Council Directive amending Directive 2011/96/EU on the common system of taxation applicable in the case of parent companies and subsidiaries of different Member States, COM(2013) 814 final (25 November 2013), at 7.
45 Additionally, Art. 6 prevents the Member State of a parent company from charging withholding tax on the profits which such a company receives from a subsidiary.
46 Art. 4(2).

Article 1(2) also includes an anti-abuse provision, which expressly addresses *both* tax evasion, by safeguarding national or DTCs provisions intended to fight it, *and* abusive practices, by inserting a new general anti-abuse rule (GAAR). This GAAR requires Member States to withdraw the benefits of the directive in case of arrangements or series of arrangements put in place for the main purpose or for one of the main purposes of improperly obtaining tax advantages whilst defeating the object or purpose of the directive, and, in light of all facts and cirumstances, not reflecting economic reality.[47] It reflects the ECJ's case law on abusive practices in the exercise of the freedom of establishment – where the ECJ regarded a tax-driven creation of subsidiaries in another Member State without economic integration there as a wholly artificial arrangement justifying the application of national anti-abuse measures[48] – and is consistent with the anti-abuse clause of the Merger Directive.[49]

Finally, the directive does not prevent the advance payment of corporation tax paid to the Member State of the subsidiary, in connection with distribution of profits to the parent company,[50] and Article 7(2) safeguards national or DTCs provisions 'designed to eliminate or to lessen economic double taxation of dividends and the payment of tax credits to the recipient of dividends'.

2.3.2 The directive's text against the benchmarks

Literature found, in the 1990 text, important limits,[51] which also emerge if the current text of the Directive is assessed against at least three specific benchmarks:[52] legal certainty, elimination of double taxation and double non-taxation; reduction of administrative compliance costs.

First, owing to the lack of a definition of the key concepts of 'distributions of profits' and of 'fiscal residence', these gaps are deemed to be filled by national tax laws and by DTCs provisions. The crucial role for national tax laws of Member States and for DTCs *with a third state* is particularly evident with regard to the 'tax residence' under Article 2.[53]

This may cause the effectiveness of the directive to be undermined whenever national laws apply different definitions of companies' 'tax residence' – e.g. the place of incorporation, or the place of management and control – which may cause situations of *dual residence* within the EU both for the distributing subsidiary and for the parent company if these companies have registered office in one Member State and head office/place of management in another Member State. In effect,

---

47 COM(2013) 814 final (n 44), proposed new Art. 1, at 9.
48 See e.g. Case C-196/04, *Cadbury Schweppes* [2006] ECR I-7995, paras. 51, 55 and 68; Case C-524/04, *Test Claimant in the Thin Cap Group Litigation* [2007] ECR I-2107, paras. 72 and 74. See also ch 3.
49 See 2.4 below, about the Merger Directive.
50 Art. 7(1).
51 Inter alia: IBFD, Survey on the Implementation of the EU Corporate Tax Directives, 1995, IBFD, at 11; W. Williams, EC Tax Law (Longmans, London, 1998), at 143–44.
52 See ch 1, at 1.2.
53 Art. 2(a)(ii).

under the ECJ's rulings on the freedom of establishment, companies can transfer to another Member State the head office *alone* as a form of exercise of the freedom of establishment, under Articles 49 and 54 TFEU, when allowed by their national laws.[54]

Because the directive does not mention DTCs between the two Member States, in these situations legal uncertainty arises as to which one amongst the two countries claiming the tax residence should grant the benefits of the directive, and as to whether enjoying either the exemption on received dividends or the tax credit *in both states* could go beyond the purpose of the directive. The tiebreaker criteria used in Article 4 of the OECD Model and of most DTCs to allocate companies' tax residence as between contracting states, i.e. the 'place of effective management' criteria – which, in essence, is the company's decision-making centre – tends to be increasingly difficult to apply in the current global and computerised economy, where decisions can be taken by directors residing in different countries and communicating by electronic means. If two contracting states both claim the 'place of effective management' in their jurisdiction, the OECD Model and many DTCs require the countries concerned to seek to determine the tax residence by mutual agreement, but not to *manage to reach* the agreement: if agreement is not reached, the company may end up being considered as resident of none of the countries under the DTC.[55]

Such a situation may also occur in case of unresolved tax residence conflict between one Member State and a third country:[56] the wording of Article 2 – due to its requiring a cumulative condition of being resident of a Member State under its law and not being resident outside the EU under a DTC with a third country – would leave doubt as to whether or not, in this situation, the company could benefit from the directive. In fact, the non-residence outside the EU under a DTC with a third country might be read as implying that, under such DTC, the company is supposed to be resident in a Member State, rather than being resident in *neither* the Member State *nor* the third country.

Apart from the importance of the options *expressly* granted, another limit from the viewpoint of legal certainty can be found in the crucial choices left to Member States in answering the doubts raised by the text of the directive. For example Article 4(1) excludes from the concept of 'distribution of profits' those profits which are received by the parent company at the winding up of the subsidiary, which raises the question as to whether, in the country of origin, these distributions should be exempted from withholding tax when they are considered – by the relevant national law – as equivalent to dividends.[57]

In turn, the GAAR in Article 1(2), by reflecting the concept of wholly artificial arrangement emerging from the ECJ's case law on the freedom of establishment,[58]

---

54 See ch 3, at 3.1.3.
55 For example, this is the case of under Art. 4(4) of the 2008 UK–Netherlands DTC.
56 For example, Art. 4(5) of the 2001 UK–US DTC.
57 Member States' discretion in this respect creates further space for differences concerning important aspects between national legislations.
58 See ch 2 at 2.3.1.1 and ch 3 below.

suggests that a Member State of the parent company could deny the exemption or tax credit if the creation of a subsidiary in another Member State were driven only by tax saving reasons with no genuine economic integration there. However, under the ECJ's case law, this would require a case-by-case examination,[59] which would not help an *ex ante* legal certainty in the application of the directive.

Moreover, the choice left to Member States between exemption and indirect tax credit method would contrast with the broadest concept of tax neutrality.[60] In fact, this choice would produce the same outcome – in terms of eliminating economic double taxation on the distributed profits – only if the level of taxation of the parent company is either *equal* or *higher* than that of the subsidiary and of any lower-tier subsidiary. Otherwise, only the exemption method would fully eliminate economic double taxation, because the indirect tax credit method – by limiting the deduction of the tax paid by any (lower-tier) subsidiary up to the amount of the corresponding domestic tax[61] – would offer no relief to the parent company for any exceeding tax amount paid by the subsidiary. The option for the credit method by a Member State also determines administrative compliance costs for resident parent companies, as this method can be difficult to apply.[62]

The choice offered by the directive between these two different methods used by national legislators is consistent *neither* with the admission (in the preamble) that restrictions, disadvantages and distortions are being created by those differences, *nor* with the intention to create conditions analogous to those of a *unique* internal market. Such methods reflect two different ideas of prevention of international double taxation at the parent company level, the 'capital import neutrality' (CIN) and 'capital export neutrality' (CEN), which both make sense across *distinct markets*.[63] Conversely, creating a *unique* internal market implies the broadest concept of tax neutrality, which would cause the distinction between CIN and CEN to disappear.

The directive may also lead to a *(juridical) double non-taxation* of the parent company, in case of a full participation exemption in its state of residence and abolition of withholding tax in the subsidiary state of residence. This would apparently create the kind of situation that the Commission, in its 2012 Recommendation against aggressive tax planning, highlighted the need to overcome.[64]

Amongst other provisions of the directive, the possibility of replacing the criterion of a holding in the capital by that of a holding of voting rights, can

---

59 See ch 3 at 3.1.3.
60 See ch 2 at 2.3.1.1.
61 Art. 4(1)(b).
62 See 2.3.3.5 and 2.3.5 below.
63 The exemption method is based on the idea of a 'capital import neutrality' (CIN), i.e. equal treatment of local investors and foreign investors in the same national or foreign market. The indirect tax credit method represents 'capital export neutrality' (CEN), i.e. equal treatment in a given State of resident taxpayers investing at home and of resident taxpayers investing abroad. See Terra and Wattel, *European Tax Law* (n 6), at 213–15.
64 Commission Recommendation of 6 December 2012 on aggressive tax planning C(2012) 8806 final, Preamble, Recital (5).

obviously generate different tax effects – given a certain amount of profits received by a parent company – in the case of subsidiary companies having different categories of shares. For example, preference shares typically entitle the holder to receive in preference to all other classes of share capital a dividend but either exclude voting rights or bear limitations on such rights. Two companies, possessing the first one 10 per cent of voting rights, the second 10 per cent of share capital composed of preference shares without voting rights, and receiving the same amount of profits distributed by their subsidiaries, would – if located in a Member State adopting the criterion of holding of voting rights – be treated in a different way. The first company would be a 'parent company' and would benefit from the directive; however, the second one would not qualify as a parent company and would still risk double taxation on the profits distributed by its subsidiary. The second company would thus be disadvantaged in comparison with competing companies located in a Member State following the criterion of holding in the share capital.

Moreover, the current range of eligible legal forms does not yet include all possible beneficiaries of the right of establishment falling within Article 54(2) of the TFEU. This provision refers to *all* profit-making 'companies and firms', not only to those listed in the Annex of the directive (which are mainly limited liability companies). Therefore, even from the viewpoint of the choice of legal forms by businesses wishing to form groups within the EU, the directive text does not achieve complete tax neutrality.

2.3.3 The case law on the Parent–Subsidiary Directive

The ECJ's case law, in assessing alleged infringements of the directive by national implementing measures, has been dealing with: (a) the scope of the option for Member States to require a minimum holding period and of the anti-abuse clause, in the 1996 *Denkavit*[65] decision; (b) the 'direct effect' of the directive's provisions, in *Denkavit*, in the 2001 *Zythopiia* case[66] and in the 2009 *Cobelfret*[67] ruling; (c) the concept of 'withholding tax' to be abolished by Member States under Article 5(1) of the directive, in the 1998 *Epson* case,[68] in *Zythopiia*, in the 2003 *Van der Grinten*[69] ruling, in the 2006 *Test Claimant in the FII Group Litigation* ruling,[70] in the 2008 *Burda* ruling[71] and in the 2010 *Ferrero* ruling[72] and, by way of exception from Article 5(1), the application of the clause in Article 7(2) safeguarding domestic or DTC provisions designed to eliminate or to lessen economic double taxation of dividends,

---

65 Joined Cases C–283/94, C–291/94 & C–292/94, *Denkavit, Vitic Voormer* [1996] ECR I–5063.
66 Case C–294/99, *Athinaiki Zythopiia* [2001] ECR I–6797, 6813.
67 Case C–138/07, *Cobelfret* [2009] ECR I–731.
68 Case C–375/98, *Epson Europe* [2000] ECR I–4243.
69 Case C–58/01, *Océ van der Grinten* [2003] ECR I–9809.
70 Case C–446/04, *Test Claimant in the FII Group Litigation* [2006] ECR I–11753.
71 Case C–284/06, *Burda* [2008] ECR I–4571.
72 Joined Cases C–338/08 & C–339/08, *Ferrero* [2010] ECR I–5743.

in *Zythopiia* and in *Van der Grinten*; (d) the non-deductibility of charges relating to participation as a possible option allowed to Member States and, in this regard, the general relationship between the options granted by the directive and the freedom of establishment, in the 2003 *Bosal Holding* ruling,[73] in the 2006 *Keller Holding* decision[74] and in the 2008 *Banque Fédérative du Crédit Mutual*[75] case; (e) the scope of the eligibility condition with regard to the shareholding in the subsidiary, in the 2008 *Les Verges du Vieux Taves* ruling,[76] and, with regard to legal forms, in the 2009 *Gaz de France* ruling;[77] (f) the method of granting the participation exemption for inbound dividends received by resident parent companies, in the *Cobelfret* and *KBC and BRB*[78] rulings.

2.3.3.1 The option of requiring a minimum holding period and the anti-abuse clause

In *Denkavit*, a Dutch parent company – holding a qualifying participation in a Germany subsidiary – had to await the elapsing date of the minimum holding period under German law to receive dividends with exemption from withholding tax, even though the dividends distribution had originally been planned to take place before that date. If dividends had been distributed before the elapsing of the minimum holding period, withholding tax would in fact have been charged. The ECJ found that Article 4(2), allowing Member States to set a two-year minimum holding period as a condition for granting the benefits of the directive, does not require this period to have elapsed on the date of dividends distribution, for the parent company to be entitled to the exemption from withholding tax.

Nevertheless, the ECJ also left Member States free to determine national rules ensuring compliance with this period,[79] since the directive does not specify whether a Member State should grant exemption from the beginning of this period without being certain of obtaining a later payment of the tax. The ECJ based this position on the directive's anti-abuse clause, which it regarded as a 'provision of principle' whose content is explained in detail by the provision allowing Member States to set the minimum holding period to avoid abuses whereby temporary holdings are taken in the capital of companies for the sole purpose of benefiting from the tax advantage available.[80]

2.3.3.2 The 'direct effect' of the directive's provisions

In *Denkavit*, the ECJ also ruled that a parent company can rely on Article 5(1) granting exemption from withholding tax before the courts of the subsidiary's

---

73 Case C–168/01, *Bosal Holding* [2003] ECR I–9409.
74 Case C–471/04, *Keller Holding* [2006] ECR I–2107.
75 Case C–27/07, *Banque Fédérative du Crédit Mutual* [2008] ECR I–2067.
76 Case C–48/07, *Les Verges du Vieux Taves* [2008] ECR I–10627.
77 Case C–247/08, *Gaz de France* [2009] ECR I–09225.
78 Joined Cases C–439/07 & C–499/07, *KBC and BRB* [2009] ECR I–4409.
79 Joined Cases C–283/94, C–291/94 & C–292/94, *Denkavit* (n 65) para. 34.
80 Ibid., para. 31.

Member State, when this Member State wrongly interprets the minimum holding period requirement. The ECJ was thus willing to recognise 'direct effect' to Article 5(1), but it did not go as far as considering the plaintiff as entitled to damages suffered as a result of a wrongful interpretation of the minimum holding period, mainly due to the absence, up to that moment, of any case law on the matter and to the circumstance that many other Member States had adopted the same reasoning as the Member State concerned.[81]

In *Zythopiia*, the ECJ, in finding that a Greek tax payable by a resident subsidiary at the time of profits distribution to its Dutch parent company constituted a withholding tax prohibited by Article 5(1), although not formally classified as such, also dealt with the financial liability of a Member State for the refund of an unduly collected (withholding) tax. In this ruling, the ECJ rejected a request from the Greek Government for a limitation in time of the effects of its ruling for the national administration to lessen the noticeable financial liability otherwise deriving from the refund of the unduly collected withholding tax. It found that the situation in *Zythopiia* was not an exceptional case justifying the limitation in time of the effects of the ruling, because Greece had *not proved* that, when introducing the national provisions establishing the contested tax, there was objective uncertainty about Article 5(1) and it was reasonably possible to suppose that Article 5(1) allowed such a tax.[82]

The ECJ simply stressed that, if the financial damages arising for Member States from the unlawful nature of a tax justified the limitation of the effects of an interpretative ruling such as *Zythopiia*, the final outcome would (paradoxically) be a better treatment for the worst violations, and that, in addition, a limitation of the effects of the ruling based solely on financial reasons would substantially reduce the enforcement of the rights conferred to taxpayers by EU tax law.[83] This ECJ reasoning can certainly discourage Member States from introducing taxes whose lawfulness may appear doubtful in light of EU law, and it implicitly suggests that both Article 5(1) and other directives' provisions which are formulated as clearly as Article 5(1) and confer enforceable rights to taxpayers, are considered as having 'direct effect'.

The ECJ's conclusions in *Zythopiia*, and their implications, can be coordinated with *Denkavit*. The implicit recognition – in *Zythopiia* – of the 'direct effect' is undoubtedly consistent with the finding in *Denkavit* of the parent company's right to rely directly on the fundamental tax relief provisions of the directive before the national courts of another Member State. Moreover, in *Zythopiia*, by affirming – outside exceptional cases – the financial liability of Member States for the refund of the withholding tax collected from the time of entry into force of the national provisions establishing it, the ECJ has also accepted, as a *general rule*, the right of companies to the full refund of a tax which they ought not to have paid under a *fundamental* directive's provision. Consequently, as a *general principle*, after *Zythopiia*,

---

81 Ibid., paras. 51 and 52.
82 Case C–294/99, *Athinaiki Zythopiia* (n 66), para. 38.
83 Ibid., para. 39.

companies are entitled to compensation for *direct damages* which consist of the payment of clearly undue taxes under Articles 4 and 5 of the directive, whereas, in the cases of *indirect damages* – such as, in *Denkavit*, the postponing of the receipt of the income until the expiry of the minimum holding period – the situation may be the opposite.

Furthermore, in the 2009 *Cobelfret* ruling, the ECJ held that the right given to a Member State to choose options for achieving the results required by the directive – in that case, the choice left between the exemption and the indirect tax credit method – does not preclude the possibility for taxpayers to enforce before national courts rights whose content can be determined with sufficient precision,[84] i.e. it does not prevent the direct effect of a directive provision which is worded in unconditional and sufficiently precise terms.[85]

2.3.3.3 *The concept of 'withholding tax' under Article 5(1) and the application of Article 7(2) safeguarding DTC provisions designed to eliminate or lessen (economic) double taxation*

In a number of cases, the ECJ considered the concept of 'withholding tax' as a concept to be interpreted autonomously and substantively under EU law, regardless of national law.

In the *Epson* case, a Portuguese 'succession and donation tax' (ISD), which was intended as a substitute for an inheritance and gift tax on assets such as shares, tax was levied on income from shares owing to the impossibility of recovering otherwise a tax on the succession of shares, and was applied in parallel with regular dividend withholding tax. The ISD was levied on a dividend distribution, falling within the scope of the directive, from a Portuguese subsidiary to its Dutch parent company, although Portugal considered this tax as a special regime, different from corporate income tax, as it was levied on the value of the securities on the basis of a dividend capitalisation factor. However, the ECJ noted that the term 'withholding tax' in Article 5(1) of the directive is not limited to certain specific types of national taxation[86] and set out three conditions for a tax to be a withholding tax: the chargeable event is the distribution of *dividends* or *any other income* from shares; the taxable amount is the income from shares, and the taxable person is the shareholder.[87]

On these grounds, the ECJ regarded the ISD as a 'withholding tax' falling within the scope of Article 5(1), and considered its name as immaterial.[88] It stressed that the effectiveness of the directive would be undermined if Member States deprived parent companies resident in other EU countries of the benefits of the directive by subjecting them to taxes having the same effects as a tax on

---

84 Case C–138/07, *Cobelfret* (n 67), para. 61.
85 Ibid., para. 63, and below in the text.
86 Case C–375/98, *Epson Europe* (n 68), para. 22.
87 Ibid., para. 23.
88 Ibid.

income, even if the names given to these taxes placed them in the (different) category of taxes on assets.[89]

In *Zythopiia*, the Greek company, whose share capital was held as to 92.17 per cent by its Dutch parent company, claimed from the competent national tax authority the refund of a part of the corporate income tax which it had paid – in accordance with national law provisions – at the time of the distribution of profits to its Dutch parent company. The distribution of profits from a Greek subsidiary to its parent company was used to make the subsidiary subject to tax on two categories of income which would not have been made taxable without the distribution, and the plaintiff claimed that this taxation was a withholding tax prohibited by Article 5(1). Greece had contended that, those profits being taxed as *subsidiary's profits*, the tax paid was an advance payment of the corporation tax by the subsidiary, made in connection with a distribution of profits to its parent company. As such, the tax would be allowed by Article 7, as the Directive does not provide for an exemption from the corporation tax on the subsidiary.[90]

Nonetheless, the ECJ, after stressing the importance of the exemption from the withholding tax for eliminating double taxation, emphasised that Article 5(1) does not limit the notion of withholding tax to specific types of national taxes, and that whatever national tax must be examined on the basis of its objective features, irrespective of the way in which it is classified by national legislation.[91] In that case, these features evidenced that the tax was generated by the *distribution of dividends* rather than by the production of income,[92] and led the ECJ to exclude the nature of an advance payment of the corporation tax. In *Zythopiia* the ECJ, by overlooking the fact that the taxable person was not the shareholder but the subsidiary, neglected one of the three conditions that it had regarded as necessary in *Epson*[93] for the existence of a 'withholding tax'.[94]

However, even if it was considered that the taxable person was the subsidiary, the ECJ could still have found this tax incompatible with the directive by refusing the further Greek argument that the taxation of the dividends by the subsidiary state of residence was allowed, up to a rate of 35 per cent, by the DTC concluded with the Member State of the parent company and therefore that the tax was authorised by Article 7(2) (which safeguards DTCs designed to eliminate or lessen double taxation of dividends). The ECJ rejected this argument by highlighting that this DTC had not eliminated or lessened, but had *created* the double taxation of dividends, because, despite the ceiling on the overall tax rate, it ultimately did authorise both states to tax the distributed dividends. Consequently, the ECJ ruled

---

89 Ibid., para. 24.
90 Which tax is, indeed, supposed by the very choice left by Art. 4 to opt for the indirect tax credit method for the corporation tax paid by the subsidiary on distributed profits.
91 Just like it had done in *Epson* (n 68).
92 Case C–294/99, *Athinaiki Zythopiia* (n 66), paras. 28 and 29.
93 Case C–375/98, *Epson* (n 68), para. 23.
94 That is, the distribution of dividends or any other income from shares as chargeable event, the income as taxable amount and the shareholder as taxable person. See Terra and Wattel, *European Tax Law* (n 6), at 639.

that such DTC could not be safeguarded by Article 7(2) and, after stating that, *outside* the application of this provision, the right to abolition of withholding tax under Article 5(1) is absolute and unconditional, it definitively concluded that the taxation at stake was a withholding tax, in breach of the directive.

Arguably, this finding in *Zythopiia* indicates that – although, by definition, all DTCs are designed to eliminate or lessen economic double taxation – the ECJ intends analysing, in each specific case, whether the DTC at stake actually produces the result of eliminating or lessening economic double taxation. If not, Article 7(2) – the only possible exception to Article 5(1) – becomes inapplicable and a tax generated by profits distribution, even allowed by a DTC, is a prohibited 'withholding tax'.

These indications, to be drawn from *Zythopiia*, can be read together with the ECJ's finding in the 2003 *Océ van der Grinten* ruling. In this last decision, the ECJ held that the payment of a partial imputation credit, by the subsidiary state of residence, to the parent company in another Member State, in connection with a dividend payment by the subsidiary, does not qualify as a 'distribution of profits' due to the very nature of a tax credit as an instrument designed to avoid economic double taxation.[95]

Consistently with the imputation credit being regarded as a tax refund and not as a profit distribution, the ECJ also found that a 5 per cent withholding tax on the aggregate amount of this tax credit and of the dividends was not a prohibited withholding tax under Article 5(1) for the part of it which related to the tax credit. After reaffirming that a prohibited 'withholding tax' exists when the tax meets the three conditions set out in *Epson*,[96] the ECJ found that the part of the 5 per cent charge related to the dividends distributed to the Dutch parent company was indeed, in principle, a withholding tax, but also accepted it under Article 7(2) in that particular case. Specifically, it found that Article 7(2) was drafted in light of the UK system, under which the distribution of dividends was accompanied by a partial tax credit where the DTC with the state of residence of the parent company so provided. Moreover, it stressed that the 5 per cent charge did not cancel out the lessening of economic double taxation of dividends that had been generated by the payment of the tax credit under the DTC, and that, in any case, the 5 per cent charge, under this DTC, was offset against the tax owed by the parent company in the Netherlands.[97]

This last deductibility of withholding tax ultimately allowed the UK–Netherlands DTC to eliminate juridical double taxation on the Dutch parent company as if the 5 per cent charge had not been levied, whilst still maintaining the lessening of economic double taxation. If this is considered together with the facts in *Zythopiia*, it could be argued that, when Article 7(2) of the directive is invoked by Member States, the ECJ analyses whether the specific DTC actually

---

95 Case C–58/01, *Océ van der Grinten* (n 69), para. 56.
96 Ibid., para. 47.
97 Ibid., paras. 85–89.

lessens economic double taxation *and* eliminates juridical double taxation. If it does not, a charge levied at the occasion of dividends distribution can be regarded as a prohibited withholding tax even where one of the three conditions is lacking (*Zythopiia*); conversely, when the DTC does so, a charge meeting the three conditions – and otherwise forbidden by Article 5 – may be justified under Article 7(2) (*van der Grinten*).

In a 2006 decision concerning, inter alia, an alleged withholding tax on inbound dividends received by a resident parent company from subsidiaries resident in other Member States, prohibited by Article 6 of the directive, and where Article 7(2) was not at stake, the ECJ held that the three conditions required for the existence of a withholding tax under Article 5 of the directive also apply under Article 6 as the concept of 'withholding tax' must have the same interpretation.[98]

In the 2008 *Burda* and the 2010 *Ferrero* rulings, the ECJ had to assess whether equalisation taxes levied at the time of dividends distributions were to be considered as 'withholding' taxes under Article 5. In *Burda*, Germany had levied an equalisation tax – that was similar to the Greek tax in *Zythopiia* – on the distributing subsidiary at the time of dividends distribution to a parent company resident in the Netherlands. The ECJ expressly stated that the three conditions set out in *Epson* for a withholding tax to exist are cumulative[99] and refused to consider the tax as a 'withholding tax' owing to the absence of the third condition, i.e. given the lack of the requirement that the taxable person be the shareholder[100] and not the distributing subsidiary.

In *Ferrero*, concerning a 5 per cent tax on the refund, pursuant to the applicable DTC, of an Italian adjustment surtax on dividends distributions to Dutch corporate shareholders, the ECJ maintained its *van der Grinten* and *Burda* findings. Although the Italian distributing subsidiaries had challenged the 5 per cent charge on the refund of the adjustment surtax, by alleging that the DTC expressly defined this refund as a 'dividend', the ECJ regarded this characterisation as not decisive[101] in light of the objective characteristics of the refund itself. In fact, it found that the adjustment surtax was merely a corrective mechanism, that was intended to prevent a tax credit from being granted for an unpaid tax,[102] which applied irrespective of whether the parent company was resident in Italy or in another state,[103] and consequently the refund could not be regarded as a distribution of profits. The second condition for the existence of a prohibited withholding tax, i.e. the income from shares as a taxable base, was therefore lacking, just as the third condition because the taxable person was the distributing subsidiary[104] rather than the Dutch shareholders.

---

98 Case C–446/04, *Test Claimant in the FII Group Litigation* (n 70), paras. 108–109.
99 Case C–284/06, *Burda* (n 71), para. 62.
100 Ibid., para. 63.
101 Joined Cases C–338/08 & 339/08, *Ferrero* (n 72), para. 20.
102 Ibid., para. 30.
103 Ibid., para. 33.
104 Ibid.

38 *The European Union and Direct Taxation*

Overall, the ECJ has therefore identified an independent EU concept of 'withholding tax'. However, doubts may arise as to whether the fact that case law subsequent to *Zythopiia* has been consistently identifying the three conditions as necessary for a 'withholding tax', implies that *Zythopiia* was wrongly decided.[105] In fact, adhering to this view may mean neglecting the case-by-case analysis carried out by the ECJ, in *Zythopiia* as well as in *van der Grinten*, about the ability of DTCs to lessen economic double taxation under Article 7(2), when this provision was invoked by national governments. Indeed, the fact that the ECJ regards the *characterisation* of a tax refund as a 'dividend' in a DTC as immaterial in *Ferrero*, may not (necessarily) imply that the ECJ has given up its previous *Zythopiia* and *van der Grinten* approach of ascertaining whether the ultimate *outcome* of a DTC, for it to be safeguarded under Article 7(2), is the lessening or the elimination of double taxation.

2.3.3.4 *The possible non-deductibility of charges relating to participation and the relationship between the options granted by the directive and the freedom of establishment*

In *Bosal Holding*, the ECJ had to assess a Dutch provision making a deduction of costs relating to a holding owned by a resident parent company, subject to the condition that the relevant subsidiary made taxable profits in the Netherlands and not in other Member States. The Netherlands argued that a refusal to allow the deductibility of the costs at issue was legitimate as it was allowed by Article 4(2), leaving Member States the option of providing that any charges relating to the holding may not be deducted from the taxable profits of the parent company.

The ECJ admitted that, in so far as the Dutch provision merely implemented the possibility offered by Article 4(2), it was compatible with the directive, but it also found that such option may be exercised only in compliance with the freedom of establishment. From this viewpoint, it found that the limitation on costs deductibility might dissuade a parent company from carrying on its activities through a subsidiary established in another Member State – since non-resident subsidiaries do not generate taxable profits in the Netherlands – and that such a limitation contrasts with the directive's objective of eliminating the disadvantaged treatment of relations between parent companies and subsidiaries of different Member States.[106]

The ECJ noted that the directive does not provide for any exception concerning the territory where the profits of the subsidiaries might be taxed, and it concluded that the national provision breached directive, interpreted in the light of Article 49. Although the Commission argued that the *Bosal* ruling 'opens up new legal possibilities for tax planning and could create further difficulties for Member States',[107] the ECJ reiterated its finding in the subsequent and almost identical

---

105   In this sense, Terra and Wattel, *European Tax Law* (n 6) at 640–41.
106   Case C–168/01, *Bosal Holding* (n 73), para. 28.
107   Commission Communication 'An Internal Market without tax obstacles achievements, ongoing initiatives and remaining challenges', COM(2003) 726 final, at 8.

Keller Holding ruling, where it struck down a German provision whereby costs relating to holding in subsidiaries are deductible only if they are instrumental in making taxable profits in the parent company's state of residence.

The Commission's concern about the possibilities for tax planning opened up by the *Bosal* (and *Keller*) could well be justified, as the *ratio* of the option for Member States to refuse the deductibility of any costs related to the holdings in subsidiaries resident in other Member States, lies in the fact that these costs relate to exempt income. The option would thus be consistent with a symmetry between deduction of costs and taxation of profits, but the ECJ's position in *Bosal* and *Keller Holding* appeared to set a limit of *general character* to Member States' discretion in implementing the options left by the directive: this implementation must be tested against the directive's objective of eliminating the disadvantaged treatment of the relations between parent companies and subsidiaries of different Member States, and against the freedom of establishment.

With regard to the option granted by Article 4(2), a further limit on Member States derives from the indication that, where the non-deductible management costs related to the holding are fixed at a flat rate, the fixed amount must not exceed 5 per cent of the profits distributed by the subsidiary. In the 2008 *Banque Fédérative du Crédit Mutual* ruling, the ECJ accepted that, in calculating the 5 per cent ceiling, Member States could apply this limit to the gross amount of distributed profits,[108] rather than to profits net of withholding tax at source, which is consistent with the prohibition as a general rule of withholding tax itself.

2.3.3.5 The eligibility conditions with regard to shareholding and legal forms

In the 2008 *Les Verges du Vieux Taves* ruling, the ECJ had to decide whether a company owning a right of usufruct over shares in another company may be regarded as a parent company for the purpose of the directive. The ECJ noted that the legal position of a usufructuary of shares in a subsidiary does not confer the status of shareholder, as the usufruct solely derives from the transfer, by the full owner of the shares, of a right to the distributed profits, but it carries *neither* an entitlement to undistributed profits *nor* voting rights. Given the directive's requirement of a holding in the capital, involving a specific legal relationship between parent and subsidiary, the ECJ found that the usufructuary was not a parent company under the directive.[109]

In the 2009 *Gaz de France* ruling, the ECJ had to solve an eligibility issue concerning the legal form: a company having the legal form of French simplified joint-stock company (*société par actions simplifiée*), which was introduced *after* the adoption of the 1990 version of the directive, had received dividends from her German wholly owned subsidiary and suffered withholding tax at source. Although this legal form was listed in the 2003 proposed amendments to the directive, these

---

108 Case C–27/07, *Banque Fédérative du Crédit Mutual* (n 75), para. 47.
109 Case C–48/07, *Les Verges du Vieux Taves* (n 76), paras. 38–39.

amendments had not yet entered into force when the distribution took place, and the ECJ held that the directive is *not aimed* at introducing a common system for *all* companies or for *all* types of holding.[110] It thus found that eligible legal forms only include the legal forms of companies expressly listed in the Annex of the directive at the time of the distribution.

The ECJ clarified that the principle of legal certainty required the list of companies in the directive's Annex to be exhaustive,[111] and therefore regarded an extension by analogy of the directive's scope to other forms of comparable companies as inadmissible.[112] *Les Verges du Vieux Taves* and *Gaz de France* are therefore consistent with each other in strictly adhering to the directive's literal wording as regards the eligibility conditions relating to the shareholding and to the legal forms.

2.3.3.6 *The method of granting the participation exemption*

In the 2009 *Cobelfret* ruling, the ECJ had to assess a particular method, a 'dividends deduction system', used by Belgium to grant the participation exemption. Inbound dividends – from both domestic subsidiaries and subsidiaries resident in other Member States – were first included in the parent company's taxable base and subsequently deducted, for 95 per cent of their amount, only if the parent company had taxable profits in the relevant period. No deduction was available in tax years when no profits was earned and unused deductions could not be carried forward: the ECJ regarded this Belgian rule as a unilateral measure restricting the access to the advantages provided for in the directive, and conflicting with it.[113] It found that the system did not allow the directive's objective of prevention of economic double taxation to be fully achieved.[114] For this reason, the ECJ also refused to consider the application of this system to both domestic and foreign dividends as a justification for such wrongful implementation of the directive into national law.[115] It also specified that, because Belgium had not chosen the indirect tax credit method, it could not rely on the fact that its own system leads to the same results as the indirect tax credit method.[116]

The ECJ admitted that the choice between the exemption method and the indirect tax credit method does not necessarily lead to the same results for parent companies receiving dividends,[117] but it clarified that, when a Member State has opted for one of the two alternative systems, it cannot rely on effects which might have arisen from an implementation of the other system.[118] Finally, the ECJ stated

110 Case C–247/08, *Gaz de France* (n 77), para. 36.
111 Ibid., para. 38.
112 Ibid., para. 43.
113 Case C–138/07, *Cobelfret* (n 67), para. 36.
114 Ibid., paras. 39, 40 and 45.
115 Ibid., para. 46.
116 Ibid., para. 47.
117 Ibid., paras. 31 and 48.
118 Ibid., para. 50.

that the choice, by Belgium, of the exemption system under Article 4(1) was sufficient for interested parties to rely on the 'direct effect' of this provision, which is worded in unequivocal and unconditional.[119]

In the *KBC and BRB* ruling, the ECJ extended its *Cobelfret* findings to internal situations in cases where national laws adopt for domestic operations the same solutions provided for by the directive for intra-EU operations,[120] and, potentially, to dividends received from extra-EU subsidiaries where they are subject to a less favourable treatment than national dividends and the national courts find that the TFEU's provisions on the free movement of capital are applicable.[121]

The *Cobelfret* case, whilst offering legal certainty to parent companies whose state of residence *have chosen* the exemption method, would need to be considered together with other rulings – concerning the application of direct taxation to the free movement of capital[122] – which leave Member States *the freedom to opt* for the credit method only in respect of foreign dividends and *to switch* from the exemption method to the credit method. Given these possibilities for national legislators, *Cobelfret* paradoxically risks creating a disincentive for Member States to continue adopting the exemption method and, indirectly, risks reducing the effectiveness of the directive.[123]

2.3.4 The implementation of the Parent–Subsidiary Directive in Member States: overview

With regard to resident parent companies receiving dividends from subsidiaries resident in other Member States, or to PEs of non-resident companies receiving such dividends, all Member States have implemented Article 4(1) by choosing the exemption method, except for: Austria, which provides for a shift from the exemption to the tax credit method when the foreign-source income has been subject to a tax burden of less than 15 per cent; the Netherlands, which also applies the tax credit method only when the subsidiary is subject to a less than 10 per cent corporate tax rate and carries out a passive investment activity; Ireland, which still applies the tax credit method.

However, there are differences between the national exemption regimes relating to the underlying conditions, to the percentage of the exemption (which is not always a 100 per cent exemption) and to the scope of the exemption itself (which may be restricted to dividends or may include other receipts too). For example, Bulgaria, Cyprus, Croatia, Germany, Hungary and Latvia offer an *unconditional* and full participation exemption, with *neither* minimum period requirements *nor* minimum holding quota, whereas other countries make the participation

---

119 Ibid., paras. 63–65: see 2.3.3.2 above.
120 Case C–439/07 and 499/07, *KBC and BRB* (n 78), para. 60.
121 Ibid., paras. 72–74.
122 See ch 3.
123 See 2.3.1.

exemption conditional to a minimum holding quota and/or to a minimum holding period or to other requirements or limit the percentage of the exemption. Austria, Belgium, Greece, Poland, and Sweden, require a 10 per cent minimum holding quota, whereas France, the Netherlands and Spain only set a 5 per cent minimum holding requirement. Belgium, Germany and Italy grant a 95 per cent participation exemption. Belgium, Italy and the Netherlands also apply the participation exemption to capital gains and – in the Dutch case – to hybrid loans. Slovakia still requires a 25 per cent minimum holding period, despite the directive's provision setting 10 per cent as a limit. Austria, Belgium, Denmark, Italy and Spain, require a one-year minimum holding period; France, Greece and Poland a two years minimum holding period.

The UK applies a participation exemption from 1 July 2009 without requiring a minimum holding quota or period. Italy and the UK require, as a further condition for the participation exemption, that the dividends must not be deductible for the distributing company in its state of residence; the UK and the Netherlands add further qualification relating to the origin of the dividends, which must be of an income nature (for the UK) or be related to a participation held for business reasons (for the Netherlands).

The implementation of Article 5(1), requiring abolition of withholding tax for outbound profits distributions, also varies from one Member State to another. Some East European Member States – Bulgaria, Estonia, Hungary, Latvia – as well as Belgium and Malta, grant an *unconditional* exemption, but most others – amongst which major EU jurisdictions such as France, Germany, Italy, Poland, Spain – make the exemption conditional upon the non-resident parent company meeting not only the legal forms and residence requirements set out in the directive, but also minimum holding period and minimum holding quota conditions. For example, France makes the exemption subject to the condition that the non-resident parent company directly holds at least 10 per cent of capital *and* of the voting rights of the resident distributing subsidiary continuously for at least two years; if the minimum holding period has not yet expired at the distribution date, the exemption is still granted provided the parent company undertakes to keep the shares for at least two years.

Germany makes the exemption conditional upon the non-resident parent company holding at least 10 per cent of the capital of the distributing subsidiary continuously for at least 12 months; if this holding period has not yet expired at the distribution date, the withholding tax must initially be paid and is later refunded on completion of the minimum holding period. Italy and Poland grant the exemption provided that the non-resident parent company continuously holds at least 10 per cent of the distributing subsidiary's capital respectively for one year and for two years. Spain makes the exemption conditional upon the non-resident parent company holding at least 5 per cent of the subsidiary's capital for a minimum continuous period of one year prior to the declaration of the dividends; if dividends are declared before the elapse of the one-year holding period, the distribution is subject to a provisional withholding tax payment, which is subsequently refunded on completion of the minimum holding period.

France, Germany and Spain even require further conditions to be met by the non-resident parent company and which relate to business carried out by the parent company and/or to the identity of the shareholders: France and Spain require that the non-resident parent company is not controlled by shareholders not resident in a Member State or that, if it is so controlled, the participation is held for business reasons and not for benefiting from the withholding tax exemption; Germany, in case of dividends paid to a PE of the non-resident parent company, grants the exemption only if the participation in the subsidiary forms part of the business capital of the PE. In the particular case of the Netherlands, which requires the non-resident parent company to hold at least 5 per cent of either the capital or voting rights, without any minimum holding period, the exemption from withholding tax applies to outbound dividends, liquidation proceeds and any other profits distributions.

Overall, the comparative overview demonstrates that – despite similarities in the implementing legislation *within groups of* Member States – on the whole national legislators have *not* been coordinating with each other in introducing implementing national laws. Consequently, the directive has been leading to a diffusion of participation exemption regimes within the EU, but has certainly *not* managed to achieve neutrality for the location of parent companies and subsidiaries in a Member State or in another one.

2.3.5 The Parent–Subsidiary Directive, the related *case law and its implementation against the benchmarks*

2.3.5.1 *Complete elimination of double taxation and of discrimination*

In light of the ECJ's case law and of the implementation in Member States, the elimination of double taxation seems to have been achieved to a different extent for international juridical double taxation and for international economic double taxation.

Juridical double taxation on parent companies meeting the eligibility conditions set out in the directive can be regarded as *almost* entirely eliminated, thanks to the development by the ECJ of a specific definition of withholding tax to be abolished under Article 5(1), to the recognition of this provision's direct effect, and to the manner in which Article 5(1) has been implemented by most Member States, in some cases as a reaction to the ECJ's case law. In fact, whereas most of the Member States grant the exemption from withholding tax irrespective of a holding period, those Member States that provisionally withhold a tax, in the event of distribution before the elapse of the minimum holding period, allow a later refund of the tax once the minimum holding period is complete. In these cases, the provisional withholding tax fulfils the role of a guarantee that the minimum holding be maintained for benefiting from the exemption, and can therefore be seen as consistent with the *Denkavit* decision.[124]

---

124 See 2.3.3.1 above.

A clear shortcoming which prevented a uniform elimination of *juridical double taxation* lies in the absence in the directive of a definition of 'distribution of profits', as a result of which a few Member States (eg the Netherlands) also exempt liquidation proceeds and other forms of distributions, but the vast majority of countries currently limit their exemption to dividends. As the ECJ's case law concerning the meaning of 'withholding tax'[125] refers to dividends or any other income from shares,[126] an exemption only covering dividends could be regarded as partially *failing* to achieve the elimination of juridical double taxation. In addition, the wording of Article 5, despite requiring exemption from withholding tax irrespective of the business carried out by the parent company and of the identity of its shareholders, has not prevented a few Member States (Denmark, France, Ireland and Spain) from making the exemption subject on these elements.

These kinds of provisions result in juridical double taxation not being eliminated when the conditions they set in terms of shareholders qualification or business purpose *are not met* by the non-resident parent company. In light of the ECJ's finding that the right to abolition of withholding tax is absolute and unconditional,[127] which suggests that Member States may not unilaterally impose restrictive measures setting out additional conditions, these national provisions give rise to legal uncertainty, a priori, as to whether or not they would be covered by Article 1(2) safeguarding DTCs or domestic provisions required for preventing fraud or abuse. Arguably, if considering the case law on abusive practices[128] and the proportionality test applied by the ECJ, they could be admissible under Article 1(2) only if, on a case-by-case basis, it could be demonstrated that they do no more than is necessary to prevent abuse.

The *elimination of economic double taxation* has been completely achieved in the numerous Member States that have opted for a full exemption for inbound distributions received from eligible subsidiaries resident in other Member States. On the contrary, it has not (necessarily) been achieved in those states which have introduced either the indirect tax credit method *or* a switchover from the exemption to the indirect tax credit method in case of distributing subsidiaries resident in a low tax state. In fact, the ECJ admitted that the outcomes of the two methods may be different at parent company level[129] and, as noted by the literature, the indirect tax credit method is cumbersome and difficult to apply, particularly in cases of sub-subsidiaries, as it makes it necessary to trace the corporation tax that was paid by the distributing sub-subsidiaries[130] and implementation guidance would probably be needed. Accordingly, the directive's most evident shortcoming toward the elimination of economic double taxation lies in the very freedom for

---

125 See 2.3.3.3.
126 For example, Case C-446/04, *FFI Group Litigation Order* (n 70), para. 109.
127 See 2.3.3.3.
128 See ch 3, at 3.3.
129 See 2.3.3.5 below.
130 See Terra and Wattel, *European Tax Law* (n 6), at 650.

Member States to choose the (less effective) indirect tax credit method instead of the (more effective) exemption method.[131]

As regards the *removal of discriminations*, an objective set by the Commission together with the elimination of double taxation,[132] this goal was indicated in the directive's preamble, in terms of creation of equal conditions for the grouping together of companies of different Member States in comparison with companies of the same Member State.[133] Nonetheless, at least two of the ECJ's positions suggest that this objective has not been achieved by the directive and the related case law. One is the acceptance by the ECJ that a Member State granting a full tax credit to domestic parent companies, to *eliminate* economic double taxation, may instead grant non-resident parent companies a half tax credit as established in the relevant DTC, to *lessen* economic double taxation.[134] Another is the position admitting that a Member State applying the exemption method to parent companies receiving *domestic dividends* may apply the (more disadvantageous) indirect credit method to parent companies receiving dividends from subsidiaries resident in other Member States.[135]

These disparities have been accepted by the ECJ without justifying them on the bases of different situations of either non-resident parent companies vis-à-vis resident parent companies *or* of parent companies receiving domestic dividends as compared with parent companies receiving foreign dividends, and without attaching importance (in contrast with its own finding in *Bosal*[136]) to the possible effect (of this difference of treatment) *of discouraging* the exercise of the freedom of establishment through the creation of subsidiaries in other Member States.

2.3.5.2 *The elimination of unintended double non-taxation*

As many Member States have introduced a full participation exemption[137] and have also abolished withholding taxes on outbound dividends, there can easily be situations of juridical double non-taxation to the benefit of a parent company. For example, in case of distributions from a Belgian or a Maltese subsidiary to a Hungarian parent company, the parent company would pay *neither* the withholding tax in Belgium or in Malta *nor* the corporate income tax in Hungary.

It could be questioned whether this juridical double non-taxation is *unintended* or is one of the possible results (of the directive's implementation) *accepted* by the EU legislator. The directive's stated goal was to eliminate the disadvantages on cross-border groupings together as compared with domestic ones, but not necessarily to offer cross-border grouping a more advantageous treatment, which would

---

131 See 2.3.3.5 below.
132 Communication COM(2006) 823 final, Coordinating Member States' direct tax systems in the internal market, at 5.
133 See 2.3.1.
134 Case C–58/01, *Océ van der Grinten* (n 69), paras. 12–13, 20–23 and 87.
135 Case C–446/04, *Test Claimant in the FII Group* (n 70), paras. 44–57.
136 See 2.3.1.3.
137 See 2.3.4.

exist whenever parent companies would not benefit from a juridical double non-taxation on domestic dividends. More importantly, even if the juridical double non-taxation was accepted at the time of introduction of the directive, this situation would currently contrast with the 2012 Commission Recommendation against aggressive tax planning.[138]

Accordingly, the directive and its implementation currently fail against the benchmark of eliminating (juridical) double non-taxation, whenever exemption from withholding tax in the source state coexists with full participation exemption in the parent company's state of residence. In itself, a 100 per cent participation exemption in this state effectively eliminates economic double taxation, given that the dividends have already been taxed in the subsidiary's hands, and this objective is not fully achieved when the participation exemption is limited to 95 per cent of inbound dividends (already taxed as subsidiary's profits in the source state). However, in cases of 100 per cent participation exemption in the parent company's state of residence, the granting of a partial exemption from withholding tax in the subsidiary's state of residence – e.g. a 95 per cent exemption – would have managed to reconcile *elimination* of economic double taxation with avoidance of a juridical double non-taxation for the parent company.

2.3.5.3 *The reduction of administrative costs for direct tax compliance within the EU, and the achievement of greater legal certainty*

A reduction of administrative compliance costs is certainly achieved in cases where the parent companies' states of residence have chosen the exemption method and the subsidiaries' states of residence have granted an unconditional exemption from withholding tax. To a minor extent, it has also been achieved when the exemption method and the exemption from withholding tax have been made conditional to minimum holding quotas and/or holding periods, which only requires the parent company to show documentation proving that these requirements are met. However, it has not been achieved in those subsidiaries' states of residence which, in addition to requiring a minimum holding period, apply a provisional withholding tax in case of distributions prior to the elapse of this period, and require the non-resident parent companies to apply for a refund of the tax once the period has elapsed: here the implementation of the directive has indeed increased the administrative onus for parent companies.

Administrative costs reduction was prevented, in these cases, by the ECJ's *Denkavit* finding[139] (which left subsidiaries' states of residence free to adopt their preferred measures to ensure completion of the minimum holding period, without requiring less cumbersome modalities than provisional withholding tax payments and subsequent applications for refund). Moreover, no evident administrative simplification has been achieved in parent companies' states of residence adopting

---

138 C(2012) 8806 final (n 64), Preamble, Recital (2).
139 See 2.3.3.1.

the indirect tax credit method, either on their own or by way of possible switchover from the exemption method. This holds true due to the difficult steps involved in applying this method (tracking the corporate income tax paid by the subsidiaries on distributed profits, determining the corresponding domestic tax), particularly when distributions by second tier subsidiaries are involved.

Such difficulties were even pointed out by the UK in the *FII* case, where this Member State argued, in justifying its denying the indirect tax credit to parent companies with less than 10 per cent holding in distributing subsidiaries, that 'such a tax credit could be granted only after lengthy and complex checks had been carried out'.[140] Arguably, the major shortcoming, in preventing reductions in administrative compliance onus, lies therefore (just as regards the elimination of economic double taxation) in the possibility of opting for the indirect tax credit method (and potentially, in the incentive to switch to this method that the ECJ's *Cobelfret* ruling might create[141]).

In terms of achievement of *greater legal certainty* for inter-corporate profits distributions within the EU – despite the directive, its related ECJ case law and its implementation have managed, to a large extent, to ensure similar participation exemptions from one Member State to another with regard to inbound dividends – issues generating legal uncertainty, left by the directive's text about the concepts of 'distributions of profits', of 'fiscal residence' and the potential reach of the anti-abuse clause,[142] appear still unresolved after the case and in light of the implementation. For example, with regard to the concept of profits distributions given by the ECJ for the purposes of Article 5(1), i.e. the concept of dividends and *any other income* from shares,[143] it might be argued that the same definition should apply to inbound distributions under Article 4, but the ECJ appears to have used, with regard to Article 4(1), the terms 'profits distributed' interchangeably with the term 'dividends'.[144] Should the widest possible interpretation of 'distribution of profits' ('... any other income from shares') apply under Article 4(1) too, the doubt may arise as to whether most Member States – in applying the benefits of Article 4(1) to inbound *dividends* – have not sufficiently implemented the directive.

As regards the 'fiscal residence', because the directive only refers to national laws of Member States and to DTCs with third countries and implementing laws of parent company residence states generally refer to subsidiaries resident in other Member States, an important issue is unresolved. This is whether the benefits of Article 4 should be granted for distributions received from subsidiaries which, under domestic laws, are resident both in the same Member State as the parent company and in another Member State, especially where this second country is

---

140 Case C–446/04, *FII Group Litigation* (n 70), para. 66.
141 See 2.3.3.5.
142 See 2.3.1.2.
143 See, 2.3.1.3.
144 For example, Case C–27/07, *Banque Fédéerative du Crédit Mutuel* (n 75), paras. 21, 24 and 44; Case C–446/04, *Test Claimant in the FII Group Litigation* (n 70), paras. 41 and 43; Case C–138/07, *Cobelfret* (n 67), paras. 27, 30 and 31.

granted tax residence by the DTC.[145] For example, under the German implementing legislation, the distributing subsidiary must have its place of effective management and its registered office cumulatively outside Germany for inbound dividends to qualify under the directive; this was considered to be in breach of the directive with regard to cases of distributing subsidiaries having the registered office in Germany and the place of effective management in another Member State or vice versa.[146]

Moreover, only some subsidiary residence Member States have also granted the exemption from withholding tax to dividends distributed to PEs (in their own jurisdiction) of non-resident qualifying parent companies. Therefore, the Member States which have not exempted these distributions may be regarded as having insufficiently transposed the directive if one assumes that Article 5(1) would cover these distributions too (the local PE being part of the non-resident parent company). It is also uncertain whether – even in case of distributions to PEs located in other Member States – dividends paid to agency PEs or services PEs can be entitled to exemption,[147] because the definition of PE given in the directive (unlike the one given in DTCs) does not cover agency PEs or services PEs.

Finally, owing to the ECJ's ruling in *Denkavit*, which regarded the previous anti-abuse clause in Article 1(2) as specified in detail by the option for Member States to require a minimum holding period, the new anti-abuse clause[148] raises the question of *whether*, in cases of distributions from subsidiaries where the parent company keeps the holding for the minimum period, but which do not carry out genuine commercial activity in their state of residence, the benefits of the directive should still apply.

2.3.5.4 *The fight against cross-border tax evasion and fraud, against abusive practices and against aggressive tax planning*

The Commission's proposal leading to the latest amendments – which have modified both the condition for granting the participation exemption under Article 4(1) and the anti-abuse clause in Article 1(2)[149] – was one of the initiatives scheduled in its 2012 Action Plan against tax fraud and tax evasion.[150] It was thus based on the awareness that the directive could risk failing to help the fight against cross-border tax evasion, abusive practices and, in general, against aggressive tax planning.

---

145 T. Kollruss, 'Dual Resident Companies and the Implementation of the Parent–Subsidiary Directive in Germany in Light of European Union Secondary Legislation and Primary Legislation: An Analysis and Review' in 21 *EC Tax Review*, 4, 2012.
146 Ibid., at 197.
147 Panayi, *European Union Corporate Income Tax* (n 8), p. 37.
148 See 2.3.1.
149 See 2.3.1.1.
150 Communication COM(2012) 722 final, An Action Plan to strengthen the fight against tax fraud and tax evasion, para. 4.1.1, at 9.

Nevertheless, apart from the elimination of *economic double non-taxation* arising in the case of hybrid financial instruments, even the amended version of Article 4(1) fails to overcome the numerous possible situations of *juridical double non-taxation*, to the benefit of the parent company, which have *actually* been created by its implementation whenever the abolition of withholding taxes in the subsidiary state coexists with a full and unconditional participation exemption in the parent company state.[151]

The directive still appears to leave scope for aggressive tax planning, since a group management could completely avoid taxation on the parent company by locating it in a state granting a full exemption and by choosing to have profits distributed by subsidiaries resident in states granting an unconditional exemption from withholding taxes. This would hold true *unless* such a strategy, in the event of distributing subsidiaries carrying out their activities without any genuine economic integration in their state of residence, were regarded as 'artificial' under the new GAAR and Member States were allowed to deny the benefits of the directive.

Arguably, this could be only established on a case-by-case basis, which would lead to the question whether the benefits of the directive would need to be withdrawn by the subsidiary state *or* by the parent company state, i.e. to a question left unresolved by the amendment of the anti-abuse clause. However, the question would be of utmost importance because, if the benefits of the directive were withdrawn by *both* states, the ultimate outcome would be juridical double taxation: the achievement of one benchmark (fight against aggressive tax planning) would lead to a complete failure against another benchmark which, on the contrary, at least as regards the elimination of juridical double taxation, is to a good extent met by the current implementation of the directive by Member States and by the current stage of the ECJ's case law.

2.4 The Merger Directive

2.4.1 The directive's key provisions

To prevent a disadvantaged tax treatment of intra-EU mergers, divisions and other restructuring operations in comparison with the same kinds of domestic operations, the current Merger Directive introduces a common system to avoid taxation at the time of a merger, division, partial division, transfer of assets, exchange of shares and transfers of the registered office of an SE or of an SCE. Eligible companies are defined in the identical manner as in the Parent–Subsidiary Directive in terms of tax residence and subjection to corporate income tax.[152] At the same time, the directive intends protecting the financial interest of the Member State of the transferring or acquired company.[153] Its preamble states that the directive aims

---

151 See 2.3.5.2 above, about the shortcomings preventing the avoidance of double non-taxation.
152 Merger Directive, Art. 3.
153 Merger Directive, Preamble, Recitals (4) and (5).

at eliminating obstacles to the functioning of the internal market, such as double taxation[154] and that, if this is not fully achieved, Member States should take the necessary measures to do it.[155]

In a cross-border *merger, (partial) division* or *transfer of assets*, a company A resident in a Member State X, without being dissolved, transfers its assets and liabilities to a company B resident in a Member State Y in exchange for the issue, to the shareholders of company A (in a merger or division) or to company A (in a transfer of assets), of shares in the capital of the receiving company B. All such operations are expected by the directive to result either in the transformation of company A in a PE of company B in Member State X *or* in the assets becoming connecting with a PE of the receiving company B in this state.[156] In an exchange of shares, a company C acquires the majority of shares in a company D resident in another Member State from this second company's shareholders, by paying them with shares of company C. In the event of transfer of registered office of an SE or SCE to another Member State, the assets of the company in the original Member State normally become connected with a PE in that state.

The directive introduces a tax deferral regime, whereby: (a) under Article 4(1), a merger, division, partial division or transfer of assets does not cause any taxation of the receiving companies on the capital gains, i.e. on the difference between the 'real value' of the assets and liabilities transferred and their 'values of tax purposes' at the time of the operation;[157] (b) under Article 8(1) and (2), on a merger, (partial) division or exchange of shares, the allotment of securities of the receiving or acquiring company to a shareholder of the transferring or acquired company implies no taxation of such shareholders on the 'income, profits or capital gains' until they are actually realised; (c) under Article 12, the transfer of registered office or of tax residence of an SE or SCE to another Member State, entails no taxation of capital gains.

The directive makes the tax deferral subject to two cumulative conditions. First, the assets and liabilities transferred must remain *effectively connected* with a PE of the receiving company in the Member State of the merged or acquired company, or – in case of a seat transfer of an SE or SCE – with a PE of the transferring SE or SCE in its origin Member State, and must generate the taxable profits or losses.[158]

Secondly, the receiving company must ensure, for the assets and liabilities involved, continuity of the tax values with the merged or acquired company;[159] this continuity is also necessary for the shareholder of the transferring or acquired company with regard to securities he receives in the receiving or acquiring company.[160] Owing to the tax deferral regime, the capital gain can be taxed, by

---

154   Ibid., Recital (14).
155   Ibid.
156   Merger Directive, Preamble, Recital (6).
157   See Art. 4(1) for the definition of *value for tax purposes*.
158   Art. 12(1).
159   Art. 4(5) and Art. 9.
160   Art. 8(4) and (5).

the Member State of the transferring company, where the PE is located, only at the time of later realisation and only in the hands of the receiving company. Member States must also allow any PE of the receiving company situated in the Member State of the transferring company to carry forward tax-exempt 'provisions or reserves' properly constituted by the transferring company.[161]

Nonetheless, the directive leaves the concepts of 'real value' and of 'provision or reserves' undefined, and it is also silent about the case where the Member State of the receiving company applies the worldwide taxation system and taxes the profits of her PE located in the Member State of the transferring company. However, given Member States' obligation to take the necessary measures to eliminate double taxation when the directive does not,[162] it is for the DTC between the two Member States to eliminate the risk of international juridical double taxation on the receiving company on the realisation of these capital gains.

The elimination of the risk of juridical double taxation is also pursued by Article 10(1), concerning a situation where the assets transferred in a merger, a division, a partial division or a transfer of assets include a PE (of the transferring company) situated in a Member State other than that of the transferring company. The state of location of the PE (whether this state is the receiving company state or a third state) must not tax it, and the transferring company state may include, in the taxable profits of that company, those losses of the PE as may have been previously offset against the company's taxable profits in its jurisdiction. The state of the transferring company can tax any profit or capital gains of the PE, provided it gives a 'notional tax credit', i.e. a relief for the tax that – but for the directive – would have been charged in the Member State where the PE is situated.[163]

The directive also intends eliminating the risk of juridical double taxation in restructuring operations involving specific entities – e.g. certain kinds of partnerships – which can be regarded as corporate taxpayers in their state of residence, but which may have participants/shareholders resident in another Member State considering these entities as fiscally transparent. The participants/shareholders may be not only natural persons, but also companies involved in the restructuring operations, such as the receiving company. Therefore, where non-resident transferring companies are regarded as fiscally transparent by the Member State of the receiving company, this state must *either* exempt any unrealised profit or capital gains of the receiving company subject to this company ensuring continuity of valuation rules (as if the operation had not taken place),[164] *or* grant the participant/shareholder of the non-resident transferring company a tax credit as if the gains had actually been realised and the tax had actually been paid by them in the state of residence of the transferring company.[165]

---

161 Art. 5.
162 Preamble, Recital (14).
163 Art. 10(2).
164 Art. 4(3) and (4).
165 Art. 11(1) and (2).

Where the Member State of the transferring company considers the non-resident receiving company to be fiscally transparent, this state may tax the allotment of shares to its resident participants of this non-resident company,[166] provided it grants them any relief available on the allotment of shares to participants in a resident receiving company.[167]

Other provisions of the directive leave Member State options affecting the scope of application of the tax relief. In this respect, Article 7 specifies that, where the receiving company has a holding in the capital of the transferring company, any gains accruing to the receiving company on the cancellation of its holding shall not be taxed, but Member States may derogate from this general rule where the receiving company's holding in the capital of the transferring company does not exceed 10 per cent. It also allows Member States to maintain, in their provisions concerning domestic operations, more favourable rules than the relief provided for by the directive, while requiring them to extend such rules to operations involving non-resident companies.

Finally, Article 15(1) sets an anti-abuse clause whereby Member States *may* deny the benefits of 'all or any part' of the directive when the principal objective, or one of the principal objectives of a restructuring operation, is tax evasion or avoidance, and specifies that if an operation 'is not carried out for valid commercial reasons', such as restructuring or rationalisation, this 'may constitute a presumption that the operation has tax evasion or avoidance as its principal objective.'

2.4.2 The text of the Merger Directive against the benchmarks

The literature, in commenting on the Merger Directive, stressed that the wording of the directive left uncertainty on essential *subjective features* of the operations:[168] e.g. under Article 2(a) to (c), the definitions of mergers, (partial) divisions and exchanges of shares – in stating that cash payment to shareholders may not exceed 10 per cent of the value of shares used as a consideration – do not specify whether the 10 per cent applies to each shareholder individually or to the shareholders as a group (in which case any particular shareholder could get a cash payment of more than 10 per cent). Article 2, by referring to the 'issue' of shares in mergers, divisions and exchange of shares[169] and to the '*transfer*' of shares in transfers of assets,[170] does not clarify whether the shares to be used as a consideration for the transfer of assets must be new or already existing shares, which makes it uncertain whether or not the receiving company must necessarily increase its share capital.[171] Therefore, the directive – if assessed against the 'benchmarks'[172] – does not fully meet the objective of legal certainty.

---

166 Art. 11(3).
167 Art. 11(4).
168 IBFD, Survey on the Implementation of the EC Tax Directives (n 51), at 20–24.
169 Art. 2(a), (b), (c) and (e).
170 Art. 2(d).
171 IBFD, Survey on the Implementation of the EC Tax Directives (n 51), p. 23.
172 See ch 1, at 1.2.

Moreover, in a *transfer of assets*, owing to the continuity of valuation rule laid down by Articles 4 and 9, the transferring company may be requested, by its state of residence, to value the received shares at the book value of assets and liabilities transferred. In this case, the same capital gain would be taxed both at the time of disposal of securities received by the transferring company and at the time of disposal of assets by the receiving company.

In an *exchange of shares* too, if the acquiring company were not allowed, under its national legislation, to attribute market value to the shares of the acquired company, the same capital gain could be taxed by the state of residence of the shareholders of the acquired company at the time of their disposal of these securities, and by the Member State of the acquiring company when this company sells its shares in the acquired company. As a 2003 Commission proposal to eliminate these possible economic double taxation cases was rejected, the risk of economic double taxation on transfers of assets and exchanges of shares still arises (as subsequently indicated, it is a matter of interpretation whether the ECJ's case law, in dealing with additional conditions for tax neutrality imposed by Member States, has partly mitigated it[173]).

A further shortcoming may lie in the assumption, underlying Article 4(1), that intra-EU mergers, (partial) divisions or transfers of assets result *either* in the transformation of the transferring company into a PE of the company receiving the assets *or* in the assets becoming connected with a PE of the latter company. There may be particular assets – e.g. intangible assets, specific equipment – which, in some cases, are even more important in the overall businesses' profitability than fixed assets, but which, by their very nature, might be transferred without becoming 'connected' with a PE. In these cases, in addition to the administrative onus of distinguishing those assets remaining connected with a PE from the others, the operation would still imply the risk of taxation on latent capital gains for some assets, which risk may not occur in a corresponding domestic operation: this disparity would fully contrast with the goals stated in the preamble.

The directive also turns out being inadequate in providing for a tax relief at the time of seat transfer of an SE or SCE, due to its setting the requirement that, in a transfer of the registered office of the SE or the SCE, assets and liabilities transferred remain connected with a PE of the transferring company in the origin state. In fact, the ECJ has regarded the transfer of head office of certain companies created under national laws, even without the registered office and without the need to keep a PE in the origin country, as falling within the freedom of establishment, and as deserving an exemption from the payment of exit taxes at the time of the transfer and until the time of later disposal of assets.[174] The directive could thus paradoxically place the seat transfer of a SE at a disadvantage in comparison with that of a national law company.

---

173 See 2.3.3; also Terra and Wattel, *European Tax Law* (n 6), at 678.
174 Case C-371/10, *National Grid Indus* [2011] ECR I-12273, paras. 37–38.

Furthermore, the directive's definition of mergers and total divisions, when requiring that the transferring company be 'dissolved', appears to *exclude* the transformation of this company into a subsidiary of the receiving company, despite a subsidiary may also become a PE of its parent company in certain cases.[175] As a result, whenever the receiving companies would prefer creating not a branch but a subsidiary in the Member State of the transferring company, the required connection of assets and liabilities transferred with a PE of the receiving company in this Member State, ends up distorting the exercise of the freedom of establishment of the receiving company in this state. Therefore, it would contravene the principle, affirmed by the ECJ's case law, whereby the choice of the form of secondary establishment should not be affected by tax provisions,[176] i.e. the principle of 'tax neutrality' between branches and subsidiaries.[177]

A much more far-reaching effect would thus have been secured – in terms of removal of tax obstacles and achievement of tax neutrality – if the 'transferred assets and liabilities' had been defined as all assets, all rights and all obligations which, due to the operation, are transferred to the receiving company and, on their whole, make it possible the carrying out of a business activity. Taken against the 'benchmarks' of abolition of double taxation and of administrative simplification, the directive therefore shows pitfalls lying in the very conditions which are still required for the receiving company (or the transferring SE or SCE) to enjoy the tax relief at the time of the operation, whereas it would meet these benchmarks had such a wider definition of 'transferred assets and liabilities' been adopted.

Apart from Member States' freedom to maintain, in their national provisions concerning domestic operations, different and/or more *favourable rules* than the relief provided for[178] *each provision* of the directive offers national legislators both an *explicit choice* on important aspects,[179] and an *implicit option*. For example, that of deciding when the assets and liabilities connected with a PE play a part in generating taxable profits or losses and can thus be regarded as 'transferred'.[180] Individual states are thus left even more space than in the Parent–Subsidiary Directive: national legislators are given the task both of implementing this greater number of options and of exactly defining the underlying technical notions (such as 'provisions', 'reserves', 'real value'), for which (like the Parent–Subsidiary Directive) the Merger

---

175 For example, W. B. Taylor, V. L. Davis and J. McCart, 'Policy Forum: A Subsidiary as a Permanent Establishment of its Parent' in *Canadian Tax Journal/Revue Fiscale Canadienne* (2007) Vol. 55, 2, 333–45.
176 Case 270/83, *Commission v France (avoir fiscal)* [1986] ECR 273.
177 C. Sacchetto, 'Imposizione tributaria e sede del soggetto nel diritto comunitario' in *Rivista di Diritto Tributario Internazionale*, 1, 2001, at 77 ff.
178 For example, Art. 4(5).
179 For example, Art. 7 and Art. 10.
180 Or the *necessary measures* to be taken to ensure that provisions or reserves partly or wholly exempt from tax may be carried over by the PEs of the receiving company in the Member State of the transferring company, inevitably including the right to freely decide *which* measures are necessary and *when* they are: Art. 5.

Directive does not provide uniform definitions. Additionally, for the Merger Directive too, the problem arises as to whether situations of dual resident companies and unresolved tax residence conflicts may prevent access to the benefits of the directive.[181]

Overall, the text of the directive appears thus unable to achieve at least three benchmarks – i.e. legal certainty, the elimination of double taxation and administrative simplification – as well as tax neutrality.

2.4.3 The case law on the Merger Directive

The ECJ's case law has been dealing with: (a) the definition of relevant operations such as 'exchange of shares', in the 1997 *Leur-Bloem* ruling[182] and 'transfer of assets', in the 2002 *Andersen og Jensen* ruling;[183] (b) the scope of the directive's anti-abuse provision, in *Leur-Bloem* and in the 2007 *Kofoed*[184] ruling, where the relationship between the directive's anti-abuse clause and national rules was also at stake, in the 2008 *AT v Finanzamt Stuttgart-Körperschaften*[185] ruling, in the 2010 *Zwijnenburg* ruling[186] and in the 2011 *Foggia* decision,[187] with further indirect indications offered by a ruling concerning the deductibility by a parent company of losses incurred by a subsidiary resident in another Member State in the event of a merger between the parent company and the subsidiary, in the 2013 *A Oy* ruling;[188] and (c) the possibility of making the tax neutrality in a cross-border exchange of shares and transfers of assets subject to conditions not expressly set out by the directive, in the *AT v Finanzamt Stuttgart-Körperschaften* ruling itself and in the 2012 *3DI Srl*[189] ruling.

2.4.3.1 The definition of the relevant operations: exchanges of shares and transfers of assets

In *Leur-Bloem*, the sole shareholder and director of two private Dutch companies was planning to use its shares in both companies to acquire the shares of a holding company, thereby implementing a transaction after which, as the owner of the new holding, he was to become, indirectly, the sole shareholder in the first two companies, which would become fully owned subsidiaries of the holding company. This latter would carry out no commercial activity; the holding, together with these two subsidiaries, would subsequently be consolidated into a domestic 'fiscal unity'

---

181 See ch 2, at para. 2.3.1.2.
182 Case C–28/95, *Leur-Bloem* [1997] ECR I–4161.
183 Case C–43/00, *Andersen og Jensen* [2002] ECR I–379.
184 Case C–321/05, *Kofoed* [2007] ECR I–5795.
185 Case C–285/07, *AT v Finanzamt Stuttgart-Körperschaften* [2008] ECR I–9329.
186 Case C–352/08, *Modehuis A. Zwijnenburg* [2010] ECR I–4303.
187 Case C–126/10, *Foggia* [2011] ECR I–10923.
188 Case C–123/11, *A Oy*, ruling issued on 21 February 2013.
189 Case C–207/11, *3 DI Srl v Agenzia delle Entrate – Ufficio di Cremona*, ruling issued on 19 December 2012.

scheme that would allow horizontal offsetting of profits and losses, and therefore reduce the overall tax exposure.

The shareholder had asked the Dutch tax authorities to treat the proposed transaction as a 'merger by exchange of shares', which, under Dutch provisions, enjoy tax exemption for gains arising on major shareholdings. The Dutch tax authorities had refused because, owing to the new holding company not running a commercially active business, the operation did not meet the requirement for the tax relief, set out by national law, to carry out an active business which is enduringly united both financially and economically with the business of the new subsidiaries. Although the situation was a merely internal one, a national provision introduced when implementing the Merger Directive stated that the operation at issue had to be treated in the same manner as a situation falling within the directive's scope.

The situation was similar in *Andersen og Jensen*, where a Danish limited liability company claimed the benefit of the tax exemption granted for 'transfers of assets' by a national provision – implementing the Merger Directive – which, in regulating domestic situations, had adopted the same definitions as the directive. In that case, the tax exemption was claimed for the planned transfer of all the business of the claimant to a new company, created by its own shareholders, under an arrangement which dissociated an asset – i.e. the proceeds of a large loan, which was to remain with the transferring company – and the related liability, i.e. the obligation arising from such loan, to be transferred to the new (receiving) company, and which required a security for the benefit of the receiving company. The Danish tax authority made the tax exemption conditional upon the operation being made without this particular arrangement.

In both cases, at the outset the ECJ stated that its jurisdiction, under Article 267 TFEU, extends to situations which are not governed by EU law but for which Member States, in implementing a directive into domestic law, has chosen to apply the same treatment to purely internal situations and to those governed by EU law. This ECJ's jurisdiction limits the extent to which Member State may restrictively interpret the directive's provisions in the domestic situations at stake.

In *Leur-Bloem*, the ECJ then had to decide: whether there can still be an 'exchange of shares' under the directive in particular circumstances concerning either the acquiring company or the identity of its shareholder or the ultimate effect of the operation, and whether the clear purpose of the companies involved to obtain tax advantages can be sufficient to resort to the anti-abuse clause. In *Andersen og Jensen*, the ECJ had to ascertain whether the operation at stake, with its particular arrangement, could fall within the definition of 'transfer of assets' provided for by the directive.

In *Leur-Bloem*, the ECJ, by literally interpreting the concept of 'exchange of shares', stated that this concept requires general conditions to be fulfilled *neither* by the participating companies *nor* by the shareholders.[190] In *Andersen og Jensen*, it

---

190 Case C–28/95, *Leur-Bloem* (n 182), para. 48.

relied on the literal definitions of 'transfer of assets' and 'branch of activity' and found that 'a transfer of assets must encompass *all* the assets and liabilities relating to a branch of activity', and that 'if the transferring company retains the proceeds of a large loan contracted by it and transfers the obligations deriving from that loan' to the receiving company, 'those two elements are dissociated'[191] (so that the definition given by the directive is not met).

Accordingly, the two rulings complement each other. *Leur-Bloem* suggests that – because *general* conditions are not envisaged by the directive – there is also no other *particular* condition which national legislators could require, in addition to the literal wording of the directive. Furthermore, although this outcome concerns 'exchange of shares', the rulings impliedly indicates that the same should apply to the concepts of all three other operations governed by the directive: in fact, its text does not suggest in any part that with regard to one of the envisaged operations Member States might adopt restrictive interpretations, of the relevant concepts, which are not admitted for the other operations.

Nevertheless, whereas Member States cannot impose conditions other than those literally set out in the directive, *companies* – given the *Andersen og Jensen* findings – cannot rely on the benefit granted by the directive and by national laws adopting the same concepts if the conditions emerging from the literal definitions of the directive are not exactly met. In turn, the concrete assessment as to whether these conditions are exactly fulfilled does not seem to be based on a purely formal criteria: the ECJ's wording in *Andersen og Jensen* suggests that, perhaps, if the transferring company had retained the proceeds of a *small* (rather than of a large) loan while transferring the related obligations to the receiving company, the *formal* dissociation would not have been considered as important as the transfer of *substantially* all assets and liabilities to the receiving company.

In this respect, it is significant that the ECJ, in *Andersen og Jensen*, asserted that the retention by the transferring company of a small number of shares in a third company would be immaterial, because such retention 'cannot exclude the transfer of a branch of activity unrelated to those shares'.[192] As the ruling did not indicate how small a formal dissociation between assets and liabilities elements should be for an operation to remain within the definition of transfer of assets, it paved the way for a case-by-case basis assessment left to national courts. This was expressly indicated with regard to one last issue concerning the arrangement of the operation,[193] where the ECJ just provided national courts with some general guidelines.[194]

However, companies may infer that, to meet the requirements for enjoying the benefits of the directive, they only need to avoid designing operations which have such a structure as to make it evident that literal definitions are not complied with,

---

191 Case C-43/00, *Andersen og Jensen* (n 183), paras. 24, 25 and 27, emphasis added.
192 Ibid., para. 29.
193 Case C-43/00, *Andersen og Jensen* (n 183), paras. 30-31.
194 Ibid., paras. 33-37.

from both a formal and a substantial viewpoint. Ultimately, this occurred in *Andersen og Jensen*, owing to the dissociation between the proceeds of a *large* loan and the related obligations. In doubtful cases, the case-by-case solution – in assessing whether or not the relevant definitions are literally met – may lead to different evaluations of (almost) similar situations from one Member State to another.

2.4.3.2 The scope of the directive's anti-abuse clause

The operation in *Leur-Bloem*, which ultimately would generate only tax savings due to the horizontal offsetting of losses, led the ECJ to examine the scope of the directive's anti-abuse clause. The ECJ found that the anti-abuse clause requires a *general examination* – open to judicial review – of *each particular case*, and that general rules *automatically* excluding certain operations from the tax advantage '*whether or not there is actually tax evasion or tax avoidance* . . . would undermine the aim pursued by directive'.[195]

Accordingly, Member States must *neither* set a general presumption that certain operations have tax evasion or tax avoidance amongst their principal objectives *nor* introduce more *specific* presumptions, i.e. establish that in particular cases such operations have, owing to the very nature of the concrete situations, tax evasion or tax avoidance objectives. This finding raises the question as to whether there might be some situations (and, if so, which ones) where the lack of valid commercial reasons, referred to in Article 15(a) as a possible (but not necessary) ground for establishing a presumption, may instead just be considered as a particular case of which a general examination is necessary. A response to this issue would have been an important contribution towards the achievement of a tax system common to all Member States, but the ECJ omitted to deal with it.

In the last part of *Leur-Bloem*, the ECJ found that a restructuring operation carried out for the *unique* purpose of benefiting from a tax advantage – of which horizontal off-setting of losses is just an example – cannot be considered as having valid commercial reasons.[196] This indicates Member States a case where they may establish a (rebuttable) presumption of tax avoidance or tax evasion objectives, i.e. a particular case of which a general examination is not necessary.

After *Leur-Bloem*, in *Kofoed* the ECJ dealt with a situation where income tax had been charged on an exchange of shares with particular features, and where the Member State concerned had not enacted specific measures to transpose the directive's anti-abuse clause into its national law. With regard to the specific features of the exchange of shares, the ECJ reiterated the *Leur-Bloem* and *Andersen og Jensen* approach of a case-by-case examination.[197] In the situation at issue, the ECJ found no element in the case-file demonstrating that the operation did not

---

195 Case C–28/95, *Leur-Bloem* (n 182), para. 48(b).
196 Ibid., para. 48(c).
197 Case C–321/05, *Kofoed* (n 184), para. 31.

fall into the definition of exchange of shares:[198] therefore, it regarded the operation as covered by the directive.[199]

Secondly, the ECJ stated that the anti-abuse clause reflects the general EU law principle of prohibition of abuse of rights, whereby the application of EU law cannot cover transactions carried out not in the context of normal commercial operations but solely for obtaining advantages offered by EU law provisions.[200] In taking this position, the ECJ referred inter alia to its landmark rulings regarding the exercise of the freedom of establishment[201] – such as the 1999 *Centros* ruling[202] or the 2006 *Cadbury Schweppes* ruling,[203] where it had affirmed this principle – despite the fact that the directive's anti-abuse clause, whose wording has remained unchanged since the 1990 version of the directive, was introduced earlier than these rulings. Arguably, the ECJ intended to ensure consistency between the interpretation of the anti-abuse clause and the principle of prohibition of abuse of rights developed in its case law concerning other EU law provisions. As regard the lack of specific national provisions implementing the anti-abuse clause, the ECJ found that in any case national courts need to verify whether there is in national law any principle or provision that might be interpreted in accordance with the directive's anti-abuse clause and therefore justify its application.[204]

Ultimately, when the outcome of this examination by national courts is positive, the *Kofoed* ruling makes the anti-abuse clause applicable without the need of a specific implementing provision. Nonetheless, because the ECJ also found, in its company law jurisprudence on the freedom of establishment, that intra-EU mergers are one of the modalities of exercising the freedom of establishment,[205] the ECJ statement in *Kofoed* that the anti-abuse clause reflects the general EU law principle of prohibition of abuse of rights raises an interpretative question.

In *Cadbury Schweppes*, concerning the application by a parent company's state of residence of its national anti-abuse legislation to tax the profits gained by subsidiaries created in a low-tax Member State, the ECJ regarded, as a decisive element for excluding wholly artificial arrangements, the genuine economic activity of the subsidiary in the host Member State,[206] which should be proved on the bases of factors ascertainable by third parties such as premises, staff and equipment.[207] Therefore, the question is whether these criteria (applied in *Cadbury Schweppes* for verifying the absence of wholly artificial arrangements) could also be used, in light of *Kofoed*, for ascertaining the existence of 'valid commercial reasons' for the non-application of the anti-abuse clause. This issue – i.e. whether, in essence, an intra-

---

198 Ibid., paras. 33–34.
199 Ibid., para. 35.
200 Ibid., para. 38.
201 Ibid.
202 Case C–212/97, *Centros* [1999] ECR I–1459, paras. 26 and 27.
203 Case C–196/04, *Cadbury Schweppes* (n 48), para. 51.
204 Case C–321/05, *Kofoed* (n 184), para. 46.
205 Case C–411/03, *SEVIC Systems* [2005] ECR I–10805, paras. 18 and 19.
206 Case C–196/04, *Cadbury Schweppes* (n 48), paras. 65–66.
207 Ibid., at para. 67.

60   *The European Union and Direct Taxation*

EU merger (or other restructuring operation) would escape the anti-abuse clause if resulting in a genuine economic activity in a Member State other than that of the merging (or transferring or acquiring) company – was left unanswered by *Kofoed*.

Subsequently, in *AT v Finanzamt Stuttgart-Körperschaften*, the ECJ examined a situation where Germany, in a cross-border exchange of shares, had made the continued use by shareholders of the acquired company of the book value of the shares transferred in exchange for the shares received in an acquiring company resident in another Member State (and made therefore the tax neutrality of the transfer), conditional upon the carrying over of that value in the tax balance sheet of the acquiring company. Under German legislation, the resident shareholders of the acquired company would thus be taxed on the *capital gains* arising from the transfer of shares, i.e. on the difference between the initial cost of acquiring the shares transferred and their market value, unless the foreign acquiring company carried over the historical book value of the shares transferred.

As one of the justifications by Germany was based on the need to prevent taxation from being circumvented, even at a stage later than the exchange of shares, the ECJ found that a Member State must grant the tax advantages provided for by the directive for exchanges of shares, unless those operations fall within the anti-abuse clause, and stated that this clause could be applied only by way of exception and in specific cases.[208] It reiterated its *Leur-Bloem* statement that, to determine whether the planned operation has tax evasion or tax avoidance as the principal objective or as one of the main objectives, national authorities must carry out a general examination of *each particular case*.[209]

Accordingly, the ECJ held that the anti-abuse clause cannot justify a national tax legislation refusing in a general way to grant the directive's tax advantages in respect of exchange of shares, solely on the ground that the foreign acquiring company has not valued the shares transferred at their historical book value[210] and, in consequence, concluded that such legislation was incompatible with the directive.[211] As highlighted below,[212] the importance of the ECJ's conclusions in this ruling goes beyond the anti-abuse clause.

In contrast with *Kofoed*, *Zwijnenburg* concerned the limits of the scope of the anti-abuse clause, even where implemented by a specific national legislation. The ECJ had to decide whether the anti-abuse clause implies that the tax benefits introduced by the directive could be denied to a taxpayer who has carried out a merger to escape *a tax not covered* by the directive (whose Annex lists the national corporate income tax to which eligible companies must be subject). The ECJ gave a negative reply, by finding that the anti-abuse clause constitutes an exception to the tax regime established by the directive and must be subject to strict interpretation

---

208   Case C–285/07 *AT Finanzamt Stuttgart-Körperschaften* (n 185), paras. 30–31.
209   Ibid.
210   Ibid., para. 32.
211   Ibid.
212   See 2.4.3.3 below.

regarding its wording, purpose and context.[213] Consequently, this clause could be used only to withdraw the exemption provided by the directive from national corporate income taxes that, otherwise, would arise from the restructuring operations falling within its scope.[214]

In *Foggia*, the ECJ went further in clarifying the scope of the anti-abuse clause, by explaining the concept of 'valid commercial reasons'. Just as in *Leur-Bloem*, there was an internal situation where domestic legislation adopted the same solutions as the directive: a Portuguese holding company had, through a merger by acquisition, acquired three loss-making Portuguese companies and had been denied, by the national tax authorities, the deduction of losses of one of these companies that had carried out no business activity, had earned no profits, had invested only in securities and had incurred about €2 million losses. Portuguese legislation – by reproducing the directive's anti-abuse clause – allowed the acquiring company to use the losses of the acquired companies subject to the operation being motivated by valid commercial reasons, and this uniform treatment of national and intra-EU restructuring operations made the anti-abuse clause applicable to purely internal situations as well.[215]

As the acquiring company had argued that the merger generated savings in administrative and management costs and that these savings constituted valid commercial reasons, the ECJ – after reaffirming the need for a case-by-case assessment[216] – accepted that valid commercial reasons could still exist despite the lack of activities carried out by the acquired company and despite the acquiring company's intention to exploit the acquired company's losses,[217] provided that *non-tax reasons are predominant*. It admitted that, in principle, a merger allowing a *reduction in administrative and management costs* could be considered as having a 'valid commercial reason'. However, it stressed that, in *Foggia*, the group's savings in costs structure were quite *marginal* if compared with the anticipated tax benefits: for this reason, it concluded that the operation could not be regarded as having valid commercial reasons.[218] Specifically, owing to reductions of administrative and management costs being inherent in any merger by acquisition, the ECJ reasoned that, if *automatically* accepting that reduction in administrative and management costs constitute a valid commercial reason, without considering the tax advantages, the anti-abuse clause would be entirely deprived of its purpose.[219]

In *Foggia*, whilst repeating its *Kofoed* statement that this clause reflects the general EU law principle of prohibition of abuse of rights,[220] it adopted a quantitative assessment, by comparing the amount of tax advantages (generated by the losses to be offset by the acquiring company) with the amount of managerial

---

213 Case C-352/08, *Modehuis A. Zwijnenburg* (n 186), para. 46.
214 Ibid., paras. 47-50.
215 Case C-128/10, *Foggia* (n 187), paras. 16-20.
216 Ibid., para. 37.
217 Ibid., para. 38.
218 Ibid., paras. 47-48.
219 Ibid., para. 49.
220 Ibid., para. 50.

and administrative cost savings. This suggests that the ECJ would have considered 'valid commercial reasons' as existing – and the anti-abuse clause as inapplicable – if administrative and management cost savings had been *greater* than tax savings *or* if the non-tax reasons had consisted of other benefits *not already inherent* in *any* merger by acquisition.

If this interpretation, that can be drawn from the *Foggia* ruling, were applied to cross-border mergers, falling within the scope of the directive, which constitute a modality of exercising the freedom of establishment, the doubt arises as to whether *Foggia* provides a response to the issue raised by *Kofoed*: whether a genuine economic integration in a new Member State, can per se constitute 'valid commercial reason' and make the anti-abuse clause inapplicable. A cross-border merger by acquisition falling within the directive is, by definition, an operation resulting in a PE of the acquiring company in the state of the merged company. Consequently, if assuming that a PE would necessarily imply an effective economic activity in the territory of this last state, the anti-abuse clause would completely lose its purpose as regards mergers by acquisition, but this outcome conflicts with the ECJ's reasoning in *Foggia* (which refused an argument depriving the clause of its purpose) and with the realisation that the anti-abuse clause covers all restructuring operations.

Indirectly, different responses could be given in light of the 2013 *A Oy* ruling, where the ECJ had to assess a Finnish law which, in a merger by acquisition, prevented an acquiring company from deducting losses incurred in previous tax years by an acquired subsidiary in another Member State, whilst allowing the deduction for domestic subsidiaries' losses. The merged subsidiary had ceased its business activity following trading losses and, as a result of the operation, the assets, liabilities and residual obligations of the merger subsidiary would be transferred to the acquiring company, which latter would no longer have a subsidiary or a PE in the (former) subsidiary's state of residence. Nonetheless, because the subsidiary had remained bound by two long-term leases of business premises in her state of residence, the merger would be justified from an economic viewpoint and would allow the merged subsidiary's leases to be transferred to the acquiring company.

At the outset, the ECJ noted that the directive did not address the question of the taking over in such a situation of any losses that the merged subsidiary may have made:[221] the lack of a PE of the acquiring company in the Member State of the subsidiary placed the operation outside the scope of the directive. Finnish legislation (just like the Portuguese legislation at stake in *Foggia*) allowed the deduction of losses by an acquiring company in a domestic operation subject to the condition that the operation was not carried out for the sole purpose of obtaining tax advantages, but it did not specify the conditions under which that deduction could be made if the merged company was situated in another Member State. In response to the argument that freedom of establishment did not apply to the case because the merged company ceased its economic activity before the

---

221 Case C–123/11, *A Oy* (n 188), para. 22.

merger and the sole motive for the restructuring was the search for a tax advantage,[222] the ECJ recalled that cross-border mergers are a method of exercising the freedom of establishment.[223] It also distinguished between the application of the freedom of establishment that was not prevented by the carrying out of a merger by acquisition solely for tax saving reasons and the adoption by Member States of measures to prevent abusive practices.[224]

On these bases, the ECJ admitted that the non-deductibility of losses incurred by a merged subsidiary in another Member State made the establishment in the latter state less attractive,[225] and therefore that it constituted an obstacle to the exercise of the freedom of establishment, but, eventually, the ECJ also regarded that legislation justified by overriding reasons of public interest. Specifically, in light of its case law on cross-border intra-group loss offsetting,[226] it considered the Finnish legislation suitable for maintaining a balanced allocation of taxing rights between Member States,[227] and for preventing *both* the double use of the same losses in different Member States[228] *and* the risk of transfer of losses to the jurisdiction where they would maximise tax savings.[229] This would apply unless the possibility of deducting losses was exhausted in the subsidiary's state of residence, in which case the parent company would be entitled to deduct them, but the ECJ left national courts the task to determine whether this situation had occurred.[230]

Finally, it specified that when the takeover of subsidiary losses by the parent company were to be allowed, the rules for calculating the non-resident subsidiary's losses for this purpose, in a merger by acquisition, must not constitute unequal treatment compared with the rules of calculation applying to resident subsidiary losses.[231]

A Oy did not deal with the directive's anti-abuse clause and the ECJ had clarified that the situation at stake was not covered by the directive. Nonetheless, since according to the ECJ the anti-abuse clause reflects the general principle of prohibition of abuse of rights, *A Oy* could, indirectly, indicate a response to the ultimate issue left unresolved by *Foggia*. This issue is whether, in cross-border mergers by acquisition (which constitute a modality of exercising the freedom of establishment), predominant tax-savings reasons would necessarily imply the lack of valid commercial reasons for operations not resulting in a PE of the acquiring company in the Member State of the merged company. The response appears to

---

222 Ibid., para. 23.
223 Ibid., para. 24.
224 Ibid., paras. 25–26.
225 Ibid., para. 32.
226 Case C–446/03 *Marks & Spencer* [2005] ECR I–10837, a landmark ruling that will be analysed in ch 3 when assessing the ECJ's case law on the application of fundamental freedoms to direct taxation.
227 Ibid., paras. 41–42.
228 Ibid., para. 44.
229 Ibid., para. 45.
230 Ibid., paras. 52–54.
231 Ibid., para. 61.

be negative, because the ECJ admitted that the deduction of subsidiary losses would still be possible for the parent company in cases of terminal losses, and because, in *A Oy*, it noted that the merged subsidiary had been trading in the past and there would be an economic advantage in the operation.

Specifically, in the absence of a PE, sole or predominant tax savings reasons would not necessarily imply the lack of valid commercial reasons *provided that* the absorbed subsidiary has been trading in the past, i.e. provided that the operation resulted in an effective economic integration given by the subsidiary's business activity. When this condition is met *and* the subsidiary's losses are terminal ones, the absence of a PE does not prevent the acquiring parent company from deducting subsidiary's losses: this deduction is consistent with the freedom of establishment, even if the savings in managerial and administrative costs were marginal in comparison with tax savings (and thus, to a greater extent, if these costs savings are greater than tax savings).

Conversely, the fact that in *A Oy* the merged company had been effectively trading in the past, together with the ECJ's statement in *Cadbury Schweppes* that the subsidiary's economic integration in the host country must be proved by objective elements ascertainable by third parties, suggests that – even if tax savings largely exceeds administrative and managerial costs savings – an operation resulting in a PE could imply valid commercial reasons (and escape the anti-abuse clause) only where the *activity concretely carried out* by the PE indicates, on a case-by-case basis, an effective economic integration.

2.4.3.3 *The possibility of attaching additional conditions for tax neutrality*

In *AT Finanzamt Stuttgart-Körperschaften*, the ECJ also held that, owing to the mandatory and clear wording of Article 8(1) and (2), Member States are not permitted to set additional conditions for the fiscal neutrality in favour of the shareholders of the acquired company.[232] In this respect, it added that leaving Member States such discretion would conflict with the directive's very objective of creating a *common* tax system instead of extending at EU level the systems currently in force in the Member States.[233] It also found that making the fiscal neutrality under Article 8(1) and (2) – in relation to the intra-EU exchanges of shares – subject to the *additional condition* that the non-resident acquiring company carry over the *historical book value of the shares* transferred in its tax balance sheet, would contrast with the directive's purpose of eliminating fiscal barriers to cross-border restructuring of undertakings by ensuring that any increases in the value of shares are not taxed until their actual disposal.[234]

The ECJ rejected an argument, by Germany, that its provisions made taxation possible in cases of gaps in the taxation system: it held that to permit a Member

---

232 Case C-285/07, *AT Finanzamt Stuttgart-Körperschaften* (n 185), para. 26.
233 Ibid., para. 27.
234 Ibid., para. 28.

State unilaterally to fill such gaps would risk undermining the directive's very objective of setting up a common tax system.[235]

The German legislation in *AT v Finanzamt Stuttgart-Körperschaften* could have implied economic double taxation, because the taxation of shareholders of the acquired company on latent capital gains could have been followed by the taxation of the acquiring company in its state of residence on the capital gains from shares at the time of disposal. Accordingly, the ECJ's finding might be seen as avoiding this risk. Moreover, as the directive pursues the same objective for all operations, this finding – if generalised to all operations – would mean that Member States cannot require additional conditions for tax neutrality, even where these would fill gaps in the taxation systems, outside the cases falling within the scope of the anti-abuse clause.

Nonetheless, the question arises as to whether such a conclusion may apply after the *3 DI Srl* ruling, where the ECJ had to assess an Italian provision which, in a cross-border transfer of assets falling within the directive, made the tax deferral for these unrealised capital gains conditional upon the transferring company carrying over in its own balance sheet a special reserve fund equivalent to the amount of the capital gains themselves. The ECJ noted that Article 4(1) and (2), read in conjunction with Article 9, require the *receiving company*, if it wishes to benefit from fiscal neutrality, to maintain the continuity of the valuation of the assets and liabilities transferred, and that this requirement is intended to prevent that neutrality from leading to a permanent exemption, which is not provided for in directive.[236]

On those grounds, it went on to stress that the directive does not establish the conditions which govern the *transferring company's ability to benefit from tax deferral* for capital gains relating to the securities representing the capital of the receiving company and issued in exchange for the transfer of assets and, in particular, it does not indicate what value the transferring company must attribute to those securities.[237] For this reason the ECJ concluded that the directive leaves Member States free to decide whether or not the fiscal neutrality from which the transferring company benefits is to be made subject to obligations to evaluate the securities received in exchange, provided that those obligations do not cause the issue of those securities during the transfer of assets to give rise to taxation of the capital gains relating to those assets.[238]

The ECJ also noted that the Council had rejected the 2003 Commission proposal pursuant to which the real value that the business transferred had immediately prior to the transfer would be attributed to those securities. The ECJ highlighted this proposal's objective of avoiding economic double taxation which could arise, at the time of the disposal of the securities, where the receiving company had maintained the continuity of the valuation of the assets and liabilities

---

235 Ibid., para. 34.
236 Case C–207/11, *3 DI Srl v Agenzia delle Entrate – Ufficio di Cremona* (n 189), para. 28.
237 Ibid., para. 29.
238 Ibid., para. 30.

transferred as requested under Article 4(2) and the transferring company had attributed the value which the business transferred had immediately before the operation to the securities received.[239] The rejection of this Commission proposal was used by the ECJ to demonstrate the discretion left to Member States as regards the conditions that could be imposed on the transferring company.

Given these ECJ's arguments, the question arises as to whether the *3 DI Srl* reasoning could be reconciled with *AT v Finanzamt Stuttgart-Körperschaften*: in this latter the ECJ position would appear to eliminate economic double taxation for exchanges of shares, whereas in *3DI Srl* it would appear to tolerate it for transfers of assets. The ECJ dealt with different directive provisions, i.e. with Article 8(1) and 8(2) concerning exchange of shares in *AT v Finanzamt Stuttgart-Körperschaften*, and with Articles 4(1), 4(2) and 9, regarding transfer of assets, in *3 DI Srl*: accordingly, it might be argued that one provision of the directive may not leave discretion to Member States whereas another provision may do so.

Nonetheless, the directive aims at creating a common system of tax deferral for *all* restructuring operations falling within its scope, and Article 8(1) and (2) are silent on the valuation rules to be adopted by the acquiring company in an exchange of shares just as Articles 4(1), 4(2) and 9 are silent about the valuation rules for the shares received to be attributed by the transferring company in a transfer of assets. Thus, if this omission means that Member States *cannot* impose further conditions on a company involved in exchange of shares (other than those expressly required by the directive), there would be an inconsistency if the same omission meant that Member States *can* do so on a company involved in a transfer of assets.

The two rulings might perhaps be reconciled by noting that, whereas in *AT v Finanzamt Stuttgart-Körperschaften* a Member State made a tax deferral for resident shareholders subject to valuation criteria adopted by a *non-resident* acquiring company, in *3 DI Srl* another Member State made a tax deferral for its resident transferring company subject to a condition to be fulfilled by this *resident* company itself. However, if these two rulings could be reconciled only in the sense that Member States, in all aspects on which the directive is silent, may impose additional conditions on resident companies or shareholders but are not allowed to make tax reliefs for their residents dependent upon choices made by the non-resident counterparts, this would aggravate the uncertainty arising in cases of *dual resident companies* involved in any operation.[240]

2.4.4 The implementation of the Merger Directive

A comparative study on the implementation of the Merger Directive[241] showed considerable differences between national implementing provisions, with regard

---

239 Ibid., para. 31.
240 See ch 2, at 2.4.2.
241 Ernst & Young, *Survey of the implementation of Council Directive* 90/434/EEC (The Merger Directive, as amended), 2009.

to the *subjective scope* of the tax deferral regime in terms of eligible companies and shareholders, to the objective *conditions* for benefiting from it, and to its *interpretation* both of concepts left undefined and of requirements set by the directive.

As regards the *subjective scope*, there are Member States – Austria, Cyprus, Finland, Germany, Poland – where the range of eligible companies is broader than the list indicated in the directive's Annex as it includes companies from extra-EU countries too, thus extending the tax deferral regime to operations where companies and shareholders from third countries are involved (in the Austrian case, even corresponding operations involving partnerships and conversions of companies into partnerships are covered). On the contrary, in Belgium, the range of eligible companies is limited to specific legal entities as listed in company law provisions and is narrower than the Annex to the directive.

The *objective conditions* for benefiting from the tax neutrality regime set out by the directive – the continuity of tax values; the existence of a PE – are accompanied, in certain Member States, by *further conditions* to be fulfilled by the transferring companies or by shareholders in specific operations; these additional requirements restrict the access to the regime.

In this respect, the most significant examples appear to be found in Belgium, in Denmark, in France, in Germany, in Italy and in the UK. Belgium grants the tax relief subject to the condition that the operation be carried out for sound economic and financial needs, and its tax authority asserts that the merging companies should be able to demonstrate that the operation is of economic or financial benefits for the companies involved. In Denmark, in cases of exchanges of shares, all shares need to be exchanged within a period of six months after the first share has been exchanged, a prior approval is necessary and the operations must be carried out within six months after obtaining the approval. In France, in case of (partial) divisions or transfers of assets, the shareholders of the divided company or the transferring company must commit themselves to hold the newly obtained shares of the receiving company for at least three years; in an exchange of shares, the shareholder of the acquired company must commit themselves to hold the shares received for three years, and the acquiring company must commit to the same holding period for shares of the acquired company. Moreover, an advance ruling, to the effect that the envisaged operations can benefit from the tax neutrality regime, is required as regards exchanges of shares aimed at consolidating an existing majority. In Germany, exchange of shares qualify for the tax deferral regime provided that the shares issued to the shareholders of the acquired company are new shares.

In Italy, the tax deferral regime is applicable for exchanges of shares only if at least one of the shareholders involved is resident in Italy or the exchanged shares are held by a qualifying company of another Member State through an Italian PE. In the UK, exchanges of shares qualify for the tax neutrality regime provided that they take place exclusively for securities (shares or debentures), unlike the definition given by the directive (which admits a cash payment not exceeding 10 per cent of the nominal value of shares exchanged).

The imposition of additional requirements for the operations to benefit from the tax neutrality regime at the level of companies or shareholders is typically motivated by anti-avoidance reasons, i.e. as a form of a priori reassurance that the operation will not be carried out mainly for tax savings reasons: this approach appears, therefore, to overlap with the rationale of the anti-abuse clause. For example, in France, the provisions implementing the directive's anti-abuse clause require an advance ruling, which is granted if, cumulatively, the operation is justified for economic reasons, is not motivated by tax evasion or fraud and the operational modalities ensure future taxation of latent capital gains; in Germany, specific anti-abuse provisions set, for each operation, from five to seven year holding period requirements for the shares received as a result of the operation at stake.

This kind of national implementing provisions arguably contrasts with the ECJ's *Leur-Bloem* case law (where the ECJ considered general presumption of abuse as unacceptable and required examination of each individual case), but its persistence indicates that, to date, the ECJ's rulings on the directive have not led to coordinated responses by Member States. On the opposite end of the spectrum of implementation-related choices, other Member States – in addition to not introducing further requirements for benefiting from tax neutrality – have not even introduced anti-abuse provisions, as in the case of Cyprus and Luxembourg. Furthermore, a few countries – Ireland, Italy and Luxembourg – have not fully introduced the 'notional tax credit' requested by Article 10 for PEs, in other Member States, of the transferring company.

With regard to interpretation, the terms left undefined by the directive – such as 'securities', 'branch of activities', 'real value', 'provisions and reserves' – have been subject to local interpretations, and this gap has been filled, under national laws, with (partially) different understandings from one Member State to another (eg the concept of 'real value' is identified with the 'fair market value' in Germany, but with the 'selling price' in Belgium). Partially different interpretations also concern important requirements set by the directive. In this respect, whereas the obligation to apply it to fiscally transparent entities was properly regarded as inapplicable by countries which do not have fiscally transparent entities, the requirement that assets and liabilities remain connected with a PE of the acquiring or receiving company in the Member State of the acquired or merged company (or with a PE in the origin state, in the event of a seat transfer of an SE or SCE) has been interpreted, by most Member States, as meaning that, when as a result of a restructuring operation assets leave their jurisdictions, they can levy 'exit taxes' on latent capital gains arising on those assets and require immediate payment.

As the directive does not expressly deal with exit taxes, this interpretation arguably needs to be assessed against the ECJ's case law (on companies' freedom of establishment) concerning exit taxes, which has been requiring Member States to grant the option of deferred payment of exit taxes.[242] The interpretation that,

---

242 See ch 3, at 3.1.3.

in a restructuring operation, a Member State can levy exit taxes on assets leaving its territory and require immediate payment can thus be regarded as contrasting with such case law.

2.4.5 The directive, its implementation and the case law against the benchmarks

2.4.5.1 Complete elimination of double taxation and of discriminations

The directive, in light of its text, of its implementation by Member States as highlighted by a comparative perspective and of the case law, fails to meet the benchmark of complete elimination of economic double-taxation and of juridical double taxation. The assessment against this benchmark could consider that the directive's key purpose was limited to providing a system for tax deferral; nonetheless, the key provisions and their implementation have been failing to eliminate double taxation, even in those respects in which they could have done so.

As already stressed,[243] due to the rejection of the 2003 Commission proposal to introduce valuation rules designed to eliminate it, *economic double taxation* of capital gains *at the time of realisation* still arises in transfers of assets whenever the Member State of the transferring company, by using his discretion recognised by the ECJ in the *3 DI Srl* ruling, requires this company to value the shares of the received company that it obtained in exchange at the book value of assets and liabilities transferred. This risk also arises in exchange of shares whenever the state of residence of the acquiring company does not allow it to attribute a market value to the shares of the acquired company received.

Accordingly, the ECJ's ruling in *AT v Finanzamt Stuttgart-Körperschaften* – by disallowing a national rule providing for taxation of latent capital gains on shareholders of the acquired company in the event of failure by the acquiring company to maintain continuity of value – has only *mitigated* the risk of economic double taxation, but has certainly not avoided it. In fact, *economic double taxation* has only been postponed since, without that ECJ ruling, it could have inevitably occurred at the time of realisation of capital gains by the acquiring company (given the previous taxation of capital gains, as they emerged, in the hands of shareholders of the acquired company).

Moreover, *juridical double taxation* might still occur whenever Member States, in their implementing laws, have not fully transposed the provisions on PEs of the transferring company located in other Member States, which are intended to overcome juridical double taxation.[244] In these cases, the interested parties would need to invoke the 'direct effect' of the directive's provisions – such as Article 10(1) as regards PEs of the transferring company that are located in other Member States – that are formulated in a clear and precise wording.

---

243 See 2.4.3.3 above.
244 See ch 2 at 2.4.1 and 2.4.4.

The impossibility for the directive to completely overcome double taxation also derives from limitations of its very scope, which covers *neither* PEs of the transferring or acquiring companies (unlike the Parent–Subsidiary Directive[245] and the Interest and Royalties Directive[246]) *nor* transfers of assets by individuals owning a business without the legal form of a company.[247]

2.4.5.2 The elimination of unintended double non-taxation

Although the directive, as clarified by the ECJ, does not intend to introduce a permanent exemption for capital gains deriving from restructuring operations, individual Member States remain completely free to maintain or to introduce rules exempting realised capital gains to the benefit of shareholders of a resident acquired company and/or of an acquiring resident company in an exchange of shares, or to the benefit of a resident transferring company and/or of a resident receiving company involved in mergers, divisions or transfers of assets. Therefore, the directive leaves potential room for an unintended double non-taxation, which may occur whenever the Member States of residence of all of the parties involved introduce a rule exempting *both* the realised capital gains on shares received (residence state of transferring companies in mergers, divisions or transfer of assets, or of shareholders of the acquired company in exchanges of shares) *and* the realised capital gains on assets received (residence state of the receiving company in mergers, divisions or transfer of assets, or of the acquiring company in exchanges of shares).

In other words, due to the lack of valuation rules in transfers of assets and exchanges of shares and to the discretion left to Member States and recognised by the ECJ,[248] the directive risks generating (not only economic double taxation but also) *unintended* double non-taxation if Member States use their discretion to exempt capital gains with a view to building a more competitive corporate or individual taxation system than other EU countries. For example, in an exchange of shares where Belgium-resident shareholders of a Belgian company sold their shareholdings to an Austrian company in exchange for shares of this latter company, and where they maintained continuity of valuation as requested by the directive for tax deferral, Belgium would exempt the capital gains in the hands of its resident shareholders when these gains are realised, whereas Austria would exempt realised capital gains in the hands of its resident acquiring company. This situation of unintended economic double non-taxation, which may derive from a lack of coordination between Member States' provisions exempting capital gains in their implementation of the Merger Directive, was not pointed out in the Commission's Action Plan against Tax Fraud and Evasion, unlike situations of

---

245 See ch 2 at 2.2.2.
246 See ch 2, at 2.5.3.
247 C. H. J. I. Panayi, *European Union Corporate Tax Law* (n 8), at 286.
248 See 2.3.4 above.

unintended double non-taxation that could derive from the implementation of the Parent–Subsidiary Directive.[249]

2.4.5.3 *The reduction of administrative costs for direct tax compliance within the EU, together with the achievement of greater legal certainty*

As some Member States require application and evidence-based documentation for granting the tax deferral required by the directive, implementation of the directive does not appear to have fully resulted in a reduction of administrative costs for compliance with direct tax-related obligations. In turn, legal certainty is compromised not only by the doubts raised by the wording of the directive, but also by all unresolved issues left by case law, all of which are of utmost importance for the application of the directive. Specifically, uncertainty still arises as to: (a) whether or not *AT v Finanzamt Stuttgart-Körperschaften* and *3 DI Srl*, taken together, can offer a definitive indication about the cases when the lack of indications in the directive means that Member States are free to require conditions additional to those expressly set out by the directive from the 'subjective' viewpoint, i.e. with regard to the companies or shareholders involved; (b) whether or not – by taking these two rulings together with *Leur-Bloem* and *Andersen og Jensen* (where the ECJ strictly adhered to the literal definitions of the relevant operations) – the ECJ's case law may be interpreted as meaning that additional conditions may be legitimate from the 'subjective' viewpoint but not with regard to the *operations* carried out; (c) whether or not *Foggia* and *A Oy*, if read together, sufficiently clarify the conditions for the existence of 'valid commercial reasons' and thus for the deductibility of losses by an acquiring company in a cross-border merger by acquisition.

In turn, the uncertainty left by the case law as regards Member States' freedom to set additional conditions results in uncertainty as to whether or not the various national implementing provisions requiring additional conditions from the subjective and/or from the objective viewpoint could be suspected of being incompatible with the directive. Furthermore, in light of these uncertainties left by the ECJ's case law, the doubt remains as to whether the conversion of a branch into a subsidiary is covered by the directive.[250] Technically, this conversion could be carried out, by a company resident in a Member State, by creating a new subsidiary in another Member State where it has a PE and by transferring all PE assets to this new subsidiary, which could thus be described as a transfer of assets. Nonetheless, the definition of 'transfer of assets'[251] does not clarify whether the receiving company can be a new one, specifically set up to implement the operation, and the conversion would not imply a cross-border transfer of assets.

---

249 COM(2012) 722 final (n 150), para. 4, p. 9.
250 Panayi, European Union Corporate Tax Law (n 8), at 286.
251 Art. 2(d).

2.4.5.4 *The fight against cross-border tax evasion and fraud, against abusive practices and against aggressive tax planning*

The comparative overview of implementing provisions shows that, whereas some Member States have set additional requirements for the tax deferral, others have introduced more liberal conditions, i.e. more favourable rules than the directive itself. Significant examples of this different national approaches can be found. Some Member States have not used the option, allowed by Article 7, to tax gains accruing to the receiving company on the cancellation of a less than 10 per cent holding in the capital of the transferring company, whereas others still require an even higher threshold.

Germany has implemented the anti-abuse clause by introducing minimum holding periods in connection with transfers of assets, exchanges of shares, divisions and partial divisions, thus widening the scope of this clause as compared with Article 15 of the directive, which choice raises doubts of incompatibility with the ECJ's case law, whereas – on the opposite end of the spectrum of national legislators' choices – Cyprus has not used the anti-abuse clause and does not withdraw the benefits of the directive on abusive grounds. Moreover, some Member States have used their discretion to exempt realised capital gains, obtained by transferring companies, receiving companies or by shareholders of acquired companies in exchanges of shares that were latent at the time of the operation, thereby creating situations of unintended economic double non-taxation.[252]

These uncoordinated national choices offer multinational groups – when planning restructuring operations amongst affiliated companies – the occasion to carry out a 'forum-shopping' by relocating the tax residence of companies involved, through the transfer of the registered office and place of effective management in the Member States offering the most favourable conditions, so as to match the most favourable conditions for transferring companies with the most favourable conditions for receiving companies. Under ECJ company law rulings, the seat transfer could be carried out by companies formed in Member States adopting the 'incorporation system' simply by moving to another country the head office/place of effective management,[253] and, by companies formed in Member States adopting the real seat criteria, by transferring both head office and registered office and converting their legal form into a form offered by the destination state.[254]

Arguably if, with a view to restructuring operations within a multinational group, there were a set of transfers of tax residences of the intended transferring and of the intended receiving companies aimed at minimising or avoiding the tax liability on capital gains by matching the most favourable conditions offered by the new states of residence concerned with the transferring and receiving companies, this would fall within the concept of aggressive tax planning as defined

---

252 See 2.4.5.2 above.
253 Case C–371/10, *National Grid Indus* (n 174), paras. 35–37.
254 Case C–210/06, *Cartesio* [2008] ECR I–9641, paras. 111–113; Case C–378/10, *VALE Epitési*, ruling issued on 12 July 2012, paras. 36–41.

by the Commission recommendation. The general anti-abuse clause that the Commission has recommended Member States to adopt,[255] and which would make such a set of transfers of tax residences ineffective, would not apply within the scope of the directive.[256] In the Action Plan against tax fraud and tax evasion, the Commission anticipated that it would review the anti-abuse clause of the Merger Directive too,[257] with a view to implementing the principle underlying the recommendation against aggressive tax planning, but, to date, it has not yet proposed a rephrasing of the Merger Directive's anti-abuse clause along the wording of this recommendation, and has not yet proposed to turn the anti-abuse clause from an option into an obligation for all Member States. As a result, neither the directive nor its implementing legislation appear to be able to achieve the objective to counter aggressive tax planning strategies.

2.5 The Arbitration Convention on Transfer Pricing

The 'Arbitration Convention',[258] signed in 1990 under Article 220 EEC, is a multilateral agreement under international law, as such – unlike directives or regulations – it is not subject to ECJ jurisdiction, but only to national courts' jurisdiction. After an extension of an initial five-year duration period, its duration currently extends automatically every five years if not otherwise objected to by Member States.

This Convention, which applies to all taxes on income, is based on the arm's length principle, just as Article 9 of the OECD Model for DTCs and the 2010 OECD Transfer Pricing Guidelines for Multinational Enterprises and Tax Administrations, under which prices for goods or services exchanged between associated companies should reflect the prices that would be practiced between unrelated parties for the same or similar transactions under the same or similar conditions. In exchanges of goods or services between affiliated companies of different Member States, economic double taxation arises if state A – the state of residence of the selling company – makes an upward adjustment in taxable profits (as it does not consider prices as reflecting arm's length prices), and this adjustment is not matched by an equivalent downward adjustment to taxable profits in state B, the buying company's state of residence (which considers these prices, i.e. purchasing costs for the buyer, to be arm's length prices). This situation may also occur for transfers of goods and services between a company and its PE in another Member State.

The Arbitration Convention applies when, as in this case, profits of an enterprise of a Member State are (likely to be) included in the profits of an enterprise of

---

255 Commission Recommendation C(2012) 8806 final (n 64), Art. 4.
256 Ibid., Preamble, Recital (9).
257 COM(2012) 722 final, (n 150), at 9.
258 Convention 90/436/EEC of 23 July 1990 on the Elimination of Double Taxation in Connection with the Adjustment of Profits of Associated Enterprises (Arbitration Convention), OJ 1990 L 225/10.

another Member State too (Article 1), although it omits defining the concepts of 'enterprise' and of PE which are therefore left to definitions given by national laws or DTCs. The Convention establishes a three-phase procedure for eliminating economic double taxation. First, a Member State must notify the enterprise concerned about its intention to make an upward adjustment and, in this initial phase, it has to hear any complaint and allow this enterprise to inform its associated party for this, to notify its state of residence authorities accordingly. The tax authority of the Member State of the complaining company may still make the upward adjustment but, *if* the complaint appears to be well founded (Article 6(2)), a second phase follows. In this case, upon request within three years of its resident complaining company, it needs to seek a mutual agreement with the tax authority of the associated company's state of residence, irrespective of any possible remedies under national laws of the countries concerned, *unless* legal or administrative proceedings (if initiated) resulted in a final ruling that one of the enterprises is liable for a serious administrative or criminal penalty as a consequence of the transactions giving rise to the adjustment (Article 8(1) and 8(2)).

If the competent authorities fail to reach an agreement within two years, they must establish an Advisory Commission that must deliver its opinion (about how to eliminate economic double taxation) within six months, after which, within a further six months, the two national authorities must either act according to the Advisory Commission opinion or take a different decision eliminating economic double taxation. In any case, this objective is regarded as achieved if either the tax chargeable on the adjusted profit in one state is reduced by the amount of tax chargeable on the same profits in the other state, or if the profits are included in the taxable base in one Member State only. Overall, the three possible procedural phases have to terminate within six years.

A limitation of this procedure, toward the achievement of the objective of eliminating economic double taxation, certainly lies in the fact that, in the first phase, the assessment (as to whether the complaint is well founded) appears to be only left to the same tax authority making the adjustment, and that it could be delayed or even stopped by a decision to appeal in national courts. So far, the Arbitration Convention has been applied only in a few cases and no arbitration award was disclosed.[259] For this reason, and because Article 25 of the OECD Model since 2008 recommends an arbitration clause in mutual agreements procedure (MAPs) set out by DTCs – which arbitration clause has started being included in new DTCs – the importance of the Arbitration Convention, as an alternative to MAPs contemplated by DTCs, is likely to diminish in the future.[260]

---

259 L. Hinnekens, 'European Arbitration Convention: thoughts on its principles, procedures and first experience', 19 *EC Tax Review* 3, 109–16 (2010).
260 See Panayi, European Union Corporate Tax Law (n 8), at 74.

Nonetheless, if compared with the numerous DTCs which still do not include the arbitration clause envisaged in the OECD Model, the Arbitration Convention still offers associated companies more effective protection against the risk of economic double taxation arising from transfer pricing adjustments. Even the maximum time length of the arbitration procedure, although not negligible, can prove preferable for interested parties than the length of MAPs set out by DTCs, which have often lasted for considerably longer periods.

Moreover, there have been attempts at improving the working of the Arbitration Convention through an expert group charged by the Commission with examining the key issues for its implementation, the EU Joint Transfer Pricing Forum (JTPF),[261] and a number of soft-law pieces partly derived from the work of the JTPF. For example, in 2006 a Council resolution, following a 2005 Commission Communication on the work of the JTPF and on a code of conduct on transfer pricing documentation for associated enterprises in the EU,[262] adopted this Code of Conduct.[263] The code politically commits Member States to accept a standardised and partially centralised transfer pricing documentation in the EU, for the purpose of reducing administrative compliance costs for associated enterprises that must prepare transfer pricing documentation to support their positions in dealing with national tax authorities.

In 2006, a code of conduct for the effective implementation of the Arbitration Convention was also issued,[264] followed in 2009 by a Revised Code of Conduct[265] after a Commission proposal.[266] This code recommends Member States to suspend the collection of taxes during the dispute resolution procedure; it also indicates common rules of conduct that national tax authorities are expected to follow in implementing the key phases of this procedure and in dealing with trilateral cases within the EU. It thus contributes to the effective implementation of the Convention and, subject to tax authorities following its recommendations, also helps legal certainty, despite the limitations deriving from its nature as a non-legally binding instrument and the scarce application, to date, of the Arbitration Convention itself.

---

261 After working informally for some years, the JTPF was formally established by a 2006 Commission Decision (Commission Decision of 22 December 2006, 2007/75/EC, OJ 2007, L 32, at 189) and its mandate was extended in 2011 (Commission Decision of 25 January 2011, OJ 2011 C 24, p. 3). In addition to business representatives, its members include representatives appointed by the concerned (tax) authority of each Member State.

262 Commission Communication COM(2005) 543 final, on a code of conduct on transfer pricing documentation for associated enterprises in the European Union.

263 Resolution of the Council and of the representatives of the Member States, meeting within the Council, of 27 June 2006 on a code of conduct on transfer pricing documentation for associated enterprises in the European Union, 2006/C, 176/01.

264 Code of Conduct for the Effective Implementation of the Arbitration Convention, 2006/C, 176/02.

265 Revised Code of Conduct for the Effective Implementation of the Arbitration Convention, 2009/C, 322/01.

266 Commission Communication COM(2009) 472 final, proposal for a Revised Code of Conduct for the Effective Implementation of the Arbitration Convention.

2.6 The Interest and Royalties Directive

2.6.1 The text of the directive against the benchmarks

The Interest and Royalties Directive, introduced in 2003, exempts intra-EU interest and royalties payments between 'associated companies' from 'any tax' in the source country (ie in the country where the payments arise).[267] The basic provisions of this directive show strong similarities with those of the two other corporate tax directives and, in particular, of the Parent–Subsidiary Directive.

Article 3 covers in fact the same typologies of companies, in terms of legal forms, residence and subjection to corporate income tax requirements (Article 3(a)). The difference lies in the notion of 'associated company' under Article 3(b), which includes, together with a company in which another holds a direct minimum quota of 25 per cent, each of two companies where a third company holds at least 25 per cent in the capital of both. Moreover, the Interest and Royalties Directive leaves identical options for Member States as in the Parent–Subsidiary Directive with regards to: the replacement of the criteria of holding in the capital with that of holding in the voting rights;[268] the setting of a two-year minimum holding period requirement;[269] the anti-abuse clause[270] and the safeguard of national or DTC provisions.[271] In turn, the anti-abuse clause in Article 5(2), denying the exemption in cases of transactions having tax evasion, avoidance or abuse as the principal or one of the principal objectives, has similar wording to the corresponding provision of the Merger Directive.[272]

The directive covers – like the Parent–Subsidiary Directive – the payments made and received between separate legal entities, both directly and through a PE situated in a third Member State.[273] The definition of PE – very similar, but not identical, to the definition given by the Parent–Subsidiary Directive – follows closely Article 5 of the OECD Model, without reproducing the provisions of Article 5(2) to 5(7). Under Article 1(3), for interest and royalties payments to be considered as made by (a company through) a PE, they must be tax-deductible in the Member State of location of the PE; under Article 1(5), for these payments to be received through the PE, the title for payment must be effectively connecting with the PE and the PE must be subject to corporation tax in its state of location.

---

267 Council Directive 2003/49/EC of 3 June 2003, 'on a common system of taxation applicable to interest and royalties payments made between associated companies of different Member States' in OJEC L 157, pp. 49–54 of 26 June 2003.
268 Ibid., Art. 3(b).
269 Art. 1(10).
270 Art. 5(1) of the Interest and Royalties Directive as compared with Art. 1(2) of the Parent–Subsidiary Directive.
271 Art. 9 of the Interest and Royalties Directive as compared with Art. 7(2) of the Parent–Subsidiary Directive.
272 Art. 5(2) of the Interest and Royalties Directive as compared with Art. 15 (2) of the Merger Directive.
273 Art. 1(2) and (5), Art. 3(c) of the Interest and Royalties Directive; Art. 5 of the OECD Model. Preamble, Real (1).

Its preamble recognises that any disadvantage on intra-EU interest and royalties payments in comparison with domestic payments must be eliminated 'in a single market having the characteristics of a domestic market',[274] and that DTCs do not always ensure that double taxation is eliminated, in addition to involving burdensome administrative formalities.[275] However, although this directive in Article 2 defines 'interest and royalties' as widely as Article 11 (for interest payment) and Article 12 (for royalties) of the OECD Model,[276] its wording does not suffice to ensure the achievement of this goal stated in its preamble, for at least three reasons.

First, it (currently) excludes payments to second-tier associated companies – due to the requirement of *direct* minimum holding – as well as to unrelated companies, despite the exemption from withholding tax of the corresponding domestic payments.

Secondly, the importance of some (implicit) options left to Member States may give rise to doubts about the boundaries of a proper implementation. This may be seen, in particular, in Article 4(2) which limits the scope of the directive to the amount of these payments that is supposed to be agreed by the parties involved in the absence of a 'special relationship', *without* indicating when the relationship between associated companies should be regarded as 'special', and in Article 4(1) granting national legislators the option not to apply the directive to particular categories of payments.

Thirdly, Member States may set a number of substantive and procedural conditions directly affecting the scope of the tax exemption granted. For example, under Article 1(11), the source state can require that conditions laid down in terms of eligibility for the exemption be substantiated by an attestation; under Article 1(12), it may make the exemption subject to a decision currently granting the exemption following an attestation certifying the fulfilment of the requirements for eligibility.

Furthermore, although the text of this directive offers greater legal certainty than that of the Parent–Subsidiary Directive because it defines 'interest and royalties', it risks failing in preventing 'aggressive tax planning' strategies which may result in double non-taxation. In fact, the directive requires the source country to abolish withholding tax, but it does not impose the obligation on the state of residence of the recipient company to tax interest and royalties, thereby leading to double non-taxation if this state exempts inbound interest and/or royalties.

In order to eliminate this risk, in 2011 the Commission, submitted a proposal for a recast of the Interest and Royalties Directive,[277] requiring Member States to

---

274 Ibid.
275 Ibid., Recital (2).
276 And, in so doing, overcomes a limit of the Parent–Subsidiary Directive given by the absence, in that directive, of the definition of 'distribution of profits'.
277 Communication COM(2011) 714 final, proposal for a recast of the Interest and Royalties Directive (11 November 2011).

abolish withholding tax only where the interest or royalty payment concerned is not exempt from corporate taxation in the hands of the beneficial owner in its state of residence.[278] Further to the extension of two other corporate tax directives to new types of companies, amongst which are the SE and the SCE, the Commission proposed to include the SE and the SCE in the scope of the Interest and Royalties Directive too, to lower the participation threshold to 10 per cent, just as it currently applies to the two other directives,[279] and to extend the directive to payments between unrelated companies.

2.6.2 The case law on the Interest and Royalties Directive

The 2011 *Scheuten Solar* ruling[280] concerned a situation where loan interest paid by a German subsidiary to a Dutch parent company, and initially deducted by the paying company, was added back for 50 per cent of its amount to the subsidiary's taxable base for German trade tax purposes. The German subsidiary submitted that this would determine an economic double taxation in contrast with Article 1(1). The ECJ noted that the directive exempts interest and royalty payments arising in their source state when the beneficial owner is a company of (or a PE situated in) another Member State,[281] and that only the actual beneficial owner can receive interest constituting income from debt-claims as defined by the directive.[282]

On these grounds, the ECJ found that Article 1(1) concerns *solely* the tax position of the interest *creditor* and is only aimed at eliminating juridical double taxation.[283] Accordingly, it concluded that, because the German legislation did not reduce the creditor's income and concerned only the determination of the basis of assessment of the business tax to be paid by the *debtor*, this legislation was outside the scope of Article 1(1).[284] The ECJ also highlighted that, without a provision determining the basis of assessment of the debtor, the scope of Article 1(1) cannot extend beyond the exemption it lays down.[285]

In light of its reasoning, the ECJ appears to have meant that Article 1(1) *never* intends eliminating economic double taxation (caused by the non-deductibility of interest or royalty payments by the debtor in conjunction with taxation on the creditor in its residence Member State), unlike the Parent–Subsidiary Directive. However, the ECJ reasoning in the case law on the Parent–Subsidiary Directive would seem – at least as regards the direct effect and minimum

---

278 Ibid., at 5.
279 After a first Commission proposal COM(2003) 841 final, submitted on 30 December 2003 [2003/0331(CSN)], the 2011 proposed recast of the Interest and Royalties Directive would again bring these amendments: COM(2011) 714 final (n 277), at 7–8.
280 Case C-397/09, *Scheuten Solar Technology* [2011] ECR I-6455.
281 Ibid., para. 25.
282 Ibid., para. 25.
283 Ibid., para. 29.
284 Ibid., para. 30.
285 Ibid., para. 34.

shareholding requirement,[286] as well as the eligibility conditions in terms of legal forms and the status of full share owner of the recipient company[287] – applicable by analogy to the Interest and Royalties Directive too, because this directive is formulated in clear and unconditional terms and sets out the same kind of eligibility conditions as the Parent–Subsidiary directive.

2.6.3 The implementation of the Interest and Royalties Directive

Whereas some Member States did not levy withholding tax on interest payments and/or royalty payments before the deadline (1 January 2004) for implementation, others generally abolished withholding taxes on interest and royalties payments as a result of the implementation. However, the most noticeable differences from one Member State to another lie: in the eligible payments, particularly as regards the concept of royalties; in the requirement regarding residency, legal forms, subject-to-corporate income tax and beneficial ownership of the payment; in the transposition of the criteria for identifying 'associated companies' and PEs; and in the chosen procedure for granting exemption.

With regard to the concept of interest and royalties in implementing laws, whereas the definition of interest never appears to deviate from the concept specified in the directive, the concept of royalties mentioned in implementing measures is narrower than the directive's definition of royalties in some countries – i.e. Belgium, Denmark, Hungary, Slovakia and Slovenia – whereas it is broader in two other Member States, Spain and Sweden.

Moreover, some countries – including Hungary, Luxembourg and Malta – *never* apply taxes on outbound interest or royalties payment to any non-resident entity, and therefore offer a more quite 'liberal' regime than provided for by the directive. These countries have implemented none of the requirements set by the directive in terms of residence, of legal forms, of subjection to corporate income tax, etc. In other countries, only part of these requirements were transposed – e.g. in Cyprus and Estonia only the residence requirement; in the Netherlands and the UK, solely the residence and subjection-to-tax requirements – whereas, amongst countries that have transposed all of the requirements, there are significant differences. France and Italy have introduced the subject-to-tax condition in objective terms, i.e. by requiring that the recipient company be subject to tax on interest and royalties, unlike the majority of other countries who have transposed this condition in subjective terms (making reference to the company as taxable entity).

The residence requirement, which in most Member States has been implemented in the sense that the recipient company must be resident in a Member State, has been transposed in Austria and in France by requiring the place of effective management of the recipient company to be in a Member State. This particular choice is useful in case of dual resident companies within the EU.

---

286 See ch 2, at 2.3.3.2.
287 See 2.3.3.5 above.

Moreover, Austria, Finland, Germany, Ireland and the UK have introduced specific definitions of PE for the purpose of exemption of interest and royalties paid to qualifying companies, whereas other Member States use domestic law definitions.

With regard to the identification of 'associated companies', the 25 per cent participation threshold has been implemented by most countries; exceptions are Hungary, Luxembourg, Malta and the Netherlands, which set neither capital nor voting rights requirements. Ireland and Italy require the minimum threshold in terms of voting rights; the Czech Republic and the UK in terms of either capital or voting rights; the remaining countries in terms of capital. The two-year minimum holding period has been implemented by a few countries – the Czech Republic, France, Ireland, Slovakia and Slovenia – whereas some other countries – Austria, Belgium, Denmark, Italy and Spain as regards royalties only – have set a one-year holding period requirement, and the remaining countries impose no minimum holding period.

Most Member States have exercised the option not to apply the directive to the specific types of payments indicated by Article 4(1) and, as authorised by Article 4(2), use transfer pricing and/or thin capitalisation rules to deny the exemption to excess amounts of interest or royalty payments (by defining the non-deductible amount under their domestic law). However, in respect of Article 4(1), exceptions are Cyprus, Denmark, Estonia, Malta, Slovenia and Spain, who apply the exemption even to the particular categories of payments listed in that provision.

Finally, in respect of formalities and methods for obtaining the exemption, apart from countries (like Hungary, Luxembourg or Malta) never applying withholding taxes, a number of countries – Cyprus, Estonia, Finland, the Netherlands, Slovakia, Spain and Sweden – requires neither an attestation of the existence of the necessary conditions nor a previous decision. On the contrary, Belgium, the Czech Republic, Germany and the UK require both the attestation and the previous decision and some other countries – e.g. Austria, Denmark, France, Ireland and Italy – only require the attestation. In countries requiring a minimum holding period, the exemption is immediately available, subject to a commitment to keep the participation until the expiry of the minimum holding period.

All countries apply a general anti-abuse provision under domestic law, but some have implemented specific anti-abuse rules: Austria and Germany have introduced provisions closely following the wording of Article 5(2) of the directive; France, Italy and Spain allow tax authorities to refuse granting the exemption in case of recipient companies controlled by residents in third countries.

Overall, pending the adoption of the proposed recast and amendments, it could thus be argued that the Interest and Royalties Directive and its implementation were capable of introducing a *common method* of taxation of intra-group interest and royalties payments within the EU, rather than a truly *common system*, because of the considerable differences still existing between national treatments of these payments.

2.6.4 The Interest and Royalties Directive and its implementation against the benchmarks

Pending the adoption of the proposed amendments, the directive seems to achieve part of the objectives taken as benchmarks (elimination of double taxation, of discriminations and of double non-taxation; reduction of administrative compliance costs; greater legal certainty; fight against aggressive tax planning, tax avoidance and tax evasion).

The directive, owing to the very abolition of withholding tax, effectively manages to eliminate juridical double taxation on the recipient associated companies covered by it, but there are a number of shortcomings if assessing the directive against a uniform abolition of withholding tax on intra-group interest and royalties payments throughout the EU. First, as the Commission highlighted in a 2009 report on the functioning of the directive,[288] the risk of juridical double taxation also arises in respect of interest and royalties payments between *unrelated* parties,[289] which are currently not covered by the directive. The same holds true with regard to indirectly associated companies (ie second-tier associates); as the Commission noted, since both this directive and the Parent–Subsidiary Directive share the same purpose of eliminating double taxation, the limitation of the scope of the Interest and Royalties Directive to first-tier associates is also inconsistent with the extension of the Parent–Subsidiary Directive to indirect holdings.[290]

In effect, Articles 11 (Interests) and 12 (Royalties) of the OECD Model do not distinguish between payments to related and to unrelated companies, thus acknowledging that both may give rise to a double taxation to be eliminated. Moreover, a discrimination toward unrelated parties contrasts with the non-discrimination principle enshrined in Article 6 of the TFEU, and the risk of abusive practices aimed at benefiting from the exemption of withholding tax is less likely to exist for payments to unrelated companies.[291]

Because some Member States – generally exempting interest and royalties payments to non-resident entities – have not introduced any association requirements and, owing to the different implementations of the minimum holding period as between those countries that have introduced the 25 per cent direct holding requirements, the scope of the elimination of juridical double taxation is wider or narrower in different groups of Member States. Finally, the directive still excludes intra-company payments, made e.g. by a branch to its head office in another Member State, despite the possible imposition of a withholding tax by some Member States on these payments as well. In this case, the taxation at source would create, for intra-company payments, the same risk of juridical double taxation that the directive eliminates *only* for payments between associated

---

288 COM(2009) 179, Report from the Commission to the Council in accordance with Art. 8 of Council Directive 2003/49/EC on a common system of taxation applicable to interests and royalty payments made between associated companies of different Member States (17 April 2009).
289 Ibid., at 8–9.
290 Ibid.
291 Terra and Wattel, *European Tax Law* (n 6), at 761.

companies,[292] and the directive would show a further pitfall if not extended to intra-company payments.

After the ECJ's statement, in *Scheuten Solar*, that the directive is not intended to eliminate economic double taxation and to prevent limitations on interest deduction at the paying company level, it is even clearer – as it is from Article 4(2) – that the directive does not oppose thin capitalisation rules or transfer pricing upward adjustments (on the paying company) concerning interest and royalty payments. Consequently – despite the directive being unable to contribute to eliminating economic double taxation – the achievement of this objective as regards interest payments is made dependent only on the ECJ's case law on abusive practices in the exercise of the freedom of establishment. As will be seen,[293] the ECJ has in fact banned Member States' thin capitalisation rules intended to limit deductions of interest payments to group companies located in other Member States (without limitations on payments to domestic group companies), except for the case of wholly artificial arrangements.

With regard to the (unintended) double non-taxation, as already highlighted the current version of the directive leaves this risk, by not imposing an obligation to tax interest and royalty payments on the Member State of the receiving company, and the Commission aims at eliminating such a loophole. Specifically, the directive currently fails to contrast double non-taxation only in the case of payments which are *not* received through a PE because, in cases of payments received by a company through a PE, the objective of eliminating double non-taxation is already achieved by the requirement, under Article 1(5), that the PE must be subject to corporation tax in its state of location.

Moreover, the directive has been contributing to the *reduction of administrative compliance costs* in comparison with the regime otherwise applicable to interest and royalties under the DTCs. In fact, under the typical DTCs regime of reduction of withholding tax in the source state coupled with credit in the state of residence of the recipient, or of exemptions from withholding tax, the reduction or the waiver is usually not automatically granted, but must be requested by the recipient to the tax authority of the payer's state of residence, after an initial full withholding. The refund of the withholding tax is a time-consuming and cumbersome administrative procedure, which may take some years to be completed. The directive eliminates this situation for eligible companies, but the differences in the implementation of procedural provisions of Article 1(11) to 1(14)[294] demonstrate that the objective of contributing to the reduction of administrative burdens (just like the objective of eliminating juridical double taxation) has been achieved to a different extent in different Member States.

With regard to *legal certainty*, the directive – owing to its providing a detailed definition of interest payments and royalties and to the degree of clarity of several other provisions – goes further than the Parent–Subsidiary Directive, although it

---

292 Ibid.
293 See ch 3.
294 See ch 2 at 2.6.3.

still leaves interpretative uncertainties. These could arise with regard to the implication of the different beneficial ownership definitions for companies and for PEs (where only the PE must be subject-to-tax on received payments),[295] as well as with regard to a definition of PE. In fact, despite being similar, but not identical, to that of the Parent–Subsidiary Directive and being based on the OECD Model definition, the PE definition does not reproduce the examples listed in Article 5(2) to 5(7) of the OECD Model and therefore raises doubts as to whether dependent agents' PEs fall within the directive.[296]

Finally, the amendments proposed by the Commission, by closing the current loophole given by a combination of exemption from withholding tax in the source state and exemption in the recipient state of residence, would eliminate the scope for a possible double non-taxation planning strategy and would ensure that interest and royalties payment between associated companies would be taxed (at least) once within the EU. Nevertheless, the lack of coordination between Member States in the implementation process – and the difference between states which unconditionally exempt interest payments and royalties and those which require the minimum holding period, the attestation, a prior decision – could still leave margins for aggressive tax planning strategies lying in 'cherry picking' the jurisdictions with the most favourable rules.

The higher the amount and the importance of interest and royalties payments within a corporate group, the higher could be the incentive to concentrate loans and licensing in those subsidiaries resident in Member States applying the more 'liberal' implementing regime *or* to move their tax residence to those states, whilst moving the tax residence of the recipient companies in Member States with the lowest corporate tax rates. The difficulty of proving abuse that was explained as regards the Merger Directive, deriving from the ECJ's case law,[297] could occur in this case as well.

2.7 The Savings Directive

Together with the Interest and Royalties Directive, in 2003 the Council adopted Directive 2003/48/EC (Savings Directive),[298] which is still the only directive on individuals' taxation. As savings income, in the current globalised economy, is a very mobile source both within the EU and towards third countries, this directive was introduced as part of a 'package to tackle harmful tax competition'.[299] It is broadly aimed at fighting cross-border tax evasion on this income source and intends overcoming the distortions of capital movement between Member States

---

295 COM(2009) 179 (n 288), at 3–4.
296 Ibid., at 7.
297 See ch 2 at 2.4, 2.4.3 and 2.4.5.
298 Council Directive 2003/48/EC of 3 June 2003 on taxation of savings income in the form of interest payments, OJ L 157/38 of 26 June 2003.
299 Including the Code of Conduct on Business Taxation and the Interest and Royalties Directive too.

that would arise if residents of a Member State were able to escape any form of taxation in this state.[300]

The directive currently applies to 'interest' paid by a 'paying agent' resident in a Member State to a 'beneficial owner' resident in another Member State and ensures effective taxation of interest payments under the legislation of the beneficial owner's state of residence. The Commission, as a result of a specific duty under Article 18 to report every three years on the operation of this directive and to propose amendments, submitted an amending proposal in 2008, eventually adopted in 2014.[301]

Unlike the Interest and Royalties Directive, the Savings Directive still allows the source state to apply withholding taxes on outbound interest payments as established under national laws and bilateral DTCs (Article 16); it creates a system of automatic exchange of information between national tax authorities (Articles 8–9) and requires the state of residence of the 'beneficial owner' to eliminate any double taxation that might arise from withholding taxes. The directive's application as between Member States would leave economic operators wide scope for circumventing its provisions if interest payments were routed from third countries' paying agents to individuals resident in Member States. To avoid this, the EU agreed with five European non-Member States (Andorra, Liechtenstein, Monaco, San Marino and Switzerland) and with ten dependent or associated territories of Member States[302] that, as from the directive's entry into force (1 July 2005), those countries and territory apply equivalent measures to those set out by the directive.

With regard to the exchange of information system, Article 8 requires the 'paying agent' to transmit personal details concerning the beneficial owner, its residence, its account number or the identification of the debt-claim giving rise to the interest, and the category of interest payments, to its Member State's tax authority. Under Article 9, this tax authority must automatically transmit these details, at least once a year and within six months following the end of its tax year, to the tax authority of the residence Member State of the beneficial owner. All Member States introduced this system of information reporting, except for two Member States[303] which, for a transitional period, rather than exchanging information, can levy a (currently) 35 per cent withholding tax and transfer 75 per cent of this tax amount to the beneficial owner's state of residence.

This system of withholding tax and revenue sharing is also currently being applied by the five European non-Member States which agreed to apply 'equivalent measures', whilst Member States' dependent and associated territories

---

300 Ibid., Preamble, Recitals (5) and (6).
301 Council Directive 2014/48/EU of 24 March 2014 amending Directive 2003/48/EC on taxation of savings income in the form of interest payments, in OJ L 111/50, 15.04.2014.
302 Anguilla, Aruba, the British Virgin Islands, the Cayman Islands, Guernsey, the Isle of Man, Jersey, Montserrat, the Netherlands Antilles and the Turks and Caicos Islands.
303 Originally Austria, Belgium and Luxembourg, but only Austria and Luxembourg as of 1 January 2010.

have been switching to information exchange. The transitional period will end *if and when* the EU manages to ensure specific conditions concerning exchange of information on request with third countries,[304] which are intended to achieve as far as possible a level playing field regarding information exchange with extra-EU jurisdictions.

The directive's specific definitions of the concepts of 'paying agent', 'beneficial owner' and 'interest payments' are widely framed. Under Article 4, 'paying agent' can be *either* the debtor of the debt-claim generating the interest *or* any operator, i.e. typically a bank *or* other financial intermediary, who is charged, by the debtor *or* by the beneficial owner, with paying interest or securing the payment of the interest. This provision aims to make the directive applicable irrespective of whether the debt-claim producing interest was issued inside or outside the EU, to catch the last intermediary in the payment chain (resident of a Member State) before reaching the beneficial owner.[305]

The 'beneficial owner' is presumed to be the individual receiving the interest payment, unless he proves that he does not receive the payment for his own benefit but represents either a recipient legal person or another individual and discloses the identity of the ultimate recipient to the paying agent (Article 4(2)), to minimise the administrative burden on the paying agent itself. Moreover, Article 6(1) provides for a definition of 'interest payment' which is considerably broader than the definition given by Article 11 of the OECD Model for DTCs.

The beneficial owner's state of residence must eliminate double taxation, either by fully crediting withholding tax levied by the paying agent's state *or* by entirely refunding it (Article 14). Unlike the treatment of corporate dividends under the Parent–Subsidiary Directive, a full tax credit must be granted, by refunding the excess withholding tax in case the tax rate of the beneficial owner's state of residence is lower than the withholding tax. However, if the source state's domestic withholding tax is levied in addition to the 35 per cent withholding tax for non-exchange of information, a specific order applies for the offsetting of both withholding taxes, depending on whether or not the beneficial owner's state of residence income tax on interest payments is sufficient to cover both of them.[306]

Within its scope of application in terms of both taxable persons involved and categories of interest income, this directive is effective in eliminating juridical double taxation thanks to the *full* tax credit or to the *full* refund, which are actually equivalent methods. Within this scope, it can also manage to pre-empt tax avoidance schemes thanks to its wide definition of 'interest payments', to prevent cases of double non-taxation as it ensures that interest payments to individuals are taxed in at least one Member State and, given its detailed provisions, to offer legal certainty with regard to both the obligations imposed and the kinds of interest involved.

---

304 See Art. 10(2).
305 Terra and Wattel, *European Tax Law* (n 6), at 788–89.
306 S. Heidenbauer, 'The Savings Directive' in M. Lang, P. Pistone, J. Schuch and C. Staringer (eds), *Introduction to European Tax Law: Direct Taxation*, 2nd edn (Spiramus Press, London, 2010).

Before the amendments, the Directive's *scope* in terms of *geographical application* and of *income category* still offered occasions for circumvention. In the first respect, the lack of agreements with many third countries made it still possible to escape the directive's provisions by channeling interest payments from these countries through the use of non-EU paying agents or by interposing legal entities, resident in any such extra-EU countries, between the paying agent and the ultimate recipient individual. In the second respect, savings income substantially equivalent to interest – but not falling within the directive – could be obtained through investments in some innovative financial provisions and in certain life insurance products.

Consequently, the amendments addressed these loopholes to better prevent possible circumvention techniques. On the one hand, certain untaxed intermediate structures within the EU – e.g. foundation and non-charitable trusts, which are listed in an Annex – have been required to apply the directive reporting or withholding tax when receiving an interest payment from an upstream economic operator even if established outside the EU, i.e. would be required to act as 'paying agents upon receipt'.

Moreover, paying agents established in a Member State and subject to anti-money laundering obligations[307] would be required, when making payments to certain specifically listed intermediate structures in selected extra-EU jurisdictions, to identify the actual beneficial owner, and – if he were resident in a Member State – they would need to apply the directive as if the payment were made directly to him. A 'look through approach' was therefore adopted to identify the ultimate recipient of payments. On the other hand, the amendments extended the directive's scope to investment income that could be obtained from certain innovative financial products and some life insurance products.[308] The inclusion of income from such other financial products could prove effective in ensuring the taxation in the state of residence for all savings income.

2.8 The Recovery Assistance Directive

2.8.1 *The directive's key provisions*

Directive 2010/24 on the mutual assistance between Member States for the recovery of claims relating to taxes, duties and other measures[309] (Recovery Assistance Directive) has replaced a 2008 directive on mutual assistance between

---

307 That is, subject to Directive 2005/60/EC of 26 October 2005 on the prevention of the use of the financial system for the purpose of money laundering and terrorist financing, OJ L 309/15, as subsequently amended.
308 C. H. J. I. Panayi, 'The proposed amendments to the Savings Directive', *European Taxation* 49, 4, 179–84 (2009).
309 Council Directive 2010/24/EU of 16 March 2010 concerning mutual assistance for the recovery of claims relating to taxes, duties and other measures, OJ L 84/1 of 31 March 2010.

national tax administrations[310] resulting from the consolidation of a pre-existing directive on the recovery of the EU's traditional own resources with subsequent amendments expanding its scope to indirect and to direct taxes.[311] The 2008 Directive covered neither all natural and legal persons nor all forms of claims, and required mutual recognition of national enforcement titles; cumbersome procedures proved to be largely ineffective as only 5 per cent of the request for recovery assistance actually managed to ensure recovery.

To overcome these situations, the Recovery Assistance Directive has, first, broadened the scope of recovery assistance in terms of both the kinds of claims covered and the taxpayers concerned. Article 2 includes within the directive's coverage all taxes and duties of any kind levied by or within Member States, even if on behalf of the EU, as well as refunds, intervention, levies and other listed duties and charges.[312] Only the social security contributions, the fees not expressly listed, the contractual duties and the criminal penalties are excluded from its scope.[313] In turn, Article 3 introduces a very broad definition of 'person', including – in addition to individuals and legal persons – other associations of persons and other 'legal arrangements' who are subject to any of the taxes covered.

The directive establishes four main instruments of assistance from a requested Member State to an applicant Member State: exchange of information; notification to the debtor of documents issued by the applicant state; recovery upon request; precautionary measures. The exchange of information can take three forms: (a) mandatory transmission *upon request* of information 'foreseeably relevant' for the recovery, where the wording 'foreseeably relevant' provides for exchange of information to the widest possible extent, except for irrelevant information;[314] (b) *spontaneous* transmission of information on upcoming refunds of tax to persons resident in another Member State (Article 6); (c) presence of officials of the applying state in administrative offices in the requested state, during administrative enquiries and court proceedings in this state, under arrangements laid down by the requested authority (Article 7), to interview individuals and examine records if so permitted under the requested state legislation.

The notification to the taxpayer of documents related to the claims at stake, issued by the applicant state, must be accompanied by a standard form containing

---

310 Council Directive 2008/55/EC of 26 May 2008 on mutual assistance for the recovery of claims relating to certain levies, duties, taxes and other measures (Codified version), in OJ L 175/17 of 10 June 2008.
311 Council Directive 76/308/EEC of 15 March 1976 on mutual assistance for the recovery of claims resulting from operations forming part of the system of financing the European Agricultural Guidance and Guarantee Fund, and of the agricultural levies and customs duties, in OJ L 73/18 of 19 March 1976, subsequently extended to VAT and excise duties (1979) and to direct taxes (2001).
312 Directive 2010/24 (n 309), Art. 2(1) and (2).
313 Ibid., Art. 2(3).
314 The wording was taken from Art. 4(1) of the OECD–Council of Europe Convention on Mutual Administrative Assistance in Tax Matters of 1988, and from Art. 26 of the OECD Model.

all details about the debtor, the claim and the responsible office (Article 8), and must be carried out by the requested tax authority in accordance with its own laws, regulation or administrative practices (Article 9). The recovery upon request, which consists of collection and enforcement by the requested state tax authority (Articles 10–15) as if it were collecting its own claims (Article 13), must be made according to the rules of the requested state concerning its similar domestic claims or the personal income tax recovery in case of absence of similar claims. Although, under Article 13, the applicant state's claim must therefore be granted 'national treatment', it does not benefit from the same legal preferences as corresponding domestic ones, unless a bilateral agreement or the requested state unilaterally grants legal preferences to claims of another EU country. In this last case, it must grant the same preferences to similar claims of other Member States.

Precautionary measures upon request toward the debtor, such as conservatory measures, must be taken by the requested Member State, if allowed by its legislation and in accordance with its administrative practices, where the claim or the enforcement instrument is contested by the taxpayer in the applying state or where there is not yet an enforcement instrument (Articles 16–17).

Whatever form of recovery assistance is requested in any concrete case, the responsibility for communications with the applying state lies with a 'central liaison office', to be designated by the competent tax authority of each Member State (Article 4) for allowing quicker and more effective communications. For the same reason, all types of assistance requests must be sent by electronic means, using a standard form, unless this is impracticable for technical reasons (Article 21).

Importantly, all requests for recovery assistance must be accompanied by a uniform European enforcement instrument – a major innovation introduced by the directive – which, under Article 12, is the sole base for enforcement in the requested Member State, where it is not subject to any act of recognition, supplementing or replacement, and may be enforced without delay. Accordingly, this provision marks, from Member State's viewpoint, a key step towards administrative simplification in cross-border tax recovery. The Commission, to the benefit of both legal and procedural certainty, has introduced a detailed implementing regulation for Article 5, Article 8, Article 10, Article 12, Article 13, Article 15, Article 16 and Article 21 of the directive, i.e. for the key provisions concerning the forms of recovery assistance.[315]

However, *neither* the power of the applicant state to request assistance *nor* the obligation on the requested Member State to provide it are unconditional. First, under Article 11, a state may not make a recovery assistance request *if* the claim or the enforcement instrument is contested in its jurisdiction by the debtor,[316] or *if* the recovery possibilities within its own jurisdiction have not yet been exhausted, except where using its national remedies would be disproportionately difficult or where the debtor has recoverable assets only in the requested state. Secondly, the

---

315 Commission Regulation No. 1189/2011, in OJ L 302/16.
316 Except the case where pro-tempore enforcement measures are permitted and under the condition set out in Art. 14.

requested state is obliged to provide none of the forms of recovery assistance if the amount for which assistance is sought by the applicant state is below €1500 or if the claim is more than five years old. Furthermore, specific grounds for refusal apply to each form of assistance.

The requested information, and/or the presence of the applicant state officials, can be refused if the requested state would be unable to obtain the information under its domestic law for its own recovery purposes, or if information would disclose a commercial, industrial or professional secret.

The notification of documents can be refused if disproportionately difficult or if the applicant state has not used its own notification means. The recovery upon request, as well as precautionary measures, can be refused if recovery would create serious economic or social difficulties in the requested state due to the situation of the debtor, subject to national law also allowing this exception for this state's own claims.

In case of litigation brought by an interested party against an act of the recovery procedures, litigation must be brought before courts of either the applicant state or the requested state according to the subject-matter as specified by Article 14. The applicant authority may ask the requested authority to recover a contested claim if the laws, regulations or administrative practices in the requested state allow such action, but in this case, should the debtor win the litigation, the applicant authority will be liable for refunding any sums recovered, together with any compensation due, in accordance with the legislation of the requested state. This obligation applies if, by the time the litigation ends with a taxpayer's victory in last instance, the claim is not more than 10 years old dating from the due date of the claim in the applicant state (Article 18).

Therefore, in case of litigation, the normal exemption of the requested state from giving assistance for claims more than five years old is derogated, but this provision appears to suppose that, in all Member States, tax litigation in all its instances is concluded within 10 years from the due date of the claim, which might not necessarily be the case in some countries. In those instances, this time-limit might risk creating an incentive for taxpayers to litigate and jeopardising the applicant Member State's possibility of recovery. In any case, the obligation to refund and to pay compensation in the event of a loss of the contestation should discourage the applicant authority from requesting recovery assistance for contested claims, especially when the final litigation outcome appears uncertain.

Furthermore, the directive's preamble expressly states that the provision of information and assistance in tax recovery under the directive refers to *claims arising in the applicant* Member State.[317] As regards direct taxation, this implies that the applicant state can only be the state of residence of the debtor, because only this state – in applying the worldwide taxation principle – could claim tax on income arising in another state, and could need assistance from such state for recovering

---

317 Preamble to Directive 2010/24/EU, Recital (7).

this tax.[318] Accordingly, the higher the sources of income that the taxpayer accrues in another state, the higher the claim that the state of residence can have on these income sources and the higher the extent to which it may need recovery assistance under the directive from that other state.

2.8.2 The directive against the benchmarks

Amongst the objectives laid down by the Commission,[319] the Recovery Assistance Directive, due to its purpose, can be assessed against three benchmarks: legal certainty; fight to cross-border tax evasion and administrative simplification. The directive, which is sufficiently clear and precise in its key provisions above indicated, entered into force in 2012, and it was implemented by Member States without significant deviations from its provisions.

With regard to *legal certainty*, the directive seems to show a pitfall in situations where a state of residence requires recovery assistance from a source state in which the taxpayer has high income sources and/or recoverable assets. This is because, the stronger the economic interests of the taxpayer in this last state, the higher the possibility that this state, under its national laws, regards the taxpayer as its own tax resident[320] and, therefore, that a tax residence conflict arises.[321]

In this situation, until the tax residence conflict remains unsolved, this state may consider that any claim to tax on income sources in its own territory, submitted by the applicant state, is not a legitimate one under its own legislation, which latter, thus, would *not provide* any recovery procedure for this claim under Article 13. Although a pending tax residence conflict is not listed amongst the grounds for refusal of a request for recovery assistance, this possible situation may well compromise the application of the directive if a requested state considers that *no legitimate claim* to tax on sources located in its jurisdiction could arise in the applicant state. Arguably, the taxpayer concerned, in this case, could be aware of the unresolved residence conflict and contest both the claim and the initial enforcement instrument in the applicant state. This would bring the case within the situation of contested claims under Article 18, but it would not help achieving the necessary legal certainty, a priori, about whether the requested state could refuse assistance (as it would seem).

On the whole, the Directive offers legal certainty about the covered claims and the applicable procedures, at least *if tax residence is not contested*.

---

318 Despite a trend to shift corporate taxation from worldwide taxation to territorial taxation by some countries within the EU, this will still hold true with regard to natural persons until the worldwide taxation principle will be applied to them.
319 See ch 1 at 1.2.
320 For example, under French tax law, one of the alternative criteria for considering an individual as a resident taxpayer is the concentration in France of the main centre of economic interests.
321 For example, under Italian law, an individual is regarded as tax resident if he has his family links in Italy even though its economic links – and therefore its (main) income interests – may arise in another state.

Regarding the fight against cross-border tax evasion, this is directly dependent on the success in recovery assistance and on its deterring effect against non-compliance, which, in turn, depends on Member States' willingness to cooperate. It was properly argued that this willingness is affected by administrative burden and financial costs involved by cooperation.[322] Administrative simplification for Member States in cooperating – and cost reduction – can be regarded as complementary to the possibility of success in fighting cross-border tax evasion. As regards the costs, innovations such as the uniform instruments for recovery measures permit administrative simplification and certainly allow costs reduction. However, owing to the continuous increase of information requests, it was noted that administrative burdens risk increasing, and that, for minimising this risk, exchange of information on request should be accompanied by direct access of officials of one Member State to databases managed by authorities in other Member States, without intervention of officials of the latter state.[323]

According to one interpretation, the legal basis for such a direct access could be found in the wording 'foreseeably relevant information' used by Article 5,[324] but *exchange* of information – which would suggest a transmission from the requested state – would appear to be conceptually different from 'direct access' (without the intervention of officials of this last state). The lack of a specific provision for direct access could be seen as a shortcoming against the benchmark at stake. Moreover, this directive suffers from a general limit whenever it relies on the national procedures of the requested state. In fact, national procedures concerning tax recovery, as well as taxpayers' protection rights standards, are (not harmonised and) are widely different from one state to another. Consequently, this has the potential of incentivising mobile taxpayers to concentrate their assets and activities in those jurisdictions offering them comparatively higher procedural protection levels.

2.9 The Administrative Cooperation Directive

2.9.1 *The directive's key provisions*

Directive 2011/16 on the administrative cooperation (Administrative Cooperation Directive) replaced Directive 77/799/EEC,[325] which required transmission of information allowing a correct assessment of 'taxes on income and capital'[326] and provided for three modalities for information exchange between Member States.

---

322 I. De Troyer, 'Recovery Assistance in the EU: Evaluation of Directive 2010/24/EU: Time for an Update?' 23 *EC Tax Review*, 5, 284–92, at 286 (2014).
323 Ibid, 287–89.
324 Ibid.
325 Council Directive 2011/16/EU of 15 February 2011 on administrative cooperation in the field of taxation and repealing Directive 77/799/EEC, in OJ L 64/1 of 11 March 2011.
326 More precisely, after a number of amendments to the original version, the scope of Directive 77/799/EEC included taxes on income and capital, and taxes on insurance premiums listed by Art. 3 of Directive 76/308/EEC.

These modalities were: exchange of information on request, enabling the requesting authority to effect a correct assessment of taxes on income and capital, and imposing the requested authority to respond as swiftly as possible;[327] automatic exchange of information, relating to 'categories of cases' to be determined by the authorities concerned under the consultation procedure;[328] spontaneous exchange of information, i.e. transmission of information without a prior request.[329]

The Administrative Cooperation Directive, whilst retaining these three information exchange channels, introduces key innovations in its scope, in the exchanges of information on request and in the automatic exchange of information, as it was stressed by the literature at the time of the Commission's proposal[330] and after its introduction.[331]

Specifically, Article 2(1) broadens the scope of administrative cooperation as it includes all taxes of any kind levied within Member States, and Article 4 requires the designation, in each Member State, of a 'single central liaison office' which must take principal responsibility for contact with other Member States in the areas of administrative cooperation covered by this directive. With regard to both its scope and the responsible office, this directive mirrors the Recovery Assistance Directive.[332] Indeed, administrative cooperation through exchanges of information and assistance in the recovery of claims concerning the same taxes, are complementary to each other in countering the risks of tax evasion and fraud. Arguably, a single central liaison office can make information exchange quicker and more effective because other Member States know where the main responsibility for the exchange lies.[333]

Article 5, relating to exchange of information on request, allows the requesting authority to ask for *any information* that is 'foreseeably relevant' to the administration and enforcement of its domestic laws, just as Article 26(1) of the OECD Model Convention. As in the Commentary to this provision, the preamble of the Administrative Cooperation Directive explains that the standard of 'foreseeable relevance' permits exchange of information in tax matters to the widest possible extent, whilst, at the same time, preventing Member States from requesting useless information.[334]

---

327 Directive 77/799/EEC, Art. 2.
328 Ibid., Art. 3.
329 Ibid., Art. 4.
330 A. Caram, 'Enhancing International Cooperation among Tax Authorities in the Assessment and the Recovery of Taxes: The Proposals for New European Directives', 37 *Intertax* 11, 630–53, (2009).
331 I. Gabert, 'Council Directive 2011/16/EU on Administrative Cooperation in the Field of Taxation' in 51 *European Taxation* 8, 342–347 (2011).
332 Art. 1(a) of the Recovery Assistance Directive. The central-office approach also mirrors the approach already followed by Art. 3(2) of Regulation 1798/2003 for VAT purposes and by Art. 3(2) of Regulation 2073/2004 for excise duties.
333 I. Gabert, 'Council Directive 2011/16/EU on Administrative Cooperation in the Field of Taxation' (n 331), at 343.
334 Commentary on Article 26(1) and Preamble, Recital (9).

Article 7(1) imposes the requested authority to respond within six months after receiving the request, or within two months if it already has the information. Article 7(3) to 7(6) sets out in detail the procedural steps to be followed by the requested authority, which latter, if unable to respond by the time limit, should inform the requesting authority – within three months after receiving the request – of the reasons for its failure to respond 'and the date by which it considers it might be able to respond'. The requested tax authority, under Article 17, can refuse providing information only if: the requesting authority has not exhausted its usual sources of information; it would be contrary to *its legislation* to conduct enquiries or to collect the information requested for its own purposes; the requesting state is unable to provide similar information on a reciprocity basis; the information would lead to the disclosure of a commercial, industrial or professional secret. Whilst this last possible reason for refusal mirrors Article 26(2)(c) of the OECD Model, the reliance on national laws (in respect of enquiries to be conducted and information to be collected) – which might justify a refusal to transmit information – could jeopardise the goal, set out in the preamble, of setting up the *same* rules, obligations and rights for all Member States.[335]

This risk also appears to exist as regards the new cooperation form introduced by Article 11, which allows officials of the requesting authority to be in the administrative offices of the requested authority and to participate in audits *if permitted by the legislation of the requested state*. In fact, national rules concerning the tax audits procedures remain unaffected by the new directive, just as Member States' freedom to (unilaterally) change these national provisions. Moreover, the ECJ, specified that exchange of request under Directive 77/799 did not confer on a taxpayer the right to be informed or to participate in the formulation of the request or in the examination of witnesses,[336] on the ground that assistance as between tax authorities is part of the investigation stage during which taxpayers' right to be heard does not apply. It added, however, that there is *nothing to prevent* a (requested) Member State from extending taxpayer's rights to be heard or even directly involved.[337]

Such a possibility for Member States to provide different taxpayer protection standards remains unaffected under the new directive. A cogent provision – overriding any contrasting national legislation – can be found, under Article 18(2), only in the impossibility for Member States to refuse information on grounds of bank secrecy; this was regarded as the directive's 'most arresting fact'.[338]

The directive innovates as regards mandatory automatic exchange of information, which it considers to be 'the most effective means of enhancing the correct assessment of taxes in cross-border situations and of fighting fraud'.[339]

---

335 Preamble, Recital 2(2).
336 For example, Case C–276/12, *Jiri Sabou*, ruling on 22 October 2013.
337 Ibid.
338 D. Weber, 'Comment on the Proposal for a Council Directive on administrative cooperation in the field of Taxation. Bank secrecy', 4 *Highlights and Insights on European Taxation* 4, at 44 (2009).
339 Preamble, Recital (10).

Article 8(1) initially required the competent authority of each Member State in which a non-resident taxpayer obtains income or owns capital, with effect from 2015, to communicate at least annually, to any state of residence, information on five specific categories of income and capital: employment income; directors' fees; life insurance products, pensions; immovable properties ownership and related income. Although these income categories are taken as defined under the source state legislation, under the DTCs based on the OECD Model they are – except for public employment income falling within Article 19(1) of the Model – generally taxable in the state of residence of the taxpayer receiving them,[340] whilst the source state has a concurrent taxing power for three of them.[341] Therefore, by entitling any residence Member State to get information on these specific income categories from source states, automatic information exchange facilitates the residence country in assessing the taxpayer's overall income on the basis of the world-wide taxation principle. It would do so, by minimising the general, abstract risk that these specific categories of foreign-sourced income might not be disclosed by the taxpayer.[342]

However, the directive allows Member States to adjust automatic exchange of information to their preferences: under Article 8(3), any Member State who does not wish to receive information can advise accordingly any other Member State; under Article 8(6), Member States may include, in DTCs, automatic exchange of information for *additional* categories of income and capital. Moreover, Article 8(6) sets a time limit for automatic exchange, i.e. six months following the end of the tax year during which the information becomes available. As regards spontaneous exchange of information, Article 9 reaffirms the specific circumstances – already stated in the 1977 Directive – under which the tax authority of a Member State is expected to communicate information, without prior request, to the tax authorities of another Member State.

In 2012, the Commission adopted an implementing regulation for the directive's provisions on exchange of information on request, as well as on spontaneous exchange, to lay down standard forms to be used for these purposes.[343] National implementing provisions were introduced by 2013 and mainly consisted of a literal transposition of the directive; no Member State, to date, appears to have advised other Member States that it does not wish to receive information automatically.

---

340 See Art. 6, Art. 15(1), Art. 16, Art. 21 (for life-insurance products related income), Art. 18, Art. 19(2).
341 Art. 15(1) for private employment income, Art. 16 for directors' fees, Art. 6 for immovable property income.
342 R. Seer and I. Gabert, 'European and International Tax Cooperation' *Bulletin for International Taxation*, 2 (2011), 88 at p. 95; I. Gabert, 'Council Directive 2011/16/EU on Administrative Cooperation in the Field of Taxation' (n 331), at 343.
343 Commission implementing Regulation (EU) no 1156/2012, of 6 December 2012, laying down detailed rules for implementing certain provisions of Council Directive 2011/16/EU on administrative cooperation in the field of taxation, OJEU L 335/42, 7.12.2012.

In 2014 the Administrative Cooperation Directive was amended, to extend automatic exchange of information under Art. 8(1) to additional items of income: dividends, interests, gross proceeds from the sales of financial assets and other capital income, as well as account balances which are paid, secured or held by a financial institution for the direct or indirect benefit of a beneficial owner who is a natural person resident in other Member States.[344] These amendments were driven by the conclusion of bilateral agreements between individual Member States and the USA relating to US legislation on Foreign Account Tax Compliance (FACTA).[345] These agreements resulted in wider cooperation with a third country under Article 19 of the directive, and triggered the obligation to offer such wider cooperation to other Member States too. As uncoordinated agreements by Member States under Article 19 would lead to distortions within the internal market, the Commission regarded an EU legislative measure expanding automatic information exchange as necessary for removing the need for Member States to invoke Article 19.[346]

2.9.2 The directive against the benchmarks

Given its purpose, the directive can be assessed against two interconnected benchmarks: the effective fight against cross-border tax evasion, and the legal certainty with regard to the kind of cooperation that a Member State can expect from other Member States. Despite the improvements in comparison with the previous directive, at least three shortcomings emerge.

First, the directive *does not clarify* whether the 'central liaison office' should coincide or not with the central liaison office for VAT purposes under Regulation 1798/2003 and/or with the one to be designated under the Recovery Assistance Directive. The discretion impliedly left to individual Member States does not help an effective and coordinated application of the different pieces of EU legislation for administrative cooperation between Member States.

Secondly, Member States' freedom to maintain different levels of taxpayers' protection standards, with regard to their possible involvement in exchange of information on request, certainly does not help achieving the uniformity of rules, obligations and rights for Member States as stated in the directive's preamble, and does not contribute to an equally effective use of exchange of information on request as an instrument to fight cross-border tax evasion.

Thirdly, whereas the expanded scope for automatic exchange of information can be assessed positively, a weakness lies in the fact that Article 8(6) does not specify what occurs if the time-limit for automatic exchange of information elapses without the information being transmitted. Unlike the case of information exchange on request, in case of mandatory automatic exchange no reason for

---

344 Council Directive 2014/107/EU of 9.12.2014 amending Directive 2011/16/EU as regards mandatory automatic exchange of information in the field of taxation, in OJ L 359 16.12.2014, Art. 1.
345 COM(2013)348 final, at 8.
346 Ibid.

refusal can exist, outside the lack of interest notified by a Member State under Article 8(3). Therefore, an elapse of the time-limit without information transmission would imply a breach of obligation by the source state, but even a breach would be difficult to establish if time limit uselessly expires due to a tax residence conflict, in which, e.g. the two states involved both consider the taxpayer to be their own resident and the tie-breaker rules contained in Article 4 of the DTCs prove inconclusive to allocate the tax residence. This risk may occur as a result of the tie-breaker rules – in particular, the 'centre of vital interest' criteria – being interpreted and applied in different ways according to different national laws and case law.

Unresolved tax residence conflicts or lengthy mutual agreement procedures (MAPs) between the countries concerned may paralyse the application of Article 8,[347] unless Member States agree *ex ante* – in advance of the deadline for information exchange – which one of them will be regarded as the state of residence of those taxpayers who have cross-border links and interests. The directive, by not imposing an obligation in this respect, has missed the chance to ensure in a uniform way throughout the EU an important condition for its effectiveness and, in this possible situation, it appears to fail at least against the two benchmarks.

Moreover, even the Commission's proposal for amendment fails to address the need for an *ex ante* solution of tax residence conflicts, thus running the risk that the paralysing effect of unresolved tax residence conflicts or lengthy MAPs would negatively reverberate on an even wider scale (owing to the new items that would be included) on the possibility of effectively resorting to automatic information exchange under Article 8.

2.10 Concluding remarks

The approved harmonising legislation – despite marking a step toward the objectives of eliminating double taxation and double non-taxation, of reducing administrative compliance costs, of achieving greater legal certainty, of fighting aggressive tax planning – has managed to achieve fully *none* of these objectives throughout the EU because, ultimately, it had to compromise between two conflicting needs: first, on the one hand, the tax sovereignty of Member States, which would require Member States' freedom to establish their individual tax systems as it would best suit their own tax and economic policy goals; and, secondly, on the other hand, the free movement rights set out by the TFEU, which, if literally interpreted (without any further exception other than the derogations expressly indicated by the TFEU's provisions), would drastically undermine Member States' powers since any direct tax measure may potentially create an obstacle to free movement. As will be shown in Chapter 3, the ECJ's case law on the application of fundamental freedom to direct taxation also shows shortcomings if analysed in light of the benchmarks.

---

347 L. Cerioni, 'The new EU tax directive on administrative cooperation between Member States: a key step against tax distortions in the internal market?' 12 *Diritto e Pratica Tributaria Internazionale*, 878–923 (2011), at 898–99.

Bibliography

R. S. Avi-Yonah, *International Tax as International Law, An Analysis of the International Tax Regime*, Cambridge Tax Law Series (CUP, 2007).

A. Caram, 'Enhancing International Cooperation among Tax Authorities in the Assessment and the Recovery of Taxes: The Proposals for New European Directives', 37 *Intertax* 11, 2009, 630–53.

L. Cerioni, 'The new EU tax directive on administrative cooperation between Member States: A key step against tax distortions in the internal market?', 12 *Diritto e Pratica Tributaria Internazionale*, 2011, 878–923.

I. De Troyer, 'Recovery Assistance in the EU: Evaluation of Directive 2010/24/EU: Time for an Update?' 23 *EC Tax Review* 5, 2014, 284–92.

Ernst & Young, 'Survey of the implementation of Council Directive 90/434/EEC (The Merger Directive, as amended)', 2009.

IBFD, *Survey on the Implementation of the EC corporate tax directives*, 1995, Amsterdam.

J. Fairhurst, *Law of the European Union*, 8th edn, Longman, 2010, ch 2, 56–85.

I. Gabert, 'Council Directive 2011/16/EU on Administrative Cooperation in the Field of Taxation' in 51 *European Taxation* 8, 2011, 342–47.

S. Heidenbauer, 'The Savings Directive' in M. Lang, P. Pistone, J. Schuch, C. Staringer (eds), *Introduction to European Tax Law: Direct Taxation*, 2nd edn (Spiramus Press, London, 2010).

L. Hinnekens, 'European Arbitration Convention: thoughts on its principles, procedures and first experience', 19 *EC Tax Review* 3, 2010, 109–116.

Hans Van der Hurk, 'The European Court of Justice Knows its limits (a discussion inspired by the *Gilly* and *ICI* cases), 8 *EC tax review* 4, 1999, 211–23.

E. Kemmeren, *Principle of Origin in Tax Conventions: A Rethinking of Models* (Pijenburg, Dongen, 2001).

E. Kemmeren, 'After Repeal of Article 293 EC Treaty under the Lisbon Treaty: the EU of eliminating double taxation can be applied more widely', 17 *EC Tax Review* 4, 2008, 156–58.

T. Kollruss, 'Dual Resident Companies and the Implementation of the Parent–Subsidiary Directive in Germany in Light of European Union Secondary Legislation and Primary Legislation: An Analysis and Review' in 21 *EC Tax Review* 4, 2012, 183–99.

C. H. J. I. Panayi, *European Union Corporate Tax Law* (CUP, Cambridge, 2013).

C. H. J. I. Panayi, 'The proposed amendments to the Savings Directive', 49 *European Taxation* 4, 2009, 179–84.

C. Sacchetto, 'Imposizione tributaria e sede del soggetto nel diritto comunitario' in *Rivista di Diritto Tributario Internazionale*, 1, 2001, 77–91.

R. Seer and I. Gabert, 'European and International Tax Cooperation: Legal Bases, Practice, Burden of Proof, Legal Protection and Requirements', *Bulletin for International Taxation*, 2, 2011, 88–98.

T. O'Shea, 'European Tax Controversies, A British-Dutch Debate: Back to Basics and Is the ECJ Consistent?' 5 *World Tax Journal*, 1, 2013, 100–27.

W. B. Taylor, V. L. Davis and J. McCart, 'Policy Forum: A Subsidiary as a Permanent Establishment of its Parent' in 55 *Canadian Tax Journal/Revue Fiscale Canadienne* 2, 2007, 333–45.

B. M. Terra, P. J. Wattel, *European Tax Law*, 6th edn (Wolters Kluwer, 2012).

D. Weber, 'Comment on the Proposal for a Council Directive on administrative cooperation in the field of Taxation. Bank secrecy', 4 *Highlights and Insights on European Taxation* 4, 2009.

W. Williams, *EC Tax Law* (Longmans, London, 1998).

3 The ECJ's case law on the application of fundamental TFEU's freedoms of movement to direct taxation versus Member States' competence

3.1 The freedom of establishment and the ECJ landmark rulings on the key issues

As regards the exercise of the freedom of establishment, four main issues – analysed in each of the paragraphs below – have been dealt with by the ECJ.

3.1.1 The treatment of branches versus subsidiaries in the host Member State

In the first ruling concerning the application of the fundamental freedoms to corporate direct taxation, the 1986 *avoir fiscal* ruling,[1] the ECJ had to decide whether branches of companies from other Member States could qualify for tax credits which national rules did reserve to resident companies. In fact, a French provision, aimed at mitigating economic double taxation, granted (corporate or individual) resident shareholders of companies having their registered office in France, upon receipts of dividends, a tax credit (*avoir fiscal*) which, on the contrary, was denied to companies resident in other Member States and holding shares in French distributing companies as part of the assets of a local branch or agency. The same rules for determining the taxable income applied to resident companies and to branches of non-resident companies. The ECJ regarded French provisions as incompatible with the freedom of establishment due to their being a covert form of discrimination against companies resident in other Member States. It stressed, in particular, that, since resident companies and branches of non-resident companies were placed on the same footing for the purpose of taxing their profits, there was no objective difference between their situations and, in consequence, the tax credit could not be denied to non-resident companies.[2]

---

1 Case 270/83, *Commission v France (avoir fiscal)* [1986] ECR 273.
2 Ibid., para. 20.

Additionally, it held that the possibility for non-resident companies to create subsidiaries instead of branches could not justify the different treatment, because the freedom left by Article 49 TFEU to opt amongst the different forms of secondary establishment could not be limited by discriminatory tax provisions[3] and the rights conferred by the TFEU's provisions on the freedom of establishment are unconditional and cannot be made subject to a condition of reciprocity included in DTCs.[4] The ECJ admitted that there could be 'certain circumstances' – regarded as absent in the specific case – under which a different treatment based on a (subjective) criteria, such as the tax residence, can be justified in tax law,[5] although it left these 'circumstances' undefined.

Avoir fiscal paved the way to subsequent rulings in which the ECJ – in assessing again national rules treating branches of foreign companies (resident in other Member States) differently from resident companies – reiterated its reasoning and its conclusion. This occurred, e.g.: in the 1993 *Commerzbank* ruling, for UK provisions denying local branches of non-resident companies, on refund of overpaid corporation tax, a repayment supplement that was granted to resident companies;[6] in the 1999 *Royal Bank of Scotland* ruling, for Greek provisions applying a higher tax rate on branch profits than on profits of resident companies;[7] in the 2006 *CLT-UFA* ruling, for German rules setting a higher tax rate for branch profits than for resident companies' distributed profits.[8] The ECJ consistently rejected justifications based on the worldwide tax liability for resident companies as opposed to territorial tax liability of non-resident companies and found that the two categories of taxpayers were in objectively comparable situations as they were subject to the same way of calculating corporation tax.

In *CLT-UFA*, where the *distributed* profits of resident companies enjoyed a more favourable treatment than branch profits remitted to non-resident companies, it also added that the fact that profit distribution by subsidiaries required a formal decision to that effect, unlike profit remittance by branches, was a mere technicality which could not affect the comparability between the situation of resident subsidiaries and branches of non-resident companies.[9]

A clarification about the issue as to when ('certain circumstances') resident and non-resident companies could be considered to be in non-comparable situations (that was left undefined by this *avoir fiscal* case law stream), can apparently be deduced from the 1995 *Schumacker* ruling on the free movement of workers.[10] This was considered by the literature[11] as applicable by analogy to companies, as it dealt

---

3 Ibid., para. 22.
4 Ibid., para. 26.
5 Ibid., para. 19.
6 Case C-330/91, *Commerzbank* [1993] ECR I-4017.
7 Case C-311/97, *Royal Bank of Scotland* [1999] ECR I-2651.
8 Case C-253/03, *CLT-UFA* [2006] ECR I-1831.
9 Ibid., para. 37.
10 Case C-279/93, *Schumacker* [1995] ECR I-225, at 249.
11 J. Wouters, 'Fiscal Barriers to Companies' Cross-Border Establishment in the Case Law of the EC Court of Justice', *Yearbook of European Law* 14, (1994), pp. 73–109, at 105.

with the status under EU law of the residents/non-residents distinction drawn by all Member States, for all taxpayers, in the direct taxation area. The ECJ had to examine German tax rules which denied a Belgian resident, who had worked in Germany and obtained there the major part (ie more than 90 per cent) of its overall family's taxable income in the relevant period, tax advantages granted to German residents and connected with personal and family circumstances. It found that, in principle, different treatments of non-residents in the host Member State (in that case, in the employment state) could be based on fiscal residence when the major part of taxable income of non-residents is concentrated in the state of residence.[12]

Nonetheless, it also held that, in the specific situation, the different treatment of the non-resident worker created an unlawful discrimination, in comparison with German residents, because his personal and family circumstances were considered *neither* in the state of residence – which, given the lack of sufficient taxable income in its jurisdiction, was in no position to grant tax advantages corresponding to these circumstances – *nor* in the state of employment.[13] Therefore, in the ECJ's assessment, the fact of obtaining the major part of the taxable income in the employment state made the situation of the non-resident worker comparable with that of resident workers and made it necessary for the employment state to grant personal deductions to the non-resident worker too.

The ECJ's reasoning in the 1999 *St Gobain* ruling[14] can be seen as complementary to both the *avoir fiscal* case law and *Schumacker*. In *St Gobain*, the German tax authorities had denied a non-resident company – having a branch in Germany, through which it held shares in companies established in non-member states and through which it receives dividends on such shares – certain tax concessions, granted to resident companies by the DTC between Germany and the extra-EU countries concerned and by German legislation. The ECJ again considered the situations of resident companies and of non-resident companies as *objectively* comparable because the difference in treatment concerned only the tax concessions, so that tax liability of non-resident companies having a PE in Germany, *theoretically* limited to national income and assets, 'comprises in fact actual dividends from foreign sources and shareholdings in foreign companies limited by shares'.[15]

In *St Gobain*, just as in the other *avoir fiscal* case law, the ECJ adopted therefore an objective criteria, based on the tax treatment of the source of income at issue, whereas in *Schumacker* it had refused, in the specific case, a *subjective* criteria (the status of resident or non-resident), as a justification for a difference of treatment. It can therefore be argued that, only in the case of a branch of a non-resident company which obtains a minor part of the overall income in its jurisdiction (and thus which is not in a *Schumacker*-type situation), the host state may apply a different treatment based on specific rules and methods for determining that minor

---

12 Case C–279/93, *Schumacker* (n 10), paras. 33–34.
13 Ibid.
14 Case C–307/97, *Compagnie de Saint Gobain* [1999] ECR I–6161.
15 Ibid., para. 48.

part of the taxable income attributable to this branch, as the *subjective* status of non-resident companies would correspond to an *objectively* non-comparable situation with the resident ones.

Another important ECJ finding in *St Gobain* concerns the relationship between DTCs and EU law. The ECJ, after accepting that – in the absence of EU law harmonising measures – Member States are free, via bilateral DTCs, to allocate powers of taxation between themselves, distinguished the *allocation* of the power of taxation from its exercise. In this regard, it stated that, once allocated the power of taxation through DTCs, Member States must exercise it consistently with EU law. Accordingly, it found – in the case of DTCs concluded by a Member State with a non-member country – that the concerned Member State must, under the 'national treatment principle', grant PEs of companies resident in other Member States the advantages contemplated by the treaty for its resident companies, on the same conditions.[16]

St Gobain therefore implies that, after placing branches (or agencies) of non-resident companies on the same footing as resident companies for the determination of taxable income – by adopting the same rules *regardless* of the part of the overall taxable income of the non-resident company deriving from such PE – a Member State can never refuse branches (or agencies) of non-resident companies the same tax treatment available to domestic companies, even if this treatment includes advantages offered by DTCs with third countries.

This holds true since, as branches are forms of exercising the freedom of establishment under Articles 49 and 54, any difference in treatment – in the ECJ words – would 'make it less attractive' for non-resident companies to create branches and would thus restrict their freedom to choose the most appropriate legal form to exercise their right of establishment.[17]

3.1.2 The cross-border compensation of costs and losses for individual and corporate taxpayers

The cross-border deductibility of costs and losses within the EU – both for individuals and for companies – is another key issue dealt with by the ECJ.

With regard to individuals, in the 1992 *Bachmann* ruling[18] concerning the free movement of capital, the ECJ accepted the non-deductibility of costs for preserving the cohesion of a national tax system. The relevant national law offered two choices about life insurance premiums paid abroad – either deducting premiums but taxing future benefits, or not deducting premiums and having future benefits exempted – and the cohesion of that system required the certainty to tax the benefits *if* the premiums had been deducted: this certainty did not exist if the benefits were paid in another Member State. The ECJ had accepted this position, and defined the cohesion as involving three cumulative elements: a direct link between the tax

---

16 Ibid., paras. 58–59.
17 Ibid., para. 42.
18 Case C–204/90 *Bachmann* [1992] ECR I–249.

advantage – in that case, a deduction – and the taxation of a related element; the application of one type of tax; its application to a single taxpayer. This principle, which in essence identifies the cohesion of a national tax in terms of symmetry at taxpayers' level between costs deduction and related profit taxation, could by its very nature be regarded as complementary to the territoriality principle.

The *Bachmann* reasoning was also applied in the 2013 *K* ruling,[19] concerning a Finnish provision which did not allow a resident taxpayer to deduct a loss on the sale of immovable property situated in France from the gain made in Finland on the sales of securities. Under the DTC between Finland and France, in conjunction with Finnish tax law, income from immovable property was taxable only in France, where no deduction was granted from the loss suffered on the property sale. The ECJ found that, because the French immovable property income was neither taxed nor otherwise taken into account for Finnish income tax purposes, the non-deductibility of loss from the sale of French immovable property ensured the cohesion of the Finnish tax system: a direct link existed, for the same taxpayer and the same tax, between (the denial of) a tax advantage (deductibility of loss generated by a capital investment) and (absence of) the related taxation (on returns on that investment). In essence, in *K* the ECJ expanded the scope of *Bachmann*, as it implied that the direct link between taxation and tax advantage, for the same taxpayer and the same tax, can be created either by national provisions alone (*Bachmann*) or by national provisions in conjunction with an allocation of taxing power under a DTC (*K*).

Moreover, the ECJ found that the refusal to allow the deduction of that loss in Finland was a proportionate measure for achieving the objective of cohesion of the tax system, but the ECJ's reasoning in this respect, and its significance, need to be seen against the ECJ's approach as regards corporate losses deductibility.

As regards corporate losses, after the withdrawal of a 1991 Commission proposal on cross-border corporate loss compensation within the EU,[20] the ECJ has been examining several cases involving both different companies within a group (ie intra-group loss relief), and head office and branches within a multinational company (ie intra-company loss relief). In both cases, the ECJ often had to decide whether principles of cohesion of the tax system, and of territoriality, could justify limitations on cross-border loss relief.

As regards *intra-group loss relief*, the first relevant rulings appeared to restrict the scope of these principles. In the 1998 *ICI* ruling,[21] the ECJ found that *neither* the risk of tax avoidance *nor* the principle of cohesion of the tax system can justify a refusal to grant resident companies forming a consortium, through which they hold shares in loss-making subsidiaries in other Member States, a relief at consortium level for trading losses available to holding companies wholly or mainly holding

---

19 Case C–322/11, *K*, ruling of 7 November 2013.
20 Proposal for a Council Directive concerning arrangements for the taking into account by enterprises of the losses of their permanent establishments and subsidiaries situated in other Member States (COM(90) 595 final, OJ No C 53 of 28 February 1991, at p. 30).
21 Case C–264/96, *ICI* [1998] ECR I–4711.

shares in resident subsidiaries. The ECJ, after stressing that the TFEU's rules on the freedom of establishment are not only addressed to a host Member State, but also prevent the Member State of origin from hindering outbound movements towards other Member States,[22] held that the national provisions could not be justified on tax avoidance grounds. This is because foreign subsidiaries are taxed in their states of residence[23] and cohesion of the tax system does not apply when, unlike the *Bachmann* situation, more legal persons are involved.[24]

In the 2001 *Metallgesellschaft* ruling,[25] it regarded as incompatible with Article 54 of the Treaty a refusal to grant a tax relief to resident subsidiaries of parent companies having their seat in another Member State, where that advantage is available to resident subsidiaries of resident parent companies. The ECJ neglected an argument based on the territoriality principle invoked as a justification to prevent the risk of tax avoidance at group level, and simply repeated that establishing a company outside the Member State concerned would not necessarily entail this risk, because that company would in any event be taxed in its state of residence.[26] When the territoriality principle is invoked against the risk of tax avoidance, its application appears to be accepted by the ECJ only at the EU level, rather than at the national level.

Considered together with these previous rulings, the *Bosal Holding* ruling[27] marked one step forward in this direction. The Member State in question, the Netherlands, submitted in fact that, according to the territoriality principle, the costs in connection with activities abroad, including financing costs and costs in relation to holdings in subsidiaries in other Member States, should be offset against the profits generated by those subsidiaries, rather than against those of parent companies in the Netherlands. The ECJ rejected this argument by stressing that the difference in tax treatment concerned not the subsidiaries but the *parent companies*, according to whether or not they have profit-making subsidiaries in the Netherlands, even though those parent companies are all established in the Netherlands.

In *Bosal Holding*, the ECJ seems thus to have paid attention to the *difference in treatment* caused by the application of the territoriality principle (rather than to the *merit* of this principle which, in *Bachmann*, it had accepted at the level of the single taxpayer). Consequently, the question could well arise as to whether *Bosal Holding*, together with *ICI* and *Metallgesellschaft* would imply the definitive application of that principle at EU level – rather than at national level – at least when invoked against tax avoidance. A response came from the 2005 landmark *Marks & Spencer* ruling.[28]

---

22 Ibid., para. 21.
23 Ibid., para. 26.
24 Ibid., para. 29.
25 Joined Cases C–397/98 & C–410/98, *Metallgesellschaft and Hoechst* [2001] ECR I–1727.
26 Ibid., para. 57, where the ECJ repeated in the identical terms a statement already formulated in the ICI (n 21) ruling (para. 26).
27 See ch 2, at 2.4.3.
28 Case C–446/03, *Marks & Spencer* [1995] ECR I–10837.

104   *The European Union and Direct Taxation*

In the situation at stake, the UK tax authority had denied a resident parent company the deduction, from its own tax base, of losses incurred by subsidiaries in other Member States, which subsidiaries had ceased trading or had been sold at the time of the claim to deduction by the parent company under the national 'group relief' scheme. The ECJ noted that refusing the deduction of losses incurred by non-resident subsidiaries was a restriction to the freedom of establishment (an 'exit restriction' applied by the origin Member State, discouraging the creation of subsidiaries in other states).

Nonetheless, it accepted *three cumulative justifications* submitted by the UK: the need to preserve a balanced allocation of taxing powers between the different Member States by ensuring a symmetry between taxation of profits and deduction of losses in the same tax system; the need to prevent a double deduction of the same losses (which might otherwise occur if a non-resident subsidiary's losses were also deducted in the parent company state of residence); the need to prevent intra-group tax planning strategies aimed at exploiting losses where they would generate the highest tax savings (which strategies might be implemented if losses of subsidiaries located in low-tax states could be transferred to a higher tax jurisdiction where the parent company is resident). The ECJ found that these justifications would constitute 'overriding reasons in the public interest' for restricting the freedom of establishment and that, therefore, the non-deductibility of losses incurred by foreign subsidiaries would pursue legitimate objectives, but it also noted that this non-deductibility would be disproportionate and would breach Articles 49 and 54 of the TFEU if losses could no longer be used in the subsidiary state of residence,[29] i.e. if they were terminal losses.

This ECJ conclusion, taken together with the underlying arguments, certainly prevents double deduction of losses, but it does not maintain the symmetry between profits taxation and losses deduction if losses are no longer deductible in the subsidiary state of residence. In this case, the territoriality principle is made applicable at *EU* level, in the sense that terminal losses incurred by subsidiaries must be always deductible *somewhere within the EU*, rather than at *national* level. Moreover, it does not necessarily prevent the transfer of terminal losses to the Member State where they would generate the highest tax value, if this jurisdiction is the parent company's state of residence. Accordingly, it could be argued that *Marks & Spencer* complements *ICI* and *Bosal Holding*.

In fact, whereas in *ICI* and *Bosal Holding* the ECJ had focused on the specific treatment of the parent company in its state of residence, irrespective of the possibilities available to subsidiary companies in their states of residence and therefore regardless of the overall tax treatment of the group at EU level concerning cross-border losses, in *Marks & Spencer* it impliedly shifted the focus onto the overall treatment of an international group of companies within the EU, as compared to the overall treatment of a national group operating within one single Member State. Just like, in a domestic group of companies, subsidiaries losses

---

29   Ibid., paras. 34, 39–51 and 55.

would normally be deducted within the state concerned, so in an EU group subsidiaries losses must be deducted *somewhere* within the EU, either in the state of residence of the subsidiary or (if no longer possible) in the parent company's state of residence.

The literature referred to this ECJ approach as the 'always somewhere approach'[30] and highlighted that this position aims at ensuring consistency between tax systems at EU level,[31] to express, in essence, the idea that it applies the territoriality principle within the EU. Moreover – and for the same reason – the ECJ position in *Marks & Spencer* may also be regarded as symmetrical with ICI from the perspective of the need of preventing tax avoidance. The establishment of a subsidiary in a Member State other than that of the parent company does not necessarily entail the risk of tax avoidance, because the subsidiary is subject to tax in its state of residence (according to *ICI*), just as the impossibility of deducting subsidiary companies' losses in the parent company's state of residence would not entail the risk of preventing loss deductions if the subsidiary company can deduct losses in its state of residence (according to *Marks & Spencer*).

Since *Marks & Spencer*, the ECJ's case law has covered virtually every possibility relating to the recognition of cross-border losses.[32] In *Rewe-Zentralfinanz*, the ECJ allowed the deduction by a parent company of a write-down to book-value of shareholdings in a wholly owned subsidiary resident in other Member States, in a situation where the deduction of the write-down was fully and unconditionally allowed by national laws solely for shareholdings in subsidiaries resident in the Member State concerned.[33] This is mainly because, unlike the *Marks & Spencer* situation, the losses relating to the write-down were incurred by the parent company, and not by subsidiaries resident in other Member States.[34] In *Oy AA*, the ECJ accepted a national law allowing the deduction, by a subsidiary resident in a Member State, of an intra-group financial transfer solely in favour of a resident parent company.[35] Specifically, it found that allowing the deductibility of financial transfers to parent companies resident in other Member States would permit corporate groups to choose the most favourable jurisdiction where to make their profits taxable,[36] thus paving the way to tax planning strategies similar to a choice of the jurisdiction where to maximise the tax value of losses (unacceptable under *Marks & Spencer*).

In *Papillon*, the ECJ found that national provisions preventing the inclusion in a 'tax consolidation group' of a domestic sub-subsidiary which was held through

---

30 M. Cruz Barreiro Carril, 'Los Impuestos Directos y el Derecho de la Uniòn Europea. La armonizaciòn negativa realizada por el TJUE', *Instituto de Estudios Fiscales*, 2012, at p. 376.
31 G.Bizioli, 'Balancing the fundamental freedoms and Tax Sovereignty: Some Thoughts on Recent ECJ Case Law on Direct Taxation', 3 *European Taxation*, 2008, 133–40, at p. 137.
32 L. Leclercq, P. Tredaniel, 'Impact of ECJ's judgment in *Lidl Belgium* on the Deduction of Foreign Branches Losses in France', *Bulletin for International Taxation* 5/6 (2009), p. 237.
33 Case C–347/04, *Rewe Zentralfinanz* [2007] ECR I–2647.
34 Ibid., at paras. 47–48.
35 Case C–231/05, *Oy AA* [2007] ECR I–6373.
36 Ibid., paras. 56 and 64.

an intermediary subsidiary located in another Member State,[37] with the consequent impossibility of deducting losses incurred by this sub-subsidiary, was incompatible with Article 49. The 'tax consolidation group' allowed the intergroup offsetting of profits and losses, and the elimination of intergroup transactions. In this case too, the ECJ had accepted that, in principle, national law could legitimately prevent the losses recorded by the sub-subsidiary from being deducted twice, i.e. first, by the intermediate subsidiary and, secondly, by the parent company as a depreciation of its holding in that subsidiary.[38] Nonetheless, it also found that this objective could be achieved by the national tax authorities through less restrictive measures, such as resorting to the Administrative Cooperation Directive to obtain information from the subsidiary residence Member State and requesting relevant documentation from the parent company.[39]

In *X Holding*, the ECJ held that a 'single entity taxation scheme', whereby a subsidiary would be included in the perimeter of tax integration just like as a foreign branch, may be reserved for resident subsidiaries.[40] It stressed again that allowing companies to choose to deduct their losses in the Member State where they are established, or in another one, would seriously undermine a balanced allocation of the taxing power between the Member States.[41] It also stated that acceptance of the possibility of including a non-resident subsidiary in the tax entity would allow the parent company to choose freely the Member State in which the losses of that subsidiary are to be deducted, as dimensions of the tax entity could be altered through the creation or the dissolution of subsidiaries.[42]

The ECJ regarded the national provisions excluding subsidiaries in other EU countries from the tax entity as proportionate for preventing these outcomes, because, under the relevant DTC, PEs and subsidiaries located in another Member State were not in a comparable situation: only PEs were subject to the fiscal jurisdiction of the origin Member State.[43] This state would thus not need to apply the same tax scheme to foreign PEs and to non-resident subsidiaries.[44]

The Dutch 'single tax entity' scheme – at stake in *X Holding* – was again under scrutiny, for another aspect, in the 2014 *SCA Group Holding and Others* ruling.[45] Unlike in *X Holding*, here the different treatment did not concern resident subsidiaries (and foreign branches) versus non-resident subsidiaries, but existed as regards the inclusion of resident sub-subsidiaries. The scheme, whilst allowing resident parent companies to include resident sub-subsidiaries held through resident intermediate companies, did not permit the integration of resident

---

37 Case C–418/07, *Papillon* [2008] ECR I–8947.
38 Ibid., paras. 47–51.
39 Ibid., paras. 55–56.
40 Case C–337/08, *X Holding* [2010] ECR I–1215.
41 Ibid., para. 29.
42 Ibid., paras. 31–33.
43 Ibid., para. 38.
44 Ibid., para. 40.
45 Joined Cases C–39/13, 40/13 & 41/13, *SCA Group Holding, X and Others, MSA International Holding*, ruling of 12 June 2014.

sub-subsidiaries held through intermediate companies resident in other Member States and not having a PE in the Netherlands.[46] The ECJ, after considering the two situations as comparable from the viewpoint of the objective of the 'single tax entity' scheme, rejected the different treatment and did not accept the justification based on risk of double loss deductions, because in the specific case national law applied a participation exemption (banning both profit taxation and loss deduction), which, per se, excluded the double use of losses.[47] Consequently, *SCA Group Holding* was consistent with *Papillon* and with *X Holding*, simply because, owing to the different national provisions, a key concern (double deduction, free choice of the jurisdiction for loss deduction purposes) did not emerge in *SCA Group Holding*. Therefore, this is also in line with the *Marks & Spencer* case law.

The continuity of the case law with *Marks & Spencer* is also evident in the 2013 *A Oy* ruling,[48] where the ECJ reiterated both the arguments and the *Marks & Spencer* conclusions and it specified that, when the deduction must be allowed, the rules for calculating the non-resident subsidiary's losses for the purpose of their being deducted by the resident parent company, in a merger by acquisition, must not constitute unequal treatment compared with the rules of calculation that would be applicable if the merger were with a resident subsidiary.[49] This should be regarded as applicable in all cases of deductibility of a non-resident subsidiary's terminal losses by the parent company even if no merger is involved.

Another situation examined by the ECJ was a 'horizontal' loss compensation, with a cross-border element, inside a single Member State, which was at issue in two rulings. The first was the 2012 *Philips Electronics*,[50] where the ECJ held that a resident company belonging to a group, headed by a non-resident parent company, could deduct losses incurred in its Member State by a PE of an associated non-resident company, even though these PE losses could also be deducted by the non-resident company in its own state of residence. The ECJ argued that, in the specific case, the possibility that the PE losses be deducted also in this latter state would not affect the right of the Member State of the PE to tax its future profits. Therefore, the deduction of PE losses by a resident associated company would not prevent the symmetry between taxation of profits and deduction of losses, unlike the *Marks & Spencer* situation of final losses incurred in another Member State.

The second case was the 2014 *Felixstowe Dock and Railway Company* ruling,[51] where the ECJ reiterated the same reasoning. Here, UK law allowed the transfer of losses between a resident company belonging to a consortium and a resident company belonging to a group where the two companies were connected by a resident 'link

---

46 A further complaint was that the scheme did not apply to resident associated companies having a parent company located in another Member State.
47 Ibid., paras. 34–36 and 54.
48 Case C–123/11, *A Oy*, ruling issued on 21 February 2013 and see ch 2, at 2.4.3 as regards the case law on the Merger Directive.
49 Case C–123/11, A Oy (n 48), para. 61.
50 Case C–18/11, *Philips Electronics*, issued on 6 September 2012.
51 Case C–80/12, *Felixstowe Dock and Railway Company*, ruling on 1 April 2014.

company' that was member of both the consortium and the group, but did not allow this loss transfer if the connecting 'link company' was resident in another Member State. The ECJ held that, despite this different treatment created a restriction to the outbound freedom of establishment, the symmetry between taxation of profits and deduction of losses was not altered, because the loss transfer took place as between resident companies and thus the UK retained its power to impose tax on the loss-absorbing company.[52]

In *Philips Electronics* and in *Felixstowe Dock*, the ECJ did not refer to the concern, expressed in *Marks & Spencer*, to prevent the intra-group transfer of losses to jurisdictions where they would generate the highest tax value. This risk could exist in the case of a choice of deducting foreign subsidiaries' losses in the parent company's Member State if this country is a higher tax jurisdiction and is unable to tax any subsequent profit of the non-resident subsidiary. Nonetheless, it could not exist, in the *Philips Electronics* situation, if, after the losses of a PE of a non-resident company were deducted both from the taxable profit of its parent company in its state of residence and from that of an associated group company in the PE's Member State, the subsequent profits of the PE could also be taxed in both countries. Apparently, if the jurisdiction where the losses of the PE (or of the subsidiary) are deducted – even if a high tax jurisdiction – could tax its future profits, there would be neither the risk of tax planning strategies maximising the tax value of losses nor the alteration of the balanced allocation of taxing rights. Neither could this risk exist in the *Felixstowe Dock* situation, where – owing to the loss transfer as between resident companies – there was not even the possibility of a potential double deduction followed by a potential double taxation.

If *Marks & Spencer* could be so reconciled with *Philips Electronics* and *Felixstowe Dock*, a twofold ECJ objective emerges: (a) *always* to ensure the deduction of losses incurred by EU companies in *one* Member State (ie either in the state of residence of the subsidiary *or* in the state of residence of the parent company), without creating the scope for tax planning strategies aimed at exploiting the tax value of losses; (b) to maintain, outside the particular case of 'terminal losses', the symmetry between the taxation of profits and the deduction of losses.

As a result, a balanced allocation of taxing rights could justify the restriction even of a 'single entity taxation scheme' (ie a fiscal consolidation) to one jurisdiction (*X Holding*), but, conversely, could allow the deduction of losses suffered by domestic sub-subsidiaries held through a non-resident subsidiary (*Papillon*) and the deduction of losses of a PE of a non-resident company by an associate company resident in the same Member State (*Philips Electronics*).

As regards *intra-company* cross-border *loss* compensation, initially the ECJ, in the 1997 *Futura*[53] and in the 1999 *AMID*[54] rulings, had to examine the case of branch profits being used to offset head office losses. In *Futura*, it accepted that a host Member State could make the carrying forward of previous losses, requested by

---

52 Ibid., para. 30.
53 Case C–250/95, *Futura Participations* [1997] ECR I–2471.
54 Case C–141/99, *AMID* [2000] ECR I–11619.

a non-resident taxpayer having a branch in its territory, conditional upon the losses being economically related to the income earned by the taxpayer in that state,[55] provided that resident taxpayers do not receive a more favourable treatment. This position appears consistent with the territoriality principle, just as the conclusion in *AMID*, where the ECJ banned the state of the head office from requesting a domestic company to offset its losses against income of a foreign branch – which income was exempt under a DTC – before carrying forward these losses against future head office profits.

Subsequently, the reverse situation, i.e. the use of branch losses to offset head office profits, comes into issue. In *Deutsche Shell*, the ECJ permitted the deduction by a parent company resident in a Member State of a currency loss incurred on repatriating start-up capital previously granted to its PE, although the PE had realised tax free profits.[56] The ECJ noted that currency losses could otherwise be considered *neither* by the parent company's state of residence *nor* by the Member State in which the PE is based, since the accounting records in that Member State drawn up in the national currency could not show the currency depreciation of the start-up capital.[57] The 'always somewhere approach' adopted from *Marks & Spencer* onwards was thus applied to PE losses too.

In *Lidl Belgium*, the ECJ refused the deduction by a parent company of losses incurred by a branch in another Member State because, under the terms of a DTC, the income of that branch was taxable in its Member State and the losses could be offset against future profits in that Member State.[58] In *Krankenheim*, the ECJ allowed the application of a recapture rule by the Member State of the parent company, which resulted in taxation of the profits of the PE located in another Member State only up to the amount of losses of the PE previously deducted by the parent company.[59] Although the recapture gave rise to parallel taxation in two Member States, the ECJ regarded the reintegration of the amount of the PE losses in the results of the parent company as inevitable because they had previously been deducted, and therefore reflected a logical symmetry.[60]

The symmetry-related argument was also at stake in the 2014 *Nordea Bank Danmark* ruling.[61] Here the ECJ struck down a national law under which, in case of a resident company transferring a PE situated in another Member State to an associated non-resident company, the losses of the PE previously deducted by the transferring company had to be reincorporated into this company's taxable profit in its state of residence, which had taxing power on both profits of the PE before the transfer and capital gains (on PE assets) made upon the transfer.

Despite admitting that the reincorporation of previously deducted losses would serve to prevent the transfer of the PE from eroding the tax base in this Member

---

55 Case C–250/95, *Futura Participations* (n 53), para. 22.
56 Case C–293/06, *Deutsche Shell* [2008] ECR I–1129.
57 Ibid., para. 52.
58 Case C–414/06, *Lidl Belgium* [2008] ECR I–3601.
59 Case C–157/07, *Krankenheim* [2008] ECR I–8061.
60 Ibid., paras. 42 and 54.
61 Case C–48/13, *Nordea Bank Danmark*, ruling of 17 July 2014.

State, as it would otherwise occur owing to the loss of taxing power on any future profits of the PE transferred to the affiliated non-resident company,[62] the ECJ considered it disproportionate. It regarded as sufficient, for maintaining the symmetry between deduction and taxation, that the Member State at issue would tax profits made before the transfer and gains made at that time.[63] Arguably, in this case the ECJ only ensured a *limited* symmetry – not a *full* symmetry as in *Krankeinheim* – because, before the transfer, the PE was actually making losses (not profits): the ECJ appears to have de facto left only taxation of on-time capital gains to ensure the symmetry with the deduction of annual losses.

Overall, as regards intra-company loss compensation too, the ECJ thus intends to ensure the symmetry (even a partial one, after *Nordea Bank Danmark*) between 'profits' taxation and loss deduction, subject again to the 'always somewhere approach'.

This approach appears to have been ignored only as regards the deductibility, by resident individual taxpayers, of losses from the sale of immovable properties in another Member State. In the *K* ruling described above,[64] the ECJ regarded the refusal by the state of residence to allow the deduction of such losses as meeting the proportionality test, because the possibilities to have the losses deducted in the Member State where the property was located (ie it could not claim that losses are 'terminal') had *never* existed. Therefore – the ECJ reasoned – the taxpayer could not claim to have exhausted this possibility. The ECJ explained that, if the state of residence in these circumstances were obliged to allow deduction of foreign immovable property losses, it would bear the adverse consequences arising from the application of the law of the Member State where the property is situated, and that the free movement of capital does not require a Member State to adjust its tax rules to those of another Member State to ensure, in all circumstances, a taxation removing disparities between national laws.

From the taxpayer's viewpoint, the ECJ's reasoning in *K* makes irrelevant the 'terminal losses' case of the *Marks & Spencer* jurisprudence when neither of the states involved grants loss deduction: in this situation, the 'always somewhere approach' is given up to the benefit of the symmetry between profit taxation and loss deduction.

K may therefore be regarded as formally consistent with the *Marks & Spencer* case law from the perspective of a residence Member State revenues (no deduction of foreign losses if these are not 'terminal' ones), but *not* from the taxpayer's viewpoint. For taxpayers, the fact that the 'always somewhere approach' does not apply in this particular situation appears to imply that their overall ability-to-pay at cross-border level is neglected, in contrast with the ECJ's position in the *Schumacker* case law stream concerning the obligation of an employment state where a non-resident worker accrues most of his or her income.[65]

---

62 Ibid., paras. 30–31.
63 Ibid., para. 36.
64 Case C–322/11, *K* (n 19); see at the start of this paragraph.
65 See 3.2 below.

3.1.3 The application of exit taxes

A further important issue dealt with the ECJ is the applicability of 'exit taxes', i.e. the taxation of latent capital gains accrued to companies or individuals at the time of transfer of their tax residence to other Member States.

In the 2004 *Lasteyrie du Saillant* ruling,[66] where a taxation of unrealised capital gains at the time of the transfer of the tax residence of a French national to Belgium had been justified by the French Government on anti-avoidance grounds, the ECJ struck down such exit taxation, because this went *beyond* preventing wholly artificial arrangements only. In the 2006 *N* ruling,[67] concerning the transfer, from the Netherlands to the UK, of an individual having substantial shareholdings in Dutch companies, the ECJ accepted that Dutch provisions, which levied tax on increase in value of the shares upon the tax residence transfer, could be justified for maintaining a balanced allocation of taxing rights between Member States, but found that the exit tax levied in the specific case failed the proportionality test.

This was because the Dutch rules did not take full account of the reduction of value capable of arising after the transfer of the tax residence in situations where such reduction was not taken into consideration by the host Member State either,[68] and the migrating taxpayer needed to provide security for him to be granted deferral in the payment of the exit tax. These rulings concerning migrating individuals, on their own, may suggest that Member States could levy exit taxes only for very specific reasons – i.e. the prevention of wholly artificial arrangements and/or the maintaining of a balanced allocation of taxing rights between Member States – and provided no less restrictive means would be available to achieve these objectives.

Nonetheless, if read together with the rulings relating to exit taxes on migrating companies, interpretative issues arise as to what extent the ECJ has been equally treating individuals and companies, which are both indicated by Articles 49 and 54 as beneficiaries of the right of establishment, although the Commission, in its 2006 Communication on exit taxes, had already considered *Lasteyrie du Saillant* as having direct implications for exit taxes on companies.[69] In the 1988 *Daily Mail* ruling[70] and in the 2008 *Cartesio* ruling,[71] the ECJ had focused not on the tax law issue created by tax residence transfers but, rather, on a (preliminary) company law issue: whether Articles 49 and 54 TFEU permit a company to transfer its head

---

66 Case C–9/02, *Lasteyrie du Saillant* [2004] ECR I–2409.
67 Case C–470/04, *N* [2006] ECR I–7409. On this ruling, see inter alia M. Lang, 'Die gemeinschaftsrechtlichen Rahmenbedingungen für 'Exit Taxes' im Lichte der Schlussanträge von GA Kokott in der Rechtssache N.' in *Steuer und Wirtschaft International* 2006, pp. 213–26; E. Kemmeren: *Pending Cases Filed by Dutch Courts I: The Van Dijk and Bujura Cases, ECJ: recent developments in direct taxation* (e. Linde, Wien) 2006 pp. 219–60.
68 Case C–470/04, *N* (n 67). paras. 54–55.
69 Communication COM(2006) 825 final (19 December 2006), Exit taxation and the need for co-ordination of Member States' tax policy, at 5 ff.
70 Case C–81/87, *Daily Mail* [1988] ECR 5483.
71 Case C–210/06, *Cartesio* [2008] ECR I–9641.

office to another Member State, whilst keeping its status as a legal person governed by the law of the Member State of origin. The ECJ had reached a negative conclusion but, in *Cartesio*, it had specified that, if a company wishes to move its registered office by converting its legal form into a form offered by the destination state, the company could rely on the freedom of establishment once the law of the destination state permits the transfer.[72]

In turn, in the 2012 *VALE* ruling,[73] the ECJ ruled that Articles 49 and 54 TFEU preclude a national law which, although enabling a company established under national law to convert, does not permit a company established in another Member State to convert into a company governed by national law by incorporating such a company.[74] In essence, after *Cartesio* and *VALE*, despite several Member States within the EU adopting the 'real seat criteria' – a criteria requiring registered office and head office to be maintained in the same jurisdiction – the ECJ regards the transfer of the registered office with conversion into a legal form offered by the destination Member State as a form of cross-border conversion, protected by Articles 49 and 54 TFEU whenever the national provisions of the destination state allow domestic conversions.

From the tax viewpoint, the transfer of the registered office with cross-border conversion, which needs to be accompanied by the transfer of the head office for a company created in a jurisdiction following the 'real seat' criteria, would normally imply the transfer of the tax residence: the head office would usually coincide with the decision-making centre ('place of effective management') which, under Article 4 of the bilateral DTCs based on the OECD Model, is generally the tie-breaker rule for identifying companies' tax residence. However, some other Member States (eg, Finland, Ireland, the Netherlands and the UK) adopt the 'incorporation criteria' allowing a domestic company to keep the registered office in their jurisdiction, and its legal personality under national law, even if transferring abroad the head office alone, which would determine the transfer of the tax residence.

The 2011 ECJ *National Grid* ruling[75] dealt with the transfer to the UK of the head office alone of a Dutch company, which was allowed by the Netherlands and by the UK, both of which apply the incorporation system, but which resulted in Dutch exit tax levied on a latent capital gain at the time of the transfer. The company involved did not keep a PE in the Netherlands, and the Dutch provisions required immediate payment of exit taxes. The ECJ found that, whilst it is legitimate to assess exit tax on unrealised gains at the time of a company leaving its country of tax residence, it is disproportionate to require immediate payment of the tax at that time, and the transferring company must be allowed to defer payment when capital gains are actually realised, although the origin state may require a bank guarantee for the increasing risk of non-recovery with the

---

72 Ibid., paras. 111–113.
73 Case C–378/10, *VALE Epitési*, 12 July 2012.
74 Ibid., paras. 43–47.
75 Case C–371/10, *National Grid Indus* [2011] ECR I–12273.

passage of time.[76] In reaching this conclusion, the ECJ found that, in the case at stake, the transferring company continued to exist as a company validly incorporated under Dutch law after the transfer to the UK of the 'place of effective management', owing to the Netherlands adopting the incorporation system, and that, exactly for this reason, the company was able to rely on the freedom of establishment.[77]

This reasoning reversed that which the ECJ had adopted in *Daily Mail*, concerning an intended transfer of the head office from the UK to the Netherlands, where the contested national provisions required the migrating company to obtain from the UK Treasury a prior consent conditional upon the sale of the part of the company's assets[78] triggering capital gains tax in the UK. In *Daily Mail*, the (ultimate) tax issue was whether the tax authorities of the home Member State are allowed, under Articles 49 and 54 of the Treaty, to require settlement of a company's tax position prior to its tax residence transfer to another Member State, but the ECJ had avoided dealing with it by focusing on the (preliminary) company law question as to whether Articles 49 and 54 allow a company to transfer the head office alone, whilst retaining its legal status.[79]

On the contrary, in *National Grid* it made the scope of the Treaty's provisions dependent upon the possibilities offered by national company law: the ECJ appears to have switched *from* the impossibility of relying on Articles 49 and 54 owing to the lack of harmonisation, and irrespective of company law in the origin Member State (in *Daily Mail*),[80] *to* the possibility of benefiting from Articles 49 and 54 *if* national company law allows the transfer (*National Grid*). This implies that solely those companies which can transfer the place of effective management alone under their national company law, can also challenge exit taxes levied on this occasion.

Secondly, the ECJ accepted a justification for the exit tax based on preserving a balanced allocation of taxing rights, by recognising, as in *N*, that the Member State of origin – in accordance with the principle of fiscal territoriality linked to the tax residence within its territory during the period in which the capital gains arise – can tax those latent gains when the taxpayer leaves the country,[81] and thus can establish the amount of the tax due on the basis of a final settlement drawn up at the time of the tax residence transfer. Nonetheless, unlike its finding in *N*, it also ruled that a failure by the destination Member State to deduct decreases in value of the assets (occurring after the transfer) does not impose any obligation to do so on the origin Member State, towards which the debt was definitively determined at the time of transfer of the tax residence.[82] Specifically, it considered the *corporate* taxpayer's assets as directly connected to its taxable profits generated

---

76 Ibid., paras. 46 and 74.
77 Ibid., paras. 28 and 32.
78 Case C–81/87, *Daily Mail* (n 70), para. 8.
79 Ibid., paras. 19–25 and 30.
80 Ibid., paras. 20–23.
81 Ibid., para. 46.
82 Ibid., para. 61.

by its economic activity[83] and it found that, because the profits are taxed only in the host Member State after the tax residence transfer, the taking into consideration by the origin Member State of either gains or losses occurring after the transfer, could hinder the balanced allocation of taxing powers between Member States and lead to double taxation *or* double deduction of losses.[84]

The ECJ motivated this position by arguing that the Treaty offers no guarantee to a *company* covered by Article 54 TFEU that the transfer of the place of effective management (thus, of the tax residence) will be neutral as regards taxation.[85] Although this last statement reiterated a position that the ECJ had already expressed in previous case law concerning individuals too,[86] this last case law, cited for application by analogy in *National Grid*, was not cited in *N*.

Thus, it appears difficult to reconcile *National Grid* with *N* by distinguishing between different categories of taxpayers, i.e. companies (*National Grid*) rather than individuals (*N*). Instead, the ECJ seems to have shifted the emphasis from taxpayers' interests to Member States' financial interests. Whereas, whilst accepting in principle a justification based on the balanced allocation of taxing powers between Member States, in *N* it had attached importance – in assessing the proportionality – to the interest of the taxpayer to have tax levied only on the residual increase in value resulting after deduction of any losses subsequent to the transfer, in *National Grid* it has attached (utmost) importance to the interest of Member States not to grant a deduction for losses incurred by a taxpayer no longer subject to their tax jurisdiction. The ECJ reasoning in *National Grid* seems to be difficult to reconcile with previous rulings concerning individuals in other respects as well.

First, although a key reason for the ECJ's finding in *National Grid* that the Dutch provisions were disproportionate lays in the fact that the company lacked a choice between the immediate payment of the tax and the deferral of payment with the related administrative burden, this choice was impliedly available to the taxpayers concerned both in *N* and in *Lasteyrie du Saillant*. In both those cases, the taxpayers – natural persons – could have decided, rather than asking for the deferral of payment by providing guarantees, to pay immediately at the time of transfer of the tax residence, or could have asked for deferred payment (even if implying administrative formalities) if that were more convenient for them. Yet, the ECJ in both those cases appeared to have overlooked, in its assessment of the proportionality, this possible option, to which it later attached the utmost importance in *National Grid*.

Secondly, whereas in *National Grid* the ECJ has accepted that the Member State could require a bank guarantee for deferred payment to allow for an increasing

---

83 Ibid., para. 57.
84 Ibid., paras. 58–59.
85 Ibid., para. 62.
86 Case C–365/02 *Lindfors* [2004] ECR I–7183, para. 34; Case C–403/03 *Schempp* [2005] ECR I–6421, para. 45; Case C–194/06, *Orange European Smallcap Fund* [2008], para. 37, referred to in *National Grid Indus* (n 75), para. 62.

risk of non-recovery with the passage of time,[87] in both *Lasteyrie du Saillant* and in *N* it had regarded the provision of guarantees (which was requested as a condition for deferred payment) as generating a restrictive effect owing to its depriving the taxpayer of the enjoyment of the assets given as a guarantee.[88] In *N* it had also considered it as a reason why Dutch taxation was disproportionate,[89] as well as such an obstacle that could not be retrospectively lifted merely by releasing the guarantee.[90]

An attempt to reconcile the two ECJ rulings might be based on the possibly different degree of difficulty in tax recovery for the Member State of origin in case of tax residence transfer. It might be assumed that the transfer of tax residence of an individual would not involve the same possible complexities concerning the cross-border tracing of all assets as the transfer of tax residence of a company disposing of those assets in its business activity, and that therefore it would be easier and quicker for the Member State of origin to obtain assistance from the host Member State in case of tax recovery from individuals than in case of companies. Consequently, the requirement to provide guarantees for obtaining deferral of exit taxes payment might be considered as disproportionate in the case of individuals, but acceptable in the case of companies. This distinction could make sense the higher the number and the wider the range of assets involved in a transfer of tax residence of companies, but not in the event of transfer of companies having a limited range of assets and not involving more difficulties for tax recovery than the transfers of individuals.

On the other hand, as regards the guarantees for deferral of payment, it would not seem possible to reconcile the ECJ's position in *National Grid* with the one in *N* (and in *Lasteyrie du Saillant*) by looking at the different types of guarantees. In fact, although in *N* the guarantee to be provided consisted of the deposit of company shares held by the transferring individual and in *National Grid* the ECJ allowed the Member State to request a bank guarantee, the risks and costs related to the constitution of guarantees indicated by the ECJ in *N* – i.e. the reduction of confidence in the solvency of the taxpayer, to whom less favourable credit conditions might be applied[91] – can exist for a bank guarantee too.

After *National Grid*, other rulings relating to exit taxes on companies resulted from Commission's infringement procedures against Member States: the 2012 *Commission v Portugal* ruling,[92] the 2013 *Commission v Netherlands*,[93] *Commission v Spain*[94] and the *Commission v Denmark*[95] rulings. Moreover, a 2012 ruling, *DI VI*

---

87 Ibid., para. 74.
88 Ibid., Case C–470/04, *N* (n 67), para. 36; Case C–09/02, *Lasteyrie du Saillant* (n 66), para. 47.
89 Case C–470/94, *N* (n 67), para. 51.
90 Ibid., paras. 57 and 67.
91 Ibid., para. 57.
92 Case C–38/10, *Commission v Portugal*.
93 Case C–301/11, *Commission v Netherlands*.
94 Case C–64/11, *Commission v Spain*, ruling of 25 April 2013.
95 Case C–261/11, *Commission v Denmark*, ruling of 18 July 2013.

Finanziaria SAPA,[96] although not strictly relating to exit taxes, concerned a national law determining a higher tax liability in terms of capital tax for a company transferring its registered and head office to another Member State,[97] and therefore generating an effect comparable to that of an exit tax. In these subsequent rulings the ECJ reiterated its *National Grid* finding about the disadvantage caused by national provisions requiring immediate payment at the time of the transfer and about justifying the measures at issue with a balanced allocation of taxing rights, which justification, however, could not be used in the event of withdrawal of an advantage that the Member State had agreed in advance to grant.[98]

Amongst these decisions, *Commission v Portugal* and *Commission v Spain* related to national provisions that taxed capital gains not only in the event of transfer of tax residence to another Member State, but also in the event of a company transferring some or all of its assets of a domestic PE to another Member State. In this case, by taxing latent capital gains, the national law equated the tax treatment to that of a cessation of activity of the PE within the Member State concerned, but, in both rulings, the ECJ found that a disconnect between the assets of a PE from any economic activity in a Member State due to cessation of activity is different from the transfer of such assets to another Member State. The ECJ highlighted that a cessation of activity creates no restriction to the freedom of establishment,[99] and that the taxation in that case could not justify the taxation of latent capital gains upon the transfer of these assets to another Member State; it therefore extended its *National Grid* findings only to this transfer.

In *Commission v Spain*, the ECJ also examined a possibility granted by national provisions to migrating (corporate) taxpayers to defer tax payment, that was subject to meeting various conditions and that would allow the migrating companies to defer the payments only when their economic and financial condition would make it possible to meet the payment deadline. The ECJ stated that this possibility was not automatic and could not be sufficient to provide the alternative, between immediate payment and postponement, as was required by *National Grid*.[100] This left completely unanswered the issue as to whether and when the request of a bank guarantee for the postponement of a tax payment could make the postponement itself 'automatic'.

In the 2014 *DMC Beteilungsgesellschaft* ruling,[101] the ECJ allowed a German provision that imposed an immediate taxation of latent capital gains at the time of an operation of share exchange causing Germany to lose its taxing power over

---

96 Case C–380/11, *DI VI Finanziaria SAPA*.
97 In the specific case, national provisions imposed, in case of seat transfer to another Member State during a five-year gap after obtaining a capital tax reduction, the immediate withdrawal of this benefit, whereas there was no such withdrawal for a company keeping its seat in the Member State concerned.
98 Case C–380/11, *DI VI Finanziaria SAPA* (n 96) para. 45.
99 Case C–38/10, *Commission v Portugal* (n 92), para. 30; Case C–64/11, *Commission v Spain* (n 94), para. 30.
100 Case C–64/11, *Commission v Spain*, cit., paras. 36 and 37.
101 Case C–164/12, *DMC Beteilungsgesellschaft*, issued on 23 January 2014.

income accrued to Austrian companies from their participation in a German limited partnership. Although in this case an outbound transfer of tax residence was not at stake and the freedom at issue was the free movement of capital under Article 63, this ruling can be seen as significant for 'exit taxes' too: the German provision allowed the taxpayer to choose deferred payment and the ECJ, in finding that the taxation of immediate capital gains was a proportionate measure, attached the condition that, in case of choice of deferred payment by the taxpayer, 'the requirement to provide a bank guarantee is imposed on the basis of the actual risk of non-recovery of the tax'.

Arguably, this provided a response to the issue left open by *Commission v Spain*, in the sense of clarifying that the postponement of payment is not automatic if a bank guarantee is imposed in the absence of an actual risk of non-recovery, and it helps reconciling *N* with *National Grid*, but it leaves Member States with complete discretion as regards the assessment, on a case-by-case basis, about the actual risk of non-recovery. Moreover, in *Commission v Denmark*, the ECJ applied *National Grid* to the case of transfers to another Member State of assets that could not be realised after the transfer itself,[102] as it highlighted that the Member State of origin remains free to provide for a chargeable event other than realisation of capital gains to ensure that these remain subject to its tax jurisdiction.[103] Overall, these subsequent rulings, while clearly extending the scope of application of *National Grid* beyond the transfer of the tax residence and beyond taxation formally falling within the category of exit taxes, do not seem to have offered *a priori* legal certainty to either taxpayers or to Member States.

3.1.4 The application of national anti-abuse rules

The compatibility of national anti-abuse tax rules with the freedom of establishment was at stake first in the 2002 *Langhorst-Hohorst* ruling.[104] German 'thin capitalisation' rules, aimed at combating cross-border tax evasion, reclassified interest paid to non-resident shareholders as dividends, and thus prohibited the deduction of interest paid to them by their resident subsidiaries. These provisions were regarded by the ECJ as differentiating between resident subsidiaries according to the seat of their parent companies, which could discourage such companies based in other Member States from exercising their freedom of establishment by creating, acquiring or maintaining a subsidiary in Germany.[105]

The ECJ stressed, first, by reiterating settled case law, that the reduction in tax revenue is not an overriding reason in the public interest which may justify a measure that is contrary to a fundamental freedom.[106] It subsequently highlighted

---

102 Case C–261/11, *Commission v Denmark* (n 95), para. 35.
103 Ibid., para. 37.
104 Case C–324/00, *Langhorst-Hohorst* [2002] ECR I–11779.
105 Ibid., para. 32.
106 Ibid., para. 36; see also Case C–264/96 *ICI* (n 21), para. 28; Case C–307/97 *St Gobain* (n 14), para. 51.

that the legislation at issue applied generally to any situation in which the parent company has its seat, for whatever reason, in another Member State, and that this situation could not, of itself, entail a risk of tax evasion, since such a company will in any event be taxed in its state of residence.[107] In so doing, the ECJ specified that, for the subsidiary's state of residence too, the impossibility of presuming tax evasion on the sole basis of the location of the other group company in another Member State (ie a reasoning that, in *ICI*, had applied to the parent company's state of residence).[108] For this reason, and since *no abuse* had been proved in the specific case[109], the ECJ rejected the justification based on tax evasion. *Langhorst-Hohorst* therefore indicated that national anti-abuse measures must have the specific purpose of preventing wholly artificial arrangements intended to circumvent national provisions,[110] and that the existence of these arrangements must always *be proved* on a case-by-case basis. The ECJ also rejected a justification based on the coherence of the tax system, and another on the effectiveness of fiscal supervision.

As regards the coherence argument – accepted in *Bachman*[111] but subsequently rejected in ICI[112] when corporate groups (instead of single taxpayers) are involved – in *Langhorst-Hohorst* the ECJ considered the requirement of a direct link between cost deduction and profit taxation at the level of single taxpayers to be absent. This is because the subsidiary of a non-resident parent company suffered less favourable treatment as a result of the thin capitalisation rules and Germany did not indicate any tax advantage to offset such treatment.[113]

Exceptions are thus admitted to none of the three strict requirements for coherence and, if Germany had granted those tax advantages, it is evident that the effectiveness of its anti-abuse rules would have been at least partly offset. Consequently, *Langhorst-Hohorst* made it necessary to demonstrate in the concrete cases, with no exception, both the existence of wholly artificial arrangements and the suitability of anti-abuse clauses to do no more than prevent them. Moreover, the ECJ's statement that these clauses made the exercise of the freedom of establishment less attractive,[114] generalised, to whatever situation of either inbound movement (to the destination state) or outbound movement (from the origin state), an assessment based on the effects of a national measure.[115]

In a subsequent landmark ruling, the 2006 *Cadbury Schweppes* ruling,[116] the ECJ had to deal with the application of a UK controlled foreign companies

---

107 Case C–324/00, *Langhorst-Hohorst* (n 104), para. 37.
108 Case C–264/96, *ICI* (n 21), para. 26.
109 Case C–324/00, *Langhorst-Hohorst* (n 104), para. 38.
110 Ibid., para. 37.
111 Case C–204/90 *Bachmann* (n 18).
112 Case C–264/96, *ICI* (n 21), para. 29.
113 Case C–324/00, *Langhorst-Hohorst* (n 104), para. 42.
114 Ibid., para. 32.
115 D. Gutmann, L. Hinnekens, 'The *Langhorst-Hohorst* Case: The ECJ finds Thin Capitalization Rules incompatible with Freedom of Establishment', 11 *EC Tax Review* (2003), pp. 90–97, at 93.
116 C–196/04, *Cadbury Schweppes* [2006] ECR I–7995.

(CFC) law, which would attribute to a resident parent company the profits (even if undistributed) obtained by a subsidiary set up in a low-tax Member State, in a situation in which a UK parent company set up a subsidiary in Ireland for declared tax savings reasons. At the outset, the ECJ reiterated, as it had stated in previous case law,[117] that the establishment in another Member State for benefiting from more favourable legislation – including tax advantages – does not in itself constitute abuse of the freedom of establishment.[118] It thus considered the national law at issue as creating a restriction to the outbound freedom of establishment, by dissuading parent companies from having a subsidiary in a low-tax Member State.[119]

After stressing that any advantage arising from the low taxation of a subsidiary in another Member State, cannot by itself authorise the parent company's state of residence to offset that advantage by less favourable tax treatment of the parent company,[120] it found that, in assessing taxpayer's conduct, it is necessary to consider that freedom of establishment is intended to allow any EU national to participate, on a stable and continuing basis, in the economic life of a Member State other than his state of origin and to profit therefrom.[121] Accordingly, it highlighted that the freedom to set up a subsidiary as a form of (secondary) establishment in another Member State presupposes the pursuit of genuine economic activity there.[122] For this reason, it concluded that, to be justified on the anti-abuse grounds, the specific objective of the restriction must be to prevent conduct involving the creation of wholly artificial arrangements which do not reflect economic reality, with a view to escaping the tax normally due on the profits generated by activities carried out on national territory.[123]

The ECJ regarded this type of conduct as capable, to the same extent as the tax planning strategies that it intended to prevent in *Marks & Spencer*, of jeopardising a balanced allocation of taxing powers between Member States.[124] It concluded that, although a CFC law was suitable to achieve this objective,[125] such legislation would be disproportionate, and in breach of Articles 49 and 54, if the parent company was able to show that tax savings were not the (sole or) main motive for incorporating the subsidiary[126] and the subsidiary carried on genuine economic activities in the host Member State in light of objective factors such as, in particular, its physical existence in terms of premises, staff and equipment.[127]

---

117 Case C–212/1997, *Centros* [1999] ECR I–1459, para. 27; Case C–167/01 *Inspire Art* [2003]; ECR I–10155, para. 96; Case C–364/01 *Barbier* [2003] ECR I–15013, para. 71.
118 C–196/04, *Cadbury Schweppes* (n 116), paras. 35–36.
119 Ibid., para. 46.
120 Ibid., para. 49.
121 Ibid., para. 53.
122 Ibid., paras. 54–55.
123 Ibid., para. 55.
124 Ibid., para. 56.
125 Ibid., para. 59.
126 Ibid., para. 62.
127 Ibid., paras. 66–47.

Arguably, *Cadbury Schweppes* – by requiring Member States to allow interested companies to demonstrate that the setting up of a subsidiary resulted in a genuine economic activity in the host Member States – paved the way to the *impossibility* of applying national CFC provisions in most cases, and thus ended up turning the freedom of establishment into a saving clause for tax-savings practices.[128] In fact, as the test for ascertaining the genuine economic activity in this host Member State having a more favourable taxation system is based on investments in premises, staff and equipment that are really *needed* to conduct business there and to earn profits subject to that more favourable tax regime, *irrespective of* where the business market is deemed to be, the concerned company will certainly have the interest to make the investments themselves.

The reasoning in *Langhorst-Hohorst* and in *Cadbury Schweppes* was reiterated in another ruling concerning thin capitalisation rules, the 2007 *Test Claimant in the Thin Cap Group Litigation* ruling,[129] when the ECJ found that, although national rules which treated loan interest payments to non-resident associated companies as distribution of dividends created a restriction that could be justified for combating abusive practices, these rules were nevertheless disproportionate if they were not confined to the part of loan interest exceeding would have been agreed on arm's length basis[130] (ie on the same terms that would have applied as between unrelated companies on commercial grounds). This limitation, in the specific case, would have meant contrasting wholly artificial arrangements.

In the 2008 *Lammers* ruling,[131] the ECJ applied again the concept of wholly artificial arrangement as defined in *Cadbury Schweppes* and specified it in even greater detail. The Belgian tax authority, by applying a national anti-abuse provision, had reclassified interest paid by Belgian subsidiaries to parent companies established in another Member State – but not to resident parent companies – as taxable dividends because these interest payments exceeded specific limits. The ECJ regarded again this differential treatment as creating a restriction to the freedom of establishment as it made less attractive for companies based in other Member States to create a subsidiary in Belgium. It explained that, to be justified on anti-abuse grounds, such a restriction must prevent conduct involving the creation of wholly artificial arrangements which do not reflect economic reality, with a view to escaping the tax normally due on the profits generated by activities carried out on national territory.[132]

In the specific case, the ECJ found that the reclassification of interest payments made to non-resident companies as dividends as soon as they exceed the specific limits, would also risk applying to non-artificial arrangements such as interest paid on loans granted on an arm's length basis,[133] and consequently regarded the

---

128 T. O'Shea, The UK's CFC rules and the freedom of establishment: Cadbury Schweppes plc and its IFSC subsidiaries ± tax avoidance or tax mitigation? *EC Tax Review* 1, 13–33 (2007), at 32, refers to a "road-map" for tax planners' practices.
129 Case C-524/04, Test Claimant in the Thin Cap Group Litigation [2007] ECR I-2107.
130 Ibid., para. 83.
131 Case C-105/07, *Lammers* [2008] ECR I-173.
132 Ibid., para. 28.
133 Ibid., para. 32.

national provision as disproportionate. Ultimately, *Lammers* not only confirmed the need to prove the existence of wholly artificial arrangements on a case-by-case basis, but it also made even clearer than *Cadbury Schweppes* that it is these strategies' outcome of prejudicing Member States' financial interests which, without a genuine economic reason, makes the arrangements artificial (and detrimental to the working of the internal market).

A ruling which may appear difficult to reconcile with this findings is the 2010 *SGI* ruling,[134] where the ECJ had to deal with transfer pricing[135] rules, which can be regarded as a category of rules against tax avoidance given their objective of preventing profits shifting through prices below arm's length. In *SGI*, the ECJ found that Belgian transfer pricing rules under which exceptional or gratuitous benefits given by a resident company to related companies in France and Luxembourg led to upward profit adjustments on the resident company, whereas it would not lead to any adjustments if benefits were granted to other resident companies, constituted a restriction to the outbound freedom of establishment.[136] However, it accepted justification based on both the preservation of a balanced allocation of taxing powers[137] and the need to prevent tax avoidance.[138] Specifically, the ECJ, by applying its *Marks & Spencer* reasoning,[139] held that permitting resident companies to transfer their profits in the form of unusual or gratuitous advantages to related companies resident in other Member States would undermine the very allocation of taxing powers between Member States, because the state of residence of the company granting these advantages would be forced to renounce its right to tax its income in favour of the residence Member State of the recipient company.[140] Thus, it found that the legislation at issue permitted Belgium to exercise its tax jurisdiction on activities carried out in its territory.[141]

Moreover, the ECJ held that, although the national law was not specifically designed to target wholly artificial arrangements devoid of economic reality, it could nonetheless be justified by the objective of preventing tax avoidance, taken together with that of preserving the balanced allocation of the taxing powers between the Member States.[142] In this respect, the ECJ stressed that, if resident companies were allowed to grant unusual or gratuitous advantages to related companies in other Member States, without any corrective tax measures, there would be the risk of intra-group transfers of income towards companies established in Member States applying the lowest tax rates *or* exempting such income. For this reason, it considered Belgian provisions as capable of preventing such practices, otherwise liable to be encouraged by significant disparities between the bases of

---

134 Case C–311/08, *Société de Gestion Industrielle (SGI)* [2010] ECR I–487.
135 See ch 2, at 2.2.4 about the Arbitration Convention.
136 Ibid., para. 55.
137 Ibid., paras. 60–64.
138 Ibid., para. 66.
139 Ibid., para. 62.
140 Ibid., para. 63.
141 Ibid., para. 65.
142 Ibid., para. 66.

assessment or rates of tax applied in the various Member States and designed only to avoid the tax normally due in the Member State of the company granting the advantage.[143]

Finally, it also considered Belgian rules to be proportionate,[144] consistently with its previous case law whereby taxpayers must be allowed to prove the existence of commercial justifications for a transaction and with the circumstance that, in the case at stake, the burden of proving the existence of unusual or gratuitous advantages rested with the tax authority.

In *SGI*, where the decisive element in the ECJ reasoning was the risk of artificial arrangements transferring income to low-tax jurisdictions, the ECJ did not investigate whether such a transfer actually took place and did not hold that taxpayers must be able to prove the absence, in the concrete case, of such a transfer. In other words, the ECJ did not apply, mutatis mutandis, its *Cadbury Schweppes* finding. This gives rise to uncertainty as to whether and how *SGI* and *Cadbury Schweppes* can be reconciled. It might be argued that *SGI* would only apply to transfer pricing rules, which rules, therefore, would be more 'protected' than other anti-avoidance rules, and would be allowed regardless of whether or not income transfer to a low-tax jurisdiction would concretely occur and, ultimately, of whether or not in this last state there would be corresponding (downward) adjustments. Nevertheless, this 'strengthened protection' of transfer pricing rules would seem unconvincing and inconsistent, since it would risk leading exactly to that economic double taxation, caused by transfer pricing adjustments, that the Commission and the Member States have been aiming at eliminating.

3.2 The free movement of workers or self-employed and the resident versus non-resident distinction

Apart from the *Schumacker* ruling, the free movement of workers under Article 45 TFEU and self-employed individuals under Article 49 has come at issue in several other ECJ rulings on direct taxation, which touched on the distinction between residents and non-residents in relation to key substantive and procedural aspects of personal direct taxation systems: rules of fiscal procedure; progressive tax scale; deduction of income-related expenses; deductions for personal and family circumstances and for foreign losses on immovable property; application of DTCs.

As regards fiscal procedure rules, the ECJ found, in the 1990 *Biehl* ruling,[145] that the freedom of movement of workers precluded a Member State legislation providing the non-refund of withholding tax deducted from the salaries and wages of employed persons who are resident taxpayers for only part of the year, because they take up residence in the country or leave it during the tax year. The ECJ

---

143 Ibid., paras. 67 and 68.
144 Ibid., paras. 72–76.
145 Case C–175/88, *Biehl* [1990] ECR I–1779.

stressed first that Article 45 prohibit not only overt discriminations based on nationality, but also all covert forms of discriminations leading to the same results by applying other criteria of differentiation.[146]

In this respect it found that one of such criteria was permanent residence in the national territory, because this requirement, which was necessary for obtaining any repayment of an over-deduction of tax, would work in particular against nationals of other Member States, who would often leave the country or take up residence there during the year.[147] The ECJ rejected a justification based on the need to protect the system of progressive taxation[148] since it regarded the national provision at stake as infringing the principle of equal treatment, in particular, in the situation of a temporarily resident taxpayer receiving no income during the year of assessment and being treated less favourably than a resident taxpayer due to his losing the right to repayment of the over-deduction of tax which a resident taxpayer would always enjoy.[149]

These findings were also applied in a subsequent 1995 ruling, *Biehl II*,[150] where the ECJ held that the risk of discriminating against taxpayers of other Member States also applied to legislation under which a temporary resident taxpayer who has no right to taxation by direct assessment must, during a tax year, have been employed on the national territory for at least nine months to become entitled to an adjustment on the basis of an annual calculation.[151] In that regard, the ECJ found that, although the special situation of temporary residents may objectively justify the adoption of specific procedural arrangements to enable the competent tax authorities to determine the tax rate applicable to national income, it could not justify the exclusion of those taxpayers from the entitlement to repayment of excess amounts of tax deducted where this was repayable to permanent residents.[152]

Biehl and *Biehl II* showed that, to avoid a covert form of discrimination, non-residents are always entitled within a Member State to the same opportunities as residents for correction of their tax position at the end of a tax year by way of assessment, whichever modality is used for this correction and even if special procedural arrangements may be necessary for temporary residents/non-residents only. Another aspect of fiscal procedure, i.e. the application of methods for determining profits of self-employed individuals when they do not provide tax authorities with evidence about their earning, was at stake in the 2007 *Talotta*[153] ruling, where the ECJ struck down a national provision establishing in that situation, only for non-residents, that turnover would be determined by applying a minimum tax base. In fact, the ECJ found that the income received by residents

---

146   Ibid., para. 13.
147   Ibid., para. 14.
148   Ibid., paras. 15 and 16.
149   Ibid.
150   Case C–151/94, *Commission v Luxembourg (Biehl II)* [1995] ECR I–4915.
151   Ibid., para. 16.
152   Ibid., para. 21.
153   Case C–385/05 *Talotta* [2007] ECR I–2555.

and by non-residents were in the same category of income from self-employed activities[154] and that the two categories of taxpayers were in an objectively comparable position, because they presented the same difficulties for the tax authorities concerned.[155]

The ECJ expressly established the comparability in light of the purpose of the national law at stake[156] (in that case, to overcome difficulties for tax authorities) and, in so doing, it confirmed a criterion that, impliedly, it had already adopted in *Biehl* and *Biehl II*. With regard to person-related deductions, the ECJ, in the 1995 *Wielockx* ruling,[157] extended to self-employed individuals, and to deductions from business profits, its *Schumacker* reasoning about both the comparability between residents and non-residents receiving most of their income in the work state and the discrimination against non-residents that would arise if deductions for personal and family circumstances were granted by neither the employment state nor the state of residence.[158]

In *Wielockx* the ECJ struck down a national provision of the work state that denied non-resident taxpayers receiving all or almost all of their income in its territory a deduction granted to residents, from their taxable income, of business profits which they allocated to a personal pension reserve. The ECJ ruled that denying the benefit to non-resident taxpayers could not be justified by the fact that the periodic pension payments subsequently drawn out of the pension reserve by the non-resident taxpayer would not be taxed in the work state but in the taxpayer's state of residence. It reached this conclusion because, irrespective of domestic provisions, the fiscal cohesion had been already ensured by the DTCs between the work state and the state of residence at the level of reciprocity of rules applied by the contracting states, and therefore that the coherence principle could not be invoked at domestic level.[159]

Just as in *Schumacker*, the ECJ assessed therefore the situation of a non-resident taxpayer, its comparability with a resident one and the national provision at issue, in light of the *overall legal framework* – including DTCs between the states concerned – applicable to the non-resident taxpayer. It reiterated this approach in the 1996 *Aascher* ruling,[160] where it disallowed a national law that applied to a non-resident self-employed individual, who was also self-employed in his residence Member State, a higher rate of income tax than that applicable to residents pursuing the same activity, essentially on the ground that there was no objective difference between the situation of non-resident taxpayers and that of resident taxpayers such as to justify the different treatment of non-residents. It found that this was the case because, in light of the relevant DTC, a non-resident taxpayer was not able to

---

154 Ibid., para. 26.
155 Ibid., para. 28.
156 Ibid., para. 30.
157 Case C–80/94, *Wielockx* [1995] ECR I–2493.
158 Ibid., paras. 19–22.
159 Ibid., paras. 23–25.
160 Case C–107/94, *Aascher* [1996] ECR I–3089.

escape the application of the progressivity rule and both categories of taxpayers were therefore in comparable situations with regard to that rule.[161]

The ECJ refused a justification whereby the higher rate of income tax on non-residents was intended to compensate for the fact that non-residents were not liable to social security contributions, as this non-liability resulted from a decision of the legislature itself.[162] It also rejected the justification based on the coherence of the taxation system as it found that there was no direct link between the application of a higher rate of tax to the income of certain non-residents and the fact that no social security contributions was levied on their income from domestic sources. *Wielockx* and *Aascher* essentially indicate an assessment by the ECJ of the situation of the taxpayer at cross-border level and a restrictive application of the principle of coherence of tax system, which latter could no longer be invoked at national level when *either* existing at the level of DTCs between the Member States (*Wielockx*) *or* eliminated by choices made by individual states themselves (*Aascher*).

In the 1998 *Gilly* ruling,[163] the ECJ had to assess whether the provisions of a DTC as applicable in case of a frontier worker created a forbidden discrimination. In that case, a frontier female worker, earning her entire employment income in Germany, was resident in France with her husband, who earned 45 per cent of the family income in France, where spouses were jointly assessed for the total family income. The frontier worker was granted no deduction in Germany whereas, in France, the household received an indirect tax credit set up by the DTC for the tax paid in the employment state. This tax credit was insufficient to offset the tax paid in Germany – and thus to eliminate juridical double taxation – because of the greater degree of personal income tax progressivity in this country. In France, the couple lost 55 per cent of their family allowances (to which they would be entitled if this worker were employed there), because 55 per cent of the overall family income was earned abroad and exempted in France by virtue of the DTC. The frontier worker had dual French and German nationality and, for this reason, under the relevant DTC, her employment income was subject to taxation only in Germany. The DTC would have made the income taxable only in France if she had been a French national, in which case the household would have received a tax credit capable of offsetting the tax and the entire family allowance in France.

Nonetheless, the ECJ found that any unfavourable consequences entailed by the tax credit mechanism introduced by the DTC derived from differences between the tax scales of the Member States concerned, and that, lacking any EU legislation in the field, the determination of those scales is left to Member States.[164] It also held that, if France were required to accord a tax credit greater than the fraction of its national tax corresponding to the foreign income, it would have to

---

161 Ibid., paras. 41–48.
162 Ibid., para. 53.
163 Case C–336/96, *Gilly* [1998] ECR I–2793.
164 Ibid., paras. 46–47.

reduce its tax in respect of the remaining income and would suffer a loss of tax revenues and an encroachment on its sovereignty in direct taxation.[165]

Finally, as regards the reduction in the family allowances suffered by the tax household and the fact that the personal and family circumstances were not considered in Germany, the ECJ considered the *Gilly* case as different from *Schumacker* because the frontier worker individual income was aggregated within the basis for assessing the personal income tax payable by her tax household in the state of residence, where she was therefore entitled to the tax advantages, rebates and deductions provided for in national law.[166] The ECJ thus regarded the employment state tax authorities as not obliged to consider the frontier worker personal and family circumstances in such a situation.[167]

If read together with *Schumacker*, *Wielockx* and *Aascher*, *Gilly* suggests that, when the 'taxable person' is not an individual but *a tax household*, the situation of non-residents appears to be assessed at the tax household level, and that the granting of aggregate family allowances by the state of residence excludes the obligation on the employment state of a household member to grant family allowances, *irrespective* of the amount of the allowances granted in the state of residence. Impliedly, the ECJ adopted therefore, with regard to the granting of general deductions (*Schumacker*, *Wielockx* and *Gilly*) and to the progressivity scale (*Aascher*), the approach of ensuring that these elements of personal taxation always exist in one country (by virtue of either national provision or DTCs), similarly to the 'always somewhere approach' on the deductibility of corporate terminal losses. Moreover, *Gilly* indicates that, if a disadvantage in a cross-border situation in comparison with a domestic situation – even when resulting in an inability to eliminate juridical double taxation completely (owing to the insufficiency of the tax credit) – derives from the distribution of taxing powers under a DTC and from higher or lower taxation levels within individual states, the ECJ does not regard that disadvantage as creating a prohibited discrimination.

In the 1999 *Gschwind* ruling,[168] the ECJ dealt again with a national law of the employment state denying deductions for personal and family circumstances to a non-resident taxpayer. This taxpayer resided with his family in a Member State but earned its entire employment income, amounting to 58 per cent of the overall household income, in another state, whilst his wife earned the remaining 42 per cent in their state of residence. The ECJ continued to use the *Schumacker* criteria of verifying whether there was a sufficient tax base for the household in the state of residence to benefit from deductions for personal and family circumstances there, and, having found that this was the case – unlike the situation in *Schumacker* – it accepted the national law at issue.[169] The existence of a sufficient taxable base in the state of residence therefore becomes the criteria for establishing the non-

---

165   Ibid., para. 48.
166   Ibid., paras. 49 and 50.
167   Ibid.
168   Case C-391/97, *Gschwind* [1999] ECR I-5451.
169   Ibid., paras. 27-31.

comparability, in the employment state, of the situation of a non-resident married couple, of which one member worked in such a state, with that of a resident married couple,[170] and the ECJ neglected again to consider the possibility of a *pro-quota* granting of the personal deductions.

This was expressly denied in the 2002 *De Groot* ruling,[171] where a Dutch resident earned more than 60 per cent of his total income in three other countries, France, Germany and the UK, whilst *neither* reaching the *Schumacker* threshold of 'almost all of its income' *nor* obtaining personal deductions in any of these countries. Although the Dutch law disallowed the personal deductions for a part corresponding to the fraction of the foreign-sourced income on the overall income, the ECJ rejected this pro quota granting of personal and family circumstances by the residence Member State by stressing that, as the end result, *all* the personal and family circumstances must be taken into account in one state or in another.

In the specific case – the ECJ noted – the state of residence was partially released from its obligation to do so *without* the states of employment undertaking to grant these deductions or having them imposed by the DTC with the state of residence.[172] A justification whereby it would be disproportionate in that situation to place on the state of residence the burden of granting all personal allowances even in the absence of allowances granted by the source states was rejected by the ECJ by repeating its statement, in *ICI* and *St Gobain*, that the loss of tax revenues can never be relied on to justify a restriction on the exercise of a fundamental freedom.[173]

The ECJ also specified that the cohesion of the tax system could not be a justification, because there was not a direct link between the Dutch method of exemption with progression applied to foreign income (whereby the state of residence forgoes taxing foreign income but considers it in determining the applicable tax rate) and the deduction of personal allowances only in proportion to the income received in the state of residence.[174] In this respect, it regarded the effectiveness of the progressive rates of income tax in the state of residence, which the method of exemption with progression seeks to ensure, as not dependent on the restriction, in that state, of the account to be taken of the taxpayer's personal and family circumstances.[175]

The *De Groot* ruling was criticised on the ground that it conflicts with Article 45 TFEU and with Article 7 of EC Regulation 1612/68 on the free movement of workers explicitly requiring the host states to grant national treatment to non-resident workers, which, as regards personal taxation, would mean entitling them to personal benefits in each source state in proportion to the part of the overall income earned in that state.[176] *De Groot* could be regarded as confirming

---

170 Ibid., para. 30.
171 Case C–385/00, *De Groot* [2002] ECR I–11819.
172 Ibid., paras. 101 and 102.
173 Ibid., para. 103.
174 Ibid., para. 109.
175 Ibid.
176 B. J. M. Terra, P. J. Wattel, *European Tax Law* 6th edn (Wolters Kluwer, 2012), at pp. 990–91.

the 'always somewhere approach' in respect of the full deductions for personal and family circumstances, because the ECJ's reasoning implies that the *pro-quota* deductions in the state of residence may have been accepted if each source state, through national provisions or DTCs, had granted a quota of deductions corresponding to the total income fraction taxable in that state.

Nonetheless, in this respect, *De Groot* appears difficult to reconcile with *Gilly*, where, despite the lack of personal deductions for the frontier worker in the employment state, the state of residence was not required to grant 100 per cent aggregate family deductions, i.e. deductions also corresponding to the fraction of the overall income taxed only in the employment state. The two rulings also seem to be inconsistent with each other because, despite the similarity of the underlying situations, in *Gilly* the ECJ had accepted the argument that if the state of residence accorded a tax credit greater than the fraction of its national tax corresponding to the foreign income, it would suffer a loss of tax revenues,[177] i.e. exactly the same kind of argument that it rejected in *De Groot*.[178] This raises the question as to whether *De Groot* overturned *Gilly* at least in respect of deductions for personal and family circumstances, but the subsequent rulings do not appear to provide a response.

On the one hand, in the 2013 *Imfeld* ruling,[179] the ECJ struck down the tax law of a residence Member State which had the effect that a couple earning income both in that state and in another one – where the husband was taxed separately on his earned income, which was exempt in his state of residence, and could obtain only part, not all, of the tax advantages linked to his personal and family circumstances – was denied a specific tax advantage, owing to the rules for offsetting it, even though that couple would be entitled to it if both the members earned all or most of their incomes in the residence Member State. In deciding this case, the ECJ simply applied its *De Groot* arguments to these facts, whereby the residence Member State can be released from its obligations to grant all tax advantages relating to personal and family circumstances only if either a DTC imposes the corresponding obligation to the source states or if their national laws grant these advantages.[180]

In reaching its conclusion, the ECJ rejected a justification arguing that the aim of the national tax law at issue was to ensure that the taxpayer's personal and family circumstances were not taken into account simultaneously in two Member States and drawing a parallel with the ECJ's *Marks & Spencer* argument about the need to prevent the double deduction of corporate losses.[181] The ECJ's reasoning was that, even if the different tax advantages granted by the two Member States

---

177 Case C–336/96, *Gilly* (n 163), para. 48.
178 Case C–385/00, *De Groot* (n 171), para. 103.
179 Case C–303/12, *Imfeld and Garcet v Belgian State*, judgment issued 12 December 2013 [2013] ECR I–0000.
180 Ibid., paras. 69–76,
181 Ibid., para. 77.

concerned were comparable and the member of the couple working in the non-residence state did actually receive a double advantage, such situation only resulted from the parallel application of the two Member States' tax laws, as agreed between them in the relevant DTC.[182]

Ultimately, it found that the Member States concerned are free to take into consideration the possible tax advantages granted by another Member State imposing tax, provided that – irrespective of how those states have allocated that obligation amongst themselves – their taxpayers are guaranteed that, as the end result, all their personal and family circumstances, and not only part of them, will be considered.[183] In so doing, it extended the *De Groot* findings, in terms of the obligation falling on the state of residence, to the situation where the employment state has only in part granted personal deductions owing to its own rules.

A number of other rulings concerned not person-related deductions but income-related deductions, i.e. business expenses, and business losses. In the 2003 *Gerritse* ruling,[184] the ECJ found, in that case for non-resident artists and sportsman earning a minor part of the overall income in the work state, that this state had to ensure non-residents the proportional deductibility of business expenses that are directly linked to the income-generating activity performed in its territory, i.e. to extend them the treatment offered to residents with whom, in respect of their activity, they were considered to be in a comparable situation.[185]

Some other rulings concerning business expenses, e.g. the 2006 *Scorpio* ruling[186] and the 2007 *Centro Equestre* ruling,[187] confirmed that, in the ECJ's assessment, the circumstance of these expenses being directly linked to the income-generating activity in the work state is the decisive element for this state's obligation to grant non-residents the related deductions.

Business losses were at stake in the 2002 *Mertens* ruling,[188] where an individual residing and carrying on a self-employed business in a Member State could deduct from his taxable profit for one year a loss incurred the previous year only on the condition that that loss was not capable of being offset against employment income in another Member State during that same previous year.

Although this provision applied indistinctly to all taxpayers, the loss could not be deducted from taxable income in either of the Member States concerned, whereas it would be deductible if that taxpayer had been both self-employed and employed exclusively in his or her state of residence, because the DTC allocated taxing powers to the work state for the employment income and to the state of residence for the business income. For this reason the ECJ regarded the situation of resident taxpayers carrying out all their occupational activities in the state

---

182 Ibid., para. 78.
183 Ibid., para. 79.
184 Case C–234/01, *Gerritse* [2003] ECR I–5933.
185 Ibid., paras. 27 and 28.
186 Case C–290/04, *Scorpio* [2006] ECR I–9461.
187 Case C–345/04, *Centro Equestre* [2007] ECR I–1425.
188 Case C–431/01, *Mertens* [2002] ECR I–7073.

concerned as not objectively comparable to that of taxpayers who were simultaneously self-employed in the state of residence and employees in another Member State,[189] and it found that the national provision, by treating incomparable situations in the same way, had created an unjustifiable restriction on free movement of workers in another Member State.[190]

In this specific case of business losses incurred by individuals, the ECJ seemed thus to have adopted a legal criteria (the jurisdictional difference between two categories of income under DTCs) to establish the non-comparability of situations, and to have followed the same 'always somewhere approach' as on its rulings about the deductibility of corporate losses or about personal deductions.

The different treatment in the ECJ's case law of personal deductions (as the state of residence obligation if there is sufficient taxable base there) and of income-related deductions (as the source state obligation if inextricably linked to the income-generating activity) would suppose that the distinction between these two categories would always be clear-cut. In some situations, this might not necessarily be the case.[191] Moreover, with regard to personal deductions in the work state, a further aspect concerning the type of income that a non-resident employee receives in his state of residence emerged from the 2004 *Wallentin* ruling.[192] Here the ECJ found that – in assessing whether a non-resident employee has sufficient tax base in his state of residence and thus whether the employment state must grant the personal deductions according to the *Schumacker* rule – a non-taxable income in the state of residencee must not be considered. Although the ECJ referred to income which, by its nature, is not subject to tax,[193] the literature has stressed that deciding whether or not any item of income is taxed is only a matter of national tax policy, not of the nature of the income.[194]

In this respect, if the ECJ intended certain items of income by their very nature as being exempt in Member States – as it would seem to be the case when, in *Wallentin*, it stressed that a basic tax-free allowance in the state of residence, under its case law, had a social purpose[195] – this would arguably encroach on that Member State's sovereignty in direct taxation that the ECJ itself had accepted to safeguard in *Gilly*.

The *Wallentin* reasoning was also used by the ECJ in a 2012 ruling, *Commission v Estonia*,[196] where the ECJ regarded as incompatible with the free movement of

---

189 Ibid., paras. 30 and 31.
190 Ibid., paras. 32 and 33.
191 For example, in Case C–364/04, *Conijn* [2006] ECR I–6137, the ECJ found that tax consultancy costs for filing a tax return that had been incurred in Germany by a Dutch resident earning business income in Germany, were to be regarded as income-related deductions, due to the complexity of German tax law placing the Dutch resident in a comparable situation with German residents.
192 Case C–169/03, *Florian Wallentin* [2004] ECR I–6443.
193 Ibid., para. 24.
194 Terra and Wattel, *European Tax Law* (n 176), at p. 982.
195 Case C–169/03, *Florian Wallentin* (n 192), paras. 18 and 19.
196 Case C–39/10, *Commission v Estonia* [2012] ECLI (EU), C, 212 (2012).

workers a national law not granting a personal income tax exemption to a non-resident pensioner who, in the pensioner's residence Member State, only perceived a small amount of tax-free pension. Interestingly, in this ruling the ECJ referred to *Wallentin* as a case where there was no taxable income *under the law* of the state of residence[197] – rather than 'by its nature' – but it stated that the state of residence should in principle be able to consider the taxpayer's overall ability to pay and his personal and family circumstances where nearly 50 per cent of his total income is received there.[198] It also highlighted that the person concerned was tax-exempt in his state of residence 'because of the modest amount of worldwide income'.[199]

Two interpretative issues, to which a response remains unanswered in the case law, would seem to arise. First, the statement about the state of residence being able in principle to consider the overall ability to pay when nearly 50 per cent of the total income is obtained there – if taken with the fact that the '*Schumacker* threshold' (requiring the employment state to grant personal deductions related to the non-resident overall ability to pay) was established at 90 per cent of the overall income – gives rise to the question as to which state should bear this obligation when the income received in the state of residence amounts, e.g., to 30 per cent of the total taxable income and the one in the work state to 70 per cent. A related question in this regard is whether the state bearing this obligation should be identified on a case-by-case basis. Secondly, the attention paid to the fact that the person was tax-exempt in his state of residence because of the modest amount of the worldwide income raises the question as to whether the reason for exemption in the state of residence is always bound to become important.

The ECJ has been subsequently expanding the scope of the *Schumacker* doctrine by requiring the employment state, in case of non-resident workers in the *Schumacker* situation, to take into consideration foreign losses related to immovably property and, eventually, any circumstance related to the assessment of the taxpayer's overall ability to pay. In two rulings, the 2006 *Ritter-Coulais*[200] and the 2007 *Lakebrink-Peters*[201] cases it found that the employment state must consider foreign negative income from immovable property in determining the personal tax rate applicable to non-resident workers if this negative income is so taken into consideration for resident workers. In the 2008 *Renneberg* ruling,[202] it required an employment state, where a non-resident worker receives all or almost all its income, to grant him deductions, from his taxable base, for negative immovable property income in the state of residence if deduction for foreign negative property income is granted to resident workers. It reached this conclusion despite, under the relevant DTC, positive property income would be taxable only in the state of residence.

---

197 Ibid., para. 53.
198 Ibid., para. 54.
199 Ibid., para. 55.
200 Case C–152/03, *Ritter Coulais* [2006] ECR I–1711.
201 Case C–182/06, *Lakebrink-Peters* [2007] ECR I–6705.
202 Case C–527/06 *Renneberg* [2008] ECR I–7735.

In fact, in *Renneberg*, the ECJ considered the *De Groot* arguments, about taking into account all personal and family circumstances of the non-resident worker irrespective of how the Member States concerned allocate that obligation amongst themselves, also applicable with regard to non-resident workers' *overall* ability to pay tax.[203] This is adversely affected by the negative property income which, in the *Renneberg* situation, could not be deducted in the state of residence owing to the insufficient tax base there.[204]

Ultimately, in *Lakebrink* and *Renneberg*, where the national provisions involved discrimination against non-resident workers due to their negative property income being taken into account in no state, the ECJ was willing to go *beyond* the contents of DTCs. Although for this reason such rulings, particularly *Renneberg*, were strongly criticised in the literature,[205] the ECJ arguably charged the task of granting person-related deductions and reliefs for foreign losses from immovable property the Member State that is in a *better position* to assess the taxpayer's overall ability to pay, which, in that situation, was the employment state, rather than the state regarded as the state of residence under DTCs. In itself, this transfer of the task of assessing the non-resident taxpayer's overall ability to pay to the work state when (almost) all its total income is earned there, would appear to be consistent with the fact that, in *Schumacker*, the ECJ had emphasised that the state of residence, under international tax law rules, has the task of assessing the overall ability to pay (and of granting the person-based deductions) because *normally* the taxpayer's personal and economic interests are mainly concentrated in the state of residence.[206]

Nonetheless, it would appear problematic to reconcile *Renneberg* with *Gilly* since, in *Gilly*, the ECJ had regarded a disadvantaged situation (the loss of a part of family deductions) created by an allocation of taxing powers under DTCs as *not* constituting a discrimination, whereas, in *Renneberg*, it went beyond the content of a DTC *because* of the discrimination that would otherwise arise from the loss of personal deductions.

Overall, the case law on the free movement of workers and other individuals has therefore left important questions unanswered about if and how some key rulings may be reconciled with each other, despite clarifying the irrelevance of the residents versus non-residents distinction as regards rules of fiscal procedure or progressive scale of taxation, the 'always somewhere approach' as regards person-related deductions and the different treatment of income-related deductions.

Furthermore, if *Renneberg* is taken together with *K*, concerning the (non-)deductibility by resident individual taxpayers of losses from the sale of immovable

---

203 Ibid., para. 70.
204 Ibid., para. 71.
205 E. C. C. M. Kemmeren, '*Renneberg* Endangers the Double Tax Conventions System or Can a Second Round Bring Recovery?' 18 *EC Tax Review* 1, (2009), pp. 4–15; G. T. K. Meussen, '*Renneberg*: ECJ Unjustifiably Expands *Schumacker* Doctrine to Losses from Financing of Personal Dwelling', 49 *European Taxation* 4 (2009), pp. 185–88.
206 Case C–279/93, *Schumacker* (n 10), paras. 31–32.

property in another Member State where the source state does not grant the deduction,[207] it can be noted that the ECJ has paradoxically charged with the task of assessing the overall ability-to-pay an employment state in the *Schumacker* situation (in *Renneberg*), but has exempted from it a state of residence (in *K*) in a normal situation despite, by the ECJ's own admission in the first part of *Schumacker*, that task should lie with the state of residence. The fact that in *K* the state of residence had renounced its power to take into account foreign immovable property income – owing also to a DTC – may not be a sufficient explanation, when the state of residence is the one where most of the taxpayer's overall income arises (and thus when the state of residence is in the same position as the employment state was in *Renneberg*).

3.3 The free movement of capital and the elimination of double taxation on dividends

In several rulings, the ECJ had to decide whether the free movement of capital under Article 63 TFEU banned national provisions which made disadvantageous treatments for residents receiving capital income, typically in the form of dividends, from other Member States, where either the inbound dividends fall outside the scope of the Parent–Subsidiary Directive. In other cases again falling outside this directive, it had to assess whether, in addition to Articles 49 and 54, Article 63 also precluded national rules treating outbound cross-border dividends differently from internal dividends. Finally, a further situation concerned the payment of interest to non-residents, including third country residents.

With regard to *inbound cross-border* dividends, the ECJ dealt with four main kinds of detrimental treatment for dividends sourced in – or investments in – other Member States.

A first type of detrimental treatment, *the refusal of tax incentives* for portfolio investments in shares in other Member States when these incentives were offered for investments in domestic shares, was at issue in the 2000 *Verkooijen* ruling[208] and in the 2004 *Wiedert-Paulus*[209] decision. In both rulings, the ECJ held that the national provisions had the effect both of discouraging nationals of the Member State concerned from investing their capital in companies which have their seat in another Member State[210] and of creating an obstacle to the raising of capital in the Member State concerned by companies of other Member States.[211] For this reason, it found that the national measures at issue created a restriction to the free movement of capital.

In *Verkooijen*, it also found that the possibility of applying national provisions distinguishing between taxpayers according to their place of residence *or* the place

---

207 See 3.1.2 above.
208 Case C–35/98, *Verkooijen* [2000] ECR I–4071.
209 Case C–242/03, *Wiedert-Paulus* [2004] ECR I–7379.
210 Case C–35/98, *Verkooijen* (n 208), para. 34; Case C–242/03, *Weidert-Paulus* (n 209), para. 13.
211 Case C–35/98, *Verkooijen* (n 208), para. 35; Case C–242/03, *Weidert-Paulus* (n 209), para. 14.

where their capital is invested, as contemplated by Article 65(1) TFEU, could exist respectively in case of non-comparable situations between residents and non-residents or for overriding reasons in the public interest such as to maintain the coherence of the tax system.[212] It then rejected a justification based on the promotion of the economy of the country through investments in domestic companies, by finding that aims of a purely economic nature cannot constitute an overriding reason in the general interest justifying a restriction of a fundamental freedom.[213]

It also refused the coherence argument, in *Verkooijen*, owing to the lack of a direct link between the grant of tax advantages to resident shareholders and the taxation of the profits of companies with their seat in another Member State as two separate taxes were levied on different taxpayers, and in *Wiedert-Paulus* due to a DTC shifting the fiscal cohesion to the level of the reciprocity of the rules applicable between the two contracting states as in the *Wielockx* case.[214] This first kind of detrimental treatment was thus disallowed by the ECJ, although in *Verkooijen* the comparability of situations between resident investors in domestic shares and in shares of companies from other Member States was apparently taken for granted as no analysis was carried out in this respect.

A second type of detrimental treatment on inbound dividends was the *refusal*, by the shareholder's state of residence, *of a tax credit* for the corporation tax paid by distributing companies resident in other Member States, where such tax credit was granted for dividends paid by domestic companies. This situation was at stake in the 2004 *Lenz*[215] and *Manninen*[216] rulings, as well as in the 2007 *Meilicke*[217] and in the 2011 *Meilicke II*[218] rulings. The ECJ consistently found that, where a Member State has a system for preventing or mitigating economic double taxation for domestic-source dividends, it must treat dividends paid to residents by non-resident companies in the same way.[219] In fact, the ECJ regarded the situation of shareholders resident in a Member State and receiving dividends from domestic companies as comparable to that of resident shareholders receiving dividends from a company of another Member State, inasmuch as both the domestic dividends and inbound cross-border dividends may be subject, first, in the case of corporate shareholders, to a series of charges to tax and, secondly, in the case of ultimate shareholders, to economic double taxation.[220]

---

212   Case C-35/98, *Verkooijen* (n 208), para. 43.
213   Ibid., para. 48.
214   Ibid., para. 58; Case C-242/03, *Weidert-Paulus* (n 209), paras. 22, 23 and 25.
215   Case C-315/02, *Lenz* [2004] ECR I-7063.
216   Case C-319/02, *Manninen* [2004] ECR I-7477.
217   Case C-292/04, *Meilicke* [2007] ECR I-835.
218   Case C-262/09, *Meilicke II* [2011] ECR I-05669.
219   Case C-315/02 *Lenz* (n 215), paras. 27–49; Case C-319/02, *Manninen* (n 216), paras. 29–55; Case C-262/09, *Meilicke II* (n 218), para. 29.
220   Case C-315/02 *Lenz* (n 215), paras. 31 and 32; Case C-319/02, *Manninen* (n 216), paras. 35 and 36.

In *Meilicke II*, the ECJ also clarified that the tax credit on inbound cross-border dividends – even if evidence required under national law is not adduced – must be calculated in relation to the rate of corporation tax on the distributed profits applicable to the dividend-paying company in its state of residence, although the tax credit amount may not exceed the amount of the income tax to be paid on dividends received by the shareholder.[221] The ECJ in *Manninen* rejected a justification based on cohesion of the tax system because the national law at stake, granting a tax credit solely to shareholders receiving dividends from domestic companies and aimed at eliminating economic double taxation, did not appear to be necessary for maintaining the cohesion in view of this objective.[222] It also refused an argument based on practical difficulties in determining the amount of corporation tax paid on distributed dividends by the non-resident company.[223]

Finally, in *Meilicke II* it held that, although the need to ensure the effectiveness of fiscal supervision would constitute an overriding reason of general interest and could be a justification, the national law, which strictly required the same degree of details and form of evidence to be adduced for dividends paid by domestic companies, was disproportionate,[224] and the tax authority could refuse the tax credit only if the shareholder concerned produces no information.[225] Essentially, in these rulings the ECJ required transposition to inbound cross-border dividends of the national systems for eliminating economic double taxation applicable to domestic dividends, and therefore placed domestic and inbound dividends on the *same* footing as regards elimination of economic double taxation that was the *objective* of the national provisions at issue.

A third type of detrimental treatment of inbound dividends was the case of shareholder residence states granting the recipient of dividends from other Member States a tax credit for the underlying corporation tax and granting exemption to recipients of domestic dividends, or vice versa. This situation, i.e. an *asymmetrical* elimination of economic double taxation, was at stake in cases involving corporate shareholders, i.e. in the 2006 *Test Claimant in the FII Group Litigation Order* ruling,[226] in the 2011 *Haribo and Salinen*[227] and *Accor*[228] rulings, and in the 2014 *Kronos International*[229] ruling. Just as in the *Lenz*, *Manninen* and *Meilicke* rulings, in *Test Claimant*, in *Haribo and Salinen* and in *Accor* the ECJ held that, in the context of a tax rule seeking to prevent the economic double taxation of distributed profits, the situation of a (corporate) shareholder receiving foreign-sourced dividends is comparable to that of a (corporate) shareholder receiving nationally-sourced

---

221 Case C–262/09, *Meilicke II* (n 218), para. 34.
222 Case C–319/02, *Manninen* (n 216), paras. 43–48.
223 Ibid., para. 54.
224 Case C–262/09, *Meilicke II* (n 218), paras. 41–43.
225 Ibid., para. 47.
226 Case C–446/04, *Test Claimant in the FII Group Litigation Order* [2006] ECR I–11753.
227 Joined Cases C–436/08 & C–437/08, *Haribo and Osterreichische Salinen* [2011] ECR I–00305.
228 Case C–310/09, *Accor* [2011] ECR I–8115.
229 Case C–47/12, *Kronos International*, ruling issued on 11 September 2004.

dividends, because, in each case, the profits made are, in principle, liable to be subject to a series of charges to tax.[230]

After establishing the comparability of situations, the ECJ reiterated that Article 63 TFEU requires a Member State which has a system for preventing economic double taxation as regards domestic dividends to accord equivalent treatment to dividends paid to residents by non-resident companies.[231] The ECJ was consistent with this position in *Kronos International* too, where economic double taxation was eliminated through an imputation method for domestic dividends and through an exemption method for inbound dividends, and where, as a consequence, a loss-making parent company could benefit from a refund of corporation tax paid by a distributing domestic subsidiary, but was not granted such refund for corporation tax paid by foreign subsidiaries. Here, the ECJ held that the refusal to grant such refund in case of inbound dividends could be explained by an objectively different situation.[232]

Specifically, it highlighted that the situations of a company receiving domestic dividends and of a company receiving foreign-sourced dividends were not comparable because the concerned Member State, via DTCs with the states of the distributing subsidiaries, had waived its taxing powers over inbound dividends coming from those states,[233] and that, in the context of the exemption method applying to inbound dividends, the lack of a refund was counterbalanced by not taking the dividends into account in determining the taxable base.[234]

In *Test Claimant in the FII Group Litigation Order*, in *Haribo and Salinen* and in *Kronos International*, the ECJ considered the indirect tax credit method and the exemption method as 'equivalent' in ensuring the same tax burden on the two categories of dividends, in particular when the corporation tax level in the state from which dividends come is lower than in the state of the recipient company.[235] In *Haribo and Salinen* it even stressed that, in such a case, exempting inbound cross-border dividends would give taxpayers that have invested in foreign holdings an advantage compared with those having invested in domestic holdings.[236]

It did so despite admitting that, if profits are subject in the state of the distributing company to a higher level of tax than the tax levied by the Member State of the receiving company, that Member State is not required to repay any excess tax paid in the state of the distributing company,[237] and that administrative

---

230 Case C–446/04, *Test Claimant in the FII Group Litigation Order* (n 226), para. 62; Joined Cases C–436/08 & C–437/08, *Haribo and Osterreichische Salinen* (n 227), para. 84; Case C–310/09, *Accor* (n 228), para. 45.

231 Case C–446/04, Test Claimant in the FII Group Litigation Order (n 226), para. 65.

232 Case C–47/12, *Knos International* (n 229) para. 81.

233 Ibid., para. 82.

234 Ibid., para. 88.

235 Case C–446/04, *Test Claimant in the FII Group Litigation Order* (n 226), paras. 48 and 57; Joined Cases C–436/08 & C–437/08, *Haribo and Osterreichische Salinen* (n 227), paras. 86–89; Case C–47/12, *Kronos International* (n 229), para. 66.

236 Joined Cases C–436/08 & C–437/08, *Haribo and Osterreichische Salinen* (n 227), para. 89.

237 Case C–446/04, *Test Claimant in the FII Group Litigation Order* (n 226), para. 52; Joined Cases C–436/08 & C–437/08, *Haribo and Osterreichische Salinen* (n 227), para. 88.

burdens which are imposed on the resident receiving company by a Member State applying the tax credit system to inbound foreign dividends are an intrinsic part of the very operation of this method.[238] The ECJ found that, for exactly such reasons, these administrative burdens could not be regarded as excessive.[239] It appeared to mitigate this last finding in *Accor*, where it held that production of evidence for benefiting from a tax credit may be required only if it were *not virtually impossible* or excessively difficult to furnish proof of payment of the tax by the subsidiaries in the other Member States, and left to national court to determine whether those conditions were met.[240]

Overall, the ECJ therefore accepted the asymmetrical elimination of economic double taxation, but its argument, in *Haribo and Salinen*, that extending exemption to inbound cross-border dividends coming from a low corporation tax state would give taxpayers investing in foreign holdings an advantage over investors in domestic holdings, would appear to contravene the very essence of the internal market. In fact, this should, by definition, allow operators to fully benefit from the advantages of investing in another Member State,[241] except for the only case of wholly artificial arrangements intended to circumvent national tax law which, however, were not at stake in *Haribo and Salinen* as regards the very investment in holdings in other Member States.

A fourth type of detrimental treatment of inbound cross-border dividends arose from the *refusal*, by the state of residence of the shareholder, *to credit withholding tax* paid in other Member States despite crediting withholding tax in case of domestic dividends. This situation, which resulted in juridical double taxation for inbound cross-border dividends in the hands of resident recipient shareholders, was at issue in the 2006 *Kerckhaert-Morres*[242] ruling, in the 2009 *Damseaux*[243] ruling and in *Haribo and Salinen*. In *Kerckhaert and Morres*, juridical double taxation arose as Belgian tax law made domestic dividends and dividends from shares of companies established in France subject to the same uniform level of income taxation on Belgian residents, without crediting withholding tax levied at source in France on inbound French sourced dividends. Despite a provision of the French-Belgian DTC stating that Belgium would credit the French withholding tax, Belgian courts had ruled that such provision merely memorialised a benefit previously granted under Belgian law and, therefore, that the DTC created no new rights beyond those existing under domestic law.[244]

---

238 Case C–446/04, *Test Claimant in the FII Group Litigation Order* (n 226), paras. 48 and 53; Joined Cases C–436/08 & C–437/08, *Haribo and Osterreichische Salinen* (n 227), para. 97.
239 Ibid.
240 Case C–310/09, *Accor* (n 228), para. 102.
241 Terra and Wattel, *European Tax Law* (n 176), at p. 1058.
242 Case C–513/04, *Kerckhaert-Morres* [2006] ECR I–10967.
243 Case C–128/08, *Damseaux* [2009] ECR I–6823.
244 For more detail see M. Quaghebeur, 'ECJ to Examine Belgian Treatment of Inbound Dividends', 37 *Tax Notes International*, 2005, 739,741; P. Smet, H. Laloo, 'ECJ to Rule on Taxation of Inbound Dividends in Belgium', 45 *European Taxation* 4, 158–159 (2005).

The ECJ stressed that, in *Kerckhaert and Morres*, Belgian law did not distinguish between domestic dividends and inbound cross-border dividends. It also found that, in respect of Belgian tax law, the position of a resident shareholder receiving cross-border inbound dividends was not necessarily altered by the fact that he receives dividends from another Member State which, in exercising its fiscal sovereignty, applies a withholding tax at source. After highlighting that the adverse consequences resulted from the exercise in parallel by two Member States of their fiscal sovereignty, the ECJ noted that EU law, in its current state, does not establish *general* criteria for attributing competence between Member States as regards the elimination of double taxation and, on this ground, it stated that it is for the Member States to *prevent* situations of juridical double taxation by applying, in particular, the DTCs and their apportionment criteria.[245]

In this respect, the ECJ noted that the DTC between France and Belgium apportioned fiscal sovereignty between the two states, but highlighted that such convention was not at issue in the preliminary reference.[246] In light of all these considerations, the ECJ eventually ruled that the free movement of capital did not preclude the Belgian legislation at stake and the consequent juridical double taxation. The reasoning in *Kerckhaert and Morres* about the exercise in parallel of taxing powers, about Member States' responsibility in eliminating juridical double taxation via DTCs and about the lack under EU law of a general criteria for the elimination of double taxation, was reiterated by the ECJ in the 2009 *Block* ruling in a situation of juridical double taxation relating to inheritance tax,[247] and in the *Damseaux* ruling involving again French dividends received by Belgian residents.

In *Damseaux*, these dividends were subject, according to the Franco-Belgian DTC, to taxation in both countries, with two alternative mechanisms in place to eliminate juridical double taxation, but, after the entry into force of the DTC, an amendment in Belgian law left one modality of relief of double taxation and this modality provided only a partial relief. As a result, the taxation of French dividends in Belgium ended up being more onerous than the taxation of Belgian dividends. The ECJ, after clarifying that it lacks jurisdiction to rule on the possible infringement of a DTC by a contracting Member State,[248] noted that the referring national court proceeded from the assumption that the DTC allowed a juridical double taxation of French dividends to Belgian resident partially to subsist.[249] It found that it is for each Member State to organise, in compliance with EU law, its system for taxing distributed profits, and that these dividends were liable to be subject to juridical double taxation in the event of two states' choice to exercise

---

245 Ibid., paras. 21–23. On this ruling see in particular S. Eden, 'The Obstacles Faced by the European Court of Justice in Removing the "Obstacles" Faced by Taxpayers: The Difficult Case of Double Taxation', *British Tax Review* 6, 610–28 (2010).
246 Ibid.
247 Case C–67/08 *Block* [2009] ECR I–00883, paras. 27–31.
248 Case C–128/08, *Damseux*, cit., paras. 19–22.
249 Ibid., para. 23.

their tax competence and to subject those dividends to taxation in the hands of the shareholder.[250]

After repeating, as in *Kerckhaert and Morres*, that disadvantages arising from the parallel exercise of tax competences by different Member States, if such exercise is not discriminatory, do not constitute restrictions prohibited by the Treaty,[251] the ECJ considered the abolition of double taxation within the EU as a Treaty objective, but highlighted immediately that the Member States have not concluded any multilateral convention to that effect under the former Article 293 of the Treaty, and that no general measure designed to eliminate double taxation has yet been adopted at the EU level.[252] Consequently, the ECJ reaffirmed, as in *Kerckhaert and Morres*, Member States' responsibility to eliminate double taxation through DTCs.[253]

As a result, in a situation where the Member States concerned agreed through a DTC that they would both be liable to tax dividends, the ECJ regarded itself as lacking the competence to require the residence Member State to prevent that double taxation, because EU law currently does not set any general criteria for eliminating double taxation within the EU.[254] It therefore found that the shareholder's state of residence is not required to prevent the disadvantages that could arise from the parallel exercise of taxing competence by the two Member States.[255]

The *Damseaux* reasoning and conclusion about juridical double taxation deriving from the parallel exercise of taxing powers by two Member States was repeated in *Haribo and Salinen*, where another issue dealt with (in addition to the elimination of economic double taxation on inbound cross-border dividends) was again whether the state of residence of the shareholder, in the context of application of the imputation method to these dividends, had to offset the withholding tax levied at source in the distributing company's state of residence.[256]

In two other cases, the 2013 *Beker*[257] and the 2014 *Bouanich* rulings,[258] the situation was partially different. In both cases, for a resident shareholder receiving dividends from a distributing company resident in another Member State, the dividends were taxable in both Member States, and, to eliminate juridical double taxation, the DTC provided for a tax credit in the state of residence for the withholding tax paid in the state of the distributing company. However, in *Baker*, the amount of creditable foreign withholding tax was calculated, under the applicable national law, in a manner that a resident taxpayer could not completely benefit from the personal and family allowances when part of its income was

---

250 Ibid., para. 26.
251 Ibid., para. 27.
252 Ibid., paras. 28 and 29.
253 Ibid., para. 30.
254 Ibid., paras. 32 and 33.
255 Ibid., para. 34.
256 Joined Cases C–436/08 & C–437/08, *Haribo and Osterreichische Salinen* (n 227), paras. 166–171.
257 Case C–168/11, *Manfred Baker, Christa Baker*, ruling of 28 February 2013.
258 Cases C–375/12, *Margaretha Bouanich* ruling of 13 March 2014.

received abroad, whereas he would do so when all income was received from national sources. In *Bouanich*, the applicable law provided for a mechanism capping various direct taxes at a certain percentage of income received during a tax year. Nonetheless, the foreign withholding tax was not taken into account, or taken only partially into account, for the calculating of the cap, thus making shareholders receiving inbound dividends liable to a higher taxation than shareholders receiving domestic dividends.

In *Baker*, the ECJ applied its reasoning in the *De Groot* ruling:[259] it found that the state of residence cannot escape its obligations to grant all deductions for personal and family circumstances, and that the balanced allocation of taxing power could not justify a failure to do so. In *Bouanich*, the ECJ noted that the different treatment, as regards the application of the capping mechanism, between inbound dividends and domestic dividends, made this case different from *Kerckhaert and Morres* (where national law provided for a uniform treatment).

The ECJ distinguished between the granting of a tax credit resulting from the DTC – which tax credit was part of the parallel taxation of dividends in two Member States – and the application of the capping mechanism, which served to reduce the level of income taxation within a Member State. Based on this distinction, in *Bouanich* it regarded the situation of resident taxpayers receiving inbound dividends as objectively comparable with that of resident taxpayers receiving domestic dividends, because the determination of the tax base and the calculation of the cap took into account inbound dividends as well. It thus found a restriction to the free movement of capital, due to these provisions discouraging investments in companies in other Member States, and rejected justifications based on the coherence of the tax system and on the need to safeguard a balanced allocation of taxing powers. The coherence justification was rejected because the ECJ found no direct link between the advantage granted by the tax cap and a particular tax; the balanced allocation of taxing power was not considered as a proper justification because the capping mechanism prevented the concerned Member State neither from taxing activities carried out in its territory nor from taxing income arising in another Member State.

Baker and *Bouanich*, due to the different situation at issue, are consistent with *Kerckhaert and Morres* and with *Damseux*, and showed that whenever, despite the elimination of juridical double taxation through a DTC, the *internal legislation* relating to a structural feature of the tax system creates a disparity between an internal situation and a cross-border situation which are comparable in light of the objective pursued by the national law, the ECJ is ready to find a restriction on fundamental freedoms and to strike down national provisions creating them. This applies not only for inbound dividends, but also to other forms of foreign income, such as, in the 2014 *Verests and Gerards* ruling,[260] immovable property income.[261] Even if the

---

259 See 3.2 above.
260 Case C–489/13, *Verests and Gerards*, ruling of 11 September 2014.
261 In this case, the ECJ regarded as incompatible with the free movement of capital a national law which resulted in a higher taxation for owners of deemed income from immovable property

ultimate outcome in *Baker* and *Bouanich* – a higher taxation of recipient of inbound dividends that had been subject to a withholding tax in the distributing company state – was the same as in *Kerckhaert and Morres*, the different origin of this outcome (from internal legislation in *Baker* and *Bouanich*) was decisive.

However, as noted in the literature, in *Kerckhaert and Morres* and *Damseux* a domestic creditable withholding tax was not at stake, so that after these rulings one might have doubted whether or not the ECJ would have reached the same conclusion if the shareholder's state of residence had given a credit for domestic withholding tax.[262] Arguably, this question – i.e. whether this state, irrespective of DTCs, would be obliged to eliminate juridical double taxation on inbound cross-border dividends *if* eliminating juridical double taxation on national dividends by crediting a domestic withholding tax – if answered in the positive, would have simply transposed, to juridical double taxation, the ECJ's position about economic double taxation. Nonetheless, because in *Haribo and Salinen* a domestic withholding tax could be offset against the shareholders' domestic income tax, but the ECJ did not consider this element when finding that the shareholder's state of residence was not obliged to grant a tax credit for the withholding tax level by the distributing company's state of residence, *Haribo and Salinen* seems to suggest a negative response to this question.[263]

The ECJ's findings in *Kerckhaert and Morres*, *Damseux* and *Haribo and Salinen* might be read as allowing juridical double taxation and be criticised due to the difference with the ECJ's stance on economic double taxation, which latter would also derive from parallel exercise of taxing powers. However, by examining the ECJ's *Kerckhaert and Morres* and *Damseux* reasoning, it could be argued *not* that the ECJ accepted juridical double taxation, but, instead, that it relied on DTCs for its elimination. The ECJ's arguments show that it did so as it considered DTCs – at the current stage of EU law – as the sole instrument, even if *not always effective,* for achieving this result, which result is actually the objective of the OECD Model Tax Convention, unlike the elimination of economic double taxation. Accordingly, it could be deduced that the same reasoning followed in *Kerckhaert and Morres*, *Damseux* and (as a result) in *Haribo and Salinen* would have led the ECJ to a different conclusion if the relevant DTCs had always ensured effective elimination of juridical double taxation and the parties had invoked those DTCs.

As regards *outbound* payments to residents of other Member States, the ECJ examined several cases in which the source state (ie the state of residence of the paying company): (a) applied a withholding tax on outbound cross-border dividends, without applying it to domestic dividends, which was the case in the 2006 *Bouanich*[264] and *Denkavit International*[265] rulings, in the 2007 *Amurta*

---

situated in another Member State than of deemed income from immovable property located in the State concerned, although the two situations were comparable in light of the objective of the contested national provision.
262 C. H. J. I. Panayi, *European Union Corporate Income Tax* (CUP 2013), at 250–51.
263 Ibid.
264 Case C–265/04, *Bouanich* [2006] ECR I–923.
265 Case C–170/05, *Denkavit International* [2006] ECR I–11949.

ruling,[266] in the 2009 *Aberdeen Property* ruling,[267] in the 2010 *Secilpar* ruling,[268] in the 2012 *Santander* ruling[269] or, in infringement procedures brought by the Commission against individual Member State, applied in any case rules leading to a better treatment for domestic dividends[270] or applied a withholding tax on outbound cross-border interest payments without applying it on domestic interest payments, in the 2008 *Truck Center* case;[271] (b) denied an imputation credit or any other tax relief on outbound cross-border dividends which would have been extended upon distribution to a domestic shareholder, which, after the 1986 *avoir fiscal* ruling, also occurred in the 2006 *Test Claimant in Class IV ACT* ruling[272] and in the 2008 *Burda* ruling.[273]

A first important ECJ finding was that, in respect of outbound cross-border dividends related to shareholdings which do not fall within the scope of the Parent–Subsidiary Directive, it is for the Member States to determine whether, and to what extent, economic double taxation must be avoided and, for that purpose, to establish, either unilaterally or through DTCs with other Member States, procedures intended to prevent or mitigate such economic double taxation, which discretion, however, does not allow them to impose measures contrasting with the freedoms of movement guaranteed by the Treaty.[274]

Secondly, the ECJ assessed whether or not the non-resident recipient (corporate) shareholder was in a comparable situation with a resident one and found that the key element, in this respect, was whether the non-resident shareholder was liable to tax in the source state concerned, taking into account *where necessary* the provisions of the DTC with the state of residence.[275] Specifically, in *Amurta* the ECJ accepted that a DTC with the state of residence, providing for the withholding tax in the source state to be offset by the state of residence, could be taken into account and allow the source state to avoid restrictions on the free movement of capital, subject to the condition that the DTC had been considered, by national courts, as part of the relevant legal background.[276]

In rulings related to two infringement procedures, the 2009 *Commission v Italy*[277] and the 2010 *Commission v Spain*[278] rulings, the ECJ specified that, for a DTC to

266 Case C–379/05, *Amurta* [2007] ECR I–9569.
267 Case C–303/07, *Aberdeen Property* [2009] ECR I–5145.
268 Case C–199/10, *Secilpar* [2010] ECR I–00154.
269 Joined Cases C–338/11 & C–347/11, *Santander* [2012] ECR I–0000.
270 For example, Case C–540/07, *Commission v Italy* [2009] ECR I–10983; Case C–478/08, *Commission v Spain*, [2010] ECR I–4843; Case C–284/09, *Commission v Germany* [2011] ECR I–09879.
271 Case C–282/07, *Truck Center* [2008] ECR I–10767.
272 Case C–374/04, *Test Claimant in Class IV of the ACT Group Litigation* [2006] ECR I–11673.
273 Case C–284/06, *Burda* [2008] ECR I–4571.
274 Case C–374/04, *Test Claimant in Class IV of the ACT Group Litigation* (n 272), para. 54; Case C–379/05, *Amurta* (n 266), para. 24; Case C–303/07, *Aberdeen Property* (n 267), para. 28.
275 Case C–265/04, *Bouanich* (n 264), paras. 51–55; Case C–374/04, *Test Claimant in Class IV of the ACT Group Litigation* (n 272), paras. 70–71.
276 Case C–379/05, *Amurta* (n 266), paras. 79 and 80; paras. 82 to 84.
277 Case C–540/07, *Commission v Italy* (n 270), para. 37.
278 Case C–478/08, *Commission v Spain* (n 270), para. 61.

compensate a different treatment in domestic laws and thus to ensure compliance with the free movement of capital, the DTC needs to ensure that the source state's withholding tax is fully credited in the contracting state of residence. By contrast, the tax treatment in its state of residence was regarded as irrelevant in itself, except for cases of application of the Parent–Subsidiary Directive where the obligation to eliminate economic double taxation is incumbent on this last state.[279] Apart from this last case, the ECJ consistently found that, once the source state, unilaterally or due to a DTC, taxes *both* resident shareholders *and* non-resident shareholders on dividends which they receive from a resident company, the position of non-resident shareholders becomes comparable to that of resident shareholders.[280]

It therefore focused on the position of non-resident *vs.* resident shareholders within the source state, by finding that it was only because of the exercise by that state of its taxing powers that, irrespective of any taxation in another Member State, economic double taxation would arise. After having being taxed through corporation tax on the resident distributing company, dividends would be subject to withholding tax in the hands of the non-resident recipient company. Consequently it ruled that, for non-resident companies receiving dividends not to be subject to a restriction on the free movement of capital, this state needed to ensure the elimination of economic double taxation to non-resident shareholder companies by applying them the same treatment as resident shareholder companies.[281]

The ECJ rejected justifications based on the need to safeguard the balanced allocation of taxing powers between the Member States, on the effectiveness of fiscal supervision and on the coherence of tax systems. Although it accepted that the need to safeguard the balanced allocation of taxing powers where the system in question is designed to prevent conduct capable of jeopardising the right of a Member State to exercise its taxing powers in relation to activities carried out in its territory,[282] the ECJ specified that this justification cannot hold valid when a Member State has chosen not to tax resident (corporate) shareholders in receipt of nationally sourced dividends.[283] It also rejected the effectiveness of fiscal supervision, which it regarded as unable to justify taxation affecting only non-residents[284]. Justifications based on coherence of the tax system were rejected due

---

279 Case C–284/06, *Burda* (n 273), paras. 88–92.
280 Case C–374/04, *Test Claimant in Class IV of the ACT Group Litigation* (n 272), para. 68; Case C–170/05, *Denkavit International* (n 265), para. 35; Case C–379/05, *Amurta* (n 266), para. 38; Case C–303/07, *Aberdeen Property* (n 267), paras. 43 and 54; Joined Cases C–338/11 & C–347/11, *Santander* (n 269), paras. 27, 28 and 42.
281 Case C–374/04, *Test Claimant in Class IV of the ACT Group Litigation* (n 272), para. 70; Case C–170/05, *Denkavit International* (n 265), para. 37; Case C–379/05, *Amurta* (n 266), para. 39; Case C–303/07, *Aberdeen Property* (n 267), para. 44.
282 Case C–379/05, *Amurta* (n 266), para. 58; Case C–303/07, *Aberdeen Property* (n 267), para. 66; Joined Cases C–338/11 & C–347/11, *Santander* (n 269), para. 47.
283 Case C–379/05, *Amurta* (n 266), para. 59; Case C–303/07, *Aberdeen Property* (n 267), para. 67; Joined Cases C–338/11 & C–347/11, *Santander* (n 269), para. 48.
284 Joined Cases C–338/11 & C–347/11, *Santander* (n 269), para. 49.

to the absence of a direct link between the exemption from withholding tax granted to resident shareholders and a consequent tax levied on them to compensate such exemption.[285]

A case in which the ECJ deviated from the conclusions reached as regards outbound cross-border dividends was the *Truck Center* ruling concerning outbound cross-border interest payments, where it found that imposing a withholding tax on these payments but exempting domestic interest payments did not breach EU law, on the grounds that resident and non-resident recipients were not in comparable situations. Here the ECJ noted that, when both the payer and the recipient were resident, the Member State concerned was not in the same position as in the case when only the payer was resident, and that this difference gave rise to two distinct charges resting on two different legal bases.[286]

This led the ECJ to find that both categories of taxpayers were taxed in respect of certain nationally-sourced income (such as interest) and that national law simply established different procedures for tax recovery, with only resident recipient companies being subject to the supervision of national tax authorities.[287] It thus explained the difference between *Truck Center* and the outbound dividends case on the ground that, in this last case, national provisions at issue did not simply set different taxing procedures, but provided that only non-residents were to be taxed on dividends.[288]

In other cases relating to outbound payments of interest, where thin capitalisation rules limiting the deductibility of interest payments to non-residents were at issue, such as the 2007 *Test Claimant in the Thin Cap Group Litigation* ruling[289] and in the 2013 *Italcar* ruling,[290] the ECJ based its comparability analysis on the situation of the taxpayers concerned and, when finding that a justification for the national measure existed, struck down that measure for failure to meet the proportionality test.[291]

If the rulings concerning outbound payments are considered together, it appears very difficult to reconcile the analysis of comparability of situations made in *Truck Center*, where the ECJ focused on the position of the Member State concerned with regard to resident and non-resident recipients, with that in other rulings where the ECJ focused on the position in which non-resident recipients, rather than the source state, found themselves. The *Truck Center* reasoning about the different position of this state when taxing residents and non-residents could apply *mutatis mutandis* to cases concerning cross-border outbound dividends, where, nevertheless, they were not made.

285 Case C-303/07, *Aberdeen Property* (n 267), para. 72; Joined Cases C-338/11 & C-347/11, *Santander* (n 269), paras. 51-53.
286 Case C-282/07, *Truck Center* (n 271), paras. 42 and 43.
287 Ibid., paras. 47-48.
288 Joined Cases C-338/11 & C-347/11, *Santander* (n 269), para. 43.
289 Case C-524/04, *Test Claimant in the Thin Cap Group Litigation* (n 129) see also 3.2 above.
290 Case C-282/12, *Italcar-Automóives de Aluguer Lda*, ruling of 3 October 2013.
291 For example, Case C-524/04, *Test Claimant in the Thin Cap Group Litigation* (n 129), paras. 82-83; Case C-282/12, *Italcar-Automóives de Aluguer Lda* (n 290), paras. 38-41.

In this respect, an inconsistency would thus appear to exist between *Truck Center* and the other rulings, to an even greater extent since, in cases where interest paid to residents and non-residents was not deductible if exceeding certain limits, the application of withholding tax only on payments to non-residents would in essence originate within the source state, only in respect of cross-border interests, that economic double taxation that the ECJ has been aiming at eliminating when the source states eliminate it for domestic dividends. Moreover, cases such as *Denkavit International* or *Amurta* could be regarded as concerning economic double taxation if following the 'single country' approach adopted by the ECJ in focusing on the source state, but could have been regarded as concerning juridical double taxation too if following a 'global approach' i.e. if considering that the withholding tax, when not (completely) offset in the shareholder's state of residence owing to a DTC, would cumulate with any possible taxation in this state.

From this perspective, in case of *outbound* cross-border dividends, the ECJ findings, by banning economic double taxation in the *source* state *when* this eliminates it for domestic dividends, has also, *in these cases only*, paradoxically contributed to overcoming exactly the juridical double taxation that was tolerated in *Damseaux* from the perspective of the state of residence and of inbound dividends.

3.4 An assessment of the case law against the benchmarks: which shortcomings?

3.4.1 *The complete elimination of double taxation and of unintended double non-taxation*

The Commission, in its Communication on double taxation in the internal market, stressed the failure to eliminate it and cited the *Kerckhaert and Morres*, *Block* and *Damseaux* rulings about juridical double taxation arising from parallel, non-discriminatory exercise of taxing powers, as opposed to those rulings where the ECJ disallowed economic double taxation and to other rulings, relating e.g. to anti-abuse clauses, where it stuck down national provisions giving preference to domestic situations in comparison with cross-border ones[292]. By reading together all the rulings indicated by the Commission, tensions and limitations can be found in the case law.

First, the emphasis that the ECJ placed in *Kerckhaert and Morres*, *Block* and *Damseaux* on the *responsibility* of Member States to eliminate juridical double taxation through DTCs can be read together with its findings, in rulings such as *Manninen*, *Amurta* or others concerning economic double taxation, that Member States must eliminate economic double taxation in cross-border situations *if* they do so in internal situations. The comparison between these ECJ positions impliedly shows that, on its own merit and irrespective of the effectiveness of DTCs, the elimination of juridical double taxation, as a Member States' responsibility, is

---

[292] Commission Communication COM(2011) 712 final, Double taxation in the single market (11 November 2011), at 5.

regarded as even more important than the elimination of economic double taxation, which latter is ultimately made dependent on Member States' *discretion* to pursue it in domestic situations.

Moreover, inbound dividends in the state of residence are outbound dividends in the source state and the ECJ accepted that this latter could fulfil the obligations to overcome economic double taxation through DTCs when these ensure a full offsetting of withholding taxes. Therefore, if in *Kerckhaert and Morres* or *Damseaux* the dividend recipient had challenged not the provisions of his state of residence, but those of the source state imposing the withholding tax, he could have managed to obtain the elimination of economic double taxation within the source state *if* this state eliminated it for domestic distributions and, as a consequence, to obtain the elimination of juridical double taxation too. From this perspective, the shortcomings towards the objective of eliminating juridical double taxation on recipients of cross-border income, arising from the parallel exercise of taxing powers, currently lies in the fact that – outside the directives *and* whenever DTCs fail to prevent this form of double taxation – the achievement of this goal is made incidentally dependent, on a case-by-case basis, upon the elimination of economic double taxation within the source state.

The same kind of shortcoming towards the elimination of juridical double taxation can also be noted in respect of capital gains arising out of companies' tax residence transfer from one Member State to another, to the extent that the ECJ, in *National Grid*, did not require the origin Member State, when levying exit tax, to offset decreases in values of the assets – and thus in decreases in the capital gains amount – occurring after the transfer, in the event of failure to do so by the destination state. The possibility of keeping the transferring company from being taxed twice on the same capital gains therefore depends, case-by-case, on the domestic law of the destination state.

In essence, the failure in eliminating juridical double taxation on both income and capital gains occurred whenever the ECJ adopted a *single-country approach* and stressed the lack of a general harmonising EU measure allocating the competence to eliminate juridical double taxation to either the state of residence or the source state.

Secondly, an inconsistency appears to emerge in the overall case law as regards the approach adopted for assessing taxpayers' situation and the greater or minor importance attached to the *effect* of the contested rules on the taxpayer's overall situation. This is because the ECJ, when ruling on the deductions for personal and family circumstances in the *Schumacker* case law or on the cross-border losses offsetting in the *Marks & Spencer* case law (ie, when adopting in such cases the 'always somewhere approach'), has been considering internal rules of all concerned Member States – as integrated with each other by DTCs – that were designed to generate an effect equivalent to eliminating juridical double taxation. It has therefore been following a *global approach* that was, ultimately, justified with the need to assess taxpayer's *overall ability-to-pay*, as clearly stated in *Lakebrink* and *Renneberg*.

In cases such as *Damseaux* there was not a differential treatment with the state of residence of the dividends recipient, unlike cases such as *Schumacker* or *Renneberg* where there was differential treatment of non-residents within the employment state. Nevertheless, the fact remains that, in *Schumacker* or *Renneberg*, the ECJ attributed, to DTCs and to the *combined* effect of the national rules of both concerned Member States on the taxpayer's overall situation, a decisive importance that, on the contrary, was not recognised in cases such as *Damseaux*. Therefore, cases when the ECJ *neglected* to make its assessment of the ability to pay (often owing to its adopting a single country approach and to its insisting on the lack of harmonising EU measures for eliminating juridical double taxation) contrast with those cases where it appears to have based its decisions exactly on this assessment for adopting a global approach (and requiring the Member States concerned to grant reliefs that they would not have granted on the basis of DTCs).

As recognised in the literature, the absence of legal bases in the Treaty, together with the ECJ's single country approach, has resulted in an occasional and inconsistent application of the ability-to-pay principle;[293] this limitation of the case law, ultimately, has resulted in a failure to completely overcome both double taxation and unintended double non-taxation.

In fact, the ECJ's case law shows the same shortcomings, when the ECJ adopted the *single country approach,* towards the objective of eliminating unintended double non-taxation as well. In this respect, the 2013 *Imfeld* ruling, where the ECJ admitted that a taxpayer may receive a double advantage owing to the parallel application of the two Member States' tax laws granting similar reliefs, appears to be symmetrical to *Kerckhaert and Morres* or to *Damseaux*. When the combined effect of the rules of two Member States concerned is not regarded as a decisive element in cross-border situations, taxpayers' overall ability to pay may either escape taxation twice (*Imfeld*) or be penalised by double taxation (*Kerckhaert and Morres* or *Damseaux*).

3.4.2 Administrative simplification and greater legal certainty

The ECJ's case law has certainly not been leading to administrative simplification for taxpayers when, in respect of inbound dividends, the ECJ has been recognising the burdensome indirect tax credit method as equivalent to the exemption method in *Test Claimant in the FII Group Litigation Order* and in *Haribo and Salinen*. Neither has it done so when, in the 2013 *A Oy* ruling, it specified that, when the deduction by the parent company of a non-resident subsidiary's losses must be allowed, the rules for calculating these losses must not constitute unequal treatment in respect of calculation rules applicable if the subsidiary were a resident one.[294] This requires the redetermination of a non-resident subsidiary's terminal losses according to the profit computation rules in force in the parent company's state of residence. An ECJ ruling which, conversely, resulted in administrative

---

293 F. Vanistendael, 'Ability to Pay in European Community Law', *EC Tax Review* 3, 2014, at 121–34.
294 Case C–123/11, *A Oy* (n 48), para. 61.

simplification was *Manninen*,[295] which induced several Member States to abolish imputation credit systems and to replace them with exemption systems for cross-border inbound dividends.

The achievement of greater legal certainty would appear to be ensured, in light of the overall case law, only in respect of specific points: (a) the neutrality between branches and subsidiaries in the host Member State; (b) the possibility of restricting the exercise of a fundamental freedom via national anti-abuse measures solely in the event of wholly artificial arrangements to be demonstrated on a case-by-case bases, perhaps except for transfer pricing rules (given the *SGI* decision); (c) the possibility for an origin state to levy exit taxes on transfers of tax residence but with deferred payment; (d) the 'always somewhere approach' as regards the deductibility of losses of subsidiaries resident (or of branches located) in other Member States and the granting of person-related deductions from income tax; (e) the deductibility of business expenses in the work state if inextricably linked to the activity carried on there; (f) the obligation for a source state to eliminate withholding tax for outbound cross-border dividends if no such tax is levied on domestic dividends; (g) the obligation for a residence state to eliminate economic double taxation of inbound dividends if eliminating economic double taxation of domestic dividends; (h) the cumulative requirements in order for a Member State to invoke the cohesion of the tax system as a justification for restrictive measures; (i) the impossibility, in principle, to invoke revenue losses on their own as a sufficient justification.

The methodology used by the ECJ can also be clearly deduced from the case law. As a first step, the ECJ assesses whether a national measure, in light of its effect for the concerned taxpayer and of the comparability between residents and non-residents or between domestic and cross-border situations, can constitute a (disguised) discrimination or (if discouraging anyway the exercise of a fundamental freedom) a restriction. If finding a discrimination or a restriction, as a second step the ECJ assesses whether the submitted justifications are acceptable, and eventually, if so, it assesses whether the measures at issue are proportionate to the objective to be achieved.

Nonetheless, in respect of this methodology, if different cases such as *Truck Center*, *Mertens* and *Schumacker* are taken together, uncertainty arises as to whether the ECJ can be expected, a priori, to assume a criteria of legal comparability based on jurisdictional differences (*Mertens*) or of factual comparability of situations, in presence of different legal situations between residents and non-residents (*Schumacker*), or even when it can be expected to compare the position of the state concerned with respect to these two categories of taxpayers (*Truck Center*) rather than the positions of the taxpayers themselves. Literature has actually been highlighting this kind of inconsistencies as between the different ECJ rulings.[296]

---

295 See 3.3 above.
296 M. Lang, 'Recent Case Law of the ECJ in Direct Taxation: Trends, Tensions, and Contradictions', 2009 *EC Tax Review* 3, 98–113, at 98–104.

Although the ECJ has often stated that the comparability or non-comparability between domestic and cross-border situations depends on the objective of the national provision at issue,[297] uncertainty a priori would not be minimised from the taxpayer's viewpoint, as the objective would be indicated, on a case-by-case basis, by the Member State concerned. Additionally, for a taxpayer having doubts as to whether a national provision contrasts with the freedom of establishment, the free movement of capital or the free movement of workers, it appears difficult to discern, from the overall case law, a clear and unequivocal pattern indicating when the ECJ can be expected to adopt the *single country approach* and when it can be expected to follow the *global approach*, despite the impact that the adoption of one approach or of another can have on the final ECJ decision.

A response based on the fundamental freedoms involved – e.g., single country approach in cases concerning the free movement of capital (eg, *Manninen*, *Denkavit*, *Amurta*, *Kerchaert and Morres* and *Damseaux*) and global approach in cases regarding the free movement of workers and the freedom of establishment (eg the *Schumacker* line of case law in *Mertens* and the *Marks & Spencer* case law stream) – is not convincing. In fact, apart from the realisation that in cases where both the free movement of capital and the freedom of establishment were at stake (eg *Test Claimant in Class IV of the ACT Group Litigation*) the ECJ appeared to adopt the global approach, the ECJ itself has repeatedly stated that Member States must exercise their competence consistently with EU law, by avoiding discriminations and unjustified restrictions, *whichever* fundamental freedom was involved.

Equally unconvincing was a response to the question of whether an outbound or an inbound exercise of the free movement rights is at stake *or* of whether the legislation within an individual Member State makes more disadvantageous treatments for non-residents or for cross-border situations, given that both approaches have been used in all such cases. Ultimately, it can thus be argued that, although the ECJ's case law has gone some way towards settling key principles, legal uncertainty still remains – a priori – on fundamental methodological matters such as the criteria for the comparability analysis and, in particular, the approach that the ECJ might be expected to adopt, which uncertainty sums up with the difficulty of reconciling some specific rulings with each other, as already highlighted in previous paragraphs.

3.4.3 The fight against cross-border tax evasion and fraud, against abusive practices and against aggressive tax planning

The Commission, in its Action Plan against cross-border tax evasion and fraud, as well as in its Recommendation against aggressive tax planning, acknowledged that these phenomenon, detrimental to the working of the internal market, are

---

297 For example, Case C–231/05, *Oy AA* (n 35), para. 38; Case C–337/08, *X Holding* (n 40), para. 22.

generated by mismatches between uncoordinated national direct taxation systems[298]. Consequently, an assessment of the case law against the objective of overcoming these distortions must be based on the extent to which the case law can either lead to a spontaneous convergence between national systems *or* maintain (or even increase) the differences between them.

Especially in the aftermath of a global economic crisis, the protection of the tax base and the safeguard of their revenues is a key concern of all Member States, which can achieve this objective *either* by tightening their domestic rules *or* by devising more favourable rules than other Member States to attract taxpayers and investments from other countries. Although the 'harmful tax competition' was politically banned by the Code of Good Conduct on Business Taxation, the 'fair tax competition' has been accepted[299] and even considered one of the principles of 'good tax governance'.[300]

The fair tax competition uses the normal elements of the tax systems – tax base and tax rate – in respect of which national provisions have been facing challenges before the ECJ. As the ECJ has been stating that a reduction of tax revenues is not in itself an acceptable justification for tax provisions restricting the outbound free movement to other Member States (eg *ICI* or *De Groot*)[301] or the inbound movement from other Member States (eg *St Gobain*),[302] a choice of protecting revenues by means of tighter tax rules (eg by denying deductions from the tax base or by increasing tax rates) ends up being not effective. On the contrary, the ECJ's position in *Cadbury Schweppes* – whereby a choice to exercise the outbound freedom of establishment could be driven by the more favourable tax regime of another Member State, provided an effective economic activity is carried out there[303] – guarantees those Member States choosing to protect their tax revenues by attracting new economic activities that this strategy will be an effective one.

The case law therefore ends up encouraging the 'fair' tax competition, which, in turn, contributes to creating those differences (between national taxation systems) providing the occasions for 'tax-shopping' strategies based on exploiting gaps and mismatches between national laws. This holds valid to a greater extent, the greater the differences between national systems left by uncoordinated reactions to the ECJ rulings on the part of national legislators. For example, as a response to the *National Grid* ruling concerning exit taxation, Member States which used to apply exit taxes (such as France, Italy, the Netherlands and the UK) have amended their national provisions by establishing different conditions for deferral of tax payment from one country to another. However, the recognition by the ECJ of

---

298 COM(2012) 722 final, An Action Plan to strengthen the fight against tax fraud and tax evasion, at 6; Commission Recommendation of 6 December 2012 on aggressive tax planning C(2012) 8806 final, at 2.
299 See ch 1 AT 1.1.
300 Commission Communication Promoting Good Governance in Tax Matters, COM(2009) 201 final, at 10–11.
301 Case C-264/98, *ICI* (n 21), para. 28; Case C-385/00, *De Groot* (n 171), para. 103.
302 Case C-307/97, *St Gobain* (n 14), para. 51.
303 Case C-196/04, *Cadbury Schweppes* (n 116), para. 75.

the origin state's entitlement to tax capital gains accruing during the concerned taxpayer's residence in its jurisdiction, has not incentivised Member States which did not apply exit taxes (eg, Hungary, Malta and Poland) to introduce them. Moreover, a test for excluding the existence of abusive practices which is based on objective elements ascertainable by third parties such as investments in premises, staff and equipment (as set out by the ECJ in *Cadbury Schweppes*) can indicate practices which are not abusive when these elements exist, but which are nonetheless 'aggressive' according to the Commission's recommendation against aggressive tax planning.

For example, a company could transfer both its registered office and its place of effective management, and therefore its tax residence, to another Member State offering a lower level of corporate taxation and invest there, even if all its market base remained in the origin Member State imposing a much higher effective corporate tax rate. This tax planning strategy, under the ECJ's case law, would not be deemed to be an abusive practice because the company would have a physical presence and an economic activity in the destination state, but could still be regarded as contrary to a 'reasonable commercial conduct', and as such, could be 'aggressive tax planning' under this Commission's Recommendation.[304]

Finally, because the ECJ, when adopting the 'single country approach', accepted that taxpayers could benefit of similar advantages in two Member States as a result of the parallel application of the two countries' tax laws granting similar reliefs (as stated in *Imfeld*), well advised taxpayers could also draw – from this case law and from the lack of coordination between national provisions – indications on how they could manage, a priori, to place themselves exactly in this situation.

Consequently, it could be argued that, overall, the ECJ's case law – through landmark rulings such as *Marks & Spencer* or *Cadbury Schweppes* – has been contributing *solely to identifying* the nature of distortions to be prevented such as double deductions, inter-group transfer of losses aimed at maximising their tax value and wholly artificial arrangements designed to circumventing the applicable national law. It has certainly *not* been helping the achievement of the objective of fighting distortive phenomenon that cause revenue losses to Member States and hinder the proper functioning of the internal market.

3.5 Final remarks in light of the benchmarks

All situations which have been examined by the ECJ ultimately arose because of the distinction made by all Member States between residents and non-residents (ie because of the tax residence at national level as main connecting factor for tax jurisdiction), and due to the well-settled framework of national tax rules and of DTCs based on this distinction. This occurred for: differential treatments of *resident* companies and of branches of *non-resident* companies; exit taxes arising from tax *residence* transfers; application of anti-abuse rules in situations involving *residents*

---

[304] Commission Recommendation COM(2012) 8806 final, cit., at 5.

of other Member States; differential treatments of *residents* and of *non-residents* workers; disadvantageous treatments of dividends *received* by residents from other jurisdictions etc.

This ECJ case law, from the viewpoint of the 'benchmarks', has been generating shortcomings. In addition to the impossibility to eliminate juridical double taxation arising from parallel, non-discriminatory exercise of taxing powers, there are difficulties of reconciliation between several rulings from the viewpoint of the *outcomes achieved* by the rulings, to the detriment of legal certainty. Moreover, a repeated rejection of the justification (for restrictive tax measure) that was based on the risk of revenue losses, has been offering Member States, at least to date, the certainty that the most effective strategy for protecting their tax base lies in competing with each other for attracting taxpayers and investments, i.e. in the 'fair tax competition' using the structural elements of their tax systems.

As noted in Chapter 2, the directives on direct taxation to date issued were also based on the 'tax residence' concept – as defined at national level – as a connecting factor between a taxpayer and a Member State. Accordingly, where – in situations of dual tax residence in two Member States – the tie-breaker rules of DTCs do not (easily) manage to solve tax residence conflicts between Member States, the application of the directives issued to date may be compromised and shows a clear limit. On the contrary, whenever tax residence can be unequivocally identified, the widely different taxation levels from one Member State to another, and the connection of tax residence with worldwide tax liability, turn the *national* tax residence into an element making it more convenient to be tax residents in a country rather than in another.

In turn, the inter-jurisdictional 'fair tax competition' has been multiplying the scope for aggressive tax planning strategies and for cross-border 'tax shopping' within the EU, leading exactly to those businesses practices which – even when not strictly falling within the concept of wholly artificial arrangements – have been regarded as damaging by the Commission in its recommendation against aggressive tax planning. It can also be added that arrangements mainly aimed at tax savings objectives by exploiting differences between national tax systems can exist even where, due to the way in which they are structured, their existence may be difficult to prove through a physical presence test as laid down by the ECJ.

Admittedly, the argument that the ECJ's case law has, simultaneously, left legal uncertainty and created scope for these arrangements, might be objected.

It was submitted that the ECJ's case law in the direct taxation area would become predictable, to the benefit of legal certainty, if a theoretical model for optimising the principles of tax sovereignty and free movement (ie of allowing these principles to coexist without hindering each other) were used as a conceptual framework for the analysis of the ECJ's case law.[305] This optimisation model would imply that a national tax measure restricting a fundamental freedom should be allowed only if meeting six cumulative requirements, and it would make it possible

---

305 S. Douma, *Optimization of Tax Sovereignty and Free Movement* (IBFD, 2011).

to structure and understand ECJ's case law as a coherent body of law as well as to predict its future developments.[306]

The six cumulative requirements are: leading to a tax disadvantage as a prima facie infringement of a free movement provision; having a respectful aim which would need to be unrelated to the restrictive effect of the tax measure; being suitable to achieve that aim; having a sufficient degree of fit in relation to the objectives; reflecting the most subsidiary means to achieve its aim and not going beyond what is strictly necessary to achieve the aim. Although this optimisation model could provide a proper conceptual framework within which most ECJ's case law could be fitted,[307] the consequent legal certainty would merely relate to the method of analysis and reasoning used by the ECJ and to the expected outcomes from the use of this method.

Nevertheless, what would be needed for the proper functioning of the internal market would be not only the predictability of results of the ECJ's rulings, *whatever* these results might be (ie predictability regardless of the achievement of the objectives set out by the Commission), but would be the certainty of completely eliminating double taxation, of reducing compliance costs, of having legal certainty about taxpayers' and Member States' positions and of reducing the scope for aggressive tax planning. In other words, the achievement of the objectives/benchmarks would require not merely understanding and structuring the ECJ's case law in such a manner that it is consistent with a framework but, rather, going beyond the findings of the ECJ's case law in all respects where its findings do not achieve the desired objectives.

Bibliography

G. Bizioli, 'Balancing the fundamental freedoms and Tax Sovereignty: Some Thoughts on Recent ECJ Case Law on Direct Taxation', 3 *European Taxation*, 2008, 133–40.

M. Cruz Barreiro Carril, 'Los Impuestos Directos y el Derecho de la Uniòn Europea. La armonizaciòn negativa realizada por el TJUE', *Instituto de Estudios Fiscales*, 2012.

T. O'Shea, The UK's CFC rules and the freedom of establishment: Cadbury Schweppes plc and its IFSC subsidiaries ± tax avoidance or tax mitigation? *EC Tax Review* 1, 13–33 (2007).

S. Douma, *Optimization of Tax Sovereignty and Free Movement*, IBFD, Amsterdam, 2011.

S. Eden, The Obstacles Faced by the European Court of Justice in Removing the 'Obstacles' Faced by Taxpayers: The Difficult Case of Double Taxation', *British Tax Review* 6, 2010, 610–28.

E. C. C. M. Kemmeren, '*Renneberg* Endangers the Double Tax Conventions System or Can a Second Round Bring Recovery?' 18 *EC Tax Review* 1, 2009, 4–15.

M. Lang, 'Die gemeinschaftsrechtlichen Rahmenbedingungen für "Exit Taxes" im Lichte der Schlussanträge von GA Kokott in der Rechtssache N.' in *Steuer und Wirtschaft International* 2006, 213–26.

---

306 Ibid., at 295–302.
307 Ibid.

M. Lang, 'Recent Case Law of the ECJ in Direct Taxation: Trends, Tensions, and Contradictions, 18 *EC Tax Review* 3, 2009, 98–113.

L. Leclercq and P. Tredaniel, 'Impact of ECJ's judgment in *Lidl Belgium* on the Deduction of Foreign Branches Losses in France', 63 *Bulletin for International Taxation* 5/6, 2009, 236–43.

G. T. K. Meussen, '*Renneberg*: ECJ Unjustifiably Expands *Schumacker* Doctrine to Losses from Financing of Personal Dwelling', 49 *European Taxation* 4, 2009, 185–88.

M. Quaghebeur, 'ECJ to Examine Belgian Treatment of Inbound Dividends', 37 *Tax Notes International*, 2005, 739–41.

P. Smet, H. Laloo, 'ECJ to Rule on Taxation of Inbound Dividends in Belgium', 45 *European Taxation* 4, 2005, 158–59.

B. J. M. Terra, P. J. Wattel, *European Tax Law* (Wolters Kluwer, 2012).

F. Vanistendael, 'Ability to Pay in European Community Law', *EC Tax Review* 3, 2014, 121–34.

J. Wouters, 'Fiscal Barriers to Companies' Cross-Border Establishment in the Case Law of the EC Court of Justice', *Yearbook of European Law* 14, 1994, 73–109.

PART II
Meeting the "benchmarks": a proposal for a new solution aimed at benefiting both the interest of taxpayers with cross-border economic links and Member States' revenues

4 Direct taxation and the proper functioning of the internal market

4.1 The CCCTB project versus the benchmarks

4.1.1 The salient features

The project for the introduction of a Common Consolidated Corporate Tax Base (CCCTB) for corporate groups operating within the EU, the most ambitious Commission proposal ever presented in the direct taxation area, resulted in a Draft Directive in March 2011[1] after nearly a decade since the first communication,[2] which considered it as the proper long-term strategy for overcoming company tax obstacles within the internal market. Under this proposal, multinationals having subsidiaries and PEs in different Member States could use an optional regime to determine the taxable base of all group units according to a new uniform set of rules. This tax base would then be consolidated by offsetting profits and losses of group members (and of their PEs) against each other and, after consolidation, it would be shared amongst the Member States concerned through an apportionment formula.

The CCCTB intends significantly to reduce the administrative burden, compliance costs and legal uncertainties that businesses in the EU currently face in complying with many different national systems for determining their taxable profits; furthermore, it is intended to eliminate international double taxation and definitively to ensure cross-border offsetting of losses. In fact, the proposal is based on the recognition that DTCs between Member States do not sufficiently tackle tax obstacles and that the existing EU legislation addresses only a small number of specific problems.[3] Consequently, it intends introducing a 'system allowing companies to treat the Union as a *single market* for the purpose of corporate tax',[4] i.e. as a domestic market without the obstacles created by the coexistence of many

---

1 Communication COM(2011) 121/3, Proposal for a Council Directive on the Common Consolidated Corporate Tax Base (CCCTB), 16 March 2011.
2 Communication COM(2001) 582, Towards an internal market without tax obstacles: a strategy for providing companies with a consolidated corporate tax base for their EU-wide activities.
3 Communication COM(2011) 121/3 (n 1), Preamble, Recitals (2) and (3).
4 Ibid., Recital (4).

different corporate tax systems. To create a (new and) autonomous system, the proposal deals with all key aspects which have been discussed both by an expert group set up by the Commission – the CCCTB Working Group (CCCTBWG) – and in academic literature, and which concern three salient features of the CCCTB: its coverage in terms of eligible companies; the administration of the system; the determination, the consolidation and the apportionment of the tax base.

With regard to the *coverage* of the proposed regime, the option could be exercised by companies from Member States – which have national legal forms listed in an Annex and which are subject to one of the applicable national corporate income taxes, listed in another Annex – and to companies from third countries with regard to their PEs within the EU. The option for the system, if exercised, would automatically include *all* qualifying subsidiaries in different Member States and *all* PEs within the EU, for at least five years. This option would have a twofold effect for companies belonging to a CCCTB group or for a single company opting for this regime in respect of all its PEs in other Member States: under Article 7, the companies concerned would no longer be subject to national corporate tax arrangements for all matters covered by the directive, unless otherwise stated; under Article 8, the rules concerning the CCCTB regime would override any provision to the contrary contained in DTCs between Member States.

The eligible companies mainly would be *public and private limited companies* resident in Member States, indicated in an exhaustive list, as well as companies resident in third countries having a similar form and which are indicated in a non-exhaustive list to be annually updated by the Commission. Article 5 gives a definition of PE applicable to all eligible companies, which definition mirrors in nearly identical terms the definition and the cases listed under Article 5 of the OECD Model and of DTCs based on it (as the CCCTBWG agreed to make use of the work carried out in the OECD framework[5]). Consequently, it is less favourable – for the state of location of a potential PE – than Article 5 of the UN Model, giving a broader definition of PE to the benefit of taxing rights of the source state. As a result, in the event of a DTC between a Member State and a third country based on the UN Model, there may be situations where a PE would exist under the DTC but not under Article 5 of the CCCTB Directive.[6]

In turn, companies are regarded as tax resident if they have registered office, place of incorporation or place of effective management in a Member State and are not dual residents under a DTC with a third country allocating tax residence to that country (Article 6(3)). In case of dual residence within the EU, tax residence for CCCTB purposes would be allocated to the country where the company has

---

5 Working document CCCTB/WP/046, Progress to date and future plans for the CCCTB (20 November 2006) at 6.

6 This could arise, for example, in situations of a building site or construction or installation project lasting more than six months or in the provision of services, including consultancy services, which would constitute a PE under Art. 3(a) and (b) of the UN Model, but not under Art. 5 of the OECD Model nor under Art. 5 of the CCCTB proposal.

its place of effective management, which is the same tie-breaker rule generally used by Article 4(3) of DTCs based on the OECD Model. Whereas an individual company resident in a Member State and having PEs in other Member States could always consolidate, a group member would be eligible for consolidation if, cumulatively: the parent company has, throughout the tax year, more than 50 per cent of voting rights and *either* more than 75 per cent of equity ownership *or* more than 75 per cent of rights giving entitlement to profit. Losing either of these thresholds would imply, for the company concerned, immediately leaving the group.

Subjective circumstances such as entry or exit of individual companies into a group opting for the CCCTB would extend the regime to the entering company or would discontinue it for the leaving company, but Articles 61 to 70 contain rules designed to prevent the taxing rights of Member States from being adversely affected. In fact, where a company enters the group, pre-consolidation trading losses would be offset against this company's apportioned tax base share, whereas, when a company leaves the group, no losses incurred during the consolidation period would be allocated to it; an adjustment would be made in respect of capital gains where certain assets are disposed within a short period after entry to or exit from a group.

The *administration* of the CCCTB would rely on a 'one-stop-shop' system and on a new *sharing* of information model.

The 'one-stop-shop' system would mean that, rather than dealing with 29 different national tax administrations, a group of companies opting for the CCCTB would need to deal only with a 'principal tax authority' (PTA), which would be the tax authority of the residence Member State of the ultimate parent company, i.e. of the 'principal taxpayer'. The 'principal taxpayer' would liaise with the PTA, on behalf of the entire group, for meeting all tax obligations arising from the option of the CCCTB. Specifically, a notice to opt should be addressed only to the PTA, which would also be the only tax authority in charge for receiving the group's consolidate tax returns, for issuing amended assessments and for coordinating the tax audits of a group member. Owing to this role of the PTA in terms of supervision of the administration of the scheme, the CCCTB proposal provides rules concerning the relationship between the PTA and other national tax authorities of residence Member States of group companies on the one hand, and the obligations arising from the scheme together with taxpayer's appeal possibilities on the other hand (Articles 104 to 126).

In the first respect, the tax authority of the residence Member State of a group member would be able to challenge a decision of the PTA concerning the notice to opt or an amended assessment before the courts of the Member State of PTA, where it would have at least the procedural rights as a taxpayer under the law of this country. Moreover, although tax audits would be initiated and coordinated by the PTA, the other national tax authorities may request the initiation of an audit.

As regards taxpayers' obligations and appeal possibilities, the proposal contains detailed rules about the contents of the notice to opt and of consolidated tax returns to be submitted by the principal taxpayer, who would also be allowed to appeal against a decision rejecting the notice to opt, a notice requesting the disclosure of documents and information, an amended assessment or an assessment on the failure to file a consolidated tax return. Dispute deriving from appeals against these assessments would be dealt with by an administrative body which is competent to hear appeals at first instance under the law of the state of residence of the PTA, but judicial appeals against decisions of the PTA would remain possible and be governed by the law of the Member State of the PTA.

The new system of sharing of information between national tax authorities, under Article 115, would work through a regularly updated central database to which all national tax authorities would have access. The PTA would need to file to this central database the consolidated tax returns together with all supporting documents, as well as all notices, documents and decisions issued towards the CCCTB group. This new sharing information system would create – only with regard to companies opting for the CCCTB – a far more effective mechanism than the automatic exchange of information set out by Article 8 of the Administrative Cooperation Directive, i.e. it would create for the first time within the EU, as regards direct taxation, a system of 'automatic administrative integration' in terms of *simultaneous access* to information.

The *determination*, the *consolidation* and the *apportionment* of the common tax base would be governed by autonomous rules. There would be no formal link between the new uniform tax base and the International Financial Reporting Standards (IFRS) governing the commercial accounting of publicly traded companies. Instead, the proposal, in Articles 9 to 43, contains extensive and detailed rules concerning positive and negative items of the taxable base, which it defines as less exempt revenues, deductible expenses and other deductible items (Article 10).

All these concepts are defined in the proposal, which also specifically indicates the non-deductible expenses and sets out the limits up to which certain cost items could be deducted. The proposal gives a very broad definition of the term 'revenues', by excluding from this concept only equity raised and debts paid, and in Article 11 lists specific categories of exempt revenues, amongst which inbound dividends without any shareholding quota requirement, proceeds from the sale of shares in companies outside the group, irrespective of the holding quota, and profits of extra-UE branches of group companies.

The CCCTB scheme would therefore use the exemption method for eliminating both juridical and economic international double taxation on *active income* of companies opting for this scheme, except for specific categories of income for which the tax credit method would apply. In fact, Article 73 of the proposal provides for a switch over to indirect tax credit method for inbound dividends or branch profits where the non-consolidated subsidiary or branch is subject in its state to a general tax regime at a rate lower than 40 per cent of the average statutory tax rate applicable in Member States or to a special low-tax regime. Moreover, under Article 76, interest, royalties and *any other* income taxed at source in a Member State or in a third country, received by a CCCTB group company, are included in the taxable base, with a deduction to offset withholding tax at source and thus to eliminate juridical double taxation. The apportionment formula used to share the tax base would also serve to share this deduction amongst group members located in different countries, which deduction would be calculated separately for each country and for each type of income.

In addition to these rules designed to eliminate double taxation either through exemption *or* indirect tax credit methods for income received by group companies from outside companies, the elimination of juridical double taxation on dividends, interest payments, royalties and any other transactions between group members would be ensured by Article 60, requiring the elimination of withholding tax or any other source taxation on these transactions. Payments of interest and royalties to recipients outside the CCCTB group could be subject to a withholding tax according to the applicable rules of the state of residence of the paying group member and any DTCs, which withholding tax would again be shared according to the apportionment formula.

The determination of the tax base would also be dependent upon the application of a general anti-abuse clause (GAAC) and of special anti-abuse rules (SAAR). With regard to the GAAC – addressing situations of possible abuse that were not foreseen when designing the SAAR – Article 80(1) states that artificial transactions carried out for the *sole* purpose of avoiding taxation must be ignored in determining the tax base. Article 80(2) specifies that this rule does not apply where the taxpayer carries out genuine economic activities and, in so doing, is able to choose between two or more transactions which generate different taxable income but lead to the same commercial results. Article 80(2), by permitting tax savings in cases of genuine economic activity, is wholly consistent with the ECJ's *Cadbury Schweppes* tax case law on abuse of rights in relation to the freedom of establishment.[7]

The concept of 'genuine economic activities' – which is omitted by Article 80 – could thus be extrapolated from this ECJ ruling and could be seen as referring to activities contributing to the *effective economic integration* of any subsidiary or PE (of a group opting for the CCCTB) in its host Member State. However, in targeting transactions carried out for the *sole* purpose of avoiding taxation, this GAAC would make it *more difficult* to find abuse than the anti-abuse clauses of the Merger Directive and of the Parent–Subsidiary Directive, which require this purpose to be 'principal' or 'essential'[8] (under the Merger Directive's related ECJ case law, it is also sufficient that tax savings reasons are the *predominant* ones[9]).

A choice to have a GAAC requiring the '*sole* purpose of avoiding taxation' could be justified since the very nature of the CCCTB – thanks to the consolidation and the subsequent apportionment – would remove, for transactions within the EU between CCCBT group entities, the risk of operations *mainly* aimed at maximising

---

7 Case C–196/04, *Cadbury Schweppes* [2006] ECR I–7995, para. 37.
8 Directive 2009/133, Art. 15(a), reproducing Art. 11(1)(a) of the original Directive 434/90; Directive 2011/96, Art. 1(2). See ch 2, at 2.2.1 and 2.2.3.
9 Case C–126/10, *Foggia* [2011] ECR I–10983, paras. 46 and 47.

tax savings. Owing to the elimination of intra-group transactions through the consolidation process, dealt with by Article 59, the GAAC should not apply to operations between entities which are part of the CCCTB group, but to operations between the CCCTB group entities and Member State companies or other entities that would not be part of the group. These operations could, to a greater or lesser extent, contribute to the effective economic integration of group units in their host Member States, unless they were carried out *solely* to achieve tax savings.

The SAAR, laid down by Article 81 and Article 82 of the proposal, seem to be aimed at protecting the consolidated tax base from erosion deriving from operations with third countries. In fact, Article 81 excludes the deduction of interest payments to an associated creditor resident in a third state with which there is no exchange of information on request comparable to that under the Administrative Cooperation Directive, where *either* the third country's corporate tax rate is lower than 40 per cent of the average statutory tax rate applicable in Member States *or* the associated creditor is subject to a special low-tax regime.

Article 82 sets out a CFC rule, which would include, in the consolidated tax base, the non-distributed income of a third country entity meeting four cumulative conditions: namely *being* controlled by a group member for more than 50 per cent; *being* subject to a general tax rate lower than 40 per cent of the average statutory tax rate applicable in Member States or to a special low-tax regime; *receiving* specifically listed types of mobile, passive and investment income[10] for more than 30 per cent of its overall income; and *not being quoted* on a recognised stock exchange. This CFC rule would not grant a credit for the corporation tax actually paid by the controlled entity in the third low-tax country, and would thus appear to create economic double taxation as a 'penalty' for investing in the third country (as an exception to the general elimination of both juridical and economic double taxation underlying other CCCTB proposed rules).[11]

Finally, the determination of the consolidated tax base would not be affected by reorganisations within the CCCTB group, such as mergers, divisions, seat transfers etc ... which, under Article 70(1), would not lead to the taxation of unrealised capital gains. Nonetheless, to protect the taxing right of the state of residence of the transferring company in the event of a relocation of (nearly) all its assets that would affect the outcome of the apportionment formula, these assets would still be attributed to the assets factor of this company in the five years following the transfer, *or* a fictitious branch would be deemed to still exist in this state if the company no longer existed or no longer had a PE there.

The proposal also establishes the consolidation methodology and an apportionment according to a three factors formula, based on labour, assets and sales. Under Article 59, consolidation would imply eliminating intra-group transactions, which transactions would need to be recorded through 'a consistent and adequate method' enabling all intra-group transfers and sales to be identified at the lower of costs and value for tax purposes. Article 59(3) specifies that groups could change

---

10 See Art. 82(3) of the proposal.
11 B. J. M. Terra, P. J. Wattel, *European Tax Law*, 6th edn (Wolters Kluwer, 2012), at 810.

this method only for valid commercial reasons at the beginning of a tax year; this provision would serve as an anti-abuse clause for transactions within the group, to prevent artificial changes of the method for mere tax savings reasons.

Article 59 literally refers only to transactions *within* consolidated groups, but – since the CCCTB system could be chosen not only by groups but also by a single company wishing to consolidate its profits with profits and losses of its PEs in other Member States – it should be applicable by analogy to transactions between a parent company and its PEs in other Member States. The consolidation, in addition to determining the automatic offsetting between profits and losses of group units in different countries, would also eliminate the risk of transfer pricing disputes and the related risk of economic double taxation. Indeed, transfer pricing rules would continue to apply only to the relationships between a CCCTB group member and an associated company *outside* the group, which would continue to be based on the arm's length principle. Under Article 79, these transactions could thus still give rise to upward profit adjustments by the tax authority for the group member concerned.

The apportionment of the consolidated tax base would be governed by detailed rules, laid down by Articles 86 to 103. Under Article 86(2) the consolidated taxable base would be apportioned only if positive, not if consisting of a loss; the loss would be carried forward and offset against the consolidated base of a subsequent tax year (Article 57(2)). In the apportionment formula, the three factors, i.e., labour, assets and turnover, would be equally weighted; the Commission regarded the three factors and their weightings as capable of ensuring that profits are taxed where they are earned.[12] The labour factor would consider both workforce payroll and employees number; these two factors would be equally weighted. The asset factor would exclude intangibles, financial assets and inventory; the turnover factor would be composed of sales by destination. The exclusion of intangibles from the assets factor was motivated by a concern to prevent risks of manipulations of the formula, in light of the stated difficulty to value (especially self-created) intangibles[13] and of the risk that intangibles, as a kind of very mobile assets, could be used to shift part of the asset factor from one jurisdiction to another.

A further objective of the apportionment formula would be to reflect the business activity of any group member: under Article 87, the principal taxpayer or the tax authority of the residence country of a group member could request an alternative method of apportionment if either of them believed that the outcome of the apportionment failed to reflect fairly the extent of the business activity of the group member, and this alternative method would be used if all tax authorities agreed on adopting it. After the sharing between group members of the consolidated tax base according to the apportionment formula, each state of residence of a CCCTB group company and its state of location of a PE would subject its apportioned share of the tax base to its national corporate income tax rate.

---

12 Special provisions (Arts. 98 to 101) would apply to companies of particular sectors.
13 CCCTB/WP060, para. 33.

4.1.2 The crucial issues and the CCCTB proposal against the benchmarks

If assessed against each of the benchmarks, the CCCTB proposal would mark a decisive step towards their achievement in some of its features, whereas it still shows pitfalls in other respects. In this assessment it would be necessary, however, to consider that the proposal might end up being implemented, through the enhanced cooperation procedure set out by Article 20 TEU and Articles 326 to 334 TFEU, only by a group of Member States and that, therefore, it may create a divide within the EU between participating and non-participating Member States.

4.1.2.1 The complete elimination of double taxation, of discriminations and of unintended double non-taxation

In addition to the automatic cross-border compensation between profits and losses of CCCTB group members within the EU, the consolidation and apportionment process would effectively manage, with regard to *intra-group* transactions, to eliminate juridical and economic double taxation. This is because a single formula for apportionment of the consolidated tax base amongst the Member States where the group operates would avoid tax on the same profit in more than one Member State[14] either in the hands of the same company (juridical double taxation) or in the hands of two different companies (economic double taxation).

In respect of intra-group transactions, elimination of juridical double taxation would also derive from the abolition of withholding taxes between group members as set out for consolidation purposes. Economic double taxation would be avoided for intra-group profits distributions *due to* application of the exemption method and to every elimination of intra-group operations in the consolidation (which would avoid transfer pricing adjustments). This would hold true, at least, if interpreting Article 59 (which refers to the elimination of intra-group transactions) as meaning that *all* profits and losses arising from *all* intra-group transactions would be ignored, including therefore transactions in intangibles i.e. in assets excluded from the assets factor of the apportionment formula. The elimination of economic double taxation would also derive, in cases of application of the switch-over clause to inbound dividends from lower-tax countries, from the indirect tax credit method. Obviously, the CCCTB, by its very consolidation and formula-based apportionment process, would also eliminate the risk of (covert) discrimination of branches of non-resident companies included in the CCCTB group.

Juridical double taxation, for dividends received by a corporate shareholder, would also be eliminated in potential situations of parallel, non-discriminatory exercise of taxing powers, where, up to date, the ECJ's case law has been unable to remove juridical double taxation owing to the absence of a general EU

---

14 J. Schwarz, 'Double Taxation in the European Single Market', 66 *Bulletin for International Taxation* 6, 295–99 (2012).

Direct taxation within the internal market 163

harmonising measure allocating the necessary competence between Member States.[15] Although this case law dealt with the treatment of inbound cross-border dividends in the hands of individual shareholders in their states of residence, the ECJ's reasoning would have been the same had the national provisions affected corporate shareholders. The CCCTB scheme would fully play the role of a general EU harmonising measure, for all groups opting for it in all participating Member States, and therefore would go *beyond* the current ECJ case law.

On the other hand, within the groups concerned, the CCCTB would also lead to the elimination of the risk of unintended double non-taxation. In fact, this risk derives from uncoordinated choices by Member States when freely defining their own tax bases and applying the DTCs, but the adhesion to *uniform* rules on the tax base would imply, for Member States, giving up exactly this freedom towards eligible groups opting for the adoption of the scheme.

Nevertheless, because the complete elimination of juridical and economic double taxation, just as other objectives set out by the Commission, should be achieved throughout the EU and for all taxpayers, the Commission recognised a limitation of the CCCTB because the scheme, owing to the fact that it was optional, would not overcome all double taxation cases.[16]

The scheme would also be irrelevant for participation in entities that do not qualify for inclusion. Finally, the possible implementation of the CCCTB by only some of the Member States through enhanced cooperation would imply that the risk of (juridical and economic) double taxation could still arise with regard to transactions between members of a CCCTB group resident in a participating state and affiliated companies resident in non-participating Member States. This is because, for these operations, the only legal instruments to overcome double taxation would continue to be the current DTCs between Member States, the directives issued to date as implemented by Member States and the national provisions, however amended in response to ECJ rulings.

4.1.2.2 *Administrative simplification and greater legal certainty*

From the viewpoint of multinational companies dealing with tax authorities, the proposal would certainly allow administrative simplification under the one-stop-shop regime and a reduction in compliance-related costs. The Commission, in light of survey evidence, stressed that implementation of the CCCTB would generate a 7 per cent reduction in costs for recurring corporate tax related tasks, and that tax related expenditure to open a new subsidiary would be reduced by 62 per cent for a large company and by 67 per cent for a medium-sized company.[17] Further estimates indicated overall costs savings for businesses to be around €3 billion, of which €1.3 billion would be derived from automatic full cross-border loss relief, €1 billion from lower costs for cross-border expansion within

---

15 See ch 3.
16 Communication COM(2011) 712 final, Double taxation in the single market (11 November 2011), at para. 4.
17 COM(2011) 121/4, Explanatory Memorandum, at 5.

the EU and €700 million from the one-stop-shop approach and to new uniform rules on the tax base.[18]

As these cost reductions would be achieved despite the remaining administrative compliance tasks concerning infra-group transactions (given by the need under Article 59 to accurately document and record infra-group transactions and to demonstrate that any change in the recording method would be for genuine commercial reasons), the CCCTB proposal can be positively assessed against the benchmark of administrative simplification and reduction in tax compliance costs. This would hold true even if the scheme were introduced by way of enhanced cooperation, because these objectives, although not achieved throughout the EU in this case, would at least be attained for CCCTB groups in participating Member States. In any case, administrative simplification for the entire group would be secured if the residence Member State of the parent company (whose tax authority would need to receive the notice to opt for the scheme) could readily be identified, and any tax residence conflicts concerning the parent company could easily be resolved.[19]

As regards legal certainty, however, the current version of the proposal would raise interpretative issues in a number of provisions. For example, the choice to indicate a non-exhaustive list of company forms for eligible extra-EU companies (in respect of their subsidiaries and PEs within the EU) certainly eliminates the problem of identifying which non-EU entities would fall under the personal scope of the CCCTB based on a necessarily general 'similarity' test with Member States entities.[20] Nonetheless, it could give rise to uncertainty as to whether a third country company having a legal form not (yet) included in the list of similar forms would have to *wait* for the inclusion of its form in the list in order to be able to opt for the scheme. If so, the effect of the list would be the same as that of a *periodically updated exhaustive* list, in contrast with the definition of 'non-exhaustive' list. If not, companies resident in third countries would be placed in a better position, with regard to the eligibility form requirements, than companies within the EU. In this respect, it appears uncertain whether companies from non-participating Member States, in case of adoption of the CCCTB proposal by enhanced cooperation, would be on the same footing as companies from extra-EU countries.

Furthermore, because the proposed CCCTB Directive would override any contrasting provisions of DTCs between (participating) Member States, but not DTCs with third countries, uncertainty arises as to whether or not a PE to be included in the consolidation area would exist in cases where the PE definition of a UN Model-based DTC, entered into with a third country, were wider than the definition given in Article 5 of the proposal. The fact that DTCs with third countries would not be overridden suggests that their own definition of PE would prevail, and thus that a PE would exist. Nevertheless, this interpretation would

---

18 Terra and Wattel, *European Tax Law* (n 11), at 800.
19 As subsequently argued in the text, this may not always be the case.
20 C. Staringer, 'Requirements for Forming a Group' in M. Lang, P. Pistone, J. Schuch and C. Staringer (eds), *Common Consolidated Corporate Tax Base* (Linde, Vienna, 2008), at 123.

seem to contrast with the wording of Article 5 as, in referring to a 'taxpayer'– i.e. to all companies eligible to opt for the scheme – this provision appears to indicate that its definition of PE applies to both Member State companies and third countries companies. The literature argued that Member States, as a matter of policy, should renegotiate DTCs with third countries, preferably in cooperation with each other, in order to align existing PE definitions in DTCs with the PE concept in the CCCTB proposal[21] but, until such a renegotiation occurred, legal uncertainty would remain.

Further shortcomings of the current version of the proposal, from the viewpoint of legal certainty, can be found in specific provisions concerning the taxable base and the administration of the scheme. With regard to the taxable base, the proposal – in terms of clarity, simplicity of application and competitive rules (in comparison with several national tax regimes) – shows attractive features in the provisions concerning tax accounting. It sets favourable depreciation rules, full deductions for strategic costs such as research and developments, a participation exemption regime without the minimum requirements allowed by the Parent–Subsidiary Directive, and tax neutrality for all business reorganisations between group members, not only for the operations falling within the Merger Directive.

Nonetheless, uncertainty arises in relation to the potential cases of application of the switch-over clause from the exemption to the indirect tax credit method and of the SAARs. In fact, because the draft CCCTB Directive was proposed by the Commission on the (probably unrealistic) assumption that all Member States would participate and does not define 'third countries', at least two questions arise and are currently unanswered: *whether* the switch over clause and the SAARs would be applicable to non-participating Member States as well, and *whether* the average corporate tax rate within the EU – to be used for identifying low-tax third countries – would be determined by excluding non-participating Member States. The same uncertainty inevitably arises, again due to the lack of definition of 'third countries', as regards the exclusion or inclusion, within the consolidation area of companies resident in CCCTB-participating Member States, of PEs in non-participating Member States.[22]

The interpretation whereby the GAAC of Article 80 would apply to operations with non-CCCTB entities in Member States and would extend to operations with third countries and non-participating Member States entities *only if* the SAAR were unsuitable to the operations at stake,[23] does not appear to be necessarily accepted. In fact, according to literature, the circumstance that the GAAC would be 'supplemented by measures designed to curb specific types of abusive practices',[24]

---

21 C. Staringer, 'Requirements for Forming a Group' (n 20), at 125; E. C. C. M. Kemmeren, 'CCCTB and Exemption Method for PEs and major shareholdings' in M. Lang, P. Pistone, J. Schuch and C. Staringer (eds), *Common Consolidated Corporate Tax Base* (Linde, Vienna, 2008), at 657.
22 C. H. J. I. Panayi, *European Union Corporate Tax Law* (CUP 2013), at 103–104.
23 See previous paragraph.
24 COM(2011) 121/4 (n 17), Preamble, Recital (20).

would not express a hierarchy between GAAC and SAAR, so that tax authorities may be tempted at their discretion to use the GAAC due to its being more general and vague than the SAAR.[25]

Under another interpretation, the GAAC, by using the term 'artificial transactions' rather than 'wholly artificial arrangements' as in the ECJ's case law, and by requiring the 'sole' rather than the 'predominant' tax-savings objective, would narrow down the ECJ's case law unnecessarily.[26] If this interpretation were accepted, uncertainty would even arise as to whether operations involving a CCCTB group member and a non-participating Member State would need to have *sole* (under the GAAC) or *predominant* tax saving purpose (under the ECJ's case law) to be regarded as abusive. This may adversely affect the fight against abusive practices, as subsequently indicated.[27]

Another problematic issue is the apportionment of the consolidated tax base between group members, and it appears to arise with regard to the safeguard clause (Article 87) allowing the application of an alternative sharing method. In the CCCTBWG intention, this clause would be applied only in very exceptional cases and should not mean re-introducing separate accounting and arm's length pricing to apportion the tax base.[28] However, its literal wording ('... *a* group member ... the extent of the business activity of *that* group member ...') could be interpreted as meaning *either* that the apportionment formula could be changed for the *entire* group if it failed to represent fairly the business activity of *a* group member *or* that it should be changed only for that group member if it worked properly for other group members. In the latter case, it would be unclear how the use of an alternative method for *a* group member could coexist with the use of the apportionment formula for *other* group members. It is also uncertain as to whether the alternative method, once chosen, would need to be used for *all the duration* of the option for the scheme and of the inclusion of the group member at stake. A negative answer would appear to be necessary if, after a given number of years, changes in the business activity of the group member concerned no longer justified the alternative method, but in this situation the unanswered issue would be which rules and procedures would apply for the shifting back from the alternative method to the apportionment formula laid down by Article 86.

With regard to the administration of the scheme, a first ground for uncertainty arises, for parent companies having dual tax residence in two CCCTB participating Member States under national laws, in case of impossibility of precisely locating the place of effective management in one country or in another. This may occur, for example, owing to the use of electronic communications between directors in

---

25 Panayi, *European Union Corporate Tax Law* (n 22), at 103–104.
26 Terra and Wattel, *European Tax Law* (n 11), at 809; also M. Lang, 'The General Anti-Abuse of Article 80 of the Draft Proposal for a Council Directive on a Common Consolidated Corporate Tax Base', 51 *European Taxation* 6, at 223–28 (2011).
27 See 4.1.2.3 below.
28 CCCTB/WP/060, CCCTB: possible elements of the sharing mechanism (Brussels, 13 November 2007), at 17.

different countries for taking managerial decisions. Indeed, the risk of difficulty in locating the place of effective management in a global, computerised economy was acknowledged even by the OECD.[29]

The proposal leaves completely unclear whether, in the event of unresolved tax residence conflict concerning the parent company, the notice to opt could be submitted to the tax authorities of both Member States concerned and they should decide by mutual agreement which one would act as a PTA, *or* whether the group would simply be unable to opt for the scheme. In fact, as the proposal would override conflicting provisions of DTCs between (CCCTB participating) Member States, it is also unclear whether the two tax authorities should make their best efforts to reach agreement as required by the OECD Model or even resort to arbitration.

Uncertainty for taxpayers could also arise from at least another provision, concerning the possibility of asking an advance ruling. As under Article 119(1) a company could request an advance ruling of its state of residence tax authority on the implementation of the scheme to specific transaction(s) to be carried out, but could also act according to its own interpretation if disagreeing with the opinion of the tax authority; it is unclear what would be the consequences for a company not acting in conformity with the tax authority opinion. If the company incurred a greater risk of being subject to tax audits, of being issued amended assessments and of having to initiate litigation, the very purpose of requiring an opinion to the tax authority (ie to increase, rather than to reduce, legal certainty) would indeed be jeopardised.

Furthermore, because the opinion of the tax authority would be binding on it unless the courts of the Member State of the PTA subsequently decided otherwise in case of litigation between the tax authorities, there would be the risk of a court's ruling diverging from the opinion given to the taxpayer, i.e. the company would risk acting in accordance with a potentially wrong opinion. If, under the national law of the tax authority giving the opinion in the specific case, a ruling on aspects of the national tax system were *unconditionally* binding on the tax authority (at least for some years), the CCCTB's 'advance ruling' system would therefore risk offering taxpayers *less* legal certainty than the national advance ruling system.

Moreover, because a complaining tax authority may have, before the courts of the PTA Member State, the same procedural rights as a taxpayer of that state, despite wide differences in taxpayer's procedural rights from one Member State to another, tensions could arise as between the PTA and other tax authorities.

Overall, the current version of the CCCTB proposal, in a number of important aspects concerning the application of the scheme, would therefore not achieve legal certainty.

---

29 OECD, 'The Impact of the Communication Revolution on the Application of the "Place of Effective Management" as a Tie-breaker Rule' (discussion paper), 2001, at 11–12.

4.1.2.3 *The fight against cross-border tax evasion and fraud, against abusive practices and against aggressive tax planning*

The proposal would certainly be able to contribute to the fight against cross-border tax evasion and fraud – with respect to the taxpayers opting for the scheme and in the interest of participating Member States – more than the current Administrative Cooperation Directive. In comparison with the bilateral annual automatic exchange of information on specific categories of income under Article 8 of that directive, the CCCTB system of (multilateral) information sharing,[30] which would cover the entire tax base of all CCCTB taxpayers, would make it much easier, for the tax authority of any Member State concerned, to quickly detect potential situations signalling a tax evasion risk and to require (or to initiate, should the risk be discovered by the PTA) tax audits accordingly.

However, the assessment would seem to be more difficult about the CCCTB's ability of contributing to the fight against abusive practices and other aggressive tax planning strategies including any techniques that would not fall within reasonable commercial conduct.[31] The Commission stated that the CCCTB would imply fewer opportunities for tax planning by companies using transfer pricing or mismatches in Member States' systems, and it emphasised that this positive effect would compensate the double work involved for national tax authorities in having to manage both their national corporate tax base determination systems and the CCCTB.[32] This prediction about fewer tax planning opportunities was based on rules for determination of the taxable base, for consolidation and for apportionment and would be well grounded, from this viewpoint, because these rules would eliminate, *within* CCCTB groups, the scope for implementing those tax planning strategies and those abusive practices that were regarded as distortions by the ECJ.[33]

Specifically, the double use of the same losses, the artificial transfers of losses to other jurisdictions for maximising the tax savings or the creation of subsidiaries without a genuine economic integration in the host country would be avoided within these groups (on the assumption that the CCCTB would prove more attractive than national regimes). The Commission's choice to exclude highly mobile assets – such as intangibles and financial assets – from the asset factor of the apportionment formula would also help preventing artificial assets transfers for tax savings reasons. Nonetheless, procedural rules could still result in forum-shopping strategies: the Dutch Government noted that the one-stop-shop approach (due to its relying on administrative supervision of the scheme by a national tax authority) could solicit relocation of the principal taxpayer to a jurisdiction with low fines, lenient terms of payment and lax supervision.[34]

---

30 See 4.1 above.
31 According to the Commission's Recommendation against aggressive tax planning, COM(2012) 8806 final, para. 4.4, at 5.
32 COM(2011) 121/4 (n 17), Explanatory Memorandum, at 6.
33 See ch 3.
34 Terra and Wattel, *European Tax Law* (n 11), at 802.

Furthermore, the prediction that the CCCTB would mean fewer tax planning opportunities apparently did not consider that the application of different national corporate tax rates to a uniformly determined tax base would make it even easier (than in the current context), for multinational groups tax managers, to calculate the difference in the effective tax rate from one CCCTB jurisdiction to another. It would thus become possible to estimate, for a group having the higher profit-making subsidiaries in high tax countries, whether an option for the CCCTB would be more or less beneficial, in terms of overall group liability, than a tax planning strategy simply consisting of moving the tax residence of those group companies to the countries setting lower corporate tax rates.

The prediction about fewer tax planning opportunities also relied on the (probably unrealistic) assumption that all Member States would adhere to the CCCTB. Accordingly, in case of implementation by enhanced cooperation, groups having affiliated both in CCCTB participating countries and in non-CCCTB Member States could implement tax arbitrage between participating and non-participating Member States: whether this would occur would depend on the interpretation of the CCCTB anti-avoidance provisions. If the GAAC is interpreted as narrowing down the ECJ case law on abusive practices, this GAAC would even risk soliciting arrangements that could have tax avoidance as a main objective but could be rigged out with some ancillary and peripheral business objectives to escape the GAAC.[35]

For example, if a company resident in a non-CCCTB participating Member State created subsidiaries and branches in CCCTB countries mainly in pursuance of group's tax savings strategies, and the economic activity carried out by these subsidiaries and branches were marginal in comparison with the tax savings, this company would still be able to opt for the CCCTB with respect to its branches and subsidiaries in the participating states. In this case, a possible application of national anti-abuse measure by this company's state of residence (on grounds of *predominance* of the tax saving objective), under the ECJ's case law, aimed at targeting operations between this company and its CCCTB-area affiliated, would arguably contrast with the fact that these operations would not fall under the GAAC of Article 80 due to the tax savings objective *not being the sole* one.

Application of the national anti-abuse rules by this state, even if possible under the ECJ's case law and on the basis of the Commission's recommendation against aggressive tax planning, would thus run contrary to the goal of the CCCTB scheme. As non-participating Member States would have a duty of non-impediment[36] of the scheme introduced through enhanced cooperation, it would appear unlikely that the national anti-abuse rules could still be applied if discouraging the option for the CCCTB with respect to subsidiaries and branches in the participating Member States: ultimately, the GAAC of the CCCTB scheme could risk hindering an otherwise possible application of national anti-abuse rules.

---

35 Ibid., at 809.
36 Panayi, *European Union Corporate Tax Law* (n 22), at 83.

On the whole, it could thus be argued that the current version of the CCCTB proposal, owing to the possibility of soliciting procedural forum-shopping and in a realistic possibility of implementation by only some Member States, risks *not* managing effectively to contribute to the fight against tax evasion, aggressive tax planning and abusive practices within the EU as a whole.

4.2 The other proposed initiatives: overview

The Commission, in its soft-law pieces where it highlighted the objectives yet to be achieved and that have been taken as benchmarks in the previous analysis, put forward suggestions for future initiatives aimed at achieving these objectives. For example, in the Communication on 'Removing cross-border tax obstacles for EU citizens',[37] the Commission proposed specific solutions, such as: setting up a central one-stop-shop in tax administrations where mobile workers and investors could both obtain all relevant information and directly pay taxes and receive all the necessary certificates for their home countries' tax authorities; facilitating cross-border tax compliance by seeking greater alignment of tax claims and declaration forms; encouraging Member States to adopt special rules for frontier workers and mobile workers to take into consideration tax and social security systems in different Member States.[38]

In the communication against double taxation in the internal market,[39] the Commission, after stressing the efforts already made for overcoming double taxation[40] through the adopted directives, the Arbitration Convention and soft-law pieces such as a code of conduct for the effective implementation of the Arbitration Convention, and a recommendation on withholding tax relief procedure,[41] highlighted the inadequacy of DTCs to remove double taxation and proposed a set of specific actions: completing the network of DTCs and extending their coverage to both entities and taxes not yet covered; extending the scope of DTCs to triangular situations within the EU; ensuring a more consistent interpretation of the same concepts contained in DTCs as between Member States – i.e. of concepts such as tax residence, PEs, business income, dividends, cross-border workers etc – by overcoming different national interpretations of these concepts; considering the elaboration of a code of conduct on double taxation; improving the working of the Arbitration Convention on transfer pricing by shortening the length of MAPs; easing and accelerating dispute resolution in all areas of direct taxation within the EU (eg through the introduction in all DTCs of a binding arbitration clause such as has been allowed since 2008 by the OECD Model).[42]

---

37 Communication COM(2010) 769 final, Removing cross-border tax obstacles for EU citizens.
38 Ibid., at 7–8.
39 Communication COM(2011) 712 final (n 16).
40 Ibid., 8.
41 Recommendation C/2009/7924 on withholding tax relief procedures (19 October 2009).
42 COM(2011) 712 final (n 16) at pp. 9–11.

Other initiatives were proposed in the 2012 Communication on the fight against tax fraud and tax evasion, including in relation to third countries:[43]

- preventing tax evasion by closing existing loopholes in the Savings Directive[44]
- enhancing the use of automatic exchange of information by developing new formats for income covered by the Administrative Cooperation Directive
- using a European Tax Identification Number (TIN) for all taxpayers engaged in cross-border activity and giving Member States' tax administrations direct access to relevant areas of each other's national databases
- developing and sharing tools, systems and working methods to identify trends and schemes involving tax fraud and tax evasion
- tackling aggressive tax planning via access to information on money flows, making it easier to trace significant payments made through offshore bank accounts, and through the creation, within the EU, of teams of auditors dedicated to cross-border tax fraud as well as through the promotion of regular joint audits
- facilitating the task of taxpayers in meeting their obligations, through tools such as a single tax web portal for all taxes and taxpayers and a one-stop shop for non-resident taxpayers in Member States, and decreasing the cost of compliance through the development of a European taxpayer code aimed at enhancing trust and confidence between taxpayers and tax authorities
- enhancing overall tax governance by pursuing a more joined-up approach between direct and indirect taxes.[45]

The Commission also stressed the need to ensure the application of equivalent standards by third countries, by ensuring that these countries commit themselves to these standards under international trade and cooperation agreements with the EU.[46]

Subsequently, it scheduled all proposed initiatives to be undertaken with specific timeframes, laid down in 2012 in an Action Plan,[47] where several actions were planned for 2013: revising the Parent–Subsidiary Directive;[48] aligning the anti-abuse provisions of the three corporate tax directives to the principles underlying the recommendation on aggressive tax planning; promoting the standard of automatic exchange of information at the wider OECD level; developing the European taxpayers' code.

Other actions were scheduled for 2014: developing a computerised format for automatic exchange of information under the Administrative Cooperation

---

43 Communication COM(2012) 351 final, on concrete ways to reinforce the fight against tax fraud and tax evasion including in relation to third countries (27 June 2012).
44 See ch 2.
45 Ibid., at 6–8.
46 Ibid., at 9–11.
47 Communication COM(2012) 722 final, An Action Plan to strengthen the fight against tax fraud and tax evasion (6 December 2012).
48 See ch 2.

Directive and proposing practical solutions for other types of income; introducing the European TIN; developing a central IT solution for electronic tools supporting administrative cooperation via information exchange; developing motivational incentives including voluntary disclosure programs; creating the tax web portal; setting up in each state the one-stop-shop for non-residents. For the longer term (beyond 2014), the Action Plan scheduled the development of a methodology of joint audits by dedicated trained auditors teams, the mutual access to national databases, and the elaboration of a single legal instrument for administrative cooperation for all taxes.

Although the timeframe appears not to have been fully met, these targeted initiatives, if considered together, would undoubtedly *contribute* to achieving part of the objectives/benchmarks. For example, a *uniform* interpretation of DTCs amongst Member States and a *binding* arbitration clause in all DTCs, committing one of the contracting states always to give tax relief, would both increase legal certainty for taxpayers engaged in cross-border activity and ensure the elimination of double taxation within the EU, thus overcoming even the cases of juridical double taxation deriving from the parallel exercise of taxing powers (where the ECJ, in essence, found that the DTCs at stake were ineffective in eliminating double taxation). In turn, reducing the length of MAPs in the Arbitration Convention would make it quicker and easier to eliminate economic double taxation in transfer pricing adjustments.

Moreover, the closing of loopholes in directives such as the Interest and Royalties Directive and the Savings Directive would make double non-taxation impossible in all respects in which gaps were eliminated. A European TIN and mutual access to national database would maximise the effectiveness of annual automatic exchange of information and, together with the closing of loopholes, would effectively counter cross-border tax evasion and fraud. A single web tax portal for all taxpayers with cross-border activity and a one-stop-shop approach for non-resident taxpayers in each Member State would certainly simplify tax compliance and reduce the related costs. Joint tax audits and the introduction of a general anti-abuse rule targeting artificial arrangements, as set out in the recommendation against aggressive tax planning, would help to *repress* aggressive tax planning cases.

Nevertheless, these initiatives do not appear to consider that aggressive tax planning may continue to take place due to at least two elements. First, the differences between national tax regimes (created by individual government policies) will inevitably continue to make tax base shifting and relocations from one jurisdiction to another an attractive course of action, as companies ultimately exercise rights created by individual states as a result of the fair tax competition.[49] Secondly, the developments of ECJ's case law have been ultimately paving the way for tax shopping strategies, because of: the rejection by the ECJ of revenue losses as a justification for measures restricting the exercise of free movement rights;

---

49 H. Van der Hurk, 'Starbucks versus the People', 64 *Bulletin for International Taxation*, 27–34, at 32–33 (2014).

the physical presence test used by the ECJ to establish wholly artificial arrangements in cases of exercise of the freedom of establishment; the possibility that a conduct not falling within the abuse concept but regarded as 'aggressive' tax planning (ie a transfer of tax residence to a country offering a much lower taxation level by a company realising most of its profit in an origin country imposing a higher taxation[50]) could still be protected by the TFEU's provisions on the freedom of establishment.

Arguably the proposed initiatives, if all implemented, would thus be effective in achieving other objectives/benchmarks, but would be *bound to fail* in the fight against aggressive tax planning, because, by adopting an *ex post* repressive approach, they would address the 'symptoms' of this phenomenon rather than the underlying cause, which lies in the kind of tax competition that was regarded as fair. Ultimately, only if and when this tax competition appears to be no longer convenient to individual states, the objective (benchmark) of effectively fighting against aggressive tax planning could be achieved.

4.3 The 'optimal conditions' for minimising tax-induced distortions in the functioning of the internal market

A situation where the benchmarks were achieved would obviously be a scenario where distortions induced by direct taxation in the functioning of the internal market would no longer exist, and where free movement rights would be mainly exercised for economic and market-related reasons and not for tax savings reasons. This idea that direct taxation should be as *neutral* as possible within the internal market has emerged ever since the 1960s,[51] although it was criticised by some of the literature which, on the basis of the ECJ's case law, has deduced that neutrality in the direct taxation area is not one of the objectives of the EU.[52]

Admittedly, the ECJ has accepted that 'forum-shopping' for the most advantageous tax rules does not in itself suffice to constitute abuse of the freedom of establishment[53] and that the Treaty does not guarantee to an EU citizen that a transfer to another Member State will be neutral as regards taxation, 'given the disparities in the tax legislation of the Member States'.[54] It has also specified that freedom of establishment cannot be understood as 'meaning that a Member State is required to draw up its tax rules on the basis of those in another Member State in order to ensure, in all circumstances, taxation which removes any disparities arising from national tax rules'.[55] Nevertheless, these statements are not

---

50 See ch 3, at 3.3.
51 See ch 1.
52 T. O'Shea, 'European Tax Controversies: A British-Dutch Debate: Back to Basics and Is the ECJ Consistent?' in 5 *World Tax Journal* 1, 100–27 (2013), at 104.
53 Case C–196/04, *Cadbury Schweppes* (n 7), para. 37.
54 Case C–365/02, *Marie Lindfors* [2004] ECR I–7183, para. 34; Case C–371/10, *National Grid Indus* [2011] ECR I–12273, para. 62.
55 Case C–293/06, *Deutsche Shell* [2008] ECR I–1129, para. 43; Case C–371/10, *National Grid Indus* (n 54), para. 62.

sufficient for submitting that tax neutrality in the direct taxation area is (or should) not be an objective of the EU. In fact, the specification 'given the relevant disparities in the tax legislation of the Member States' suggests that the ECJ merely took account of the *current situation* within the EU, where national tax laws show relevant disparities from one Member State to another, but certainly *did not intend to prevent* the Commission or the Member States from seeking – either through coordination or harmonisation – the convergence between national direct tax systems and the consequent tax neutrality.

In other words, it does not appear possible, from a teleological viewpoint, to interpret such statements, made by the ECJ in the *current situation* of lack of tax neutrality, as meaning that the situation should not *evolve* towards (greater) tax neutrality and that this should not be pursued as an objective consistently with programmes laid down since the early years of the (then) EEC. Otherwise, even all the objectives laid down by the Commission in its Communications (and taken as benchmarks in this work) – which by definition imply a move to a different situation – might (paradoxically) be regarded as not being EU objectives. Considering the ECJ's statements at issue merely as reflecting the current situation seems to be the only possible manner to reconcile them with other ECJ statements, which have highlighted the need to overcome *distortions* arising from the lack of sufficient tax neutrality such as wholly artificial arrangements aimed at circumventing national tax laws mainly for tax savings reasons (and which have stressed that the purpose of the freedom of establishment lies in a genuine economic integration in the host country[56]).

The importance of neutrality in the direct taxation area has been stressed by other literature, which has even argued that the very requirements of the internal market, in *primis* the non-discrimination principle and the fundamental freedoms, are fundamentally *incompatible* with the concepts that have served to build the current international tax law framework:[57] residence rather than source, unlimited worldwide income taxation, rather than limited tax liability and tax credit rather than exemption or DTCs.

In light of the limited legislative harmonisation in the direct taxation area, the ECJ has in essence accepted these concepts whilst adapting their application, from time to time, to the internal market non-discrimination principle and fundamental freedoms requirements. The current situation of partial non-achievement of the benchmarks ultimately results from loopholes left by the directives introduced and from the ECJ's adaptation and compromise-making efforts.

Accordingly, the optimal conditions for minimising tax-induced distortions in the functioning of the internal market could be specified one-by-one, in light of: the situations dealt with by the ECJ; the specific pitfalls identified by the Commission in its Communications; the mismatches between uncoordinated national

---

56 For example, Case C–196/04, *Cadbury Schweppes* (n 7), para. 53; see also ch 3.
57 F. A. Garcia Prats, 'Revisiting "Schumacker": Source, Residence and Citizenship in the ECJ Case Law on Direct Taxation' in I. Richelle, W. Schon and E. Traversa (eds), *Allocating Taxing Powers within the European Union* (Springer, 2013), at 1–8.

Direct taxation within the internal market 175

systems that persisted even after the implementation of the directives and after the ECJ rulings, as indicated in the previous chapter; the general realisation that the 'fair tax competition', by widening the differences between national tax systems, creates occasions for aggressive tax planning strategies.

A *first condition* is a uniform interpretation, in Member States, of concepts contained in DTCs between themselves and in the directives adopted to date. The Commission, in its communications, has stressed that double taxation may derive from different national understandings of concepts contained in DTCs – such as business income, tax residence, PEs – and that double non-taxation may derive from income qualification mismatches from one Member State to another.[58] Moreover, the implementation of the directives has often allowed national laws to fill with different contents the concepts left undefined,[59] thus resulting in a different effectiveness of the directives from one Member State to another. Accordingly, a uniform interpretation of all concepts contained both in the DTCs and in the directives adopted would be a necessary precondition for eliminating remaining cases of double taxation and occasions for aggressive tax planning strategies aimed at exploiting loopholes deriving from income and expenses qualification mismatches.

With regard to this second type of distortions, a general anti-abuse clause as proposed by the Commission in the Recommendation against aggressive tax planning could manage to defeat an aggressive tax planning strategy *ex post*, ie *after* it has been implemented. However, in light of the ECJ's case law, this outcome could be reached, in case of abusive practices, only if the main or sole purpose of avoiding tax were *proved*, whereas it could risk not being reached at all in case of those aggressive tax planning strategies that could not be regarded as abusive under the ECJ's case law. This last could be the case of operations not falling within normal commercial conduct, such as tax residence transfers of companies maintaining most of their market-base (or income generating-assets) in the origin country, as already mentioned in the previous chapter and in the literature.[60] Consequently, an *ex post* repression of aggressive tax planning could not equate to an *ex ante* prevention of these distortions, for which a uniform interpretation of concepts contained in DTCs and in the directives introduced would be a necessary (but not sufficient) precondition.

A *second, and related, condition* can be found in the overcoming of tax residence conflicts between Member States, which conflicts risk creating uncertainty in the application of the directives aimed at eliminating double taxation,[61] as well as hinder the application of the automatic exchange of information under the Administrative Cooperation Directive.[62] Moreover, a situation of dual tax residence in two countries adopting the worldwide taxation system and having

---

58 Such as the case of hybrid financial instruments: see ch 2, at 2.2.
59 See ch 2.
60 R. Russo, *Fundamentals of International Tax Planning* (IBFD, Amsterdam, 2007).
61 See ch 2.
62 See ch 3.

different tax rates results in potential double taxation on all income sources on which a tax credit granted by a country could not sufficiently offset tax levied by another, and in cumbersome compliance related to twofold worldwide income reporting requirements.

The tie-breaker rules of DTCs, because of different national interpretations, may not always manage effectively to solve dual tax residence cases[63] and the mutual agreement procedures (MAPs) under DTCs may take years to overcome the problem. A solution for *ex ante* preventing tax residence conflicts could thus lie in an autonomous definition of 'tax residence' introduced by an EU directive (and properly implemented by Member States), provided that this autonomous definition were such that tax residence in one Member State would automatically *exclude* tax residence in another Member State.[64] Whether Member States would accept a proposal for such a directive is a different issue. Arguably, this could have a positive response once Member States came to value the benefits of legal certainty and the smooth application of the automatic exchange of information (under the Administrative Cooperation Directive), which aim at fighting cross-border tax evasion.

A *third condition* could lie in a final ECJ position in respect of exit taxes on the transfer of tax residence of individual and of companies and in a *uniform application* of these taxes from one Member State to another, as well as in a greater approximation of Member States' specific anti-abuse rules – as already envisaged by the Commission – and of national group taxation schemes. This condition is important since differences between national exit tax regimes, anti-abuse rules and/or group taxation schemes, could offer multinational groups, together with other differences in the general features of tax systems, the occasions for tax planning strategies aimed at choosing locations of group units, in terms of tax residence of the parent company and/or of subsidiaries, and of location of branches, in such a way as to cherry-pick and combine the most favourable rules of different Member States and third countries. The well known cases of the Google or Starbucks groups and of their tax savings architecture are significant in this respect.

A *fourth condition* lies in an approximation of the taxpayers' procedural rights standards from one Member State to another. This approximation would be important as the Administrative Cooperation Directive and the Recovery Assistance Directive rely on national provisions in several important respects,[65] although these provisions for both information collection and recovery of tax claims confer wider or narrower powers to tax authorities depending on the lower or higher taxpayer's procedural rights standards in Member States. As these two directives are complementary to each other and are aimed at contributing to combat cross-

---

63 P. Mastellone, 'La residenza' in C. Sacchetto (ed.), *Principi di diritto tributario europeo e internazionale* (Giappichelli, Turin, 2011), at 119.
64 L. Cerioni, 'Tax Residence Conflicts and Double Taxation: Possible Solutions?' 66 *Bulletin for International Taxation* 12, at 647, 654–55 (2012).
65 See ch 2, at 2.8 and 2.9.

border tax evasion and fraud, their effectiveness risks being undermined without a de facto full 'mutual recognition' (of these national provisions as between Member States), which, therefore, is needed to foster mutual trust and mutual reliance as between national tax authorities.

A *fifth condition* can be found in a 'one-stop-shop' approach, already proposed by the Commission in the draft CCCTB Directive[66] and in its Communications on removing cross-border tax obstacles and on the fight against cross-border tax evasion.[67] This approach intends to reduce administrative compliance burdens and costs and to simplify cross-border compliance obligations. As the costs of dealing with several different national tax authorities for compliance with direct tax obligations risk discouraging the exercise of free movement rights, a one-stop-shop approach permitting simplification and minimisation of compliance costs must be regarded as one of the optimal conditions to be achieved. Obviously, the highest effectiveness of a one-stop-shop approach would be achieved if it led to a scheme allowing *all* mobile taxpayers (individuals and companies) receiving income in more than one Member State to deal with only one tax authority to meet all their direct tax obligations within the EU.

This scheme would go even beyond the current 'one-stop-shop' approach pursued by the Commission,[68] because it would require each national tax authority to act systematically not only in its own interest, but also as an 'agent', for tax return and tax payment collection purposes, of the national tax authorities of the country of origin of incoming workers or investors. The one-stop-shop tax authority would need to collect and to transfer in timely manner these tax returns and the collected taxes to the origin countries' tax authorities. The idea of a national tax authority acting as 'tax collector' for another national tax authority, in the form of systematic annual collection of (income) taxes and thus beyond a response to a request for assistance under the Recovery Assistance Directive, has already been partly implemented both in EU tax law (under the transitional Euro withholding tax system in the Savings Directive[69]) and, in international tax law, under the 'Rubik Agreements' entered into by two Member States with a third country, eg Switzerland.[70]

A 'one-stop-shop scheme' for the purposes of direct taxation within the EU – that, by assumption, were made available as an option to all mobile workers and investors receiving income in at least two Member States – would go well beyond these precedents and would circumscribe the application of the Recovery Assistance Directive to those recovery claims that the Member State of the one-stop-shop tax authority (in case of obligations not spontaneously met by taxpayers) might have in other Member States. Arguably, such a far-reaching 'one-stop-shop'

---

66 See 4.1 above.
67 See 4.2 above.
68 See 4.1 and 4.2 above.
69 See ch 2, at 2.6.
70 These agreements, which charged the Swiss tax authority with the role of withholding tax collector for bank accounts held by non-residents, were regarded by the Commission as compatible with EU law.

scheme could be based – just like the proposed CCCTB one-stop-shop – on a *central database* containing all data, income details and tax obligations details of mobile taxpayers opting for it, which would serve as a generalised *multilateral* automatic exchange of information between all Member States.[71]

This would be far more effective in contrasting cross-border tax evasion than the *bilateral* automatic exchange of information under the Administrative Cooperation Directive, and would be consistent with some measures proposed by the Commission, such as mutual access to national databases or the creation of a unique European TIN (tax identification number) for all taxpayers having cross-border income within the EU. Nevertheless, as regards taxpayers moving from one country to another, an obstacle towards the scheme feasibility lies in the risk of tax residence conflicts – between the Member State of the tax authority acting as one-stop-shop and other Member States where taxpayers have economic and personal links – which remain unresolved or whose resolution through MAPs was excessively lengthy. The obstacle would arise from the uncertainty as to whether the one-stop-shop should collect and transfer tax returns and payments related to taxes on worldwide income (if tax residence remained in the origin Member State) or on a territorial base (if the tax residence switched to its Member State).[72]

As the *ex ante* prevention of double tax residence situations within the EU can be regarded, in itself, as another condition to be met for removing a cause of juridical double taxation, the optimal conditions to be achieved would end up being complementary to each other.

On the whole, these five conditions could be regarded as those *necessary*, both for overcoming the remaining tax obstacles to the exercise of free movement rights *and* for fighting abusive or aggressive tax-shopping practices (ie for countering both kinds of distortions generated by the coexistence of up to 28 national direct taxation systems), within the current international taxation framework.

Nonetheless, they could not yet be sufficient for *ex ante* minimising the very incentive to undertake aggressive tax planning practices – i.e. for overcoming a priori one of the two kinds of distortions – without a further condition: the convergence between the essential features of national direct tax regimes or, in other words, the creation of 'general boundaries' to the 'fair tax competition'.[73] In fact, the catch-all term 'tax avoidance' for companies opting for the most beneficial route to reducing their tax burdens has a strong contender in the 'tax competition', i.e. states trying their best to induce companies into establishing themselves on their respective territories.[74] Unless and until Member States have a spontaneous interest in the convergence of their tax systems, the current situation

---

71 L. Cerioni, 'Removing Cross-Border Tax Obstacles for EU Citizens: Feasibility of a Far-Reaching One-Stop-Shop Regime for Mobile Workers and Investors' in 53 *European Taxation* 5, 194–206 (2013) at 199–200.
72 Ibid., at 205.
73 F. Vanistendael, 'Fiscal support measures and harmful tax competition', *EC Tax Review* 3, 152–60, at 159 (2000).
74 H. Van der Hurk, 'Starbucks versus the People' (n 49), at 32.

and even the first five conditions are bound to create complex tax governance issues from the viewpoint of taxpayers, Member States and the EU alike.

4.4 The optimal conditions for minimising tax-induced distortions in the internal market versus tax governance issues for taxpayers, for Member States and for the EU

As indicated by the review of the legislation and of the case law to date issued against the benchmarks in Chapters 2 and 3, the coexistence between uncoordinated national taxation systems, deriving from the 'fair' tax competition and from the lack of tax neutrality, distorts the working of the internal market.

Accordingly, the Commission faces a tax governance issue: the choice is as to whether to tolerate the current sub-optimal situation *or* to try to pursue *all* optimal conditions that would be necessary and sufficient for the proper functioning of the internal market. The very soft-law pieces that it has issued over the last decade[75] show a tax-policy choice to achieve all these conditions, *except for* the limitation of 'fair' tax competition (ie the elimination of the ultimate cause which, *ex ante*, creates, especially for multinational companies, the incentive for tax-shopping practices).

The 'fair tax competition' was actually regarded by the Commission as one of the three principles of good governance in tax matters, together with transparency and exchange of information,[76] and was distinguished again from the 'harmful tax competition' taking place through special business taxation regimes. The Commission called for an examination of the coherence between these principles of good governance and Member States' own tax policies, including DTCs with third countries, to ensure that Member States do not, through their bilateral DTCs, open up new opportunities for tax avoidance of other Member States' tax systems or for circumvention of EU directives.[77]

However, these opportunities could be created not only by DTCs, but also by domestic provisions adopted as a result of the fair tax competition. Together with different national tax policy objectives, the fair tax competition explains the several kinds of national direct tax provisions that are still widely different – even in the areas covered by the directives or affected by the ECJ rulings – after the EU legislation to date introduced and after the ECJ's case law. As for corporate direct taxation (more affected by EU law developments than the area of individuals' direct taxation), numerous examples of striking differences can be found.

For example, as regards tax rates, Bulgaria and Cyprus apply a 10 per cent tax rate, Ireland a 12.5 per cent rate, Germany, Latvia and Lithuania a 15 per cent rate, the Czech Republic and Slovakia a 19 per cent rate, Austria and Denmark a 25 per cent rate and Belgium and France a greater than 33 per cent

---

75 See ch 1, at 1.2.
76 Commission Communication COM(2009) 201 final, Promoting Good Governance in Tax Matters, at 5.
77 Ibid., at 12–13.

rate etc, and some Member States[78] apply progressive rates to profits not exceeding specific thresholds, rather than merely flat rates. National provisions on the taxable base considerably diverge as regards the definition of taxable profit,[79] the dependence or independence of tax rules from accountancy rules,[80] the deductibility of costs,[81] the possibilities of losses carry forward,[82] the dividends exemption regimes,[83] the anti-abuse rules,[84] the availability of group taxation schemes,[85] the application of exit taxes[86] and the prevention of international double taxation of business income.[87]

The differences offer plenty of opportunitues for tax planning strategies that could be designed to *match* the most favourable features of individual systems. For example, within groups of companies, tax-residence related choices could be based on the jurisdictions offering the most generous participation exemption regimes for parent companies, and on the jurisdictions providing the highest

78 Including Belgium, France, Luxembourg, the Netherlands, Spain and the UK.
79 Estonia completely exempts both domestic and foreign undistributed profits; the UK applies a scheduler system composed of different categories of income and capital gains; a number of other countries consider all profits accrued by a company to be business profit.
80 Austria, Belgium, Cyprus, the Czech Republic, Finland, France, Germany, Italy, Lithuania, Luxembourg, Portugal, Slovakia and Spain have been regarded as 'practically formal dependence' systems, whereas Greece, Hungary, Ireland, Malta, Sweden and the UK would be 'material dependence' systems and, finally, Denmark, the Netherlands, Poland and Slovenia could be considered as 'material independence' systems. See D. Edres and others (eds), *The Determination of Corporate Taxable Income in the EU Member States* (Kluwer Law International, 2007), at pp. 159–68; P. Essers, 'The Precious Relationship Between IAS/IFRS and the CCCTB with Respect to Provisions and Liabilities', in M. Lang, P. Pistone, J. Schuch and C. Staringer (eds), *Common Consolidated Corporate Tax Base* (Linde, 2008), at pp. 389–98.
81 Although expenses relating to the production of income are generally deductible, both the range of individual items which are allowed and the admissible ceilings (eg for depreciation and amortisation of fixed and intangible assets) vary considerably from one jurisdiction to another.
82 Certain jurisdictions, e.g. Austria, Belgium, Denmark, Ireland and the UK, allow an indefinite carry-forward of losses, but many others set specific time limits. Only a few jurisdictions allow carry-backward of losses.
83 See ch 2 as regards the wide differences in the implementation of the Parent–Subsidiary Directive.
84 For example, many countries – Cyprus, Denmark, Estonia, Finland, France, Germany, Hungary, Ireland, Italy, Lithuania, the Netherlands, Portugal, Spain, Sweden and the UK – have CFC (controlled foreign corporations) regimes, which, nonetheless, widely diverge from each other with regard to both the geographical scope of application and the underlying conditions. Moreover, a number of countries – France, Hungary, Malta, the Netherlands, Spain, Slovakia and Poland – do not apply limitations to interest expenses deduction, whereas others do.
85 Most countries have domestic group taxation schemes, which do not allow the inclusion within the group perimeter of EU subsidiaries; France, Denmark and Italy allow a group taxation including foreign subsidiaries too, but under different conditions.
86 For example, Malta, Hungary and Poland never apply exit taxation, whereas Slovenia exempts from exit tax only companies having a European Company or a European Cooperative Society form; other countries – e.g. the Netherlands, France, Italy and the UK – apply exit taxation, in addition to setting different conditions, and have had different and uncoordinated reactions when amending their national provisions in response to the 2011 ECJ *National Grid Indus* (C–371/10) ruling.
87 Although most jurisdictions apply the worldwide taxation with foreign tax credits, France applies a territoriality system, and Denmark exempts foreign PE income and property income.

allowances for depreciation for subsidiaries carrying on productive investments *or* on those jurisdictions which do not contemplate limits on interest deductions for subsidiaries in need of high amounts for loans from parent companies.

As a result, and since tax residence defined at national level is the personal connecting factor between taxpayers and individual national systems which are still mostly based on the worldwide taxation principle, tax governance issues arise *both* for taxpayers with activities, income and links in more than one Member State, *and* for Member States.

For taxpayers, the typical issue is how to legally minimise the overall tax liability, under conditions of legal certainty (and how to benefit from the higher procedural rights protection standards), by taking advantage of the differences between the substantive and procedural rules of Member States. As the ECJ has been accepting, in the direct taxation area, that tax savings reasons may be amongst the reasons (even if not the main ones) for the exercise of fundamental freedoms,[88] and has found, in the indirect taxation area, that taxpayers have the right to choose the most favourable fiscal means,[89] the literature agrees that taxpayers have, under EU law, fairly broad rights to arrange their activities in a manner such that their taxes are minimised.[90]

Taxpayers – in particular, (multinational) companies, mobile (financial) investors and self-employed professionals – face therefore a cost-benefit analysis in deciding *how* and *up to which point* to exploit the existing mismatches between national tax regimes for minimising their overall tax liability. Although the advantages in terms of tax savings are partly offset by costs in terms of tax and legal counselling, the tax-reduction strategies exploiting mismatches between national systems become more and more attractive the wider the mismatches, and the higher the income and the tax savings amount.

In turn, the exploitation of mismatches – i.e. aggressive tax planning strategies as defined by the Commission – typically takes place by segregating the taxable income (shifted to the lowest-tax jurisdictions) from the activities or elements generating it (remaining in a higher-tax jurisdiction). Even the OECD, in its 2013 Action Plan against base erosion and profit shifting (BEPS), stressed that 'No or low taxation is not per se a cause of concern, but it becomes so when it is associated with practices that artificially segregate taxable income from the activities that generate it. In other words, what creates tax policy concerns is that, due to gaps in the interaction of different tax systems, and in some cases because of the application of bilateral tax treaties, income from cross-border activities may go untaxed anywhere, or be only unduly lowly taxed'.[91]

---

88 Case C–196/04, *Cadbury Schweppes* (n 7), para. 75.
89 Case C–255/02, *Halifax* [2006] ECR I–1609, para. 73.
90 D. Weber, 'Abuse of Law in European Tax Law: An Overview and Some Recent Trends in the Direct and Indirect Tax Case Law of the ECJ – Part 1', 53 *European Taxation* 6, 251–64 (2013), at p. 251; M. Helminen, 'The Problem of Double Non Taxation in the European Union – To What Extent Could This Be Resolved through a Multilateral EU Tax Treaty Based on the Nordic Convention?' 53 *European Taxation* 7, 306–312 (2013), at pp. 307–308.
91 OECD, *Action Plan on Base Erosion and Profit Shifting*, (OECD Publishing, 2013), at 10.

The tax governance issue from taxpayer's viewpoint – i.e. the cost-benefits analysis making exploitation of mismatches more and more convenient the higher the potential tax savings – turns out being simultaneously a cause and an effect of the tax governance issue faced by Member States in a globalised economy. As the protection of tax revenues is the common goal of all national legislators, within the internal market characterised by 'fair' tax competition each Member State is induced to strike a balance between immediate budgetary requirements and the attractiveness of its territory to foreign investors.[92]

Striking this balance implies – for national tax legislators – deciding up to which point to take account of legislation of other Member States in designing their own tax provisions. The uncertainties left by the ECJ's case law on fundamental freedoms of movement and the progressive erosion of tax sovereignty have been indicating that, ultimately, the *most effective way* to protect national tax revenues currently lies in designing a *competitive* direct taxation system capable of attracting investments. Thus, the balance for *any national legislator* will tip towards increasing the attractiveness of its jurisdiction *whenever* the general tax systems of other Member States causes it to lose taxpayers and revenues due to outbound tax residence transfers.

In turn, the need to protect its tax revenues by *competing* with other Member States does not suit the need effectively to *cooperate* with other Member States, through the modalities which are possible under the Administrative Cooperation Directive and the Recovery Assistance Directive, in fighting a cross-border tax (evasion and) avoidance which is being ultimately fostered by the 'fair' tax competition. In fact, administrative cooperation in transmitting information or in giving tax recovery assistance may mean, for a requested Member State (who, by assumption, suffers revenue losses due to the tax competition by the applicant Member State) helping the revenue interests of a country whose tax competition policy is damaging its own revenue interests. Reconciling administrative cooperation (which assumes that shared goals will be jointly pursued) with legislative competition (which assumes that Member States will pursue their goals individually) could be possible, for the requested state, only by using all the options allowed by these directives to *restrict* the scope of the cooperation. For example, this could be done, as regards the Administrative Cooperation Directive,[93] by using the clause allowing a Member State to express no interest in the automatic exchange of information or by not allowing the participation of foreign officials in administrative enquiries in its jurisdiction.

As for the Recovery Assistance Directive,[94] it could be applicable by maintaining whenever existing, or by introducing, higher taxpayers' procedural rights protection standards than those of the applicant state (which could therefore see its request not fully met). Therefore, (even) a Member State which may be a 'loser'

---

92 W. Schon, 'International Tax Coordination for a Second Best World (Part I)', 1 *World Tax Journal* 4, 67–14 (2009), at 70.
93 See ch 2, at 2.9.
94 See ch 2, at 2.8.

in a tax competition in designing tax bases or tax rates, may use the options left by these two directives to become a 'winner' in designing taxpayers' procedural rights protection standards and, in so doing, to reduce its cooperation with those Member States causing it to suffer revenues losses. Nonetheless, the ultimate risk of this possible strategy of 'reconciling' administrative cooperation with tax competition would be that of ultimately undermining the effectiveness of these two directives, and thus their ability to counter cross-border tax avoidance.

Ultimately, the convenience for Member States to use tax competition to protect their revenues, as a result of the ECJ's case law on fundamental freedoms, creates therefore a crucial tax governance issue for mobile taxpayers (for whom exploitation of the mismatches created by inter-jurisdictional tax competition becomes convenient to a higher extent the higher the amount of tax savings), and this taxpayers' governance issue is bound to deepen the tax governance issue for national legislators. This vicious circle, which can further foster inter-jurisdictional competition between Member States in designing both substantive and procedural inter-jurisdictional rules, is bound to require the EU institutions to decide eventually about *whether* to continue accepting the 'fair' tax competition as currently taking place *or* to identify it as the ultimate root of aggressive tax planning strategies which may be difficult to fight, despite the Commission's recommendation, when they are not strictly abusive under current ECJ case law.

In fact, if the first five optimal conditions for the proper functioning of the internal market were read together with the tax governance issues faced by taxpayers and by Member States, it could easily be realised that achieving these conditions within the current international taxation framework would not overcome or minimise the indicated tax governance issues. This would hold true because *none* of these five conditions would affect the 'fair' tax competition and, therefore, because achieving these conditions would maintain the incentive for taxpayers (especially for multinational companies) to seek the lowest possible effective tax rate.

Neither could the result of overcoming or minimising the tax governance issues be achieved by the intended actions laid down in the 2012 Action Plan against tax evasion and tax fraud,[95] which – as already indicated – set out a timeframe for the initiatives already indicated in the 2012 Communication against tax evasion and for other initiatives.[96]

There is a wide overlap between the initiatives set out in this Action Plan or in other EU soft-law pieces and the 2013 OECD Action Plan on BEPS, since the Commission and the OECD largely expressed the same concerns about fighting aggressive tax planning and eliminating gaps leading to double non-taxation as well as to risks of double taxation. Seven amongst the objectives that were expressed by the OECD in the Action Plan on BEPS, are not specifically indicated in the 2012 Commission's Action Plan.

---

95 COM(2012) 722 final, An Action Plan to strengthen the fight against tax fraud and tax evasion (n 47).
96 See 4.2 above.

These OECD objectives are: *addressing* the tax challenge raised by the digital economy, which allows a company to have a significant digital presence in the economy of another country without being liable to taxation there owing to the lack of nexus under the current international tax rules (action 1 of the BEPS plan); *strengthening* specific anti-abuse rules such as CFC rules and interest deduction limitation rules (actions 4 and 5); *preventing* the artificial avoidance of the PE status (action 7); *establishing* methodologies to collect and analyse data on BEPS (action 11); *ensuring* that transfer pricing outcomes are in line with value creation (actions 8, 9 and 10) and *re-examining* transfer pricing documentation (action 13), which latter objective led to a Memorandum on this documentation (2013), a discussion draft on transfer pricing documentation and a template for country-by-country (CBC) reporting (2014); *requiring* taxpayers to make early disclosure of their aggressive tax planning strategies (action 12); and *developing* a multilateral instrument that would override current bilateral DTCs (action 15).

Nonetheless, four amongst these objectives have been expressly shared by EU institutions, through the Joint Transfer Pricing (JTPF) Forum and the Code of Conduct on transfer pricing documentation for associated enterprises in the EU (2006), through the creation by the Commission of a High Level Expert Group on Taxation of the Digital Economy,[97] through a 2013 'compromise proposal' for the CCCTB aimed at limiting the deduction of interest ('interest limitation rules')[98] and through a Council resolution on coordination of the CFC rules and of thin capitalisation rules within the EU.[99] Only the prevention of artificial avoidance of the PE status, the early disclosure of aggressive tax planning strategies, the collection of data on BEPS and the development of a multilateral instrument, have not been specifically indicated by EU institutions, but their goal (fighting aggressive tax planning) coincides with that of the initiatives scheduled by the Commission in the 2012 Action Plan.

The initiatives laid down by the Commission and by the OECD share a common feature, lying in the *ex ante* closing of loopholes leading to double non-taxation and in the *ex post* detection and repression of tax avoidance/aggressive tax planning strategies *once* they have been already conceived. The elimination of gaps and qualification mismatches could certainly manage to close *ex ante* some current avenues to implement such strategies, such as the lack in bilateral DTCs of 'subject-to-tax clauses', which can lead to double non-taxation of items of income not taxed in a contracting state irrespective of their treatment in the other contracting state. Owing to their underlying approach focusing only on closing loopholes and on *ex post* detection, all these initiatives could well contribute to achieving the first (uniform interpretation and application of DTCs) and the third

---

[97] Commission Decision COM(2013) 7082 final of 22 October 2013 setting up the Commission Expert Group on Taxation of the Digital Economy.

[98] Compromise Proposal for the CCCTB, doc. 14768/13 FISC 18 (14 October 2013), Art. 14a ('interest limitation rule').

[99] Council Resolution of 8 June 2010 on coordination of the Controlled Foreign Corporation (CFC) and thin capitalisation rules within the European Union [2010] OJ C156/1.

(greater approximation between national anti-abuse rules) amongst the optimal conditions.

Nevertheless, these initiatives would certainly *not* help to overcome or minimise the tax governance issues created by the 'fair' tax competition both for taxpayers (cost-benefit analysis making it convenient legally to exploit differences in tax systems between Member States) and for Member States (convenience of tax competition strategies as a winding road to protect revenues)[100] and would therefore be insufficient for eliminating or limiting the *ex ante* incentive for profit shifting and tax base erosion strategies. This holds true simply because, even if all such actions were implemented, companies, mobile investors and self-employed taxpayers would still find it convenient to transfer their tax residence to another Member State to become subject to the more favourable worldwide taxation regime, even if most of their income-generating assets and/or market base were left in the state of origin.

Although the ECJ's case law would allow this form of tax planning provided there is an economic integration in the new Member State given by physical investments, the outcome (a segregation of the taxable profit from its originators) would arguably contrast with the objectives of both the recommendation against aggressive tax planning and the BEPS Plan. In other words, given the 'fair' tax competition and the worldwide taxation linked to national tax residence, this connecting factor turns out causing a *fragmentation* of the EU single market and continuing to provide aggressive tax-shopping occasions. Against this, the first five conditions and the initiatives proposed by the Commission could not be effective, owing to their being very shaped on the current (residence-based) international tax law framework.

The CCCTB proposal – by offering a uniform and optional regime for determining the tax base, by introducing a formulary apportionment and by eliminating the need for residence-based DTCs between the participating Member States – could certainly manage, for groups opting for it, to reduce the inter-jurisdictional tax competition (that would be limited to tax rates). This would occur as the supranational scheme would compete with national regimes of (participating) Member States; nevertheless, an important limit would lie in the fact that its application could be jeopardised in cases of difficulty of solving tax residence conflicts relating to the parent company.

Therefore, despite the CCCTB, the *wider* the mismatches and the lack of coordination as between national laws, the *greater* the extent to which the indicated 'tax governance' issues would still arise from the viewpoint of taxpayers with cross-border activities (including those not opting for the CCCTB), from the viewpoint of Member States and, in the end, from the viewpoint of the EU too.

Ultimately, the argument would be a circular one: the maintaining of the current approach by EU legislator and by Member States, creates 'tax governance' issues for taxpayers, amongst which scope for profit shifting and aggressive tax planning opportunities, which, in turn, threaten Member States' revenues and

---

100 See 4.2 above.

complicate tax governance in the direct taxation area for individual Member States and for the EU. Eventually, the Commission will have to assess whether the distortions caused by the form of aggressive tax planning that the envisaged initiatives would fail to eliminate, should be ignored or whether the scale and effect of these distortions would justify, in light of the subsidiarity and proportionality test, a proposal for a new supranational solution aimed at tackling the ultimate cause of aggressive tax planning and of autonomously contributing to achieve all objectives set by the Commission.

4.5 The residence-based jurisdiction in direct taxation versus the protection of tax sovereignty of Member States

It can readily be understood, from the foregoing, that the distortions arise, in the working of the internal market, as tax residence is the main connecting factor for allocating a given country taxing rights on the worldwide income. As noted in Chapter 3, the distinction between residents and non-residents practised by Member States is also, ultimately, at the root of the issues which were dealt with by the ECJ in developing its case law, which has resulted in shortcomings if assessed against the 'benchmarks'.[101]

The concept of tax residence is well settled in the international tax law order, and it developed earlier than the original drafting of the Treaty in 1957. The drafters of the TFEU recognised the pre-existing residence-based connecting factor in the international tax law order when they inserted Article 65(1) (previously Article 58 of the EC Treaty) on the free movement of capital, which allows Member States to apply different tax treatments of non-residents and foreign investment, subject to the condition that this must not represent a means of arbitrary discrimination or a distinguished restriction. The ECJ, in its *Schumacker* case law stream[102] – whilst justifying in principle the residence-based criteria used in the international tax practice – shifted the obligation to grant tax deductions related to the taxpayers' overall ability-to-pay to the work state when the taxpayer earns most of his income there and the state of residence may not grant him both personal deductions and other deductions. The literature has highlighted that the ECJ ultimately regards the work state, in this case, as a 'virtual state of residence'.[103]

The higher the economic integration within the internal market, the higher the possibility of *Schumacker*-type cases where the non-discrimination principle forbids differences of treatment based on the tax residence. Moreover, the *higher* the economic integration within the internal market and the higher the possibility

---

101 See ch 3, at 3.5.
102 See ch 3, at 3.2.
103 M. Cruz Barreiro Carril, *Los Impuestos Directos y el Derecho de la Uniòn Europea. La armonizaciòn negativa realizada por el TJUE*, 1st edn (Madrid: Instituto de Estudios Fiscales, 2012), 375–76.

of taxpayers having links in at least two countries, the *higher* the risk of situations of tax residence conflicts, which might not be easily resolved on the bases of DTCs tie-breaker rules and which can undermine the effectiveness of the directives.[104] In other words, the more the internal market turns into a single market *having the characteristics of a domestic market* – which is an objective stated in the preambles of the corporate tax directives[105] – the higher the extent to which the very existence of different national tax-residence based jurisdictions ends up being at odds with the completion of the *single* market.

Therefore, in the current context of inter-jurisdictional tax competition and of negative integration by the ECJ's case law, it can be questioned to what extent the national tax residence-based jurisdiction can still effectively protect the (remaining) tax sovereignty of Member States in a unified market. 'Sovereignty' is traditionally intended as ultimate decision-making authority and general freedom of action of States, as limited by international law.[106] Therefore, if tax sovereignty means freedom of individual countries to design the (direct) taxation rules for all individuals or legal entities over which they can claim taxing rights if there is an internationally-recognised connecting factor with this taxpayer, a connecting factor between a state and any taxpayer is necessary for any state to assert its tax jurisdiction.

However, the connecting factor is capable of protecting a state's freedom of action (ie its sovereignty) in the direct taxation area to a higher extent, the higher the connecting factor: (a) is easily applicable and exists only with that state; (b) is impossible (or at least difficult) to eliminate by taxpayers; (c) the outcomes of its application are *immune* both from overlapping with other states' claims and from taxpayers' contestations. The national tax residence connecting factor increasingly tends to lose *all* these features in a globalised market. With regard to (a), in recent years the literature – in noting that the location of taxpayers, of activities and of markets is becoming more and more unstable and unclear – has highlighted that the identification of a 'residence country' and of a 'source country' is becoming increasingly difficult to ascertain.[107]

In addition to the tax residence concept becoming difficult to apply when a taxpayer's links are evenly spread in two or more countries, such connecting factor (a pillar of the current international tax law order) is certainly *unable* of ensuring exclusivity to a state. This is demonstrated by possible tax residence conflicts and by the risk that they become difficult to solve under DTCs tie-breaker rules due to different national interpretations of these rules or that their solution under the MAPs be a lengthy process. The possibility of tax residence transfers by both companies and individuals – within the EU, as a result of the very exercise of the freedom of establishment and of the free movement of workers – also proves that

---

104 See ch 2, 2.3.2 and 2.4.2.
105 Ibid.
106 S. Douma, *Optimization of Tax Sovereignty and Free Movement* (IBFD, 2011), at 80.
107 W. Schon, 'Internal Tax Coordination for a Second-Best World, Part I' (n 92).

this connecting factor can be eliminated by taxpayers, and that the country concerned, in this case, can only levy 'exit taxes' (within the limits allowed by the ECJ[108]).

These measures safeguard a Member State's interest to tax capital gains accrued to the taxpayer during the period of tax residence in its jurisdiction, but certainly *do not protect* the future tax revenues. Finally, the very role of DTCs, as well as the ECJ case law on the fundamental freedoms to direct taxation,[109] widely demonstrate that the outcomes of the application of the tax residence criteria at national level, are certainly not immune from overlapping with other states' claims and from contestations by non-resident taxpayers.

Both of these elements can cause erosion of tax revenues, just like the tax-planning strategies that can be implemented, especially by companies, when transferring the tax residence to another Member State offering a more favourable tax regime, whilst keeping their market-base and most income-generating assets in the origin state.[110] If accompanied by investments in the destination country in terms of premises, staff and equipment, this form of tax planning – although 'aggressive' to the extent that it would not correspond to 'reasonable commercial conduct'[111] – could *not be contrasted* through national anti-abuse rules, because it would not be an abusive practice under the ECJ's case law.[112] In addition to lower tax rates in the new residence country, this form of tax planning – in essence, a 'tax residence shopping (i.e. worldwide taxation shopping)' – could include benefits such as the non-applicability of anti-avoidance legislation at the level of the tax subject, no or lower withholding taxes on inbound and outbound income flows, and in some cases better DTCs network.[113]

It could thus prove attractive to companies, thereby creating a further element of erosion of tax revenues. Moreover, since under the current system only a resident in principle has access to a tax treaty and its benefits, it is of principal interest for a person wishing to benefit from a state's DTC network to be a resident. Therefore, the national tax-residence principle 'plays a key role in international tax avoidance, including treaty abuse, since a place of residence can be chosen or transferred in order to claim the desired treaty benefits without necessarily affecting the income-producing economic activity'.[114]

Ultimately, all these elements demonstrate that, as a connecting factor, tax residence at national level is increasingly unable to protect tax sovereignty and revenues of individual Member States. Instead of supporting the idea of stability

---

108 See ch 3, at 3.3.
109 See ch 3.
110 Russo, *Fundamentals of International Tax Planning* (n 60), at 66.
111 C(2012) 8806 final, Commission Recommendation against aggressive tax planning (n 31), Art. 4.
112 Case C–196/04, *Cadbury Schweppes* (n 7), para. 53.
113 Russo, *Fundamentals of International Tax Planning* (n 60), at 67.
114 E. C. C. M. Kemmeren, 'Source of Income in Globalizing Economies: Overview of the Issues and a Plea for an Origin-Based Approach', 60 *Bulletin for International Taxation*, 430–52, at 445 (2006).

of the (main) location of a taxpayers and of its interests in a particular jurisdiction (an idea which historically lies behind the tax residence concept), the free movement rights and the fair tax competition are creating a 'tax abode', i.e. a (temporary) location of a taxpayer in a (Member) State so far as this location fits its tax-reduction interests whilst being compatible with its other economic interests, and the ECJ's case law has been unintentionally favouring these tax-shopping phenomenon.[115]

Tax-residence based jurisdiction at national level, therefore, is at odds with the internal market, whose proper functioning would require direct taxation *not to be* the main driver of the exercise of free movement rights. Moreover, literature highlighted that, within an internal market having the features of a single market, direct taxation should be neutral also in the sense that relation between taxes and public goods should not be disturbed to the disadvantage of transnational investments.[116]

From this perspective, international tax neutrality would require income to be taxed only in the state where that income has been generated, since this state's public facilities contributed to the operation of income-earning activities.[117] This would result in an 'origin-based taxation' approach adhering to 'capital-import neutrality' (CIN) and allowing labour and capital originating in any Member State to compete on equal terms in the labour and capital markets of any other state, regardless of the residence place of the worker or investor. It was noted that this approach would create a 'level playing field' throughout the EU, consistently with the key principle of an 'open economy with free competition' under Articles 119 and 120 TFEU.[118]

4.6 The quest for alternatives to the national tax-residence: which solutions?

Whilst widely agreeing that the 'residence' and 'source' concepts are unsuitable for the proper functioning of the internal market, literature proposed different solutions to overcome the distinction between 'tax residence' and 'source' within the EU.

According to one suggestion, both residence and source states should apply worldwide taxation for both residents and non-residents (thereby taking into account positive and negative income), and should both offer double taxation relief. It was submitted that this would eliminate a territorial fragmentation of the tax base currently caused by territoriality and source taxation, which latter implies a compartmentalisation of loss relief possibilities and thus creates a major hindrance to cross-border economic activity, especially for multinational

---

115   See 4.1 and ch 3, at 3.3 above.
116   E. C. C. M. Kemmeren, 'Double Tax Conventions on Income and Capital and the EU: Past, Present and Future' in *EC Tax Review* 3, at 159 (2012).
117   Ibid., at 159.
118   Ibid., at 160.

groups of companies based in small home countries and for frontier workers earning employment income in one state and having a negative income in another state.[119]

The proponents argued that the tax relief granted by each country would be sufficient to eliminate double taxation entirely, *if* the Member States concerned had the same tax system and applied the same tax rates.[120] This solution has one shortcoming: since tax rates are widely different as a result of (both individual countries' domestic policy objectives and) 'fair tax competition', worldwide taxation of both residents and non-residents would *not* encourage Member States spontaneously to approximate their tax rates. Each individual state would adopt a 'capital export neutrality' (CEN) approach, making foreign income subject to its own tax rates, irrespective of the tax rates of other countries. Consequently, one of the necessary optimal conditions to be achieved for the proper functioning of the internal market – i.e. the spontaneous convergence of tax rates too – would not be met. Moreover, the persisting differences between tax rates would still leave the risk of a remaining double taxation of cross-border income flows whenever the foreign tax credits were insufficient to offset fully the foreign tax.

Another proposal to overcome the distinction between 'residence' and 'source' within the EU, in case of individuals earning income in two (or more) Member States, is the 'fractional taxation' of income.[121] Each state should agree to apply its progressive tax rate, as determined by considering the individual's worldwide income, to the 'fraction' of the overall net income received by the individual in his own jurisdiction, and it should also agree to grant *pro-quota* deductions for personal and family circumstances. This solution – which was defined as a 'general source taxation, but oriented to worldwide income'[122] – would obviously be effective in preventing double taxation, double non-taxation and double use of the same personal deductions.

It would also allow equal treatment, in terms of progressivity in the tax rates, of taxpayers who have earned the same amount of overall income, irrespective of whether this income has been entirely or only partly obtained in this state, and it would meet the concerns, underlying the *Gerritse* and *De Groot* ECJ rulings,[123] to ensure that Member States coordinate with each other in granting personal deductions. The overall taxpayer's 'ability-to pay', as revealed by his or her worldwide income, would therefore be considered (through tax rates) *pro-quota* in each Member State and (unlike the situation in *De Groot*) the corresponding

---

119 Terra and Wattel, *European Tax Law* (n 11), at 97.
120 Ibid. 98.
121 K. Van Raad, 'Fractional Taxation of Multi-State Income of EU Resident Individuals: A Proposal' in K. Andersson, P. Meltz and C. Silfverberg (eds), *Liber Amicorum Sven-Olof Lodin* (2001), 211; M. Mossner, 'Source vs. Residence – an EU Perspective' (2006) *Bulletin for International Fiscal Documentation*, 501, at 506.
122 M. Mossner, 'Source vs. Residence – an EU Perspective' (n 121), at 506.
123 See ch 3, at 3.3.

pro-quota granting of personal deductions would be admissible under EU law, because it would result from an allocation as between Member States of the obligations to grant all personal and family circumstances.[124]

Obviously, because each Member State would need to know the worldwide income of taxpayers obtaining *a* source of income in its own jurisdiction, effective exchange of information – concerning income obtained by the taxpayers concerned in third countries too – would be essential in making this system work. In this respect, its implementation would necessarily affect the Administrative Cooperation Directive.[125] First, it would arguably require an amendment to its Article 24(1), under which the competent authority of a Member State, receiving information from a third country, may transmit such information to other Member States *if* allowed by the DTC with the third country. The transmission to other Member States should become *compulsory* for *always* allowing each national tax administration to know the worldwide income of taxpayers receiving any income source in its jurisdiction.

Moreover, the 'fractional taxation' system would create the first two situations which, under the Article 9(1) of this directive, would trigger spontaneous exchange of information. In fact, any state taxing its own 'fraction' of the overall taxpayer's net income through the progressive rates based on the worldwide taxpayers' income, would be aware that a second state could not properly apply its own progressive rates, and would suffer revenue losses,[126] if it were not informed about the income obtained by the taxpayer in the first state. In turn, any taxpayer would obtain a reduction in tax in one Member State (due to the non-taxation of the 'fraction of income' obtained in other Member States) which would cause an increase in tax liability in other Member States[127] (owing to the application of a rate, in the progressive scale of income taxation, taking into account the part of income taxable in the first Member State).

Accordingly, each (source) state – following the disappearance of the distinction between 'residence' and 'source' – should spontaneously transmit information to any other states. Since the ECJ, in interpreting Article 4(1) of Directive 77/79/EEC, stated that this provision's wording ('. . . shall communicate') implies an obligation to transmit information in the circumstances set out there,[128] this obligation should continue under the Administrative Cooperation Directive which, as regards spontaneous information exchange, mirrors this 1977 Directive. However, spontaneous exchange of information by its nature relates to individual

---

124 Ibid.
125 Directive 2011/16/EU of 15 February 2011, in OJ L 64/1 of 11 March 2011.
126 The kind of situation envisaged by Art. 9(1)(a) of Directive 2011/16/EU.
127 The case envisaged by Art. 9(1)(b).
128 Case C-420/98, *W.N. v Staatssecretaris van Financiën* [2000] ECR I-2847 (13 April 2000), para. 13. See also S. Hemels, 'References to the Mutual Assistance Directive in the Case Law of the ECJ: A Systematic Approach' (2009) *European Taxation* 12, 583; R. Seer, I. Gabert, 'European and International Tax Cooperation: Legal Basis, Practice, Burden of Proof, Legal Protection and Requirements' (2011) *Bulletin for International Taxation* 2, 88, at 94.

cases[129] and thus, to keep this role, it could no longer be used once the circumstances otherwise triggering it were no longer to concern singular cases, but to become systematic due to the very taxation system.

In these cases, automatic exchange of information should be used. Article 8 of Directive 2011/16, which currently contemplates a unidirectional automatic transmission of information from source state to state of residence, should be amended to provide for *either* an EU-wide set of bidirectional automatic and compulsory transmissions *or* a general obligation on Member States to transmit, to a central database held by the Commission (and open for consultation by all tax authorities), the data of all individual taxpayers who, to their knowledge, carry on cross-border activities and thus receive cross-border income within the EU. This would obviously imply repealing the current Article 8(2) and (3) allowing Member States not to transmit information if they do not wish to receive it.

A further proposal to overcome the distinction between 'residence' and 'source' was formulated specifically for corporate taxation: the proposal for a destination-based corporate tax (DBCT).[130] The proponents argue that – because in a globalised world economy, both residence and source-based taxation distort the behaviour of multinational companies, their location-related choices and the competition between companies selling in the same markets – there is a need to identify an appropriate location of taxation by considering the mobility of different income-generating factors. They note that, unlike other income-generating assets or activities, consumers and customers tend to be immobile, and argue that, in consequence, taxing the income in the place of sale, whilst giving relief for costs in the place where they are incurred, would avoid distorting the behaviour of multinationals.

In their arguments, the country of destination of sales could legitimately tax corporate profits arising from sales in its territory, as sales are the real origin of corporate income, and the significance of this connection was highlighted by recent tax scandals involving Starbucks, Amazon or Google, which were criticised exactly for not paying tax where they were making sales (and earning profits). In this reasoning, inter-nation equity considerations would support a destination-based taxation principle, which would make corporate taxation similar to VAT, and the DBCT could be implemented by dissociating the *substantive jurisdiction*, ie the legitimacy to tax, from the *enforcement jurisdiction*, i.e. the availability of effective legal and implementing means of collecting the proposed tax. This proposed system would be implemented through a one-stop-shop system for all companies engaging in cross-border trade: the residence country would collect tax due on behalf of the sales destination country, taxing the corporate profits at the rate of the latter.

---

129 R. Seer, I. Gabert, European and International Tax Cooperation: Legal Basis, Practice, Burden of Proof, Legal Protection and Requirements (n 128), at 94.
130 M. Devereux, R. de la Feria, 'Designing and Implementing a Destination-based Corporate Tax', CBT Annual Symposium, Oxford (26 June 2013).

The proposal was formulated as a new international system for allocating taxing rights on corporate profits. It would certainly meet the concern underlying the first Action proposed under the OECD Action Plan on BEPS, that, in addressing the tax challenges of the digital economy, stated that issues to be examined included the ability of a company to have a significant digital presence in the economy of another country without being liable to taxation due to the lack of nexus under current international rules. In fact, the destination of sales nexus would make companies operating through e-commerce, and having most or all of their client base in another country, liable to tax in this last country. If applied within the EU, it would have the merit of eliminating double taxation, double non-taxation and the scope for those aggressive tax planning strategies lying in transfers of tax residence to another Member State, whilst leaving the market base in the previous state.

Nonetheless, the implementation of the one-stop-shop at national level would risk creating tensions between national tax authorities, given the still widely different tax collection and recovery mechanisms from one Member State to another, for at least two reasons. First, the reliance of the destination country on the procedural rules of the residence country would make the corporate tax revenues of the former country dependent upon the higher or lower effectiveness of the tax collection mechanisms of the latter country. In situations of companies resident in country A but having their entire market base in country B, country A could lack the interest to act as a corporate tax collector for country B *without reciprocity*, i.e. if country A were not, in turn, the destination country for sales of companies of other economic sectors that are resident in country B. However, in this case reciprocity – unlike under the current DTCs system – would be made entirely dependent upon customers' preferences, and would thus be completely outside national legislators' control.

Secondly, the dissociation between the taxation of corporate profits in the sales destination country and the deduction of costs in the country where they are incurred – which may be the residence country – would contrast with the symmetry between taxation of profits and deduction of costs that the ECJ's case law intended to safeguard in terms of cohesion of national tax systems.[131] The effectiveness of the DBCT implementation through a national one-stop-shop, and its consistency with the cohesion of tax systems, could therefore well be called into question. Furthermore, because the DBCT solution would still leave the state of tax residence an important role, i.e. the role of tax collector, it would not overcome the risk of dual residence under domestic laws and thus of tax residence conflicts. By contrast, where the role of the state of residence was only the role of enforcement on behalf of the destination state with no benefit for its own tax revenues (ie without a reciprocity), a dual residence situation would imply that none of the two states involved may be particularly keen to be allocated the tax residence.

---

131 See ch 3, at 3.1.2.

Each of these solutions – which would imply amending the current DTCs between Member States (and, in the case of the first two proposals, which would also cause the current DTCs tie-breaker rules for the allocation of tax residence to remain applicable *only* in the DTCs between any Member States and third countries) – would have its own distinct merit in achieving part of the conditions for the proper functioning of the internal market.

The 'origin-based taxation' proposal – as well as the DBCT proposal – would manage to achieve neutrality of competitive conditions, to avoid double taxation and double non-taxation. The 'double worldwide taxation with double foreign tax credit' would manage to avoid double non-taxation and tax base compartmentalisation and to consider overall ability-to-pay in each state. The 'source taxation with worldwide orientation' would manage to avoid double non-taxation, as well as double taxation and to consider taxpayers' overall ability to pay within the EU.

Nonetheless, each of these solutions would continue to imply administrative compliance costs for taxpayers receiving income in different Member States, which would still have to deal with different national tax administrations (even facing double worldwide reporting obligations in case of 'double worldwide taxation with double foreign tax credit'). In this respect, only the CCCTB project and the DBCT proposal would mark a step forward due to its 'one-stop-shop' approach, but would do so only for corporate groups (opting for this new regime) in the case of the CCCTB and for all companies in the case of the DBCT.

A proposal for a new solution aimed at achieving *all optimal* conditions should bring together all the merits of these solutions *and* encourage a spontaneous convergence between Member States' tax systems, whilst also simplifying cross-border tax compliance for taxpayers.

However, the new solution could not be searched by simply 'borrowing' the solutions adopted in extra-EU federal states, such as the USA or Switzerland. Although these extra-EU countries have their own single markets which, similarly to the EU single market, are characterised by free movement of goods, persons, services and capital, a different solution would be necessary in the EU, owing to the particular institutional framework of the EU, to the objectives which should be achieved *ex ante* for the proper functioning of the internal market and to the different history of tax law developments in these extra-EU countries. In fact, in the USA, there are five provisions in the Constitution specifically addressed to the federal government's substantive power to impose taxes, amongst which the most important one states, inter alia, that federal taxes must be uniform throughout the US and that no direct tax may be imposed unless it is apportioned among the states by population.[132]

Those states that existed prior to the adoption of the constitution retained all pre-existing taxing and spending powers that were not delegated to the federal

---

132 W. Hellerstein, 'The United States', in G. Bizioli, C. Sacchetto (eds), *Tax Aspects of Fiscal Federalism: A Comparative Analysis*, 25–68, IBFD (2011), at 31.

Direct taxation within the internal market 195

Government by the Constitution nor prohibited by it to the states.[133] Constitutional principles establish a framework for the distribution of taxing powers between federal and state governments, as a result of which, in principle, there is a concurrent federal and state taxation of income.[134] This situation has, in common with the European situation, the pre-existence of states with their own taxing powers, the subsequent creation of a new entity – through a constitution (in the case of the USA) instead of an international treaty (as in the case of the EU) – and the transfer of powers to the new entity, but is deeply different from the European case, where no taxing power was assigned to the EU in the direct taxation area. The level of (economic and) political integration that the founders of the USA intended to achieve from the outset, inter alia through the transfer of taxing powers to the federal level in the direct taxation area, was much deeper than the level of (economic) integration pursued by the founders of the (then) EEC.

Moreover, the US constitution does not contain detailed provisions laying down *specific* socio-economic objectives (whose achievement presupposes the proper functioning of the internal market). For all these reasons, a new solution – for the direct taxation area – aimed at contributing to achieving the objectives set out by the Commission, could borrow *neither* the USA institutional tax framework *nor* the USA solution of considering 'tax residence' as equivalent to 'citizenship' and of applying worldwide taxation to USA citizens, irrespective of their location.

However, it seems that the Swiss case cannot indicate an optimal solution for the EU. Although some problematic issues arising within the confederation's single market – namely, the conferral of powers to the confederation; the early struggle between confederation and the cantons on taxing powers; the need to avoid double taxation; and the autonomy of cantons to set their own tax rates – appear to be similar to those arising within the EU internal market, the different institutional developments mark significant differences. First, the confederation has (similarly to the USA case) taxing powers expressly allocated to it by the federal constitution, including direct taxation powers, whereas the cantons retain the original, general taxation competence to the extent not conferred to the confederation.

Secondly, the constitution confers on the confederation the task of establishing the principles on the harmonisation of taxes imposed by the confederation, the cantons and the communes, and precisely defines the object of this harmonisation, in a context where the crucial impulse for harmonisation in the direct taxation area (too) came from the cantons themselves.[135] This 'bottom-up' impulse towards tax harmonisation of the Swiss cantons contrasts with the resistance often opposed by EU Member States against attempts at 'top-down' harmonisation carried out by the Commission.[136] Whilst in Switzerland the conferral of taxing powers on

---

133 Ibid., at 30.
134 Ibid., at 38.
135 D. P. Rentzsch, The Swiss Confederation, 223–66 in G. Bizioli, C. Sacchetto (eds), *Tax Aspects of Fiscal Federalism*, cit., at 249.
136 See ch 1.

the confederation and the coexistence of different levels of government with taxing powers may have induced the cantons to seek harmonisation, the EU would arguably need a solution which, *without* requiring the EU to become a federal state and thus *without requiring* the conferral of direct taxation powers on the EU, would induce Member States to a degree of (bottom-up) convergence (with national direct taxation systems) that has not yet been in existence.

Bibliography

L. Cerioni, 'Tax Residence Conflicts and Double Taxation: Possible Solutions?' 66 *Bulletin for International Taxation* 12, 2012, 654–55.

L. Cerioni, 'Removing Cross-Border Tax Obstacles for EU Citizens: Feasibility of a Far-Reaching One-Stop-Shop Regime for Mobile Workers and Investors' in 53 *European Taxation* 5, 2013, 194–206.

M. Cruz Barreiro Carril, *Los Impuestos Directos y el Derecho de la Uniòn Europea. La armonizaciòn negativa realizada por el TJUE*, 1st edn (Madrid: Instituto de Estudios Fiscales, 2012).

M. Devereux, R. de la Feria, 'Designing and Implementing a Destination-based Corporate Tax', CBT Annual Symposium, Oxford (26 June 2013).

W. Hellerstein, 'The United States' in G. Bizioli, C. Sacchetto (eds), *Tax Aspects of Fiscal Federalism, A comparative analysis*, 25–68, 2011, IBFD.

S. Hemels, 'References to the Mutual Assistance Directive in the Case Law of the ECJ: A Systematic Approach', *European Taxation* 12, 2009, 583.

M. Helminen, 'The Problem of Double Non Taxation in the European Union – To What Extent Could This Be Resolved through a Multilateral EU Tax Treaty Based on the Nordic Convention?' 53 *European Taxation* 7, 2013, 306–12.

H. Van der Hurk, 'Starbucks versus the People', 64 *Bulletin for International Taxation*, 2014, 27–34.

E. C. C. M. Kemmeren, 'CCCTB and Exemption Method for PEs and Major Shareholdings' in M. Lang, P. Pistone, J. Schuch and C. Staringer (eds), *Common Consolidated Corporate Tax Base* (Linde, Vienna, 2008).

M. Lang, 'The General Anti-Abuse of Article 80 of the Draft Proposal for a Council Directive on a Common Consolidated Corporate Tax Base', 51 *European Taxation* 6, 2011, 223–28.

P. Mastellone, 'La residenza' in C. Sacchetto (ed.), *Principi di diritto tributario europeo e internazionale* (Giappichelli, Turin, 2011).

M. Mossner, 'Source vs. Residence – an EU Perspective', *Bulletin for International Fiscal Documentation*, 2006, 501–506.

C. H. J. I. Panayi, *European Union Corporate Tax Law* (CUP, 2013).

F. A. Garcia Prats, 'Revisiting "Schumacker": Source, Residence and Citizenship in the ECJ Case Law on Direct Taxation' in I. Richelle, W. Schon and E. Traversa (eds), *Allocating Taxing Powers within the European Union* (Springer, 2013).

K. Van Raad, 'Fractional Taxation of Multi-State Income of EU Resident Individuals: A Proposal' in K. Andersson, P. Meltz and C. Silfverberg (eds), *Liber Amicorum Sven-Olof Lodin* (2001), at 211.

D. P. Rentzsch, 'The Swiss Confederation', 223–66, in G. Bizioli, C. Sacchetto (eds), *Tax Aspects of Fiscal Federalism*, 249, 2011, IBFD.

R. Russo (ed.), *Fundamentals of International Tax Planning* (IBFD, 2007).

T. O'Shea, 'European Tax Controversies: A British-Dutch Debate: Back to Basics and Is the ECJ Consistent?' in 5 *World Tax Journal* 1, 2013, 100–27.

R. Seer, I. Gabert, 'European and International Tax Cooperation: Legal Basis, Practice, Burden of Proof, Legal Protection and Requirements', 65 *Bulletin for International Taxation* 2, 2011, 88–94.

C. Staringer, 'Requirements for Forming a Group' in M. Lang, P. Pistone, J. Schuch and C. Staringer (eds), *Common Consolidated Corporate Tax Base* (Linde, Vienna, 2008).

J. Schwarz, 'Double Taxation in the European Single Market', 66 *Bulletin for International Taxation* 6, 2012, 295–99.

B. J. M. Terra, P. J. Wattel, *European Tax Law*, 6th edn (Wolters-Kluwer, 2012).

F. Vanistendael, 'Fiscal support measures and harmful tax competition', 9 *EC Tax Review* 3, 2000, 152–60.

D. Weber, 'Abuse of Law in European Tax Law: An Overview and Some Recent Trends in the Direct and Indirect Tax Case Law of the ECJ – Part 1', 53 *European Taxation* 6, 2013, 251–64.

5 The response to the challenge of achieving on a long term basis the objectives set by the Commission

Hypothesis for a new 'comprehensive solution' in the direct taxation area

5.1 The quest for a new solution: hypothesis for an optional 'European Regime for Tax Compliance Simplification' (ERTCS) based on a new 'EU tax residence'

5.1.1 The hypothesis for a comprehensive solution for taxpayers with interests in more Member States

Given the shortcomings in the legislative and case law developments that have been described in Chapters 2 and 3, it can be argued that, to achieve all objectives, a new solution should reconcile, within the internal market, consideration of the ability-to-pay (a concern in the ECJ's case law)[1] with a degree of tax neutrality such as to prevent distortions *ex ante* and that it should make national legislators perceive that their remaining sovereignty in the direct taxation area would be best safeguarded, together with their revenue interests, if they spontaneously approximated their tax systems. This should be proposed with the stated purposes of safeguarding the remaining tax sovereignty of Member States and their fiscal revenues, of minimising in a uniform way the very incentive for aggressive tax planning strategies within the single market, and of offering *all* taxpayers bearing obligations towards at least two Member States a drastic simplification of their direct-tax compliance obligations towards *all* countries.

Inevitably, introducing such a solution would go beyond the possibilities of Member States acting alone due to the scale and effect of the potential action, and, according to the subsidiarity principle, an EU legislative measure would be necessary for this purpose. Furthermore, for *all* national legislators to consider their (remaining) sovereignty in the direct tax area as sufficiently safeguarded, this new solution should be an optional one like the CCCTB and, to generate uniform effects throughout the EU, it should be a 'supranational' one, and thus be entirely governed by an EU measure.

---

1 See ch 3, at 3.4.

As the direct-tax related distortions in the internal market are arising in the current context of tax residence-based jurisdiction at national level, and the tax residence connecting factor is becoming increasingly unable to protect Member States' tax revenues,[2] these elements should also be considered in conceiving the new supranational and optional solution.

Consequently, this new solution could be based on the idea – never explored in depth – of having, in addition to the concept of *national* tax resident and of *foreign* tax resident, a (new) concept of *European* tax resident.[3] The new solution could be a 'European regime for tax compliance simplification' (ERTCS), giving all taxpayers with cross-border interests and links in two or more Member States the possibility of meeting all their tax filing and payment obligations toward different countries by dealing *only* with a 'European one-stop-shop' (EOSS) office.[4]

This EOSS, in the author's view, could be managed by permanent representatives of national tax authorities composing a 'Joint Supranational Tax Committee' (JSTC), which could assess the relevant taxpayers' overall ability to pay. In order to make this assessment possible, Member States would need to agree to allow all taxpayers using the EOSS to consider the EU as if it were only one jurisdiction for tax residence purposes. Consequently, no Member State could continue applying the worldwide taxation system to individuals and companies choosing the new regime, which would end up introducing an 'EU tax residence' scheme.

Although the idea of an 'EU tax residence' remained an isolated one when it was first mentioned, it could currently become a topical one due to the increasing difficulty of identifying a national 'residence' of mobile taxpayers in a globalised economy, and for at least three other reasons. First, cooperation forums or expert groups that have already been set up by the Commission, such as e.g. the EU Joint Transfer Pricing Forum[5] or the recent platform on aggressive tax planning, good governance and double taxation,[6] and the creation of the EOSS would only mark a *step forward*. It would also mark a *deeper level of interaction* between national tax administrations than the regional cooperation groupings which already exist both in Europe and in third countries such as, e.g. the Intra-European Organisation of Tax Administrations (IOTA) or the Centre for Inter-American Tax Administrations (CIAT), which, ideally, at a global level should come together under an umbrella organisation.[7] In this respect, literature has actually been

---

2 See ch 4, at 4.3.
3 J. M. Arrese, F. Roccatagliata 'La Corte di Giustizia Cee ci ripensa: la "coerenza" dei sistemi fiscali nazionali non può giustificare trattamenti discriminatori verso i lavoratori non residenti', *Diritto e Pratica Tributaria*, 4, 1996.
4 Which could represent the ultimate step of development of the 'one-stop-shop' approach. See ch 4, at 4.3.
5 See ch 2, at 2.7, about the Arbitration Convention.
6 Commission Decision C(2013) 2236 of 23 April 2013 on setting up a Commission Expert Group to be known as the Platform for Tax Good Governance, Aggressive Tax Planning and Double Taxation.
7 J. Owens, 'The Role of Tax Administrations in the Current Political Climate', *Bulletin for International Taxation*, vol. 67, n. 3, 2013, at 160.

advocating the move from *cooperation* towards better *coordination* between tax administrations, i.e. moving from exchange of information to *simultaneous examinations* and *joint audits*.[8]

To this end, the EOSS – due to its very nature as a *permanent office* composed of representatives of national tax authorities acting simultaneously – could *best* manage to achieve the optimal degree of coordination between national tax authorities within the EU.

Thirdly, the new 'EU tax residence' solution could help the application of the potential CCCTB scheme, by eliminating the risk of tax residence conflicts concerning the parent company and of difficulties in identifying the 'place of the effective management'. The 'EU tax residence' would, admittedly, be a challenge to the current international tax law order, but this would occur in the case of the CCCTB regime too. In fact, literature argued that 'instead of comparing purely domestic situations with international ones, we will have to get accustomed to comparisons between 'intra-CCCTB area' situations and 'CCCTB area/rest of the world' situations. The CCCTB, in other words, will force us to develop new intellectual structures'.[9]

The EU tax residence could be exactly part of the new 'intellectual structures' which would be made necessary for a successful introduction of the CCCTB. In fact, due to the EU tax residence solution being complementary to the CCCTB, the 'intra-CCCTB area' could well coincide with the 'EU tax residence idea', and the comparison 'CCCTB area/rest of the world' could well be a comparison 'EU tax residence area/foreign tax residence area', since parent companies opting for the CCCTB could also be expected to opt for the ERTCS. This would reasonably hold true given the advantage – both for all other group members and for national tax authorities – of dealing with the EOSS rather than with the tax authority of the parent company.

Fourthly, the prospect of interacting with an EOSS alone – rather than dealing with many different national tax authorities – would certainly be attractive for all taxpayers wishing to reduce compliance onus. In fact, the EOSS, as institutional task, would collect and transmit filing documentation and payments to each concerned national tax authority; this would imply no costs for taxpayers. The ERTCS scheme would thus have the same advantages as a 'one-stop-shop' scheme in national tax authorities for mobile workers and investors, with the additional benefit of avoiding the risk of tax residence conflicts.

5.1.2 The proposed solution versus the acquis communautaire

Because the *acquis communautaire*, including the ECJ's case law on direct taxation, has been built on the current international legal order based on *national* tax-

---

8 Ibid.
9 D. Gutmann, 'Transfer of Assets to Third Countries' in M. Lang, P. Pistone, J. Schuch, C. Staringer and A. Storck (eds), *The Common Consolidated Corporate Tax Base (CCCTB) and Third Countries* (Edward Elgar, Cheltenham, 2013), at 271.

residence jurisdiction, the 'EU tax residence' might appear to be incompatible with that of the *acquis communautaire*. On a first reading, this issue does not arise for the CCCTB, which still assumes companies' tax residence at national level. Nonetheless, with regard to companies opting for it, even the CCCTB would imply overriding some pillars of the current international tax framework on which the '*acquis communautaire*' has been built, i.e. overriding the DTCs or the 'arm's length principle' which, as indicated in Chapters 2 and 3, have been accepted by the ECJ's case law. Despite this, the CCCTB would need to be regarded as compatible with the *acquis communautaire* simply because it would imply a deeper level of integration than the current one, and would help to better achieve the objectives set out in the Treaty.

The same argument would hold valid for the EU tax residence, owing to both its being complementary to the CCCTB and its implying a level of administrative integration that, on a costs-benefits analysis, may ultimately benefit both taxpayers with cross-border incomes and Member States. One further reason of compatibility of the EU tax residence solution with the *acquis communautaire* would lie in the relation between this solution and the ECJ's case law. Specifically, if the EU tax residence solution contributed to achieving all optimal conditions (and thus all benchmarks set out by the Commission), this solution would be *consistent* with the concerns underlying the ECJ's case law in terms of distortions to be avoided, as it would manage to *ex ante* minimise the very incentive for wholly artificial arrangements, i.e. for mere tax arbitrage.

On the other hand, it would go *beyond* the case law in achieving objectives that the ECJ regarded itself as unable to ensure without a general harmonising EU measure, i.e. objectives such as avoiding juridical double taxation deriving from parallel exercise of taxing powers (*Kaerchaert and Morres, Damseaux*)[10] *or* double granting of deductions for the same personal and family circumstances (*Imfeld*)[11] owing to parallel tax reliefs. Even in going *beyond* the case law, the EU tax residence solution would be consistent with the *acquis communautaire*, simply because it would further develop it (again, like the CCCTB solution). Ultimately, the way in which the EU tax residence solution would be structured would therefore be the decisive element for its compatibility with the *acquis communautaire* too.

5.2 Structuring the 'EU tax residence' scheme: suggestions

Each aspect of the new solution – e.g. how taxpayers opting for the scheme would meet their direct tax obligations and how the taxing powers on individuals would be allocated – should be targeted at an individual objective to be achieved, but all mechanisms should be complementary to each other in allowing the solution to help ensuring all optimal conditions.

---

10 See ch 3, 3.3.
11 Ibid., 3.2.

5.2.1 The EU tax residence solution vs. the simplification of tax compliance

As already noted, the objective of simplification of tax compliance would be pursued to the greatest possible extent in the ERTCS, where taxpayers, in connection with the 'EU tax residence', would deal with only an EOSS office for simultaneously meeting all direct tax obligations toward different Member States. As the EOSS would be managed by a JSTC made up by permanent representatives, at senior level, of tax authorities of Member States, the JSTC would act as a *multi-national* tax authority having three tasks: *collection of* reporting documentation and payments on behalf of national tax authorities; *immediate transmission* of reporting documentation and of payment to the concerned national tax authorities; *storage of all information* concerning taxpayers and their incomes (as indicated in reporting documents) in a central database. This latter would be always *instantaneously* and *simultaneously* accessible by each national tax authority by using a unique European TIN for all taxpayers opting for the scheme, and would, therefore, serve as a multilateral automatic sharing of information amongst all national tax authorities, just like in the CCCTB proposal.

The Commission – in addition to a central database in the draft CCCTB Directive and a European TIN for *all* taxpayers engaged at cross-border activities in its Communications against cross-border tax evasion – also suggested an approximation of tax declaration forms for simplifying cross-border tax compliance.[12] The ERTCS would share the central database approach and the European TIN, but would go farther than an approximation of different national tax declaration forms. In fact, such an approximation would still imply multiple (although easier) tax returns related obligations toward different national tax authorities.

On the contrary, in the ERTCS, because of the receipt of reporting documents by a JSTC (permanent representative of all national tax authorities), taxpayers could use a single and unified tax return form, which could be made available and sent electronically to the EOSS through the single tax web portal (envisaged by the Commission), to indicate all incomes that would be taxable by each Member State. The EOSS would need to set deadlines for its receipt of the single unified tax return and payments, which should be *earlier* than the deadlines established under national laws. It would subsequently need to transfer, to each national tax authority, the unified tax return and the payments intended for each State, by the same deadlines set for receipt of tax returns and payments under each national legislation.

With regard to individuals, the *single unified tax return form* would contain, for any income category, a specific section for each Member State, and taxpayers would fill only the sections concerning (their income categories and) the specific Member State toward which they have tax obligations. The single unified tax return form,

---

12 COM(2010) 769 final, Removing cross-border tax obstacles for EU citizens, at 7.

which would show the categories of taxable income and the determination of tax due to each Member State, would be transmitted to each national tax administration, together with the payment. Any national tax authority wishing to issue an amended assessment and/or to initiate tax audits – concerning incomes to be taxed in its jurisdiction (and indicated in the single unified tax return) – would retain its competence to decide it, and would have all related documentation sent to the taxpayer by the EOSS, which would therefore remain the only contact point for taxpayers opting for the scheme.

With regard to companies, the introduction of the ERTCS would imply an amendment to the CCCTB proposal, in the interests of multinational companies opting for both the CCCTB and the ERTCS. The *consolidated tax returns* form that is envisaged in the CCCTB proposal is already a *single unified tax return*, but the CCCTB proposal would need to be amended to the effect that the consolidated tax return – instead of being sent to the principal tax authority (national tax authority of the parent company residence Member State) – would need to be sent to the EOSS.

All administrative supervision tasks which, in the CCCTB proposal, are currently envisaged for the principal tax authority (PTA), would need to be shifted to the JSTC: the receipt of the notice to opt, the issue of amended assessments, the decision to open tax audits and the coordination of tax audits. There would be two main advantages in shifting the administrative supervision to the JSTC: the elimination of the risk of tax residence conflicts concerning the parent company on the one hand; the elimination of the risk of having the national tax authority of a group member appealing against decisions of the PTA before the courts of the PTA Member State in the event of litigation between tax authorities, on the other hand.

Once the task of deciding, e.g. to issue amended assessments *or* to initiate tax audits were conferred to the JSTC, there would no longer be scope for judicial litigation between national tax authorities (which could create situations of legal and administrative uncertainty for taxpayers). This is because different views amongst national tax authorities – all of which would be represented and would enjoy equal status in the JSTC – would need to lead to an agreement *within* the JSTC itself, in order for the latter to decide the course of action. In this respect, issues concerning the internal working of the JSTC – such as whether this permanent body would take its decisions by simple or by qualified majority or by unanimity, which decisions could be taken in either of these ways, within which deadlines the JSTC should take its decisions – would need to be governed in detail by the legislation introducing the ERTCS.

These issues would be relevant when the EOSS were used to manage the CCCTB as a formulary apportionment scheme implying the sharing of the consolidated tax base. However, these internal decision-making issues would not arise if the JSTC were to act simply on the part of a national tax authority in respect of decisions (eg amended assessments, tax audits) concerning income not to be apportioned, i.e. taxed *only* in its own jurisdiction.

Such cases may concern either individual taxpayers (earning incomes in at least two Member States), or corporate groups not eligible for the CCCTB, or multinational companies having PEs in other Member States but not opting for the CCCTB. Even these taxpayers could obviously opt for the ERTCS, but the JSTC would simply act from time to time, toward these taxpayers, as 'agent' of the appropriate national tax authority.

Overall, from a taxpayer's perspective, the introduction of the ERTCS and of its one-stop-shop approach would therefore achieve the objective of contributing to administrative simplification of cross-border tax compliance, and of increasing legal certainty in case of corporate taxpayers opting for both the ERTCS and the CCCTB. From national tax authorities' perspective, the operation of the JSTC and the central database, by creating a multilateral automatic sharing of information both for individuals and for companies opting for the scheme, would serve two purposes: administrative simplification in accessing information about *all* cross-border incomes (as requests for information or several bilateral automatic exchanges of information would no longer be necessary), and a more effective fight against cross-border tax avoidance. In fact, a multilateral automatic sharing of information through a permanent representative of national tax authorities and a permanently accessible central database would obviously be more effective for fighting cross-border tax avoidance, rather than an annual bilateral automatic exchange of information under the Administrative Cooperation Directive.

5.2.2 The 'EU tax residence' solution versus the removal of all remaining tax obstacles to cross-border business activity within the internal market and the achievement of greater legal certainty

As already indicated, a key role in the administrative simplification of cross-border tax compliance would be played by the *single unified tax return* that, in connection with the EU tax residence, should be addressed to the EOSS.

To use the single unified tax return, taxpayers opting for the scheme would necessarily need to know what *connecting factor* with each Member State would be relevant for taxing powers allocation, given that national tax residence would no longer apply due to the very concept of 'EU tax residence'.

Suggestions already formulated in the academic literature appear to be important in this respect. It was convincingly argued that tax jurisdiction with respect to income and capital should be linked, as much as possible, to the utilisation of production factors of labour and capital, and, therefore, to the territory where these factors are utilised (territory principle).[13] In this connection, taxes should be considered as a contribution for the benefits provided to an

---

13 E. C. C. M. Kemmeren, 'Source of Income in Globalizing Economies: Overview of the Issues and a Plea for an Origin-Based Approach', 60 *Bulletin for International Taxation* 11, 430–52, at 431 (2006).

individual through state activities,[14] and this direct benefits principle could be regarded as part of the ability-to-pay principle, because the benefits connected with the acquisition of wealth increase the ability-to-pay taxes.[15]

On these grounds, it was argued that the principle of 'source' should be interpreted as the origin for income taxes, and as the economic location for capital taxes: tax jurisdiction would belong to the state where income is actually produced (origin) through a substantial income-producing activity, and capital is actually established and preserved (economic location).[16] The principle of source could thus be reinterpreted as a 'principle of origin-based taxation'.[17] This literature has been suggesting a definition of 'substantial income-producing activity' as meaning an essential and significant part of the taxpayers' activity as a whole,[18] and has stressed that a connecting factor (for tax jurisdiction) based on the principle of origin would be much more difficult to manipulate than the national tax residence-based connecting factor.

This is because, in an origin-based taxation, it would not be easy to change the allocation of tax jurisdiction without affecting the economic location of a substantial income-producing economic activity.[19] This concern – i.e. to have a connecting factor that could not (easily) be moved – is the same concern underlying the suggestions for a DBCT, whose proponents stress that, as customers tend to be immobile, sales destinations could be a strong connecting factor for taxing corporate profits.[20] Sales of goods or services to a general customer base – which in the era of digital economy and e-commerce may even be entirely directed to customers located in other countries – could actually be regarded as the *origin* of business profits, just as the producing activity in itself could be regarded as the origin of other categories of income (eg employment income or income from professional services) arising out of the payment for the performance of a specific activity.

Both the origin-tax jurisdiction based on the productive activity and the destination-based proposal for a DBCT could thus be taken into account in determining, for different categories of income or profit, the connecting factors with each individual Member State, within the 'EU tax residence' area, for taxpayers opting for the ERTCS.

For these taxpayers, the ERTCS and the related 'EU tax residence' concept – due to its overriding the application of the national-tax residence connecting factor – could provide the framework for the application of these new proposed connecting factors. This is because a regime considering the EU as a *single jurisdiction* for tax residence purposes (as inherent in the 'EU tax residence' definition) could be perfectly matched with a situation where, within the EU, all items of

---

14   Ibid.
15   Ibid.
16   Ibid., p. 433.
17   Ibid., p, 437.
18   Ibid.
19   Ibid., at 446.
20   See ch 4, at 4.6.

income and capital would be taxed only once, i.e. only in the Member State where the substantial producing activity occurs *or* – in case of business profits – where the sales to customers originate business profits.

As a result, the origin-based connecting factor (whilst being more difficult to manipulate than the national tax residence and, therefore, whilst protecting more effectively Member States' tax revenues) would also automatically eliminate any residual risk of double taxation and of double non-taxation. Towards taxpayers opting for the 'EU tax residence', it would replace the current national tax residence-based DTCs (between Member States) with specific provisions, in the directive or regulation introducing the ERTCS, allocating tax jurisdictions.

These provisions would need to indicate when a Member State could be regarded as origin-State for each item of income that is currently allocated by way of DTCs – i.e. dividends, interest payments, royalties, immovable property income, independent services, dependent personal services, business profits – and when it could be considered as state of 'economic location' for capital.

With regard to the allocation of jurisdiction for *corporate tax* purposes, for all corporate taxpayers not opting for the CCCTB but nonetheless opting for the ERTCS, it would be necessary, by accepting the DBTC approach, to identify the state(s) of destination of sales as countries where – irrespective of the location of the company – business profits originate. In case of companies with registered office and head office in a state, but selling to customers located in several other countries within the EU, the allocation of jurisdiction could be made *pro-quota* to all countries of destination of the (overall) turnover. The enforcement jurisdiction – instead of being allocated to one country on behalf of another as in the original DBCT proposal – would be exercised by the JSTC under its own new enforcement powers as a 'multinational' authority.

The design of the scheme should also consider that some small Member States are currently tax residence states of businesses which may not necessarily be eligible (or opt) for the CCCTB, but which carry out their activity by using the facilities and the technological infrastructure of these states, whilst selling most of their products or services in other (larger) Member States offering the main part of the overall market base. If adopting the 'destination-based approach', these small Member States would risk losing tax revenues: to offset this risk, the ERTCS should provide for 'compensatory rights', to be paid by the Member States who would be allocated taxing rights to the Member States providing the location, the facilities and the infrastructure for carrying out the activity. The exercise of the enforcement task by JSTC and the introduction of 'compensatory rights' would avoid the risks of tensions and of lack of reciprocity between national tax authorities, which may otherwise risk undermining the practicality of a DBCT.[21]

Moreover, the very disappearance of the national-tax residence connecting factor, and the new connecting factor given by sales destination as origin of the profit, would imply that any 'transfer pricing' issue within corporate groups

---

21 Ibid.

choosing the ERTCS – even if not eligible for the CCCTB – would be eliminated within the 'EU tax residence' area. This would occur *automatically* because intra-EU transfers of goods and services, by giving rise to corporate taxation only in the country of destination of sales, would ultimately be equated to domestic transfers of goods and services.

With regard to the allocation of jurisdiction for *individual income-tax purposes*, identifying the state of origin would make it necessary to indicate *when* the substantial income-producing activity would need to be considered as occurring in one state. For some categories of income, the origin state could be easily indicated. For example, for immovable property income, it would be the state of location, since only in this state any activity on the immovable property that were necessary to make the property suitable for renting (and for producing income) could be carried out. For dependent personal services, it would obviously be the state where the employee spends his working time, for most or all of the tax year, for performing the activity agreed in the employment contract which determines the payment of salaries.

As regards independent services, the origin state would be the state where, for most or all of the tax year, the professionals carry out their activity (ie the state where the intellectual element and the skills involved in performing the activity are being spent) and where the payment is received. In case of dissociation between the state where the activity is carried out and the state where clients receive the performance and pay the service, it would be this second state, analogously to the case of business profit.

With respect to dividends and to capital gains on shares, tax jurisdiction could be allocated, just like the case of profits, to the state(s) where the profit-originating sales occur. In fact, the origin of distributed profits, as well as of increases in share values due to company's profits, ultimately derives from the favourable market response to the carrying on of the business activity.

Interests and capital gains on debt-claims could be regarded as originating in the state where the debtor produces the interest income. As regards royalties on underlying intangible property, the ultimate originator of this kind of income – which is obtained from a licence agreement setting out a pre-agreed rate – can be found in the legal system which first allowed legal protection, without which no payment could be received. Therefore, taxing rights on royalties income should be allocated to the state where the intangible property was produced and where it obtained protection.[22]

An exception to this rule should, however, exist for the EU patent and the EU trademark, which, once obtained, offer protection of intangible property for all Member States. Because in the case of an EU patent or EU trademark the legal protection – and the possibility of economic exploitation – is offered by EU law, rather than by a national legal system, the ultimate originator of royalty income

---

22 See Kemmeren, 'Source of Income in Globalizing Economies: Overview of the Issues and a Plea for an Origin-Based Approach' (n 13), at 449–50.

could not be traced back to a specific Member State legal system. By default, taxing rights could be attributed *pro-quota* to Member States from which, owing to licence agreements with different licensees, the royalties payments are received.

The allocation of deductions for income-related expenses, or for costs incurred in producing profits, could follow the allocation of the individual items of income or of profits, for consistency with a principle of symmetry between cost deduction and taxation of a related item of income.

In case of individual taxpayers obtaining more items of income (throughout the EU), the individual items of income or profit originating in each state involved would be summed up, to get, for each origin State, a *total gross amount of taxable income*. The obligation to grant personal allowances, reliefs and reductions related to individual and family circumstances could be – by a regulation or a directive introducing the ERTCS and accepting the origin-taxation principle for 'EU tax resident' individuals – allocated *pro-rata* to each state, according to the *fraction* given by the gross income originating in that state on the overall total gross income. Each origin state would apply its domestic rules for determining all deductions related to personal and family circumstances, but would grant a fixed percentage of these deductions depending on the fraction of the overall gross income taxable falling within its jurisdiction.

As individual and family circumstances affect taxpayers' ability-to-pay with individual Member States, the *pro-rata* allocation of the obligation to grant deductions would result in a *proportional application of the ability-to-pay principle*, which was invoked by literature[23] as a step that should be taken by the ECJ to overcome its currently inconsistent application of this principle[24] and to guarantee a more balanced outcome in revenue distribution between Member States.[25] Taxpayers would thus indicate, in the single unified tax return to be submitted to the EOSS, the income (net of income-related deductions) and capital to be taxed in each state according to the origin-based taxation principle, and – in case of individuals – the fraction of personal deductions for all family circumstances to be granted by each state. The power of each state to tax only the income allocated to it under the origin-taxation principle, the allocation of any items of income to one state *or* to another and the fractional granting of all personal deductions by each state, would automatically eliminate the risks of (juridical and economic) double taxation, of double non-taxation and of double granting of full deductions to individuals for the same personal and family circumstances.

The system would thus manage to remove all remaining obstacles (to the proper functioning of the internal market) that the ECJ's case law has not yet been able to overcome in the current international tax law setting, whilst managing to ensure that the taxpayers' overall ability-to-pay would be (properly) considered at

---

23 F. Vanistendael, 'Ability to Pay in European Community Law', *EC Tax Review* 3, 2014, 121–34, at 134.
24 See ch 3, at 3.4.
25 See Vanistendael, 'Ability to Pay in European Community Law' (n 23), at 134.

cross-border level, which was a concern of the ECJ in the *Schumacker* case law[26] and *mutatis mutandis*, for companies, in the *Marks & Spencer* case law.[27]

On the other hand, in the event of negative income originating for the taxpayers in one of the involved states and positive income originating in other Member States, there would be the need that negative income be taken into account *either* by offsetting it against future positive income originating from activity in the same state *or* – if this were not possible – against income originating in other Member States.

Negative income would in fact reduce the ability-to-pay, as it was impliedly recognised by the ECJ when it required the residence state of the parent company to grant deductions of terminal losses incurred by subsidiaries in other Member States (*Marks & Spencer* case law) or when (in *Schumacker*-type situations) it required employment states to grant deductions that states of residence were unable to grant. In case of taxpayers opting for the 'EU tax residence', the application of origin-taxation principle – with each state taxing only the income or the profit originating in its territory – would by definition be inconsistent with the deduction from the taxable base of negative income originated in other states.

Nonetheless, the same final outcome – i.e. taking into account by one state of negative income originating in another Member State and of the reduction of the ability-to-pay – could be achieved by way of an alternative route, i.e. through the application by each origin state of the '*source taxation with worldwide orientation*' approach proposed by literature for individual Member States, where 'source' would be intended as meaning 'origin'.

Specifically, each state – when taxing only the income originating in its territory – could take into account negative income originating in other Member States by granting a reduction in the applicable *tax rates* scale, e.g. a reduction of the tax rate scale corresponding to the fraction of the negative income originating in another state(s) against the positive income originating in its own territory. Instead of determining reduced tax rates for each taxpayers – which would make the system burdensome for tax authorities – it would be sufficient for each national legislator to establish brackets of reduced tax rates, each one corresponding to minimum and maximum thresholds of negative income originating in other states. Thanks to the central database of taxpayers opting for the ERTCS, and to the single unified tax return that would be received by the EOSS, each national tax authority would be able to know at any time the positive or negative taxpayer's income originating in other Member States and to be updated about it from one tax year to another. In fact, the central database would be instantaneously accessible by each national tax authority through the European TIN, and the single unified tax return would immediately be available through its representative in the JSTC.

This would hold true for *all* categories of income, and thus without the limitation to specific categories that would otherwise apply to the annual automatic exchange

---

26 See ch 3, at 3.2.
27 See ch 3, at 3.1 and 3.1.2.

of information under Article 8 of the Administrative Cooperation Directive. After the entry into force of the ERTCS as an optional scheme, any Member State would thus be placed in a position to apply, toward taxpayers opting for it, the source taxation with worldwide orientation, by applying – in light of information becoming immediately available after the initial taxpayer's option for the scheme – *normal* tax rates taking into account the income originated in other Member States, and reduced tax rate brackets to consider negative income originated there. Shortly thereafter, owing to its one-stop-shop approach, to the central database and to the single unified tax return, the EU tax residence would thus facilitate the implementation of the 'source taxation with worldwide orientation', which was proposed by the literature for adoption by Member States (and, already in itself, which would eliminate the risks of double taxation, of double non-taxation and of other overlapping between national taxation regimes).

Ultimately, a cross-border assessment of the taxpayers' ability to pay would still be ensured, without reducing the ability of the proposed system to achieve the other objectives indicated above.

5.2.3 The 'EU tax residence' solution vs. the safeguard of the remaining tax sovereignty of Member States

As already mentioned, the 'EU tax residence' solution would overcome the deficiencies of the national tax-residence connecting factor in protecting the remaining tax sovereignty of Member States. Whereas the national tax residence *within* the EU could be removed from one tax year to another without affecting the main income-producing economic activity or the location of the market-base – which would terminate the worldwide taxing powers on the outgoing taxpayers and would cause revenue losses to the Member State concerned – the EU tax residence scheme would not have this shortcoming, at least for two reasons.

On the one hand, the option for the ERTCS, once exercised, would remain irrevocable for its duration: just like the CCCTB proposal, the directive or regulation introducing the scheme could provide for a five year period of validity of the option, and could establish an automatic extension to subsequent equal periods in the absence of a renunciation by the taxpayer before the expiry of the original period. Therefore, the EU tax residence, and the related application of the origin-taxation principle, could not be removed for all duration of the scheme (which could be for an indefinite time, once taxpayers appreciate the advantage in terms of simplification of cross-border tax compliance). It would thus make taxing powers of individual states (and their tax revenues) *immune* to any transfer of the individual taxpayer's home or professional and family links from one Member State to another, or to any transfer of the registered office and place of effective management of a company throughout the EU.

On the other hand, the application of the origin-principle as a connecting factor with individual Member States (as a result of the EU tax residence) would make it much more difficult for a taxpayer to remove the connecting factor with an individual state. To avoid taxation in a state, any substantial income-producing

A comprehensive solution to direct taxation? 211

activity in that state would need to be terminated (which, in case of independent professional activities, would not even be in the interest of taxpayers when the activity performed in a state, thanks to the infrastructure offered in its territory and to the resources available there, were a successful one and client were located in the same country) or, in case of business profits, clients would need to move, which is unlikely and completely outside the company's control.

In essence, for individual taxpayers opting for the ERTCS, and for corporate taxpayers not eligible for the CCCTB, but still opting for the ERTCS, there would no longer be different national residence-based tax jurisdictions, but there would only be different national income or profit origin-based tax jurisdictions. As the connecting factor(s) of 'EU tax resident' taxpayers with each national origin-based tax jurisdiction, for direct taxation purposes, would be the substantial income-producing activity (and/or capital-preservation activity) or the profit-generating sales in each country, each Member State would remain free to independently exercise its tax sovereignty by setting its own tax rates and rules for calculating the tax base for taxpayers falling within its *exclusive* jurisdiction, without the risk of overlapping with other states.

Obviously, the disappearance for direct taxation purposes of the distinction between residents and non-residents in each Member State, would imply that individual Member States would no longer set different treatments between residents and non-residents, i.e. would no longer have any reason for introducing the kinds of provisions which, to date, have been causing their tax sovereignty to be eroded by ECJ rulings removing (covert) discriminations and unjustified restrictions. In other words, the exercise of taxing powers of individual Member States, toward taxpayers opting for the ERTCS, would no longer be exposed to challenges on behalf of non-resident taxpayers or of resident taxpayers complying against detrimental treatments of their cross-border investments.

Since the new connecting factors with each state, given by the substantial income-producing (and/or capital-preservation) activity and/or by the business profits originating-sales, would by its nature be much more stable than the national tax-residence, there would be implications for the protection of tax revenues. This would need to be ensured, by individual Member States, by setting two typologies of rules. First, effective rules for identifying all (individual and corporate) taxpayers carrying out this income-producing (and/or capital preservation) activity *or* earning business profits out of sales in their territory (irrespective of whether the taxpayer came from other Member States or are located there). Secondly, simple rules (concerning the computation of the tax base and the tax rate) to be equally applied to *all* 'EU resident' taxpayers whose income or profit originates or capital is produced or preserved in their jurisdiction.

As the differences between effective tax rates of Member States would apply only on locally-originating income or profits and no longer on the worldwide income, they would become less important amongst the factors determining taxpayers' location (and free movement related choices) within the EU: the choice to locate, to carry out activities and to invest in one Member State or in another could be expected to be guided by a greater extent – than in the current situation – by non-tax motives, i.e. by genuine economic reasons linked, e.g. to the infrastructural facilities, to the availability of skilled workforce, to location of the existing market-base and to the commercial penetration in new markets etc.

This would be fully consistent with the ultimate purpose of the freedom of establishment as indicated by the ECJ's case law, which consists of promoting a genuine economic integration in the economy of a Member State. Furthermore, because the differences between effective tax rates of Member States would become less important amongst the factors determining taxpayers' location choices, it would be less appealing for national legislators to compete with each other for attracting taxpayers through their effective tax rates; it would even be pointless to try to do so with regard to corporate taxpayers, owing to the sales-destination based taxation.

Conversely, the increased importance of non-tax motives, from the perspective of 'EU tax residents', in deciding whether to locate, to invest and to carry out income-generating activities, would make a spontaneous convergence between national effective tax rates more convenient for individual Member States: this convergence would make it even easier to highlight the 'competitive advantages' offered by each jurisdiction in terms of non-tax factors.

Ultimately, the EU tax residence, by replacing national residence-based tax-jurisdictions with national origin-based tax jurisdictions, and by implying for each Member State simply the need to apply the same rules on tax bases and tax rates for all taxpayers carrying out (genuine) income-producing activities in their territory, would better protect tax sovereignty of Member States from further erosion. Whilst allowing them to independently exercise this sovereignty in determining their tax bases and tax rates, it would also make it more convenient for them to spontaneously coordinate their choices in this respect. This would be fully in line with the objective of making direct taxation more neutral within the EU single market.

5.2.4 The 'EU tax residence' solution versus the minimisation of the scope for abusive practices and for aggressive tax planning strategies by multinational businesses

In its 2013 Action Plan against Base Erosion and Profit Shifting (BEPS), the OECD stated that concern arises about 'cases of no or low taxation associated with practices that *artificially* segregate taxable income from the activities that generate it'.[28] According to the OECD, '... due to gaps in the interaction of different tax systems, and in some cases because of the application of bilateral tax treaties, income from cross-border activities may go untaxed anywhere, or be only unduly lowly taxed'.[29]

---

28 OECD, Action Plan on Base Erosion and Profit Shifting (OECD Publishing, 2013), at p. 13.
29 Ibid., at p. 10.

This concern of the OECD about the occasions for practices exploiting loopholes left by overlapping of the current (national tax residence-based) tax systems echoes the concern expressed by the Commission in the recommendation against aggressive tax planning, which also recommended that Member States should fight artificial practices. It could be noted, in particular, that the concern about practices artificially segregating taxable income from the activities generating it is certainly justified in the current context, where national tax residence, as a main connecting factor for direct taxation purposes, could be switched to a second state, whilst leaving income-producing activities or the (entire) market base a first state. On the contrary, in an *origin-based* taxation system, the taxable income could *never* be segregated, by definition, from the factors originating it, just because the income-producing activities would be, by their very nature, the connecting factor with individual states for income taxation purposes, and the sales destination would be the connecting factor for corporate taxation purposes.

Because, in both cases, the *ultimate originator* of income or profit would be the connecting factor, any transfer of location (ie any transfer of those elements that currently define the national-tax residence) would be made completely irrelevant for tax purposes.

Furthermore, as previously argued, the disappearance of the national tax residence-based jurisdiction, and of worldwide taxation with regard to incomes obtained by taxpayers in other Member States, would eliminate the scope for a worldwide-taxation shopping, and would make a spontaneous convergence between national effective tax rates (more) convenient for individual states. As a consequence, the choice for the EU tax residence would also *ex ante* eliminate the incentive for (currently possible) aggressive but not abusive tax planning strategies, that could take place by transferring the tax residence to a Member State offering a lower effective tax rate on the worldwide income whilst leaving the market-base or the income-generating activity and assets in the origin Member State.

In essence, the 'EU tax residence' could therefore be made incompatible with, but more convenient than, forum-shopping and aggressive tax planning strategies. This would be due to the very features of the scheme: EOSS, single unified tax return, origin-taxation jurisdiction, greater incentive for national legislators to spontaneously approximate to each other their effective tax rate.

To enhance these features as an alternative to the currently possible forum-shopping and aggressive tax planning strategies, the introduction of the ERTCS could be devised in subsequent phases. In a first experimental phase, which may last for a ten-year period to allow for a sufficiently long period of time to assess the outcomes of the scheme, the 'EU tax residence' could be introduced as a pilot project addressed only to taxpayers meeting specific conditions: e.g. the best tax compliance records with national tax authorities; the willingness to disclose in advance the foreseen tax planning strategies within the EU, which condition would meet the goal of one of the actions indicated in the OECD Action Plan on BEPS; the commitment to give up the implementation of these strategies. As will be argued in the next Chapter, in the choice between the implementation of aggressive tax planning strategies and the option for the ERTCS, this latter could actually manage to prevail, also in light of the increasing risk that the aggressive tax planning strategies be no longer effective in achieving on a lasting base their ultimate intended outcomes.

5.3 The individual aspects of the suggested solution versus the individual objectives set out by the Commission

Each feature of the proposed solution would be conceived with a view to achieving one amongst the specific objectives that have been set out by the Commission in earliest communications and taken as benchmarks:

- the working of the scheme through a EOSS and a single unified tax return would serve drastically to simplify tax compliance from taxpayers' viewpoints, by avoiding them the need to deal with up to 29 different national tax administrations
- the allocation of exclusive taxing rights according to the origin-taxation principle for each possible item of income (and of capital) would serve to eliminate both all risks of juridical and economic double taxation and of unintended double non-taxation
- the specific rules for identifying when each particular item of income would be considered as generated in one jurisdiction (rules to be equally applied to all taxpayers, wherever located, falling within the national origin-based tax jurisdiction), would serve to ensure legal certainty and to avoid discrimination toward any taxpayers
- the central database would serve to allow each national tax authority to check the overall position of the taxpayers opting for the scheme, and to apply *either* the full tax rates to taxpayers having income originating in more Member States *or* the reduced tax rates to taxpayers having negative incomes originating in other Member States; it would therefore, as a multilateral automatic sharing of information, be more effective than a bilateral automatic exchange of information in pursuing the objective to fight cross-border tax evasion and fraud
- a choice to launch the ERTCS, in an initial experimental phase, as a pilot scheme to be offered to taxpayers having the best tax compliance records and willing to give up the implementation of aggressive tax planning strategies, would serve to contribute to the objective of fighting abusive practices and other aggressive tax planning strategies.

It could be objected that the ERTCS, whilst offering a simplification of tax compliance to eligible taxpayers, could complicate the work of national tax authorities, which would have to operate with two parallel systems towards two different sets of taxpayers. The current national tax residence-based system, to be independently managed by each national tax authority, would continue to rely on the existing domestic rules, bilateral DTCs and EU directives on administrative cooperation, as regards taxpayers not eligible for the ERTCS, whereas the ERTCS would be jointly managed with other tax authorities through the JSTC and the central database.

Nonetheless, from tax authorities' viewpoint, a duplication of applicable rules and of tasks would also arise as a consequence of the implementation of the CCCTB proposal, because corporate groups not eligible for the CCCTB (or not opting for it) would continue to be subject to normal national corporate tax rules on the determination of the taxable base. Furthermore, the additional costs for tax authorities involved in the duplication of the tasks could be offset – just as in the case of the CCCTB – by the benefits in terms of more effective protection of the tax base.

5.4 The feasibility of the 'EU tax residence' solution by enhanced cooperation

Admittedly, some Member States, which may be reluctant to proceed toward closer integration, could reject the idea of an ERTCS based on an EOSS and on 'EU tax residence'.

Notably, the CCCTB project is also finding the opposition of those Member States who are contrary to further harmonisation in the direct taxation area, and the Commission has already been considering the introduction of the CCCTB by enhanced cooperation, according to the rules provided in Article 20 TEU and on Articles 330 to 333 TFEU.

The CCCTB scheme would in fact imply, for Member States, the risk of losing (further) tax sovereignty due to resident businesses opting for new supranational rules on the determination of the taxable base. By contrast, the ERTCS, once Member States agreed on the adoption of an origin-based taxation approach, would only imply strengthening the degree of administrative cooperation to turn it into one of the day-to-day tasks of any national tax authority. As the central database would constitute an effective instrument for cross-border fight against attempts of tax evasion and avoidance,[30] the ERTCS would be well consistent with the objectives of the single market. Even this scheme, in the event of opposition by some Member States, could thus be proposed for introduction by enhanced cooperation.

The hypothesis of introduction of the ERTCS by enhanced cooperation would strengthen administrative cooperation as between participating Member States alone, since only their national tax authorities would be represented in the JSTC. Eligibility would need to be restricted to taxpayers who, at the time of exercising the option, are resident in any of the participating Member States *and* who derive income from at least *one other* participating Member State. This restriction would be consistent with the scheme's purpose to simplify tax compliance for specific categories of taxpayers and with the choice, by non-participating Member States, to exclude both their resident taxpayers and the income originating in their territory.

---

30 See 5.2, 5.2.1, above.

Therefore, incomes derived by these taxpayers in non-participating Member States, *or* income derived in participating Member States by taxpayers resident in non-participating Member States, would be irrelevant: the scheme would apply *neither* to taxpayers resident in a participating Member State but deriving income from non-participating Member States, *nor* to taxpayers resident in non-participating Member States and deriving income in participating Member States. In case of resident taxpayers, at the time of the exercise of the option, in a participating Member State and deriving income both from another participating Member State and from non-participating Member States, the ERTCS would only apply to income originating in other participating Member States.

In other words, the relations between participating and non-participating Member States, in the event of introduction of the scheme through enhanced cooperation, would equal the relations between Member States and third countries in the event of participation of all Member States in the ERTCS. Even in this case, owing to the scheme's very purpose of offering a new solution to all taxpayers who are currently tax resident in Member States *and* receive cross-border income *within* the EU, the scheme would not be accessible to taxpayers resident in third countries and deriving income from a Member State, and it would not apply to incomes derived in third countries by 'EU tax residents'.

At the time of the exercise of the option, as a result of their choice for the ERTCS, eligible taxpayers would stop being regarded as residents of individual participating Member States and start being considered as 'EU tax resident'. For these taxpayers, current residence-based DTCs would no longer apply owing to the introduction, within the 'EU tax residence' area, of origin-based national tax jurisdictions and of related rules on the exclusive allocation of taxing rights. Nonetheless, these DTCs would continue to apply as between non-participating Member States and participating Member States towards all taxpayers not falling within the scope of the ERTCS. With regard to these taxpayers, the current allocation of taxing rights set out in DTCs between participating and non-participating Member States (and between Member States and third countries in the event of adherence by all Member States) would not be affected.

Finally, the hypothesis of an ERTCS introduced by enhanced cooperation would not risk raising those issues of compatibility with the TFEU's rules on free trade, competition and state aids within the internal market. In the case of the CCCTB by enhanced cooperation, these issues might be raised owing to the exclusive tax advantages that companies based in participating Member States could end up enjoying in comparison with companies based in non-adhering Member States, in terms of cross-border compensation for loss beyond the limits set by the ECJ's case law and/or in terms of more favourable treatment resulting from the apportionment formula.[31]

---

31 L. Cerioni, 'The Possible Introduction of Common Consolidated Base Taxation via Enhanced Cooperation: Some Open Issues' in 46 *European Taxation* 5, 187–96 (2006); C. E. McLure Jr, 'Legislative, Judicial, Soft-Law and Cooperative Approaches to Harmonising Corporate Income Taxes in the US and the EU' in 14 *Columbia Journal of European Law* 3, 377–411 (2008).

Companies in CCCTB-participating Member States would enjoy these competitive advantages whilst keeping the same nexus for tax jurisdiction (with individual Member States) as companies in non-CCCTB participating countries. This would be the same nexus (ie the national tax residence-based jurisdiction) which was taken by the ECJ in its case law concerning provisions of all Member States.

Arguably, this might give rise to doubts as to whether, in the event of lower taxation as a result of the CCCTB, eligible taxpayers in participating countries would enjoy a targeted and 'selective' tax advantage – comparable to state aid – not available to competing companies resident in non-CCCTB participating Member States who would be on the same footing as eligible companies with regards to a key feature of tax systems, such as the connecting factor for tax jurisdictions. In the case of the ERTCS by enhanced cooperation, eligible individual or corporate taxpayers of participating Member States would certainly enjoy all advantages (in terms of simplification of tax compliance, of complete elimination of the risk of double taxation etc) in comparison with taxpayers of non-participating Member States, although these advantages might not necessarily consist of a reduction of tax payable to individual Member States (whether they would also imply a lower tax burden would depend on the effective tax rate in each origin-based jurisdiction).

Even when resulting in a lower tax burden toward individual states, that advantage – available only to taxpayers opting for the scheme in participating Member States – would simply be the consequence of a new and different nexus for tax jurisdiction, i.e. of a situation that, in this fundamental aspect of tax systems, would be different from the situation of non-eligible taxpayers of either non-participating or participating Member States. The advantage would not result, therefore, from any form of specific tax measures granted unilaterally by participating states only to a specific category of taxpayers, and the ECJ's case law has left Member States free to choose a nexus for tax jurisdiction different from the residence-based nexus.

Ultimately, in light of the foregoing, the ERTCS could be introduced by enhanced cooperation without losing its advantages for eligible taxpayers of participating Member States, and whist remaining compatible with the Treaty's rules on competition, free trade and state aid prohibition. A more effective achievement of the objectives set out by the Commission in at least a part of the internal market – the area of the participating Member States – would still be preferable to the risk of incomplete achievement throughout the EU.

Bibliography

J. M. Arrese, F. Roccatagliata, 'La Corte di Giustizia Cee ci ripensa: la 'coerenza' dei sistemi fiscali nazionali non può giustificare trattamenti discriminatori verso i lavoratori non residenti', 70 *Diritto e Pratica Tributaria*, 4, 1996, 683–99.

L. Cerioni, 'The Possible Introduction of Common Consolidated Base Taxation via Enhanced Cooperation: Some Open Issues', 46 *European Taxation* 5, 2006, 187–96.

D. Gutmann, 'Transfer of Assets to Third Countries' in M. Lang, P. Pistone, J. Schuch, C. Staringer and A. Storck (eds), *The Common Consolidated Corporate Tax Base (CCCTB) and Third Countries* (Edward Elgar, Cheltenham, 2013).

E. C. C. M. Kemmeren, 'Source of Income in Globalizing Economies: Overview of the Issues and a Plea for an Origin-Based Approach', 60 *Bulletin for International Taxation* 11, 2006, 430–52.

C. E. McLure Jr, 'Legislative, Judicial, Soft-Law and Cooperative Approaches to Harmonising Corporate Income Taxes in the US and the EU' in 14 *Columbia Journal of European Law* 3, 2008, 377–411.

J. Owens, 'The Role of Tax Administrations in the Current Political Climate', 67 *Bulletin for International Taxation* 3, 2013, 156–60.

F. Vanistendael, 'Ability to Pay in European Community Law', 23 *EC Tax Review* 3, 2014, 121–34.

6 Assessing the effectiveness of the proposed solution

6.1 The actions suggested by the Commission versus the proposed 'EU tax residence' solution: the EU perspective

As argued in Chapter 5, the ERTCS should contribute to the achievement of all objectives set out by the Commission. The impact of the proposed solution for the individual short-term and long-term initiatives considered by the Commission in each soft-law piece[1] can, therefore, be the criteria for assessing the effectiveness of the proposal.

In its communication on eliminating double taxation within the single market,[2] the Commission set out specific actions to be undertaken, amongst which were: an extension of the scope and coverage of DTCs to address triangular situations; the development in the EU of a common understanding of some concepts contained in DTCs between Member States, e.g. royalties, business income, dividends, PEs, tax residence, cross-border workers; the acceleration of disputes resolution within the EU, both through the improvement in the working of the Arbitration Convention on transfer pricing and through the insertion of a binding dispute resolution procedure in DTCs between Member States.

At least two amongst these initiatives would become even more important in the event of introduction of the ERTCS. One would be the development of a common understanding of some concepts currently contained in DTCs between Member States, because, due to the very fact that the ultimate originator of income would determine the connecting factor for tax jurisdiction, Member States would need to agree on identifying where this ultimate originator arises. This agreement would only be possible – with respect to items of income such as royalties, business income, dividends – if there were the same understanding of these concepts from one Member State to another. Although these concepts are currently contained in national tax residence-based DTCs as between Member States, whose application would be overridden by the ERTCS, they would also be contained in the Directive or Regulation introducing the ERTCS.

---

1 See ch 1, at 1.2 and ch 4, at 4.2.
2 Commission Communication COM(2011) 712 final, Double taxation in the single market (11 November 2011).

This EU legislative measure would need *either* to indicate the connecting factor for tax jurisdiction (ultimate originator) on each type of income *or* leave to a multilateral agreement entered into between Member States the task of specifying, for each type of income, what would be the originator and how its location should be identified. Therefore, a uniform definition for each item of income, agreed by Member States, would need to be provided, either by the legislation introducing the new scheme or by the multilateral convention.

Another initiative that would become even more important is the acceleration of dispute resolution. The Arbitration Convention on transfer pricing would remain applicable only to businesses not opting for ERTCS, and no double taxation issue would arise for taxpayers opting for the scheme within the 'EU tax residence' area (due to the exclusive origin-based tax jurisdiction). However, there may be instances where disputes could still arise as between the representatives of the national tax authorities in the JSTC in case of companies opting both for the CCCTB and for the ERTCS (for these companies, the EOSS would have the administrative supervision role that, in the current draft CCCTB Directive, is played by the 'principal tax authority' (PTA)).

As a result, in the event of any disagreement between tax authorities that may not be overcome by a majority decision-making within the JSTC, the solution (rather than via litigation brought by the tax authority of a group member before courts of the PTA Member State) would still need to be searched within the JSTC. Hence, a binding dispute resolution mechanism would be necessary for a timely settlement of all disputes that may arise within the JSTC, in order for the JSTC to issue its decisions (on matters such as, e.g. the apportionment of the consolidated tax base, the issue of amended assessments, the decision to open tax audits). The binding resolution mechanism could be provided for *either* in the legislative measure introducing the ERTCS *or* in the multilateral convention. The other initiatives considered by the Commission, i.e. the recast of the Interest and Royalties Directive and the expansion of the scope of DTCs to triangular situations, would remain important for taxpayers not opting for the ERTCS and, in any case, for non-participating Member States in the event of introduction of the scheme via Enhanced Cooperation.

In turn, in the 2012 Action Plan against tax evasion and fraud, the Commission set out several concrete actions.[3] The proposed ERTCS and the creation of the EOSS would make most of these initiatives *even more important* than in the current scenario and would broaden their scope, because they ultimately suppose – just like the ERTCS – *both* a higher level of cooperation between national tax authorities (than it appears feasible in the current context) *and* a higher degree of convergence of taxpayer's rights on an EU-wide scale. Both these two developments would be made necessary by the setting up of such a permanent body representing all national tax authorities as the JSTC would be, and by the existence of a supranational one-stop-shop as the only authority interacting with taxpayers irrespective of their being located in a Member State or in another one.

3 See ch 4, 4.2.

Specifically, a first Action Plan initiative enhanced by the ERTCS, would be the introduction of a European TIN for each taxpayer engaged in cross-border activity within the EU, and the direct access for all national tax authorities to each other's national databases.[4] In the Commission intention, the European TIN would allow all national tax authorities *to identify* each taxpayer carrying out activities in more Member States, for making the automatic exchange of information quicker and more effective. If the ERTCS were made available, in a first phase, as a pilot project for taxpayers having the best tax compliance records, the European TIN could serve a twofold purpose (at least in this initial phase of the ERTCS). In respect of taxpayers not eligible for the ERTCS, it would play the role envisaged by the Commission, whereas, towards taxpayers opting for the ERTCS, it could be used by the JSTC to manage the scheme (ie to accompany the transmission to each national tax authorities of tax returns and payments) and, by the national tax authorities, to access simultaneously all information included in the central database.

To serve this dual purpose, it would be sufficient for the European TINs of those taxpayers opting for the ERTCS to have any distinctive feature (in comparison with the European TINs of other taxpayers) indicating that they meet their tax obligations towards all Member States through the EOSS. Moreover, the direct access for all national tax authorities to each other's national databases could be the *first step* towards the realisation and the management of the central database that would record details of taxpayers opting for the ERTCS. In fact, at the time of setting up of the EOSS, the first details concerning all taxpayers opting for the scheme, to be stored in the central database, would need to be timely drawn from national databases, even though the central database, simultaneously accessible by each national tax authority through the European TIN, would be subsequently updated each year with information stored by the EOSS. The direct access for all national tax authorities to each other's national databases would thus be a preliminary step that could foster, amongst the national tax authorities, the degree of mutual trust and confidence that would subsequently be necessary for the very functioning of the EOSS.

The development of a European Taxpayer's Code[5] – an initiative which the Commission is considering in the current context of taxpayers dealing with many different national tax authorities – would also become even more meaningful in the event of introduction of the ERTCS. In fact, the Commission intends to develop a European Taxpayer's Code for the purpose of setting out best practices for enhancing cooperation, trust and confidence between tax administrations and taxpayers, for ensuring greater transparency on the rights and obligations of taxpayers and for encouraging a service-oriented approach. As taxpayers using the ERTCS would meet their tax return and payment obligations towards at least

---

4 COM(2012) 351 final, on concrete ways to reinforce the fight against tax fraud and tax evasion including in relation to third countries, p. 7; COM(2012) 722 final, An Action Plan to strengthen the fight against tax fraud and tax evasion, at para. 22, point 12.
5 COM(2012) 722 final (n 4), at 10.

two Member States *only* through the EOSS, acting in the common interest of national tax authorities, this purpose of the European Taxpayer's Code, would need to become the very *modus operandi* of both the EOSS and taxpayers using the ERTCS, to the benefit of taxpayers and all national tax authorities.

At the current stage, the Commission has been asking stakeholders' inputs for developing the European Taxpayer's Code, and the Confederation Fiscale Européenne (CFE), together with other tax professional organisations, has been drafting a Model Taxpayer Charter (MTC), i.e. a 'Charter of Taxpayer Rights and Responsibilities',[6] setting out the rights and obligations of a taxpayer as generally provided under its domestic law. The MTC may expand and/or clarify the responsibilities of the state to taxpayers.[7] This approach – should such document be used by the Commission for elaborating the European Taxpayer's Code – would be enhanced by the ERTCS, because this scheme would also expand the responsibilities of Member States to eligible taxpayers (responsibilities which, following the introduction of the ERTCS, would include allowing taxpayers to submit tax returns and payments through the EOSS). Just like the MTC, which recognises the sovereignty of the State to levy tax in accordance with its domestic law and to administer such laws,[8] the ERTCS would recognise Member States' (remaining) sovereignty and would intend offering it – through a stronger and more stable nexus for tax jurisdiction – an even more effective protection.

Furthermore, the hypothesis of testing the ERTCS – at least in a first experimental phase – as a pilot project for taxpayers having the best tax compliance records, would be consistent with the MTC's approach of presuming the taxpayer to be honest and trustful unless there is evidence to the contrary.[9] On the other hand, the MTC states that *any* Taxpayer Charter entered into by *a* Member State shall acknowledge the primacy of the four EU fundamental freedoms – in the contents that the ECJ's case law has been defining – and shall recite the rights of the taxpayers identified thereby from time to time.[10]

The MTC thus impliedly suggests that a European Taxpayer's Code should also set out (in addition to common taxpayers' rights and obligations expected in any jurisdiction) taxpayer's rights derived from the fundamental freedoms and from the *acquis communautaire*. Even from this perspective, the ERTCS – because it removes all remaining tax obstacles to the exercise of the free movement of persons and of capital, and because it marks further progress of the *acquis communautaire*, just as the CCCTB would do – would enhance the scope of the European Taxpayer's Code. In fact this code, amongst other rights, would indicate the right to opt for the ERTCS and to benefit from the simplification of cross-border tax compliance.

---

6   M. Cadesky, I. Hayes and D. Russell, *Towards Greater Fairness in Taxation: A Model Taxpayer Charter* (CFE, ADTCA, STEP, 2012), at 35.
7   Ibid., Art. 1(3).
8   Ibid., Art. 1(5).
9   Ibid., Art. 5(1).
10 Ibid., Art. 30(1).

Two other initiatives indicated by the Commission – i.e. the promotion of simultaneous controls and of the presence of foreign officials; the development of a central IT solution for electronic tools supporting administrative cooperation – would be intrinsic to the very operation of the ERTCS. This would hold true, firstly, because the scheme – by working via a single unified tax return addressed to the EOSS and stating the income to be taxed in each Member State according to the origin-based taxation principle – would require simultaneous controls whenever *any* national tax authority (represented in the JSTC) has reasons to believe that the taxpayer, in the single unified tax return, has wrongly failed to allocate to its jurisdictions income originating there.

The controls would necessarily need to be simultaneous, since the income wrongly omitted for a jurisdiction in the tax return may have been (wrongly) indicated as originated in another Member State(s): given the exclusive origin-based taxation rights, it would be of utmost interest both for the tax authority alleging the mistake and for all other tax authorities to verify whether the taxpayer might have underrepresented taxation rights of a country and overrepresented taxation rights of another Member State. Together with simultaneous controls, the presence of officials of all concerned tax authorities – both in the Member State where the taxpayer is located and in other Member States where the origin (or non-origin) of individual items of income would need to be verified – would be appropriate to maximise the effectiveness of the control. This would hold true since it would allow each tax authority's auditors participating in the control to report, in real time, the fact-findings to its own national representative in the JSTC.

Secondly, the setting up of a central electronic database which, after having received details from national databases upon initial implementation of the ERTCS, would be periodically updated by the EOSS and would remain simultaneously and instantaneously accessible by each national tax authority via the European TIN, would obviously make it appropriate to develop a central IT solution for allowing at any time the smooth working of this electronic instrument. Given the possibility of simultaneous access and the multilateral sharing of information allowed by the single unified tax return and by the central electronic database, the degree of day-to-day interaction between national tax authorities could be defined as 'administrative integration' rather than simply as 'administrative cooperation'.

This would make the development of a central IT solution even more important than in the current 'administrative cooperation' phase (still characterised by exchange of information, however automatic). Just because simultaneous controls would become of utmost importance in the event of introduction of the ERTCS, the scheme would also make it necessary to elaborate a methodology of joint audits by dedicated trained teams of auditors. Because the controls, whenever a national tax authority believes that a taxpayer has not properly indicated the income according to the origin, would need to be simultaneous, and the audits would need to be jointly carried out, a common methodology would also need to be developed.

A further initiative indicated by the Commission, i.e. the development of voluntary disclosure programs, would be appropriate in case of introduction of the ERTCS: taxpayers using the scheme would need to be incentivised to disclose spontaneously to the JSTC – before submitting the single unified tax return – details of any particular case where locating the ultimate originator of an income item in a Member State *or* in another may be difficult. This voluntary disclosure could enable national tax authorities to examine the case jointly, and could allow the JSTC to issue to the taxpayer, before the deadline for submitting the single unified tax return (and in the utmost interest of the taxpayer itself), a decision about *where* the origin of income should be located. This decision would be binding for the national tax authorities until the particular situation – which gave rise to the disclosure and to the decision of the JSTC – remains unchanged, and would thus offer taxpayers the same legal certainty as an advance ruling.

The elaboration of a single legal instrument for administrative cooperation for all taxes – the last targeted action envisaged by the Commission – could also be facilitated by the ERTCS. In fact, because this would be a scheme for 'administrative integration' in the direct taxation area (which latter, to date, has been regarded by Member States as more closely connected with their national sovereignty), it would allow national tax authorities to strengthen their experience in interacting with each other's on a routine bases, and thus to develop a closer relation than the current instruments for administrative cooperation. Exactly because it makes these instruments obsolete for the direct taxation area, the ERTCS could be a driver for the elaboration of a new single legal instrument applicable to all other taxes too.

This would appear reasonable because, in the VAT area, the Commission has already been pursuing a one-stop-shop approach[10a] and a higher degree of administrative cooperation (than in the direct taxation area) between national tax authorities has already been reached. After a first experimental phase as a pilot-project, in the longer run the ERTCS itself could serve as a 'single legal instrument' for all taxes, because the national tax authorities represented in the JSTC, amongst their tasks, would collect other taxes too. For the ERTCS to serve as a single legal instrument for 'administrative integration' for all taxes, the directive or regulation governing it would also need to contain detailed provisions concerning assistance in recovery of tax claims.

Furthermore, the ERTCS would not prevent the remaining initiatives set out in the Action Plan – such as e.g. the amendment to the anti-abuse rules of the corporate tax directives – which suppose the current international tax setting. In fact, these initiatives would still remain appropriate for taxpayers *not opting* for the ERTCS (and for non-participating Member States in case of ERTCS introduced by Enhanced Cooperation). Despite the ERTCS's purpose of creating, for all taxpayers with cross-border incomes and links, a more attractive regime than the current intra-EU tax environment, in the event of an initial phase of the ERTCS as a pilot-project only a small number of such taxpayers would, in fact, be able to opt for the scheme.

10a See COM (2011) 851 final, 6.2.2011, para. 5.1.1.

Finally, the ERTCS would be complementary to the CCCTB project. As was highlighted,[11] for corporate groups opting for both schemes the EOSS would take over the administrative supervision role that, in the current CCCTB proposal, would be entrusted to the PTA. For these corporate taxpayers, the 'CCCTB-area' would therefore coincide with the 'EU tax residence' area. The otherwise possible difficulties in locating the 'places of effective management' (tax residence) of the parent company would therefore be avoided *ex ante*, which would facilitate in all cases the option for the CCCTB. In light of the further circumstance that the role of the JSTC, and the necessity of reaching agreements between national tax authorities before issuing amended assessments, deciding audits etc would eliminate the risk of litigation as between national tax authorities, the contribution of the ERTCS to the smooth functioning of the CCCTB scheme would appear to be very important.

6.2 The proposed solution and the safeguard of Member States' revenue interests

It was argued in Chapter 5 that the very features of the ERTCS scheme would be conceived to *ex ante* eliminate the incentive for aggressive tax planning strategies, and thus to protect revenue interests of Member States. It was also submitted that, to enhance the effectiveness of the scheme for this purpose, it could be introduced in two phases, i.e.: in a first experimental phase, as a pilot project for taxpayers bearing income or corporate tax obligations towards at least two Member States and having the best tax compliance records; in a second phase, as a scheme of general application to all taxpayers facing these cross-border tax compliance obligations.

An initial introduction as a pilot project would appear to be appropriate from the perspective of national tax authorities too: in fact, because they would have to run two parallel systems – the current systems for all taxpayers not eligible for the ERTCS, and the new scheme with which they would need to become familiar – they could find the new scheme more manageable if it were initially targeted to a lower number of taxpayers bearing cross-border tax compliance obligations than to all of them. The best tax compliance records with national tax authorities for the past, and the commitment to give up the implementation of any planned aggressive tax planning strategy for the future, could be the two cumulative criteria for selecting the eligible taxpayers for the first phase as a pilot project.

The taxpayers concerned would in this case face a trade-off between two alternatives: (a) remaining within national residence-based tax jurisdictions, dealing with several different tax administrations and incurring the related costs, bearing legal and tax consultancy costs for undertaking the tax planning strategies and incurring the risk of falling within anti-abuse clause; or (b) opting for the ERTCS and committing themselves to give up any such strategies, dealing only

---

11 See ch 5, at 5.2.1.

with the EOSS and deciding the location of their income-generating activities only on the basis of non-tax motives.

In this choice, the taxpayers concerned would have, first, to consider the *tax savings* allowed by the foreseen (aggressive) tax planning strategies against the costs of these strategies and the risk they involve in terms of repressive reaction by tax authorities (by application of anti-abuse clauses) and reputational damage linked to condemnation by the public opinion. This last 'effect' would need to be considered as these strategies are being widely perceived, by governments, by public opinion and by the Commission, as contrasting with corporate social responsibility (CSR), i.e. with the increasingly global demand for business behaviour that takes into account not only profit-making needs but also the wider interest of stakeholders. Should the estimated tax saving benefits (exceed the costs and) make the risks tolerable, the option of implementing aggressive tax planning strategies would need to be seen against the alternative option for the ERTCS.

The new scheme would not necessarily lead to tax savings in particular countries, but would certainly lead to reduction in compliance costs, would offer more legal certainty, would completely eliminate the risk of repressive reactions by national tax authorities and would not cause any reputational damage, in addition to being complementary to the CCCTB proposal. The cases of multinationals whose names have been associated with aggressive tax planning strategies – Starbucks, Google and Apple – and the negative effects of these strategies, suggest that ultimately, in this comparison, the balance from taxpayers' viewpoint could tip towards the 'EU tax residence'.

In this respect, Starbucks' negative experience with aggressive tax planning can be a significant one for other (corporate) taxpayers too. The company, who had in the UK the largest European market, was blamed of implementing an aggressive tax planning strategy due to its moving its European head office (ie the tax residence of its European subsidiary) from the UK to the Netherlands, where it actually managed to reduce its tax liability. Nonetheless, in April 2014, following accusations made by the UK tax authority and pressure from both the UK Government and public opinion, the company agreed to transfer back its European unit tax residence to the UK, even though in the UK it would incur a higher level of taxation. Other governments could end up analysing the case and applying the same means of pressure towards other multinationals, with the ultimate outcome of frustrating their aggressive tax planning strategies too. The ultimate indication of the Starbucks case for the medium-term future could thus be twofold: for multinationals, the final outcome of aggressive tax planning strategies could turn out being uncertain and counterproductive; for Member States, tax competition based on the structural elements of the tax systems – i.e. what is currently known as 'fair tax competition' and unintentionally encouraged by the ECJ's case law – might *not necessarily* remain a 'winning' element to increase their revenues.

However, this potential scenario could not suffice to make the national tax residence a stronger and more stable nexus (for protecting individual States' revenues) than currently is: the risk of overlapping with other States' claims and the risk of further erosion of tax sovereignty by ECJ rulings (banning differential treatments of resident versus non-resident taxpayers), would both remain. Moreover, even if after the Starbucks case a coordinated pressure from all major jurisdictions were to persuade multinationals to renounce aggressive tax planning strategies based on tax residence transfers to countries offering the lowest taxation levels, tax residence transfers could still be implemented by smaller businesses or even by self-employed individuals as long as the ECJ's case law on the freedom of establishment does not consider them to be 'abusive practices' (and thus permits them).

In essence, the overall impact of the Starbucks case on tax competition and on the attractiveness of aggressive tax planning strategies remains hardly foreseeable, but it would certainly be in the interest of all Member States to limit aggressive tax planning even if carried out by taxpayers *other* than multinationals. In medium-term future, the spontaneous convergence (which would be fostered by the ERTCS) between national tax bases and rates could therefore be, already on its own, as a more convenient strategy than tax competition for protecting tax revenues.

On the other hand, the more aggressive tax planning strategies imply tensions with tax authority and public opinion (and, despite immediate tax savings, turn out being exposed to uncertainty and even to failure), the more it could thus become convenient, for multinationals and other taxpayers, to give up these strategies in exchange for accessing a regime – such as the ERTCS – bringing them advantages in terms of much higher degree of legal certainty, of strong and simultaneous simplification of their tax compliance obligations towards all Member States in which they operate, and of lack of risk of repressive reactions by national tax authority.

Empirical findings drawn from some tax managers of internationally-oriented businesses and/or tax advisors with international clients,[12] actually appear to confirm that the certainty in the benefits that the ERTCS would bring would be more attractive than the combination between possible immediate tax savings and risks in the ultimate outcome offered by aggressive tax planning strategies. Accordingly, Member States not adhering to the ERTCS would run the risk of being perceived, from the tax compliance viewpoint, as less attractive countries for carrying out activities and for locating income-originating investments.

The ERTCS could also contribute to greater legal certainty in the relationships between EU law and DTCs, both between Member States and with third countries. Literature proposed an 'EU Model Tax Convention'[13] for overcoming the differences still existing amongst bilateral DTCs entered into by Member States. According to his first proponents, the EU Model Tax Convention would

---

12 In a sample of 100 tax professionals (from 5 major EU countries) serving international businesses, 80 stated that the legal certainty offered by the ERTCS would be a key element for them to opt for it.
13 P. Pistone, *The Influence of Community Law on Tax Treaties: Issues and Solutions*, EUCOTAX Series on European Taxation (Kluwer Law International, 2002), 235–53.

need to be a binding set of rules to be included by Member States in their (bilateral or multilateral) DTCs, and would need to be formulated along the lines of the OECD Model regarding tax residence allocation as well.[14]

In the same terms, the idea was considered by the Commission for ensuring consistency between EU law and the provisions of bilateral DTCs entered into by Member States,[15] although the Commission indicated a preference for a non-binding instrument such as a recommendation.[16] By contrast, the latest literature, by assuming that DTCs should help developing the internal market into a truly domestic market and that, for this purpose, taxation of income should occur only on a territorial base rather than on a residence base,[17] argued that the EU Model Tax Convention, supplemented with a Commentary as a policy document, should be based on exclusive taxation of income in the state of origin.[18]

An EU Model Tax Convention based on the principle of exclusive taxation in the state of origin, and followed by newly drafted DTCs between Member States, would eliminate the distinction between state of residence and source State within the EU for direct taxation purposes, just as the ERTCS would do. It has already been noted that – because the ERTCS would imply replacing the current national *residence-based* tax jurisdiction with national *origin-based* tax jurisdiction – the legislative measure introducing the scheme should contain provisions setting out the criteria for locating the origin of any item of income in a Member State or, alternatively, Member States would need to enter into a multilateral convention for establishing these criteria. In both cases, an EU Model Tax Convention based on the principle of exclusive taxation in the state of origin, and supplemented by a Commentary on each of its provisions, could be an essential *preliminary step* either for reaching agreement on the provisions to be included in the directive or regulation introducing the ERTCS *or* for the multilateral convention to be entered into between Member States.

As the Commission itself submitted when it was first considered, the EU Model Tax Convention could take the form of a soft-law piece. It could be elaborated by an expert group whose members could be drawn from each national tax authority and could set out, for each item of income, the criteria for locating the ultimate income originator in a Member State and thus for allocating the tax jurisdiction. Once the agreement was reached and resulted in the elaboration of an EU Model Tax Convention based on the origin-taxation principle, the EU Model Tax Convention would allow either a swift adoption of the provisions of the ERTCS Directive or Regulation setting out the criteria for tax jurisdiction allocation *or* of a multilateral convention between Member States, because the contents of either the ERTCS Directive or Regulation or of the multilateral

---

14   Ibid., at 258–59.
15   Commission working document, EC Law and Tax Treaties, DOC(05) 2306, (9 June 2005).
16   Ibid., paras. 44–47, at pp. 16–17.
17   E .C. C. M. Kemmeren, 'Double Tax Conventions on Income and Capital and the EU: Past, Present and Future', *EC Tax Review* 21, 157–77 (2002), at 158–59.
18   Ibid., 176–77.

convention could be 'borrowed' from the provisions of the Model, as well as, where necessary, from any clarification by the supplementing Commentary. On the other hand, in the event of intended adoption of the scheme only by a group of Member States through enhanced cooperation, an EU Model Tax Convention based on taxation in the state of origin could be addressed only to Member States wishing to participate in the scheme.

A different EU Model Tax Convention, still based on taxation in the state of residence, could be used by non-participating Member State *or* for tax jurisdiction allocation between non-participating and participating Member States, since the scheme would apply *neither* to incomes derived in third countries by eligible taxpayers *nor* to taxpayers resident in third countries and deriving income in participating Member States. Taxpayers resident in non-participating Member States would be equated to taxpayers resident in third countries, so that the current DTCs would continue to apply between participating and non-participating Member States (as well as between participating Member States and third countries).

Therefore, the scope for a EU Model Tax Convention aimed at achieving more uniformity amongst bilateral DTCs based on the OECD Model (as in the original proposal for an EU Model Tax Convention), would still remain, and the introduction of the ERTCS via Enhanced Cooperation would ultimately require the adoption of two versions of the EU Model Tax Convention.

Finally, the introduction of the proposed scheme would increase the importance of initiatives which, with regard to relations with third countries, were planned by the Commission in its Action Plan against tax fraud and tax evasion: the adoption of measures intended to encourage third countries to apply minimum standards of good governance in tax matters[19] and the inclusion of common anti-abuse clauses in DTCs with third countries too.[20] 'Good governance in tax matters' means, according to the Commission, promoting more transparency, exchange of information and 'fair tax competition'. However debatable tax competition is, more transparency and a greater exchange of information, with third countries too, are essential for any Member State to be able to effectively contrast tax-minimisation schemes that may be implemented through operations involving third countries, including those jurisdictions applying very low tax rates and/or not exchanging information, commonly known as 'tax havens'.

Currently, Member States tend to act unilaterally towards any third countries: DTCs with third countries are stipulated by each individual Member State, and are generally based on the OECD Model (DTCs with developed countries) and on the UN Model (DTCs with developing countries). Despite the common pressure against these jurisdictions, at the OECD level, for more transparency and more exchange of information in the aftermath of the economic crisis, Member States also still tend to adopt their own individual and uncoordinated responses against

---

19 COM(2012) 722 final (n 4), para. 7, at 5–6.
20 Ibid., para. 8, at 6.

tax havens. The Commission, in the Action Plan against tax evasion, stressed that, as a result, 'the overall protection of Member State's tax revenues tends to be only as effective as the weakest response of any one Member State'.[21]

Consistently with this concern, the Commission recommended that Member States align their attitudes in respect of jurisdictions not applying minimum standards and, for this purpose, suggested measures such as blacklisting of non-compliant jurisdictions and the renegotiation, suspension or conclusion of DTCs. It also recommended that Member States should include common anti-abuse rules in DTCs with third countries,[22] emphasising that Member States should be able to use a single set of tools and instruments for exchange of information, both within the EU and in their relations with third countries, and committed itself to promote the automatic exchange of information as the future European and international standard of transparency and exchange of information.[23]

Although these targeted initiatives would help to fight global strategies of tax-minimisation, the current situation does not appear to be the optimal one for their implementation. In fact, national legislators are aware that cross-border strategies of tax minimisation or aggressive tax planning leading to double non-taxation can take place both within the EU and through operations involving any Member State and a third country, and Member States still have to outweigh the advantages of tax competition rather than tax cooperation. If attracting the location of the tax residence of more taxpayers in its jurisdiction (ie tax competition with other Member States) is assessed, by a national legislator, as more convenient than tax cooperation with other Member States, even adopting more lenient tax policies towards third countries becomes an element of a 'competitive' tax policy for making the tax residence in its jurisdiction more attractive than in other Member States.

In this respect, significant examples are offered by the implementation of corporate tax directives[24] – where, e.g. some Member States have introduced more favourable rules applying to operations with third countries too – *or* by the failure of ECJ rulings on anti-abuse clauses to induce national legislators to approximate their CFC rules or thin capitalisation rules.

Consequently, the current lack of consistent tax policies towards third countries may result in paradoxical situations of legal uncertainty even if a uniform anti-abuse clause were introduced in DTCs with third countries (as recommended by the Commission): in light of the ECJ's case law,[25] e.g. a Member State exempting dividends received by a resident parent company from a subsidiary located in a tax haven country, where the distributing company faces no taxation, would need to extend the exemption to dividends received by local branches of companies resident in other Member States. This would hold true despite the fact that an exemption may lead to situations of double non-taxation, and the taxpayer

---

21 Ibid., at 5.
22 Ibid., para. 4.1.2, at 9.
23 Ibid.
24 See ch 2, at 2.3 and 2.4.
25 See ch 3, at 3.1.

involved may find it uncertain whether or not the DTC anti-abuse clause could apply to this situation if the unconditional exemption were granted, by the Member State concerned, as a choice of its own tax 'attractiveness' policy.

On the contrary, in case of introduction of the ERTCS, national legislators of (participating) Member States – due to the replacement of the national residence connecting factor with the *national origin* nexus and due to the spontaneous convergence between national rules that the scheme would promote – would be aware that cross-border strategies of tax minimisation or aggressive tax planning leading to double non-taxation could *only* come from operations involving third countries too. In other words, the situation resulting from the introduction of the ERTCS could be described as a situation of 'EU tax residence area *vs*. rest of the world'. As the national tax residence element would become irrelevant, the location of taxpayer in a jurisdiction or in another would also become *immaterial* for individual States' taxing rights, and the current degree of competition between Member States in attracting the location of taxpayers – fostered by national tax residence and worldwide taxation – would no longer persist. As a result, all Member States (participating in the ERTCS) would have a common interest to cooperate in order not to have their national tax bases eroded by operations with third countries, the income from which would not fall within the scheme.

Specifically, any Member States having origin-based taxing rights over a taxpayer would find it more convenient that this taxpayer derives income from other Member States rather than from third countries, because it could gain *immediate* knowledge *only* of income originating in other Member States due to the single unified tax return and to the permanently accessible central database. Thanks to this immediate knowledge, it could become easier for each Member State to apply a 'source (origin) taxation with worldwide orientation', i.e. tax rates taking into account income originating in other Member States within the EU tax residence area, if taxpayers subject to its jurisdiction have income originating in other Member States than in third countries. Member States adhering to the scheme would, in essence, automatically support each other in protecting their own tax base and tax revenues, and therefore would have a common interest to make uniform choices towards the rest of the world.

Because of the common interest, it would be much more (convenient and) realistic for Member States to align their attitudes towards third countries, i.e. to adopt common measures (in the use of the already existing instruments such as DTCs with third countries, as well of automatic information exchange) such as those envisaged by the Commission, and it would also become convenient to make uniform choices in the treatment of incomes derived from third countries. Ultimately, the introduction of the ERTCS could therefore be expected to increase the effectiveness of the measures recommended by the Commission for adoption towards third countries, and to contribute to avoiding situations of *ex ante* legal uncertainty (such as the one exemplified above) otherwise deriving, in the current situation, from uncoordinated and competing national attitudes towards third countries.

6.3 An overall 'impact assessment' of the proposed solution: first indications for future research

In light of the foregoing, the ERTCS and the creation of an 'EU tax residence' for taxpayers opting for the scheme would have a positive impact on the key initiatives that the Commission intends pursuing, both with regard to the overcoming of remaining distortions induced by direct taxation within the EU and with regard to the alignment of Member States' attitudes towards third countries. In essence, the proposed solution would make some amongst these initiatives essential as preliminary steps to the introduction of the ERTCS, would make other initiatives complementary to the scheme and would facilitate common measures in respect of third countries.

A particularly important impact – on the ultimate TFEU's objective of turning distinct national markets into a truly single market – would be the ERTCS's contribution towards greater tax neutrality and thus towards a fiscal level playing field within the internal market, i.e. the contribution of the scheme to reducing the differences (and thus to a spontaneous convergence) between the national tax bases and rates.

This potential impact of the ERTCS appears to be particularly significant in light of a negative economic assessment – in the literature – of the effects of ECJ tax rulings on the actual achievement of a level playing field and of tax neutrality.[26] This literature, after stressing that the TFEU confers on the ECJ a constitutional mandate of contributing to establish the internal market, and that for this purpose it is necessary to achieve a greater level playing field and increased tax neutrality, argued that the *removal* of national measures establishing differential treatments on grounds of nationality or residence (discriminatory measures) and of measures hindering the exercise of a fundamental freedom (restrictive measures), should constitute only a means towards the achievement of a level playing field and tax neutrality.

It subsequently noted that the ECJ has been focusing on the removal of discriminatory or restrictive national provisions as an objective of its own, and it found that the ultimate effect of some landmark rulings was an increase in differences between Member States in tax bases and rates. It specifically stressed that, when only one aspect of the tax system is made more uniform – such as thin capitalisation rules or cross-border group relief rules – without systematic harmonisation of tax rates and bases, the differences in bases and rates may become more significant, with the ultimate outcome of further reducing tax neutrality and compromising the achievement of a level playing field.

Given these findings, the introduction of the ERTCS could be expected to generate a further positive impact – on the achievement of tax neutrality and thus of a fiscal level playing field – in respect of all three categories of taxpayers that would benefit from the scheme: *individuals* deriving incomes in at least two

---

[26] R. de la Feria, C. Fuerst, *Closer to an Internal Market? The Economic Effects of EU Tax Jurisprudence*, WP 11/12 (Oxford University Centre for Business Taxation, 2011).

Member States; *corporate taxpayers* with cross-border activities but *not eligible* for the CCCTB; and *corporate taxpayers* also *eligible* for the CCCTB.

The option for the ERTCS by the first two categories of taxpayers could contribute to tax neutrality and to achieving a level playing field due to the incentive that it would create for national legislators to spontaneously approximate their tax bases and rates, and owing to the fact that it would *stop exposing* Member States to challenges against their national provisions (on the part of taxpayers choosing the scheme) before the ECJ. In fact, within the EU tax residence area, the application of the new origin-based tax jurisdiction rules, regardless of the (nationality or) location of taxpayers, would by definition eliminate any grounds for discrimination or restriction.

Therefore, the higher the number of taxpayers who, after a first experimental phase as a pilot-project, decided to opt for the ERTCS, the higher the positive impact that the scheme would generate for tax neutrality and for the turning of national markets into a truly internal market. On the other hand, the option for the ERTCS by corporate taxpayers who would also be eligible for the CCCTB, by allowing a more effective functioning of such a formulary apportionment scheme and thus by making the CCCTB more attractive, would contribute to promote more tax neutrality, at least with regard to the determination of the taxable base according to uniform EU rules that would replace different national rules.

At the time of the CCCTB proposal, an 'impact assessment study', carried out on behalf of the Commission, was also published.[27] This impact assessment was based on an estimate about the change in effective tax rate in each Member State that would be caused by a switch from current national rules to the common CCCTB rules, and on assumptions about the responses of economic operators to these changes.

Although a key finding was that, from corporate taxpayers' viewpoint, the reduction in compliance costs would be the greatest benefit of the scheme,[28] the study found that only five countries – namely, Belgium, Germany, Italy, Luxembourg and Malta – would see an increase in their gross domestic product (GDP) as a result of the introduction of the CCCTB,[29] whereas, of the other Member States, GDP would fall by 1 per cent or more in four countries. The increase in the GDP was foreseen for countries where the switch to the CCCTB rules would determine a reduction in effective corporate tax rates, whereas the drop in the GDP was predicted for countries where the new uniform rules would determine an increase in the effective corporate tax rates. These outcomes of the study – which, amongst Member States, indicated potential 'winners' and 'losers' – have been generating opposition to the scheme by some Member States.

---

27 L. Bettendorf, M. Devereux, A. van der Horst and S. Loretz, 'Corporate Tax Reform in the EU: Weighing Pros and Cons, Policy Briefing' Oxford University Centre for Business Taxation (21 March 2011).
28 Ibid., at 4.
29 Ibid., at 2.

Nonetheless, these outcomes were based on the fact that, with the introduction of the CCCTB alone, there would be no convergence in nominal tax rates to be applied to national shares of the common tax base (so that the effective tax rate would increase where a given nominal tax rate applied to an increased tax base as a result of the new common rules). In fact, it was expressly stated that: 'In aggregate, European economies would only benefit if the spread of tax burdens is reduced by harmonizing the tax rate as well as the tax base'.[30]

In case of introduction of the ERTCS, this assumption could no longer be retained, because of the incentive (created by the new origin-based nexus for tax jurisdiction over individuals and over companies not eligible for the CCCTB) towards the spontaneous convergence of nominal tax rates. This convergence of national nominal tax rates would affect also the effective tax rate for companies opting for the CCCTB (as well as for all other taxpayers only operating within domestic markets). Once the ERTCS, after a first pilot-project phase, were made applicable to *all* taxpayers deriving cross-border incomes and bearing tax obligations towards at least two States, and proved to be successful in securing stability of national tax revenues, it would in fact be in the interest of simplicity of national tax systems, and of national legislators, to avoid two different sets of national tax rates (one applicable to ERTCS taxpayers, the other applicable to the remaining taxpayers).

The outcomes of the CCCTB impact assessment study and the opposition by 'losers', the changes that the ERTCS would bring to the current intra-EU direct taxation framework, the working of the scheme, the complementarity of the new scheme to the CCCTB project and the ultimate objectives of the ERTCS, seem to indicate the issues on which any future research and analysis on this proposed scheme could focus.

In relation to the changes that the ERTCS would bring to the current intra-EU direct taxation framework, by replacing the national tax-residence nexus with the national origin-based nexus, the first issue would be how to avoid some Member States becoming 'losers' under the scheme. This problem could arise (especially) on the adoption of a destination-based approach for allocating taxing rights on business profits (solely or predominantly) arising from sales in States other than the current states of residence. The solution could come from the 'compensatory rights' that, as indicated in Chapter 5, would be paid by the Member States who would be allocated taxing rights to those that would lose the tax jurisdiction:[31] the risk for these last States to become the 'losers' could be eliminated through the compensation to which they would become entitled for any taxpayer opting for the ERTCS scheme and over whom they would lose tax jurisdiction.

An important issue for future research would thus be how to identify the criteria to be used for determining the 'compensatory rights', and, from estimates and quantitative analysis too, to suggest that, thanks to this compensatory mechanism,

---

30 Ibid., at 3.
31 See ch 5, at 5.2.2.

the ERTCS would leave no 'losers' amongst Member States, whilst simplifying tax compliance for all eligible taxpayers.

A second issue appears to arise with regard to companies that would be eligible to opt for both the CCCTB and the ERTCS and which would be interested in accessing both schemes. In respect of these companies the allocation of taxing rights to Member States would be based on the formulary apportionment set out in the draft CCCTB Directive. As the ERTCS would, for these companies, contribute to the smooth functioning of the CCCTB, the issue would be whether – in case of some Member States suffering revenue losses in the event of option of the interested taxpayers for the CCCTB and other Member States gaining from this option – the ERTCS should provide for 'compensatory rights' to be paid by the 'winner' Member States to those that would be the 'losers'.

A positive response, i.e. a rule in an ERTCS Directive or Regulation providing for these compensatory rights, could probably overcome the reluctance of some Member States to accept the CCCTB regime. Nonetheless, it would make it appropriate to analyse whether the criteria for determining the ERTCS related 'compensatory rights' as a result of the simultaneous application of the CCCTB, should be the same as those to be applied in favour of Member States which, for taxpayers not eligible for the CCCTB, would not be the market-destination States but which would provide the facilities for the business activity. It would also be necessary to determine whether – for 'compensatory rights' to be paid to Member States losing from the CCCTB – the option by interested taxpayers for the ERTCS should be precedent or concomitant to the option for the CCCTB.

Further 'technical issues' to be explored would lie in the kind of legislative measure to be preferred for introducing the ERTCS – i.e. whether a Directive or a Regulation would be preferable – and in the working of the EOSS. In this respect, important operational aspects to be defined would lie in the duration of the mandate of members of the permanent representatives of national tax authorities in the JSTC, in the renewal of their members, and in the rules applicable to any tax audits to be decided by the JSTC. As regards tax audits, the issue could be whether a specific procedure – and related taxpayers' rights – should be laid down in the legislative measure introducing the scheme or whether it could be possible to rely on the national laws of the Member States having taxing rights in each individual case, which national laws could in any event be affected by the uniform provisions of a European Taxpayer's Charter.

Arguably, there is also a longer term issue for further research and analysis that would be appropriate to deal with, given the ERTCS's objective of protecting, among other, the tax sovereignty and tax revenues of Member States by offering a more stable nexus for allocating tax jurisdiction to individual Member States. Given that the scheme would create an 'EU tax residence' area where taxing rights would be based on the origin principle, and that the socio-economic structure of each Member State – in terms of prevailing activities, of dominant economic sectors, of consumers' demands etc – might be more suitable to determine the origin of a type of income rather than of another type, a longer term challenge could be to define, within the EU tax residence area, the overall structure of an origin-based allocation of taxing rights consistent with the socio-economic structure of each Member State and therefore of the single market as a whole.

Although this last challenge could more effectively be taken up by economists than by law researchers, it seems evident that – on the whole – the hypothesis of introduction of the ERTCS would offer a new and multi-faceted topic and would raise far-reaching issues that could be left to future research and analysis, both at an academic and at a decision-making level, for the benefit of the long-term 'tax sustainability' of the European integration project.

Bibliography

L. Bettendorf, M. Devereux, A. van der Horst and S. Loretz, 'Corporate Tax Reform in the EU: Weighing Pros and Cons, Policy Briefing', Oxford University Centre for Business Taxation (21 March 2011).

M. Cadesky, I. Hayes and D. Russell, *'Towards Greater Fairness in Taxation: A Model Taxpayer Charter* (CFE, ADTCA, STEP, 2012).

R. de la Feria, C. Fuerst, *Closer to an Internal Market? The Economic Effects of EU Tax Jurisprudence*, WP 11/12 (Oxford University Centre for Business Taxation, 2011).

E. C. C. M. Kemmeren, 'Double Tax Conventions on Income and Capital and the EU: Past, Present and Future', 21 *EC Tax Review* 3, 2012, 157–77.

P. Pistone, *The Influence of Community Law on Tax Treaties: Issues and Solutions* EUCOTAX Series on European Taxation (Kluwer Law International, 2002), 235–353.

7 Conclusions

In the aftermath of the economic and financial crisis, 'euro-scepticism' is spreading across public opinion in a number of Member States, partly as a consequence of austerity policies implemented to redress public finances and to their recessive effects, as well as to the constraints imposed by the Treaty on Stability, Coordination and Governance in the Economic and Monetary Union (the 'fiscal compact'). In the backdrop of this situation, the distortions in the functioning of the internal market which still arise in the direct taxation area can only contribute to threatening the future of the European project, as they risk preventing both Member States and economic operators from fully enjoying the benefits of economic integration and of the single market.

In its communications, the European Commission has indicated one by one these distortions, which are to the detriment both of Member State's tax revenues (risk of double non-taxation, of abusive practices, of aggressive tax planning strategies) and of taxpayers carrying out cross-border activities within the EU (remaining risks of double taxation, insufficient legal certainty and onerous compliance with different national tax systems). These distortions ultimately derive from the lack, within the internal market, of tax neutrality in the widest possible meaning – i.e. in the sense of creating a context where the movement of individuals, of companies and of capital could take place for *non-tax* reasons – as was envisaged in reports and programmes ever since the early years of the (then) EEC.

Over the history of the European project, the relationship between the EU and direct taxation has been a difficult one because Member States have been regarding the maintaining of their autonomy in this area and the tax competition with other Member States as the avenues for protecting their tax sovereignty and their tax revenues. Because the consequent lack of tax neutrality has resulted in the distortions highlighted by the Commission, the objectives set out by the Commission itself in terms of overcoming these distortions have been taken as 'benchmarks', in the first part of this work, for a critical review of the EU legislation issued to date and of the case law developed by the ECJ in the direct taxation area. This analysis has shown, in essence, that the three corporate tax directives – in light of their implementation and of the related ECJ case law – have largely eliminated (juridical) double taxation for the kinds of operations covered by each of these directives, but have partly failed to contribute to meeting other 'benchmarks' such as legal certainty, elimination of double non-taxation and an effective fight against aggressive tax planning strategies.

The Directives on Administrative Cooperation and on tax Recovery Assistance also show limitations lying in the reliance on divergent national laws of Member States on important aspects concerning their application, and therefore risk turning the different procedural rules of Member States into an element of international tax planning and of failing to contribute to countering aggressive tax planning. In turn, the ECJ's case law on the application of the fundamental freedoms to direct taxation has partly been failing against three 'benchmarks', i.e. the elimination of double taxation as well as of double non-taxation, legal certainty and countering aggressive tax planning.

However, by unintentionally encouraging tax competition, the ECJ's case law has even been creating further scope for specific aggressive tax planning strategies, which can be regarded as damaging in light of the Commission's recommendation against aggressive tax planning and in light of the OECD's Action Plan on BEPS, but which cannot be regarded as abusive within the ECJ criteria for identifying abuse. The analysis carried out has, ultimately, stressed that these shortcomings against the benchmarks have been occurring in the current international tax law order which, within the EU too, is still founded on national residence-based tax jurisdictions, on the distinction between residence and source and on the worldwide tax liability for residents etc.

It has also highlighted that the effort (by EU legislators as well as by the ECJ) to *adapt* the essential requirements of the internal market (such as non-discrimination and the free movement rights) to this pre-existing international tax order is bound to fail to achieve an essential condition for meeting all the benchmarks: the move toward a spontaneous approximation by Member States of essential features of their national direct taxation system. Without this move, tax neutrality would *not* be achieved and, as a result, the benchmark of effectively countering aggressive (even if not abusive) tax planning strategies would not be reached. Arguably, to achieve this benchmark, it would be necessary to eliminate or at least reduce the *ex ante* incentive for taxpayers to undertake these strategies.

All the targeted actions indicated by the Commission as well as by the OECD in its Action Plan on BEPS would be insufficient for this purpose, due to their very being based on an approach *ex post* detection and repression of these strategies after they have been conceived, and due to the fact that these strategies are ultimately being encouraged by the current national tax residence-based jurisdiction that fosters tax competition.

In light of the partial non-achievement to date of all benchmarks and of the insufficiency that even the initiatives already proposed are bound to prove, this work has formulated the hypothesis for a new supranational and optional regime to be made available to *all* taxpayers with cross-border incomes. This solution – namely, a 'European Regime for Tax Compliance Simplification' (ERTCS) based on an 'EU tax residence', which would replace the national tax residence-based jurisdiction with national origin-based tax jurisdiction – could be regarded, on a first assessment, as generating a mutual benefit to both Member States and taxpayers bearing cross-border tax compliance obligations. Member States would be offered a stronger and more stable nexus with taxpayers than the current national tax residence (and thus a stronger protection of tax revenues); at the same time, the taxpayers at issue would be offered, within the EU, two highly valued benefits: a drastic simplification of tax compliance obligations and a greater legal certainty than in the current international tax environment.

The interest for Member States to a spontaneous convergence, that this solution would determine, would *ex ante* minimise the scope for aggressive tax planning strategies. Moreover, the hypothesis of making the new scheme available as a pilot project for taxpayers showing the best tax compliance records and giving up these strategies, could further strengthen the ability of this solution to contribute to achieving all objectives.

Admittedly, much further research would be necessary on this solution: e.g. how to make the exclusive taxing powers that each (participating) state would have under the origin taxation principle, within the 'EU tax residence' area, consistent with the economic structure of the internal market. This would imply identifying: which type of income could better originate in which state, i.e. with which type of income each Member State could have the stronger nexus by virtue of its own socio-economic structure; whether the response to this question could vary from one economic sector to another. Nonetheless, at the current stage, the hypothesis for this solution seems to be already capable of offering inputs to the debate at an academic and extra-academic level, at a time both of increasing pressure on Member States to protect their revenues and increasing demand by taxpayers for legal certainty and for tax compliance simplification.

In any event, and exactly because of its ultimate purposes of reconciling states' and taxpayers' needs, the solution could be 'borrowed' for consideration by any future group of states which, in any other part of the developed or of the emerging world, may wish to proceed both to full economic integration (with free movement of capital as well as of natural and legal persons) and to a degree of political integration comparable to the degree reached by the EU – and may set for itself the same objectives that the Treaty sets for the EU – whilst protecting their revenues and offering compliance simplification and legal certainty to taxpayers. This holds true because the ultimate needs of both states (in terms of protection of their financial interests) and of taxpayers (in terms of easy compliance with tax obligations, simplification of the tax law environment and of legal certainty) tend, by their very nature, to be universal ones.

Index

A Oy (2013) ruling 55, 62–4, 71, 147
Aascher (1996) ruling 124–6
Aberdeen Property (2009) ruling 142
ability to pay principle 132, 146–7, 186, 190, 205, 208
abusive practices 14–17, 28, 120, 237; benchmark shortcomings 149–51; CCCTB and proposed initiatives 165–70, 188; ECJ case law 15, 82–3; and EU tax residence proposal 212–14, 227; and Merger Directive 72; and Parent-Subsidiary Directive 44, 48; and rights prohibition 63
Accor (2011) ruling 135
acquis communautaire 200–1, 222
administrative cooperation 7, 20–1, 172, 182–3, 214–15, 223–4
Administrative Cooperation Directive 106, 204, 210, 238; against benchmarks 95–6; and CCCTB 168; centre of vital interest criteria 96; and direct taxation internal market function 171, 176–8, 182, 191; foreseeable relevance standard 92; information exchange 158–60; key provisions 91–5
administrative simplification 46, 54, 88–91, 163–4, 204; benchmark shortcomings 147–9
aggressive tax planning 2, 14–16, 45, 81–3, 86; benchmark shortcomings 149–53; CCCTB and proposed initiatives 168–79, 181–8, 193; and Commission Recommendation (2012) 30–1; cross-border tax evasion and fraud 48–9, 72–3; and EU tax residence proposal 198–9, 212–14; strategies 77

always somewhere approach 105, 109–10, 126–32, 146–8
Amazon group 192
AMID (1999) ruling 108
Amurta (2007) ruling 142, 145, 149, 151–5
Andersen og Jensen (2002) ruling 55–8, 71
anti-abuse clause 28, 48–51, 55–65, 68, 72–6, 159–61, 175, 225–6, 230–1; benchmarks 151–3; general (GAAC) 29, 49, 159–60, 165–6, 169; and Interest and Royalties Directive 76; and Merger Directive 58–64; and minimum holding period 32, 72; national rules application 117–22; and Parent-Subsidiary Directive 32; SAAR 159–60, 165–6
anti-abuse measures 14, 17, 72–3, 120, 151–3
anti-avoidance 68, 111
Apple company 226
apportionment 138, 156, 159–62, 166–8, 185, 203, 216, 220, 233–5
Arbitration Convention on Transfer Pricing 73–5, 170–2, 220; Advisory Commission 74; and EU tax residence proposal 219–20
arm s length principle 73, 120, 161, 166, 201
artificial transactions 166
assets transfers 8, 25, 50–8, 65–72
associated companies 79; identification 80
AT v Finanzamt Stuttgart-K rperschaften (2008) ruling 55, 60, 65–71
automatic information exchange 94–6, 231
avoidance *see* tax avoidance
avoir fiscal (1986) ruling 98–100, 142

242 Index

Bachmann (1992) ruling 101–3, 118
Baker (2013) ruling 139–41
Banque F d rative du Cr dit Mutual (2008) case 32, 39
Base Erosion and Profit Shifting (BEPS) 181–5, 193, 212–13, 238
benchmarks 2, 19–97, 186, 201, 214, 237–8; abusive practices 149–51, 168–70; and Administrative Cooperation Directive 95–6; administrative simplification 147–9; aggressive tax planning 149–51, 168–70; and CCCTB project 155–70; cross-border tax evasion and fraud 149–51, 168–70; EC objectives 13–18; EU direct taxation 3–18; Interest and Royalties Directive 76–8; legal certainty 147–9; and Merger Directive 52–5, 69–73; and Parent-Subsidiary Directive 28–31; and Recovery Assistance Directive 90–1
beneficial owner 84–6
Biehl (1990) ruling 122–3
Biehl II (1995) ruling 123–4
Block (2009) ruling 138, 145
book values 53
Bosal Holding (2003) ruling 32, 38, 103–4
Bouanich (2014) ruling 139–41
branches 54, 106, 148, 151, 158, 162, 169, 176, 230; of activities 68; v subsidiaries treatment 98–101
Burda (2008) ruling 31, 37, 142

Cadbury Schweppes (2006) ruling 59, 64, 118–22, 150–1, 159
capital *see* free movement of capital
capital export neutrality (CEN) 30, 190
capital gains 7–8, 51–3, 60, 113, 146, 207; realisation 70
capital import neutrality (CIN) 30, 189
Cartesio (2008) ruling 111–12
central database 158, 178, 192, 202–4, 209–10, 214–15, 221, 231
Centre for Inter-American Tax Administrations (CIAT) 199
Centro Equestre (2007) ruling 129
Centros (1999) ruling 59
CLT-UFA (2006) ruling 99
Cobelfret (2009) ruling 31–4, 40–1, 47

Code of Good Conduct 11; on business taxation 150; Revised 75
Commission Communications 2, 24–7, 38–9, 81–96, 111, 115–17, 122, 130; Action Plan 48–9, 70, 73, 149–56, 183, 220, 229–30; Administrative Cooperation Directive 92–5; aggressive tax planning Recommendation (2012) 30–1, 46; and Arbitration Convention 74–5; and benchmark shortcomings 145; and CCCTB 161–71; cross-border corporate loss 102; and direct taxation internal market function 174–88, 192, 195; double taxation 45, 53; and ERTCS 198–218; infringement procedures 142; Interest and Royalties Directive proposal 77–8; on JTPF work 75; and Merger Directive 69–73; objectives and benchmarks 13–18; and real value proposal rejection 65–6; tax fraud and evasion 48, 171, 183; two-track strategy 11–12; valuation rules introduction 69
Commission v Denmark (2013) ruling 115–17
Commission v Estonia (2012) ruling 130
Commission v Italy (2009) ruling 142
Commission v Netherlands (2013) ruling 115
Commission v Portugal (2012) ruling 115–16
Commission v Spain (2013) ruling 115–17, 142
Common Consolidated Corporate Tax Base (CCCTB) 2, 198–211, 215–17, 220–6, 233–5; abusive practices 168–70; administrative simplification 157, 163–7; aggressive tax planning 168–70; cross-border tax evasion and fraud 168–70; crucial issues 162–70; discrimination elimination 162–3; double taxation elimination 162–3; greater legal certainty 163–7; optimal conditions 173–86; project v benchmarks 155–70; salient features 155–61; three factors formula 159–61, 168; unintended double non-taxation elimination 162–3; Working Group (WG) 156, 166
compensation: horizontal loss 107
compensatory rights 206, 234–5

competition 9; fair tax 11; harmful 11; inter-jurisdictional 9, *see also* tax competition
compliance *see* European Regime for Tax Compliance Simplification (ERTCS)
compliance costs 14, 17; administrative 46–8, 71
comprehensive solution 198–218
Confederation Fiscale Europ enne (CFE) 222
controlled foreign companies/corporations (CFCs) 118–20, 160, 180; rules 184, 230
cooperation: administrative 7, 20–1, 172, 182–3, 214–15, 223–4; enhanced 22, 163–4, 169, 215–17, 220, 224, 229
corporate social responsibility (CSR) 226
corporate tax rates 6, 9; refund 136
country-by-country (CBC) reporting 184
credit *see* tax credit method
cross-border tax obstacles 2, 7, 50; costs and losses compensation 101–10, 162, 216; and EU tax residence proposal 204–10; evasion 16–17, 22, 48–9, 72–3, 90–1; evasion and fraud benchmark 149–51, 168–70; losses offsetting 14; recovery 88; withholding taxes abolition 11

Daily Mail (1988) ruling 111–13
damages 33–4
Damseaux (2009) ruling 137–9, 145–9, 201
De Groot (2002) ruling 127–32, 140, 150, 190
deductions 12, 40, 127; and deductibility 38; income-related expenses 208; personal 130; *pro quota* 128
deferral *see* tax deferral regime 50, 65–7
Denkavit case (1996) 31–4, 43, 46–8
Destination-Based Corporation Tax (DBCT) 192–4, 205–6
Deutsche Shell (2008) ruling 109
DI VI Finanziaria SAPA (2012) ruling 115–16
differentiation criteria 123
direct taxation 3–18, 155–97; benchmark shortcomings 145–53; benchmarks 3–18; CCCTB project v benchmarks 155–70; double taxation on dividend elimination 133–45; ECJ case law and TFEU freedoms of movement 98–154; EU tax law source 19–25; free movement of capital 133–45; free movement of workers 122–33; freedom of establishment 98–122; initiatives overview 170–3; mismatch exploitation 179–86; national tax-residence alternatives quest 189–96; obstacles 7; proper functioning of internal market 155–97; residence and source concepts 189–96; residence-based jurisdiction v tax sovereignty 186–9; tax-induced distortion optimal conditions 173–86
director fees 94
discrimination 9, 43–5, 69–70, 81, 132, 139; covert 211; elimination 162–3; nationality based 123; non-discrimination principle 174; unlawful 100
dispute resolution 75, 170
distribution of profits 26–8, 47
dividends 47–8, 85, 95, 98–100, 117, 120, 152, 206–7, 219, 230; deduction system 40; and direct taxation internal market function 158–9, 162–3, 170, 180; domestic 45; double taxation elimination 133–48; foreign-sourced 136–7; inbound cross-border 133–6, 140, 148; as refund 38; taxation 9
divisions 7–8, 25, 49, 52–4, 70–2, 160; asset 67
DMC Beteilungsgesellschaft (2014) ruling 116
double tax conventions (DTCs) 7, 35–8, 44, 47–8, 94–101, 112; apportionment criteria 138; and Arbitration Convention 73–5; benchmarks assessment 151–2; bilateral 12, 22–4, 84, 101, 112, 184; and CCCTB salient features 155–9; direct taxation and internal market function 163–79, 184–8; and EU law sources 22–9; and EU tax residence proposal 201, 206, 214–20, 227–31; free movement of capital and double dividends taxation 136–47; and free movement of workers 122–32; and Interest and Royalties Directive 76–7, 82–3; PE definition of UN Model-based DTC 164–5;

244 *Index*

planning strategy 83; residence and source concepts 193–4; Savings Directive 83–6; tie-breaker rules 176, 187, 194

double taxation 3, 8, 36, 40, 81; and CCCTB proposal 162–3; direct and internal market function 14, 155–97; elimination 3–4, 13–15, 23–7, 38, 43–5, 49, 69–70, 78, 133–48, 162–3; international 5; juridical 12, 25–7, 30, 36–7, 43–5, 49–51, 69, 78, 81, 162–3; subsidiary and parent company 8; unintended non 14, 45–6, 70–1, 162–3, *see also* Common Consolidated Corporate Tax Base (CCCTB); economic double taxation; juridical double taxation

dual resident companies 48, 55, 66, 79, 97

economic double taxation 4, 7–8, 12, 25, 28–30, 36–8, 43–5, 49, 53, 65–6, 69–71, 78, 82, 98, 122, 135–48, 162–7, 172, 214

employed/self-employed workers 122–33

employment income 94, 125–9, 190, 205

enhanced cooperation 22, 163–4, 169, 215–17, 220, 224, 229

enterprise concepts 74

Epson (1998) case 31, 34–7

equalisation tax 37

establishment *see* freedom of establishment

European Commission (EC) 1–8, 19, 22, 168–71, 237; Action Plan 48–9, 70, 73, 149–56, 183, 220, 229–30; High Level Expert Group on Taxation of Digital Economy 184; objectives and analysis benchmarks 13–18; *Programme for tax harmonisation* document (1967) 5; Regulation 1612/68 (free movement) 127, *see also* Commission Communications

European company 26, 180

European Cooperative Society (SCE) 26, 180

European Court of Justice (ECJ) 1–2, 9–24, 28–49, 53–73, 93–6, 237–8; abusive practices case law 15, 82–3; and Arbitration Convention on Transfer Pricing 73; benchmark shortcomings 145–51; and compatibility grounds 12; and direct taxation internal market function 159–69, 172–93; and EU tax residence proposal 198–210, 208–12, 216–17, 222, 226–33; free movement of workers 122–33; freedom of establishment 98–122; Interest and Royalties Directive 78–9; and Merger Directive case law 55–66; national tax system interpretations 14; and negative integration 9; and Parent-Subsidiary Directive case law 31–41; and TFEU fundamental freedoms 98–154

European Economic Community (EEC) Treaty 1–3, 9; Article 220 double taxation abolition 4, 23; Article 293 (double taxation) 13, 24; Articles 56-9 (negotiation) 10; Competition, Taxation and State Aids 3

European Regime for Tax Compliance Simplification (ERTCS) 198–217, 219–38; abusive practices and aggressive planning strategy minimisation 212–14; Action Plan 221, 224; aspects v Commission objectives 214–15, 219–25; comprehensive solution hypothesis 198–200; and cross-border tax obstacle removal 204–10; effectiveness 219–36; and EOSS 200–4; feasability 215–17; impact assessment 232–6; proposed solution and *acquis communautaire* 200–1; and single unified tax return 202–4; structure suggestions 201–14; tax sovereignty safeguards 210–12, 225–31

European Tax Identification Number (TIN) 171, 202, 223

European Taxpayer Code 171, 221–2

European Taxpayer s Charter 235

evasion *see* tax evasion

exchange of information 7, 87, 200, 204, 214, 221–3, 229–30; direct taxation and internal market function 158, 168, 171–82, 191–2; multilateral automatic 178, 202–4, 214; paying agent 84; on request 85, 91–5, 160; spontaneous 191

exchange of shares 49–60, 66–70

excise duties 6

exemption *see* tax exemption

exit taxes 12–14, 14, 53, 148–53, 176, 180, 188; application 111–17; payment deferral 68–9
explicit choice 54

fair market value 68
Felixstowe Dock and Railway Company (2014) ruling 107–8
Ferrero (2010) ruling 31, 37–8
Financial and Fiscal Committee (Neumark) Report (1962) 3–8, 15
fiscal residence 47
Foggia (2011) case 55, 61–3, 71
Foreign Account Tax Compliance (FACTA) 95
forum shopping 16, 72, 170, 173, 213
fractional taxation system 190–1
fraud 14–17, 22, 72–3, 93; Action Plan 48–9, 70, 73, 183, 220, 229–30; benchmark shortcomings 149–51; and CCCTB 168–70
free movement of capital 5–12, 41, 101, 110, 116–17, 133–45, 149, 186, 239; and double taxation elimination 133–45; rights 16, 172, 177
free movement of workers 99, 149, 187; rights 16, 172, 177; and TFEU 122–33
free zones 9
freedom of establishment 9, 12, 16, 28–32, 45, 53–4, 59, 62–4, 68, 82, 159, 187; benchmarks assessment 145–53; cross-border compensation of costs and losses 101–10; cumulative elements 101–4; double taxation on dividends elimination 133–45; and ECJ landmark rulings 98–122; and EU tax residence proposal 212, 227; exit taxes application 111–17; free movement of capital 133–45; and free movement of workers 122–33; justifications 104; national anti-abuse rules application 117–22; and Parent-Subsidiary Directive 38–9; TFEU provisions 173–4; treatment of branches v subsidiaries 98–101
Futura (1997) ruling 108

Gaz de France (2009) ruling 32, 39–40
general anti-abuse clause (GAAC) 29, 49, 159–60, 165–6, 169

Gerritse (2003) ruling 190
Gilly (1998) ruling 24, 125–32
global approach 146, 149
good governance 14, 229
Google group 176, 192, 226
Gschwind (1999) ruling 126

Haribo and Salinen (2011) ruling 135–41, 147
harmonisation 3–7, 13–15, 20–4, 113, 174, 195–6, 215, 232; horizontal 7; internal market attempts 22–5; programme 15
horizontal loss compensation 107
hybrid loans 42

ICI (1998) ruling 102–5, 127
Imfeld (2013) ruling 128, 147
immovable property income 12, 94, 102, 131–3, 140, 206–7; foreign losses 122
impact assessment 232–6
implementation 7, 13, 163, 230, 237; abusive practices and aggressive tax planning minimisation 213–15; and CCCTB proposal 167–70; and ERTCS 223–5; EU tax residence sovereignty safeguard 210; internal market optimal conditions 175, 180; residence and source concepts 191–3
implicit option 54
income: employment 94, 125–9, 190, 205; foreign sourced 127; immovable property 12, 94, 102, 122, 131–3, 140, 206–7
income-related deductions 122, 130–2, 208; and expenses 122
indirect taxation 3–7, 19–22, 181
information sharing model 157, *see also* exchange of information
inheritance tax 138
integration: negative 1, 9–15, 187
Interest and Royalties Directive 76–84; case law 78–9; definition 77; implementation 79–83; text against benchmarks 76–83
interests 7, 182, 188, 198–9, 203, 207, 225, 239; and benchmarks 10–13, 90, 96, 145; and exit taxes 114; free movement of workers 132; and national anti-abuse rules 121; and royalties 81

246 *Index*

internal market 26, 30, 50, 95, 121, 137, 145, 149–53; direct taxation and proper functioning 155–97; and EU tax residence proposal 198, 204–10, 216, 228, 232–3
intra-company payments 82; cross-border loss compensation 108
Intra-European Organisation of Tax Administrations (IOTA) 199
intra-group loss relief 102; and transactions 162
Italcar (2013) ruling 144

Joint Supranational Tax Committee (JSTC) 199, 202–9, 215, 220–5
Joint Transfer Pricing Forum (JTPF) 75, 184, 199
juridical double taxation 4, 8, 12, 24–7, 36–7, 43–4, 49–51, 69, 81–2, 85, 152, 201; and direct taxation internal market function 159, 162–3, 172, 178; elimination 145–7; enforcement 192; free movement of capital 125–6, 137–41; substantive 192, *see also* double taxation; economic double taxation
justifications 60, 99, 104, 122, 140, 143, 148

K (2013) ruling 102, 110
KBC and BRB (2009) ruling 32, 41
Keller Holding (2006) ruling 32, 39
Kerckhaert & Morres (2006) ruling 137–41, 145–7
Kofoed (2007) ruling 55, 58–62
Krankenheim (2008) ruling 109
Kronos International (2014) ruling 135–6

Lakebrink-Peters (2007) ruling 131–2, 146
Lammers (2008) ruling 120
Langhorst-Hohorst (2002) ruling 117–20
Lasteyrie du Saillant (2004) ruling 111, 114–15
law: soft 15, 19, 22, 75, 170, 179, 183, 216, 219, 228
law development 19–97; sources 19–25
legal certainty 17, 28–30, 52, 55, 71, 75–7, 90, 117, 172, 176, 181; administrative costs reduction 46–7; benchmark shortcomings 95–6, 147–9, 152–3; and CCCTB 163–7; conclusions 237–9; and EU tax residence proposal 205–10, 214, 224–7; Interest and Royalty/Savings Directives 81–5; participation exemption 40–1
legal forms 39–40
Lenz (2004) ruling 134–5
Les Verges du Vieux Taves (2008) ruling 32, 39–40
Leur-Bloem (1997) ruling 55–61, 68, 71
Lidl Belgium (2008) ruling 109
life insurance 94
link company 108
Lisbon Treaty (2009) 13, 24
loans: hybrid 42
look through approach 86
loss compensation: horizontal 107
loss relief: intra-group 102, 162

Maastricht Treaty/TEU (1992) 9–10, 17–19, 162, 215; legal bases and Articles 19–22
management: place of effective 29, 48, 72, 112–14, 151, 156–7, 166–7, 210, 225
Manninen (2004) ruling 134–5, 145, 148–9
market: single 155, *see also* internal market
Marks & Spencer (2005) ruling 63, 103–10, 119–21, 128, 146, 149–51, 209
Meilicke (2007) ruling 134
Meilicke II (2011) ruling 134–5
Merger Directive 8, 12, 21, 25–6, 28, 49–73, 76, 83, 107, 159, 165; administrative costs reduction 71; anti-abuse clause 55, 58–64, 73; case law 55–66; cross-border tax evasion and fraud 72–3; implementation 66–73; key provisions 49–52; shares exchange and asset transfers 55–8; tax neutrality conditions 64–6; text against benchmarks 52–5, 69–73; unintended double non-taxation elimination 70–1
mergers 7, 25, 49, 52–4, 59, 70, 160; by acquisition 62–3
Mertens (2002) ruling 129, 148
Metallgesellschaft (2001) ruling 103
minimum holding period 26, 31–4, 42–8, 72, 76, 80–3
Model Tax Convention 227–8

Model Taxpayer Charter (MTC) 222
money laundering 86
multilateral automatic exchange of information 178, 202–4, 214
mutatis mutandis application 144
mutual agreements procedure (MAPs) 74–5, 172

N (2006) ruling 111, 113–17
National Grid Indus (2011) ruling 53, 72, 112–17, 146, 150, 173, 180
negative integration 1, 9–15, 187
neutrality 8, 15, 30–1, 43, 60, 148, 198, 232–3, 237–8; CEN 30, 190; CIN 30, 189; tax 15–16, 53–5, 64–8, 165, 173–4, 179, 194
non-discrimination 21, 174, 186
non-resident taxpayers 12
Nordea Bank Danmark (2014) ruling 109–10

OECD Model 22–3, 29, 81–3, 87, 112, 141, 228–9; Action Plan (2013) on BEPS 181–4, 193, 212–13; Article 5 (interest and royalties) 76; Article 19(1) 94; Article 26(2) 92–3; and CCCTB proposal 156–7, 167, 170; for DTCs 73–7, 85; objectives 184; Transfer Guidelines for Multinational Enterprises and Tax Administrations 73
one-stop shop system 157, 171, 177–8, 235; European (EOSS) 199–204, 208–9, 213–15
optimal conditions 16, 173–86, 190, 194, 201
origin-taxation principle 208–10, 214–15, 228, 234
over-deduction 123

Papillon (2008) ruling 105–8
parent company 26, 30–1, 37, 44–9, 103; definition 26; non-resident 41–3
Parent-Subsidiary Directive 8, 12, 25–49, 70–1, 76, 85, 133, 142–3; anti-abuse clause 32; case law 31–41; and charge deductibility 38–9; as common objective 25–6; cross-border tax evasion and fraud 48–9; direct tax compliance cost reduction 46–8; double non-taxation elimination 45–6; double taxation elimination and discrimination 43–5; implementation 41–9; key provisions 26–8; overview 41–3; participation exemption granting method 40–3; provision direct effect 32–4; shareholding/legal forms eligibility 39–40; text against benchmarks 28–31; and withholding tax 34–8
participation exemption 40–1
paying agent 84–6
pensions 94; personal 124
permanent establishment (PEs) 12, 26, 48, 50–4, 67, 97, 102, 106–9; absence 64; direct taxation and internal market function 155–7, 161, 164, 170, 175; Interest and Royalties Directive 79–80; non-taxation payments 82; and transfer pricing 73; UN Model-based DTC definition 164–5
personal deductions 100, 127–32, 186, 190–1, 208
Philips Electronics (2012) ruling 107–8
place of effective management 29, 48, 72, 112–14, 151, 156–7, 166–7, 210, 225
positive obligations 21
Principal Tax Authority (PTA) 157, 167–8, 203, 220
profit: distribution 27–8, 47; taxable 9, 27, 38–40, 50–1, 54, 73, 108, 113, 129, 155, 180, 185
progressivity rule (taxation) 123–4, 132
proportionality 22, 44, 110–14, 144, 186
provisions and reserves 68

real seat criteria 112
real value 68
receiving company 65, 72
Recovery Assistance Directive 21, 86–92, 95, 177, 182, 238; against benchmarks 90–1; and central liaison office 88; key provisions 86–90; person definition 87
Renneberg (2008) ruling 131–3, 146–7
residence *see* tax residence
restrictions 9–10, 16, 23–5, 30, 139, 142, 149, 211
restructuring operations 7–8, 25, 49–51, 61–2, 66, 70–2
Rewe-Zentralfinanz (2007) ruling 105

rights: compensatory 206, 234–5; voting 30–1, 43, 76
Ritter-Coulais (2006) ruling 131
Royal Bank of Scotland (1999) ruling 99
Royalties Directive 7–12, 21, 70, 76–84, 158–9, 172, 207–8, 219–20
Rubik Agreements 177
Ruding Report (1992) 8–9, 15

St Gobain (1999) ruling 100–1, 117, 127, 150
Santander (2012) ruling 142
Savings Directive 21, 83–6, 171–2, 177
SCA Group Holding and Others (2014) ruling 106–7
SCE 49–50, 78
Scheuten Solar (2011) ruling 78, 82
Schumacker (1995) ruling 99–100, 110, 122–7, 131–3, 146–9, 174, 186, 209
SE 49–50, 78
seat transfer 50, 53, 116
Secilpar (2010) ruling 142
securities 68
self-employed workers 122–33
SGI (2010) ruling 121–2, 148
shareholding 39, 50–3, 70–2; allotment 52; book value 64; domestic income tax 141; exchanges 53–8, 67; and Merger Directive implementation 66–9; minimum quota 158; requirement 78–9; resident/non-resident 134–5, 139, 143; taxation 65
shares: exchange of 49–60, 66–70
similarity test 164
simplification *see* European Regime for Tax Compliance Simplification (ERTCS)
single country approach 145–51
single entity taxation scheme 106–8
single market 155
single unified tax return 202–4, 208–10, 213–14, 223–4, 231
soft law 15, 19, 22, 75, 170, 179, 183, 216, 219, 228
source 39–41, 46, 76–8, 81–90, 93–6, 100, 125–48, 156–9, 238; domestic 134; of EU tax law 19–25; and EU tax residence proposal 209–11, 228, 231; foreign 41, 137; indirect/direct taxation 19–22; principle 205; and residence concepts 189–96; tax-induced distortions optimal conditions 174–6; taxation with worldwide orientation 159, 189–90, 194, 209–10
sovereignty 8, 13, 152, 187; debt crisis 1; erosion 12; and EU tax residence 210–12, 225–31; v residence-based jurisdiction 186–9
special anti-abuse rules (SAAR) 159–60, 165–6
special tax regimes 11
spontaneous information exchange 191
Starbucks group 176, 192, 226–7
subsidiaries 7–8, 12, 155–6, 164, 168–9, 176, 180–1, 210; and ECJ case law 98–108, 118–20, 136–7, 158; and Merger Directive 54–6, 59, 62; and Parent-Subsidiary Directive 25–8, 31, 37–49, 83; profit 35; state of residence 62–3; v branches treatment 98–101
subsidiarity 10–11, 22, 186, 198
succession and donation tax (ISD) 34
switch-over clause 162, 165

Talotta (2007) ruling 123
tax avoidance 58–60, 81, 121, 169, 178–9, 183–4, 188, 204; and cross-border costs and losses compensation 102–5
tax competition 9–15, 173, 182–3, 227, 230, 237–8; fair 11, 150–2, 172, 175, 178–9, 183, 189–90, 226, 229; harmful 83, 150, 178; jurisdictional 183, 187
tax consolidation group 105–6
tax coordination 1
tax credit method 27, 30, 34, 40–1, 51, 147, 158–9, 162, 165; full 85; half 45; inbound foreign dividends 135–6; indirect 44, 47; notional 68; refusal 134
tax deferral regime 50, 65–7
tax evasion 2, 28, 52, 58–60, 68, 76, 118, 202, 214–15; Action Plan 48–9, 70, 73, 149–56, 183, 220, 229–30; and Administrative Cooperation Directive 92; benchmark shortcomings 149–51; CCCTB and proposed initiatives 167–72, 176–8, 183; cross border 16–17, 48–9, 72–3, 90–1, 149, 220,

229; EC Communications 14; and fraud 48–9, 70–3, 149, 171, 220, 229–30; Interests and Royalties Directive 81, *see also* tax avoidance
tax exemption 27–35, 40–9, 53–6, 61, 65, 70, 76–83, 89, 107, 130–1, 135–7, 144–8, 158–9, 162, 165, 174, 180, 230–1; Dutch method 127; provisions or reserves 51
tax governance 14, 150, 171, 179–86
tax planning strategies 108
tax relief 9
tax residence 28, 49, 70, 73, 115, 142–4, 151–3, 175, 181, 186, 195, 225, 231-9; -based jurisdiction v tax sovereignty 186–9; conflict 29, 175, 187; dual 66, 175; EU solution 198–218, 219–25; EU/ERTCS system 198–218; fiscal 47; national tax alternatives 189–96; non- 99–101; payer s state 82; requirements 79; shareholder s 134; and source concepts 189–96
tax return: single unified 202–4, 208–10, 213–14, 223–4, 231
tax systems cohesion 3–5, 14–16, 96, 105, 237; common 64, 80; determination, consolidation and apportionment 158–61, 168; and direct taxation internal market functioning 150–6, 174–85, 193–4; ECJ justification 118; and EU tax residence proposal 198, 212–13, 217, 226, 234; justifications 143; strict requirements 118, *see also* CCCTB
taxable profit 9, 27, 38–40, 50–1, 54, 73, 108, 113, 129, 155, 180, 185
taxpayers: non-resident 12; protection rights 91
terminal losses 108
Test Claimant in Class IV ACT (2006) ruling 142
Test Claimant in FII Group Litigation Order (2006) ruling 31, 37, 47, 135–7, 147
Test Claimant in Thin Cap Group Litigation (2007) ruling 120, 144
thin capitalisation 82, 118, 230; German 117
3DI Srl (2012) ruling 55, 65, 69–71
tie-breaker rules 96, 152, 176, 187, 194

transfer pricing 7–8, 12, 80–2, 148, 161–2, 168–72; Arbitration Convention 73–5, 219–20; Code of Conduct 184; and EU tax residence proposal 199, 206, 219–20; rules 121–2
transferring company 65, 72; intra-group 121; resident 70
transfers: assets 8, 25, 50–8, 65–72
Treaty on European Union (TEU/Maastricht 1992) 9-10, 17–19, 162, 215; legal bases and Articles 19–22
Treaty on the Functioning of the European Union (TFEU, Rome 1958) 3, 17–26, 41, 96, 162, 173, 186, 189; Article 6 and non-discrimination 81; Article 45 (free movement of workers) 122–3, 127; Article 49 (secondary establishment) 99, 104–6, 111–13, 133; Article 54(2) 31, 103–4, 111–14, 133; Article 267 and Merger Directive 56; Articles 26 and 115 (double taxation) 24; Articles 63-6 (free movement) 10, 133–6; and ECJ case law on fundamental freedoms 98–154; and EU tax residence proposal 215, 232; and free movement of workers 122–33; freedom of establishment 98–122, 173–4; legal bases and Articles 19–22
Truck Center (2008) case 142–5, 148

United Nations Model 22, 156, 164, 229
United States Constitution 194–5
usufructuary 39

VALE (2012) ruling 72, 112
valid commercial reasons 59–62
Van der Grinten (2003) case 31–2, 36–8
VAT Directives 5–6, 21, 95
Verests and Gerards (2014) ruling 140
Verkooijen (2000) ruling 133–4
voting rights 30–1, 43, 76

Wallentin (2004) ruling 130–1
Werner Report (1970) 6
wholly artificial arrangements 15–16, 28, 59, 82, 111, 118–21, 137, 148, 151–2, 166, 173–4, 201
Wiedert-Paulus (2004) ruling 133–4

250 *Index*

Wielocks (1995) ruling 124–6
withholding tax 6–12, 77–86, 122, 137–48, 159, 162, 170, 177, 188; abolition 11–12, 36, 162; and Parent-Subsidiary Directive 27–49; and Savings Directive 84; under Articles 5(1) and 7(2) 34–8
workers: employed/self-employed 122–33, *see also* free movement of workers

worldwide taxation 51, 89–90, 175, 180–1, 185, 188, 199, 213, 231; double 194–5

X Holding (2010) ruling 106–8, 149

Zwijnenburg (2010) ruling 55, 60
Zythopiia (2001) ruling 31–8